Implementing Transboundary Water Agreements

Implementing Transboundary Water Agreements

Alistair Rieu-Clarke

Professor of Law, Law School, Northumbria University, UK

Edward Elgar
PUBLISHING

Cheltenham, UK • Northampton, MA, USA

Published by
Edward Elgar Publishing Limited
The Lypiatts
15 Lansdown Road
Cheltenham
Glos GL50 2JA
UK

Edward Elgar Publishing, Inc.
William Pratt House
9 Dewey Court
Northampton
Massachusetts 01060
USA

Authorised representative in the EU for GPSR queries only: Easy Access System Europe– Mustamäe tee 50, 10621 Tallinn, Estonia, gpsr.requests@easproject.com

A catalogue record for this book
is available from the British Library

Library of Congress Control Number: 2025931105

This book is available electronically in the **Elgar**online
Law subject collection
https://doi.org/10.4337/9781035337279

FSC www.fsc.org MIX Paper | Supporting responsible forestry FSC® C013604

ISBN 978 1 0353 3726 2 (cased)
ISBN 978 1 0353 3727 9 (eBook)

Printed and bound by CPI Group (UK) Ltd, Croydon, CR0 4YY

Contents

Preface

The genesis of this book is hard to trace. For quite some time, I have had a growing sense that there is a need to place a spotlight on issues of compliance and implementation within the context of transboundary water agreements. What was particularly puzzling to me was the contrast that could be found between transboundary water agreements and multilateral environmental agreements (MEAs). Why is it that compliance and implementation mechanisms are almost 'a given' within the design of MEAs but largely absent from transboundary water agreements? This contrast is mirrored in the amount of scholarship focused on MEA compliance and implementation compared to transboundary water agreements. When I started this enquiry, I was hopeful, even confident, that I would find an answer. However, what has been particularly encouraging is the more practical insights that this research has yielded. While this is not the place to set out those insights, it has become clear to me that a greater focus on compliance and implementation within the context of transboundary water agreements has much to offer.

While with hindsight I would not recommend writing a book over many years, it has had the advantage in that I have been able to shape my thinking through a range of experiences. Through research and consultancy projects, I benefited from being exposed to the practicalities of implementing transboundary water agreements in many of the world's transboundary waters. I am so grateful to the practitioners from across the globe who came along to our water law training events and asked: 'Yes, but how do we implement these rules in practice?' I am also grateful for my time at the secretariat of the Water Convention, which offered me a first-hand account of how reporting under SDG indicator 6.5.2 and the Water Convention works, and how the Implementation Committee under the Convention functions.

The work has been enriched and made much more enjoyable through numerous exchanges with friends and colleagues. I am particularly grateful to Professor Patricia Wouters and Professor Owen McIntyre for their guidance and encouragement along the way. I am also grateful to colleagues at Northumbria University for their support and encouragement, especially Professor Alan Reed and Professor Michael Stockdale. Moreover, without being given a sabbatical from the University, I would still be completing this work. Friends at the Water Convention secretariat have also been a great source of inspiration and guidance, and a special thanks to Iulia Trombitcaia for commenting on parts of Chapter 5. I am also thankful for the opportunity to present my work at an event held at Edinburgh Law School in June 2024 – thanks in particular to the organisers Dr Ana Maria Daza-Clark, Professor Patricia Wouters, Professor Owen McIntyre and Dr David J. Devlaeminck, as well as the participants for their helpful comments and feedback.

Finally, I am most thankful to Angela, Grace and Beth. Thanks for providing me with balance and much-needed distractions in my life!

1. Introduction to *Implementing Transboundary Water Agreements*

1.1 THE IMPORTANCE OF TRANSBOUNDARY WATERS[1]

States have long recognised the value of entering into agreements for their shared transboundary rivers, lakes and aquifers. As far back as 2,500 BC, two Mesopotamian states, Lagash and Umma, concluded the so-called Mesilim Treaty.[2] This treaty cemented an agreement whereby Umma leased boundary land from Lagash for agricultural purposes in return for a payment that in part helped maintain joint canal works and reservoirs.[3] Both states therefore benefited from the cooperation. Despite this ancient evidence of cooperation over transboundary waters, much work still needs to be done to promote water cooperation globally.

When viewing our blue planet, it might appear at first glance that sharing waters equitably and sustainably does not pose a particularly difficult challenge. However, only 2.5% or 35,000 million km^3 of the world's total water supply is freshwater.[4] Less than 1% of this freshwater supply is available for direct human use, with the rest being found in glaciers, permanent snow cover or deep in underground aquifers.[5] Global run-off and groundwater recharge,

[1] The term 'transboundary waters' is used to refer to rivers, lakes and aquifers that cross sovereign state boundaries.

[2] Peter H. Sand, 'Environmental Dispute Resolution 4,500 Years Ago: The Case of *Lagash v Umma*' (2019) 30(1) Yearbook of International Environmental Law 137. The agreement reached by Lagash and Umma can be seen in cuneiform inscriptions on a limestone cone and stele housed in the Musée du Louvre, Paris.

[3] Malcolm Shaw, *International Law* (CUP 2017), 10.

[4] United Nations Environment Programme (UNEP), *Global Environment Outlook 3 – Past, Present and Future Perspectives* (Earthscan 2002), 150.

[5] UN Commission on Sustainable Development, 'Comprehensive Assessment of the Freshwater Resources of the World' UN Doc E/CN.17/1997/9 (4 February 1997). Global projections suggest that glaciers may lose between 25–50% of their

i.e., the difference between precipitation on land surfaces and evaporation, amounts to approximately 47,000 km^3 annually.[6] More than half of this runoff occurs in Asia and South America, and 12% is found in a single river system – the Amazon.[7] This means that, while total global runoff is sufficient to meet our planetary needs, the variability of supply both in temporal and spatial terms leads to competition and potential disputes between different water users.[8] Of course, climate change adds another layer of complexity to already unpredictable water supplies.

Where waters cross sovereign borders, it is imperative that states work together with the aim of reconciling competing interests and ensuring that their shared waters are managed in a sustainable and equitable way. Approximately 313 transboundary river and lake basins are shared by 150 countries.[9] These basins cover nearly half of the Earth's land surface and are home to 40% of the world's population. Thirty-nine states have more than 90% of their territory within transboundary basins; and five or more states share 20 transboundary rivers.[10] Most of the world's major transboundary rivers are shared by several states, including the Danube (17 states), the Congo (13 states), the Nile (12 states), the Niger (10 states), the Amazon (9 states), the Rhine (9 states) and the Zambezi (9 states).[11] Additionally, while hidden underground and often undervalued, the importance of transboundary aquifers should not be overlooked.[12] An estimated 275 aquifers are transboundary; these aquifers account for more than 100 times the volume of global surface water.[13]

---

mass by 2100, which is likely to have significant impacts in terms of sea level rise, water resource availability and natural hazards (David R. Rounce and others, 'Global glacier change in the 21st century: Every increase in temperature matters' (2023) 379(6627) Science 78).

[6] UNEP (n 4).

[7] Ibid.

[8] The Food and Agriculatural Organisation of the UN (FAO) estimates that on average 10% of the global population live in countries with high or critical water stress. See FAO, *Progress on Level of Water Stress – Global status and acceleration needs for SDG Indicator 6.4.2* (FAO 2021), 35.

[9] Oregon State University, 'Transboundary Freshwater Spatial Database' <https://transboundarywaters.ceoas.oregonstate.edu/transboundary-freshwater-spatial-database> accessed 13 June 2024.

[10] Ibid.

[11] Ibid.

[12] UNESCO, *The United Nations World Water Development Report 2022* (UNESCO 2022).

[13] UNESCO, *Atlas of Transboundary Aquifers* (UNESCO 2009), 61.

1.2 WHY COOPERATE OVER TRANSBOUNDARY WATERS?

Certain key characteristics of water make cooperation over transboundary waters both essential and complex. Water is a finite and vulnerable resource that for many purposes has no substitute. All social and economic activities rely heavily on the supply and quality of freshwater. Water provides a range of services, including provisioning services (drinking water, domestic use, agriculture, industry, power generation and navigation), regulating services (maintenance of water quality, flood and erosion control), cultural services (recreational, tourism, and spiritual values), and supporting services (nutrient cycling, and ecosystem resilience).[14] Water is, therefore, central to sustainable development.[15]

A key feature of water is its indivisibility. For example, quantities of water stored for hydropower in one country will limit the amount of water available to a downstream country. Similarly, water quality issues flow across borders.[16] For instance, industrial and agricultural uses in one part of a river, lake or aquifer system may affect the quality of water in other parts of the system, which in turn might restrict how that water can be used. There is also a strong linkage between water and land use.[17] Converting land from natural forest or wetlands to urban or agricultural uses is likely to have a range of water-related impacts, such as increasing the likelihood and severity of floods or droughts downstream.[18] Also, land-based pollution, which includes plastics, may be transferred through rivers, lakes and groundwater to the marine environment.[19]

---

[14] Bruce Aylward and others, 'Freshwater Ecosystem Services', in Rashid Hassan, Robert Scholes and Neville J. Ash (eds), *Ecosystems and Human Well-being: Current State and Trends* (Island Press 2005), 216.

[15] The Future We Want, UNGA Res 66/288 (27 July 2012); International Decade for Action, 'Water for Life' 2005–2015, UNGA Res 58/217 (23 December 2003).

[16] See for example Sergei Vinogradov and Patricia Wouters, *Sino-Russian Transboundary Waters: A Legal Perspective of Cooperation* (Institute for Security and Development Policy 2013).

[17] Malin Falkenmark and others, *Water – A Reflection of Land Use* (Swedish Natural Science Research Council 1999).

[18] Charles Vörösmarty and others, 'Freshwater', in Kanchan Chopra and others (eds), *Ecosystems and Human Well-Being: Policy Responses* (Island Press 2005), 187.

[19] Derek A. Bigham, 'Pollution from Land-Based Sources', in Douglas J. Cusine and John P. Grant (eds), *The Impact of Marine Pollution* (Routledge 2019).

The significant pressures placed on our transboundary rivers, lakes and aquifers make cooperation among an often diverse but interconnected range of users essential. Population growth, industrialisation and the expansion of irrigated agriculture have led to a dramatic increase in water demand worldwide.[20] While at the global level water withdrawals are estimated to be only 18% of total renewable freshwater resources, there are significant regional variations.[21] Many countries in Northern Africa and Western Asia withdraw all their renewable water resources every year.[22] With the world's human population set to grow from 7.8 billion in 2020 to 9.7 billion in 2050, further pressure on the world's freshwater supplies is likely in the coming years.[23]

The overexploitation of water has already taken its toll on freshwater ecosystems. Most rivers are fragmented to a greater or lesser extent by dams, and only an estimated 23% of rivers greater than 1000 km in length flow uninterrupted to the sea.[24] As land has been converted to agricultural and urban use, half the world's wetlands are estimated to have been lost during the 20th century.[25] Also, the overexploitation and pollution of land in many regions of the world are threatening groundwater supplies.[26] These waters provide over half the world's population with drinking water.[27] It is estimated that water quality conditions have degraded in almost all regions of the world through intensive agricultural practices and from the effects of large urban and industrial areas.[28] Inland fisheries and freshwater species are also under threat due

---

20 Ibid, 168.

21 FAO (n 8).

22 Ibid.

23 UN Department of Economic and Social Affairs, 'Global Population Growth and Sustainable Development', UN Doc DESA/POP/2021/TR/NO.2 (2021), 5. Global water withdrawal was only 600 km^2 per year in 1900, but by 2017 it was estimated at 3,800 km^2 per year – this figure is set to increase by one percent each year in line with population growth (see UNESCO (n 12), 15).

24 Günter Grill and others, 'Mapping the World's Free-flowing Rivers' (2019) 569 Nature 215.

25 UN, 'The Sustainable Development Goals Report 2020' <https://unstats.un.org/sdgs/report/2020/The-Sustainable-Development-Goals-Report-2020.pdf> accessed 6 June 2024.

26 UNESCO (n 12), 19.

27 Abhijit Mukherjee and others, 'Global Groundwater: From Scarcity to Security through Sustainability and Solutions', in Abhijit Mukherjee and others (eds), *Global Groundwater: Source, Scarcity, Sustainability, Security and Solutions* (Elsevier 2021), 3.

28 UNESCO (n 12), 19.

to habitat degradation, invasive species and overharvesting.[29] A third of the world's freshwater fish are threatened with extinction.[30]

A further complicating factor is climate change. Water-related impacts of climate change are already evident in all regions of the world.[31] These impacts include increased frequency and intensity of heavy precipitation, accelerated melting of glaciers, changes in the frequency, magnitude and timing of floods, more frequent and extended – often multi-year – droughts, changes in groundwater storage and recharge, and the deterioration of water quality.[32] In addition to physical climate change, the magnitude of uncertainty and the scientific complexity of the issue pose unique resource allocation and risk management challenges.[33]

In many parts of the world, cooperation over transboundary waters offers the best means by which states can address the aforementioned challenges. Through cooperation, states can maximise and share the benefits of water across an entire basin, while safeguarding and sustaining healthy ecosystems.[34] For this reason, a basin-wide and holistic approach to water management has gained widespread support both within science and policy.[35] As far back as 1956, the International Law Association (ILA) suggested that, 'so far as possible, riparian states should join with each other to make full utilisation of the waters of a river both from the viewpoint of the river basin as an integrated whole, and from the viewpoint of the widest variety of uses of the water to assure the greatest benefit to all'.[36] This suggestion was reiterated in numerous global policy statements from the UN Water Conference of Mar del

---

[29] Abigail J. Lynch and others, 'Inland Fish and Fisheries Integral to Achieving the Sustainable Development Goals' (2020) 3 Nature Sustainability 579.

[30] WWF and others, 'The World's Forgotten Fishes' (2021) <https://wwfint.awsassets.panda.org/downloads/world_s_forgotten_fishes__final_april9_.pdf> accessed 6 June 2024, 9.

[31] Martina A. Caretta and others, 'Water', in Hans-Otto Pörtner and others (eds), *Climate Change 2022: Impacts, Adaptation and Vulnerability* (CUP 2022), 551.

[32] Ibid.

[33] UNECE and INBO, 'Water and Climate Change Adaptation in Transboundary Basins: Lessons Learned and Good Practices', UN Doc ECE/MP.WAT/45 (2015); Dan Tarlock, 'Now Think Again About Adaptation' (1992) 9 Arizona Journal of International and Comparative Law 169, 169.

[34] Claudia W. Sadoff and David Grey, 'Beyond the River: The Benefits of Cooperation on International Rivers' (2002) 4 Water Policy 389.

[35] Bruce P. Hooper, 'Integrated Water Resources Management and River Basin Governance' (2003) 126 Water Resources Update 12.

[36] 'Statement of Principles' in ILA Report of the Forty-Seventh Conference (Dubrovnik 1956), 241–243.

Plata in 1977[37] to more recently in target 6.5 of the Sustainable Development Goals (SDGs).[38]

While compelling reasons can therefore be put forward as to why states should cooperate over their transboundary waters, this begs the question, do they actually cooperate in practice?

1.3 STATE PRACTICE ON TRANSBOUNDARY WATERS

1.3.1 Evolution of Transboundary Water Agreements

Since that first agreement between Lagash and Umma in 2,500 BC, over 3,600 transboundary water agreements have been adopted.[39] Despite this significant state practice, the treaty architecture for transboundary waters remains fragmented. This fragmentation relates in part to the purpose of agreements. The majority of agreements concern navigational uses, which reflected the major use of transboundary waters up until the start of the 20th century.[40] Only 400 or so agreements address non-navigational uses of transboundary waters.[41] Additionally, many of the early agreements concerning non-navigational uses tended to have a narrow, or even singular purpose, such as hydropower development or fisheries.[42] It was not until more recent times that there was a general shift towards a holistic and integrated approach to transboundary

[37] 'Report of the United Nations Water Conference, Mar del Plata, 14–25 March 1977', UN Doc E/CONF.70/29 (1977).

[38] Transforming our World: the 2030 Agenda for Sustainable Development, UNGA Res 70/1 (21 October 2015). SDG target 6.5 calls upon countries to implement integrated water resources management at all levels, including through transboundary cooperation, by 2030 (ibid., 18).

[39] Mark Giordano and Aaron Wolf, 'The World's International Freshwater Agreements', in UNEP and others, *Atlas of International Freshwater Agreements* (UNEP 2002), 6. See also Stephen C. McCaffrey, 'The Evolution of International Law Relating to Transboundary Waters', in Alistair Rieu-Clarke, Andrew Allan and Sarah Hendry (eds), *Routledge Handbook of Water Law and Policy* (Routledge 2017).

[40] Ariel Dinar and others, *Bridges over Water: Understanding Transboundary Water Conflict, Negotiation and Cooperation* (World Scientific Publishing Company 2007), 58–60.

[41] Giodarno and Wolf (n 39); Stefano Burchi and Kerstin Mechlem, *Groundwater in International Law* (FAO 2005).

[42] See for example, the Preliminary Convention Between Bolivia and Peru for the Exploitation of Fisheries in Lake Titicaca (adopted 17 July 1935) <http://www.colsan.edu.mx/investigacion/aguaysociedad/proyectofrontera/1935.pdf> accessed 6 June 2024; Convention between Spain and Portugal to Regulate the

waters.[43] Observers have therefore questioned whether many agreements have the necessary capacity to cope with existing and future challenges, such as climate change, population growth, ecosystem degradation, and food and energy security.[44]

Fragmentation is also a concern when it comes to the territorial coverage of agreements. Some major river systems, such as the Tarim Basin (shared between China, Kyrgyzstan, Tajikistan, Pakistan and Afghanistan), the Irrawaddy (shared between Myanmar, China and India), and the Orinoco River (shared between Venezuela, Colombia and Brazil) do not have a basin-wide agreement in place.[45] There is also a tendency for states to enter into bilateral agreements even where a water system is shared by more than two states.[46] For example, several bilateral arrangements cover the Ganges-Brahmaputra-Meghna Basin, but there is no basin-wide arrangement in place.[47] In the case of the Mekong, an arrangement for the entire basin was developed, but only the four lower Mekong Basin states (Cambodia, Laos, Thailand and Vietnam) are party to it.[48] China and Myanmar, both upstream, are not party to the

---

Hydro-electric Development of the International Section of the River Douro and its Tributaries (adopted 16 July 1964), 1288 UNTS 191.

43 See for example UNGA Res 70/1 (n 38).

44 UN-Water, 'Transboundary Waters: Sharing Benefits, Sharing Responsibilities', <https://www.unwater.org/sites/default/files/app/uploads/2017/05/UNW_TRANSBOUNDARY.pdf> accessed 6 June 2024; UN, 'The Sustainable Development Goals Report 2020', <https://unstats.un.org/sdgs/report/2020/The-Sustainable-Development-Goals-Report-2020.pdf> accessed 6 June 2024.

45 UNEP and others (n 39).

46 Neda A. Zawahri and Sara McLaughlin Mitchell, 'Fragmented Governance in International Rivers: Negotiating Bilateral versus Multilateral Treaties' (2011) 55 International Studies Quarterly 835.

47 See for example, Statute of the Indo-Bangladesh Joint Rivers Commission (adopted 24 November 1972) <https://faolex.fao.org/docs/pdf/bi203668.pdf> accessed 6 June 2024; Treaty between the government of the Republic of India and the government of the People's Republic of Bangladesh on sharing of the Ganga/Ganges waters at Farakka (adopted 12 December 1996), 1066 UNTS 15; Memorandum of Understanding between India and China upon Provision of Hydrological Information of the Yaluzangbu/Brahmaputra River in Flood Season (adopted 16 December 2010) <https://mea.gov.in/Portal/LegalTreatiesDoc/CH13B0811.pdf> accessed 6 June 2024; Memorandum of Understanding between India and China on Strengthening Cooperation on Transborder Rivers, 23 October 2013 <https://faolex.fao.org/docs/pdf/bi-189111.pdf> accessed 6 June 2024.

48 Agreement on the Cooperation for the Sustainable Development of the Mekong River Basin (adopted 5 April 1995), 34 ILM 864 (Mekong Agreement). Cambodia, Laos, Thailand and Vietnam are party to the Mekong Agreement.

agreement. Along similar lines, a basin-wide agreement for the Nile Basin has been adopted, but it currently does not have the support of all Nile states.[49] Conversely, and much to the protestation of the Nile upstream states, Egypt and Sudan adopted an agreement in 1959 that allocates the entire waters of the Nile between the two furthest downstream countries.[50]

The fragmented global architecture of transboundary water agreements is at variance with calls to strengthen transboundary cooperation. SDG target 6.5, for instance, calls upon countries to implement integrated water resources management at all levels, including through transboundary cooperation as appropriate, by 2030.[51] A specific SDG indicator monitors the proportion of transboundary basin area covered by 'operational arrangements for transboundary water cooperation'.[52] In 2023, the monitoring of this indicator found that only 43 countries have operational arrangements covering more than 90% of the basin area within their territory.[53] Along similar lines, Giordano and Wolf's assessment concluded that around 60% of all transboundary rivers,

---

China and Myanmar also have territory within the basin but are not party to the Agreement.

[49] The text of the Agreement on the Nile River Basin Cooperative Framework was developed by the countries of the Nile Basin from January 1997 to May 2009; see Salman M.A. Salman, 'The Nile Basin Cooperative Framework Agreement: A Peacefully Unfolding African Spring?' (2013) 38(1) Water International 17. In April 2001, seven Nile countries took the decision to open the Agreement up for signature against strong reservations from Egypt and Sudan. Six countries have subsequently ratified or acceded to the Agreement (Burundi, Ethiopia, Rwanda, South Sudan, Tanzania and Uganda), which paves the way for the Agreement's entry into force; see Cooperative Framework Agreement (Nilebasin.org) <https://nilebasin.org/about-us/cooperative-framework-agreement> accessed 14 January 2025.

[50] Agreement between the Republic of the Sudan and the United Arab Republic for the Full Utilisation of the Nile Waters (adopted 8 November 1959), 6519 UNTS 64.

[51] UN (n 38).

[52] For a definition of 'operational arrangements for transboundary water cooperation', see UNECE and UNESCO, 'Step-by-Step Monitoring Methodology for SDG indicator 6.5.2', <https://www.unwater.org/app/uploads/2020/02/SDG_652_Step-by-step_methodology_2020_ENG.pdf> accessed 6 June 2024; see also UNECE, Guide to Reporting under the Water Convention and as a Contribution to SDG indicator 6.5.2, UN Doc ECE/MP.WAT/60 (2020), <https://unece.org/sites/default/files/2021-02/ece_mp.wat_60_eng_web.pdf> accessed 23 January 2025.

[53] UNECE and UNESCO, Progress on Transboundary Water Cooperation – Mid-term status of SDG indicator 6.5.2, with a special focus on climate change (2024), UN Doc ECE/MP.WAT/76 (2024).

lakes and aquifers lack any type of cooperative management framework.[54] Much work is therefore needed to ensure that all transboundary waters are covered by cooperative arrangements.

While the fragmented landscape of transboundary water agreements might be a cause for concern, this does not mean that these waters are not subject to international law. At the regional level, two 'multi-basin' agreements have influenced the law relating to transboundary waters, namely the Convention on the Protection and Use of Transboundary Watercourses and International Lakes (Water Convention), which is serviced by the United Nations Economic Commission for Europe (UNECE)[55] and the Revised Protocol on Shared Watercourses in the Southern African Development Community (SADC Revised Protocol).[56] Both framework instruments have played a major role in the development of basin-specific agreements across Europe, Central Asia and Southern Africa.[57] Additionally, the influence of the Water Convention has been extended due to a decision taken by its parties to open the Convention for membership to all UN member states – a decision that became operational in 2016.[58]

All states are also subject to customary international law, which sets out general rules and principles relating to transboundary waters. The International Law Institute (ILI) and ILA, two non-governmental expert groups, have been particularly influential in studying and proposing rules and principles that reflect a codification and progressive development of customary

---

[54] Giordano and Wolf (n 39), 7.

[55] Convention on the Protection and Use of Transboundary Watercourses and International Lakes (adopted 17 March 1992, entered into force 6 October 1996), 31 ILM 1312 (Water Convention). At the time of writing this book there were 55 parties to the Water Convention.

[56] Revised Protocol on Shared Watercourses in the Southern African Development Community (adopted 7 August 2000, entered into force 22 September 2003), 40 ILM 321 (SADC Revised Protocol). There are 11 parties to the SADC Revised Protocol.

[57] UNECE and UNESCO (n 53), 22–27. Member states of the European Union (EU) have also been influenced by Directive 2000/60/EC of 22 December 2000 establishing a framework for the Community action in the field of water policy [2000] OJ L 327/1 (Water Framework Directive), which seeks to ensure that all waters within the EU – both national and transboundary – achieve 'good water status'.

[58] UNECE, 'The Global Opening of the 1992 Water Convention' (2013) <https://www.unwater.org/sites/default/files/app/uploads/2017/05/Brochure_ECE_ENG_WEB_OK.pdf> accessed 7 June 2024. Detailed analysis of the Water Convention is carried out in Chapter 5 of this book.

international law in the field.[59] However, the most significant contribution to the codification and progressive development of customary international law relating to the use and protection of transboundary waters is the negotiation and adoption of the Convention on the Law of the Non-navigational Uses of International Watercourses (Watercourses Convention).[60] The International Law Commission (ILC) spent over 20 years developing 33 Draft Articles on the Law of the Non-navigational Uses of International Watercourses, which subsequently provided the basis for the adoption of the Watercourses Convention by states within the UN General Assembly in 1997.[61] A vote was taken on the adoption of the Watercourses Convention, which recorded 103 votes in favour, 26 abstentions, and 3 votes against.[62] Since its adoption, the Watercourses Convention has attracted 39 contracting states and entered into force on 17 August 2014.[63] Even prior to its entry into force, the Convention proved influential in shaping state practice, as well as the decisions of international courts.[64] For example, in the Gabčíkovo-Nagymaros Project case between Hungary and Slovakia, the International Court of Justice was quick

---

59 International Law Institute, 'Resolution on the Utilization of Non-Maritime International Waters (Except for Navigation)' (1961) 49 Annuaire de l'Institute de Droit International 370; International Law Institute, 'International Regulations Regarding the Use of International Watercourses for Purposes Other than Navigation (Madrid Declaration)' (1911) 24 Annuaire de l'Institute de Droit International 365; 'Helsinki Rules on the Uses of the Waters of International Rivers', in ILA Report of the Fifty-Second Conference (Helsinki 1966), 486 (Helsinki Rules); and Charles Bourne, 'The International Law Association's Contribution to International Water Resources Law' (1996) 36 Natural Resources Journal 155.

60 Convention on the Law of the Non-navigational Uses of International Watercourses (adopted 21 May 1997, entered into force 17 August 2014), 2999 UNTS 77 (Watercourses Convention).

61 'Draft Articles on the Law of the Non-navigational Uses of International Watercourses' in Report of the International Law Commission on the Work of its 46th Session, UN Doc A/49/10 (2 May – 22 July 1994), 89–135.

62 Convention on the Law of the Non-navigational Uses of International Watercourses, UNGA Res 51/229 (8 July 1997).

63 UN Treaty Collection, 'Chapter XXVII – Environment' (*treaties.un.org*, 27 August 2024) <https://treaties.un.org/Pages/ViewDetails.aspx?src=TREATY&mtdsg_no=XXVII-12&chapter=27&clang=_en> accessed 27 August 2024. See Flavia R. Loures and Alistair Rieu-Clarke (eds), *The UN Watercourses Convention in Force – Strengthening International Law for Transboundary Water Management* (Routledge 2013).

64 Stephen C. McCaffrey, 'The Progressive Development of International Water Law', in Loures and Rieu-Clarke, ibid.

to make reference to the Convention despite the fact that there were only five months between the adoption of the Convention and the Court's decision.[65]

The Watercourses Convention and the Water Convention are also supplemented by the work of the ILC to develop rules and principles relating to transboundary aquifers, which culminated in a set of draft articles on the law of transboundary aquifers in 2008.[66] However, the final form of those draft articles is yet to be decided.[67]

All these developments provide an important backdrop for states to consider when negotiating and implementing transboundary water agreements.

1.3.2 Transboundary Water Conflicts

Transboundary water conflicts encompass verbal, economic or military hostilities between countries sharing rivers, lakes or aquifers.[68] Petersen-Perlman, Veilleux and Wolf argue that 'given the complexity created by different economies, ecosystems, climates, politics and cultures within watersheds, transboundary water management can be considered a type of conflict management and/or conflict prevention'.[69] The former UN Secretary-General, Kofi Annan, even went as far as to suggest that 'fierce national competition over water resources has prompted fears that water issues contain the seeds of violent conflict'.[70] Along similar lines, his predecessor, Boutros Boutros-Ghali, predicted in the 1980s that, 'the next war in the Middle East will be fought over water, not politics'.[71] Others suggest that the so-called 'water wars' hypothesis is tantamount to scaremongering and ignores the reality, i.e., that conflicts are

---

[65] *Gabčíkovo-Nagymaros Project (Hungary/Slovakia)* (Judgement) [1997] ICJ Rep 7.

[66] 'Draft Articles on the Law of Transboundary Aquifers' in Report of the International Law Commission on the Work of its 60th Session, UN Doc A/63/10 (5 May – 6 June and 7 July – 8 August 2008), 19–79.

[67] Gabriel Eckstein and Francesco Sindico, 'The Law of Transboundary Aquifers: Many ways of going forward, but only one way of standing still' (2014) 23 Review of European Community and International Environmental Law 32.

[68] Jacob D. Petersen-Perlman, Jennifer C. Veilleux and Aaron T. Wolf, 'International Water Conflict and Cooperation: Challenges and Opportunities' (2017) 42(2) Water International 105, 106.

[69] Ibid, 107.

[70] UN, 'World's Water Problems can be "Catalyst for Cooperation" says Secretary-General in message on World Water Day', UN Doc SG/SM/8139-OBV/262 (26 February 2002).

[71] Jan Selby, 'The Geopolitics of Water in the Middle East: Fantasies and Realities' (2005) 26(2) Third World Quarterly 329, 339.

not primarily focused on water issues but are multidimensional.[72] Research by Wolf and others surveyed water-related disputes from 1948 to 2000.[73] They found that of 37 cases of 'acute conflict', i.e., disputes that include some element of violence, 30 were between Israel and its neighbours, and none resulted in formal war.[74] Despite these assurances, other scholars have pointed out that, 'the absence of war does not mean the absence of conflict'.[75] Zeitoun and Mirumachi, for instance, argue that many water conflicts are largely silent due to power imbalances between the states involved, and conflict and cooperation may to a greater or lesser extent operate in tandem within a particular river basin or transboundary aquifers.[76]

In terms of the issues that generate conflict, De Stefano and others reviewed 2,555 water-related events between 1948 and 1999, involving 124 countries and 122 transboundary river basins.[77] They concluded that infrastructure and water quantity are the most conflictive transboundary water issues. Others point to additional factors, including low rainfall, inadequate water supply, overreliance on a shared water source, high population growth and rapid urbanisation, modernisation and industrialisation, and a history of armed combat and poor relations between countries and among groups within countries.[78] More generally, Delli Priscoli and Wolf categorise conflicts into five central causes, namely disagreements over data, personal relationship conflicts, perceived or actual incompatible interests, problems with structure forces,[79] and perceived or actual competing values.[80]

---

[72] Jeroen Warner and Sumit Vij, 'No, there will not be a war for water' (*NewSecurityBeat*, 10 January 2022) <https://www.newsecuritybeat.org/2022/01/no-war-water> accessed 7 June 2024.

[73] Aaron T. Wolf, Shira B. Yoffe and Mark Giordano, 'International Waters: Identifying Basins at Risk' (2003) 5 Water Policy 29.

[74] Ibid.

[75] Mark Zeitoun and Jeroen Warner, 'Hydro-hegemony – a Framework for Analysis of Trans-boundary Water Conflicts' (2006) 8(5) Water Policy 435, 437.

[76] Mark Zeitoun and Naho Mirumachi, 'Transboundary Water Interaction I: Reconsidering Conflict and Cooperation' (2008) 8 International Environmental Agreements: Politics, Law and Economics 297.

[77] Lucia de Stefano and others, 'Tracking Cooperation and Conflict in International Basins: Historic and Recent Trends' (2010) 12(6) Water Policy 871.

[78] Barry S. Levy and Victor W. Sidel, 'Water Rights and Water Fights: Preventing and Resolving Conflicts before they Boil Over' (2011) 101(5) American Journal of Public Health 778.

[79] Such forces might include limited physical resources or authority, geographic constraints, time or inadequate organisational structures.

[80] Jerome Delli Priscoli and Aaron T. Wolf, *Managing and Transforming Water Conflicts* (CUP 2009), 39.

While infrastructure, water management or other factors may contribute to conflict, some authors are keen to point out the correlation between conflict and governance. For example, in surveying situations of conflict and cooperation in the world's transboundary river basins, Wolf, Stahl and Macomber concluded that:

> Co-riparian relations have shown to be significantly more cooperative in basins with treaties and high dam density than in similarly developed basins without treaties. Thus, institutional capacity together with shared interests and human creativity seem to diffuse water's conflict-inducing characteristics, suggesting that an important lesson of international water is that as a resource it tends to induce cooperation, and incite violence only in the exception.[81]

While the authors define 'institutional capacity' broadly, i.e., 'water management bodies or treaties, or generally positive international relations',[82] the research would suggest that treaties may have a positive effect on promoting cooperation and avoiding conflict, and their design and function should be carefully considered when exploring how to enhance cooperation over transboundary waters.

1.4 TREATIES, CONFLICT, IMPLEMENTATION AND COMPLIANCE

The correlation between treaties and water conflict is clear. Where conflicts do arise, states have often either turned to their existing agreements to manage those conflicts,[83] or have adopted new agreements that set out the terms of any settlement between the disputing parties.[84] An increasing body of scholarship

---

81 Aaron T. Wolf, Kerstin Stahl and Marcia F. Macomber, 'Conflict and Cooperation within International River Basins: The Importance of Institutional Capacity' (2003) 125 Water Resources Update 1.

82 Ibid, 4.

83 See Daniel Haines, 'India and Pakistan are Playing a Dangerous Game in the Indus Basin – What's Behind the Rivals' Latest Spat over Water Rights along their Shared Waters' (*United States Institute of Peace,* 23 February 2023) <https://www.usip.org/publications/2023/02/india-and-pakistan-are-playing-dangerous-game-indus-basin> accessed 7 June 2024; Salman M.A. Salman, 'The Baglihar Difference and its Resolution Process – A Triumph for the Indus Waters Treaty?' (2008) 10(2) Water Policy 105.

84 See for example, the dispute between the Netherlands, France and Germany concerning chloride concentrations in the Rhine River (Carel Dieperink, 'International Water Negotiations under Asymmetry, Lessons from the Rhine Chlorides Dispute Settlement (1931–2004)' (2011) 11 International Environmental Agreements: Politics, Law and Economics 139).

has sought to deepen knowledge and understanding of these agreements and how they enhance cooperation between countries, as well as preventing and managing conflicts.[85] While there are notable exceptions,[86] most legal scholarship in this space has tended to take a positivist perspective.[87] A body of both scholarship and the work of international organisations, including the ILC,[88] the ILA[89] and the ILI, has surveyed treaty practice as part of a broader effort to ascertain and interpret the rules and principles of customary international law that apply to the protection and use of transboundary waters.[90] Most significant in this regard was the aforementioned work of the ILC, which extensively surveyed the bilateral, sub-basin, basin, regional and global agreements applicable to transboundary waters, as part of a broader project to ascertain state practice and *opinio juris*.[91] Legal scholarship has complemented and updated this analysis by exploring treaty practice as it relates to specific topics, such as

---

85 See generally Alistair Rieu-Clarke, 'The Role of Treaties in Building International Watercourse Regimes: A Legal Perspective on Existing Knowledge' (2010) 12(6) Water Policy 822.

86 See for example, Jutta Brunnée and Stephen J. Toope, 'The Changing Nile Basin Regime: Does Law Matter?' (2002) 43(1) 43 Harvard International Law Journal 105.

87 See for example, Stephen C. McCaffrey, *The Law of International Watercourses* (OUP 2019). Conca, Wu and Mai suggest that, 'legal scholarship … has focused substantially more attention on the evolution of legal principles for shared basins …. Less clear is the extent to which these principles are taking root in specifical political relationships among river sharing states' (Ken Conca, Fengshi Wu and Ciqi Mei, 'Global Regime Formation or Complex Institution Building? The Principled Content of International Freshwater Agreements' (2006) 50 International Studies Quarterly 263, 265).

88 Draft Articles (n 61).

89 Helsinki Rules (n 59). See also Slavko Bogdanović, *International Law of Water Resources – Contribution of the International Law Association (1954–2000)* (Kluwer Law International 2001).

90 Resolution on the Utilization of Non-Maritime International Waters (n 59).

91 See generally, ILC, 'Analytical Guide to the Work of the International Law Commission – Law of the Non-navigational Uses of International Watercourses' (*legal.un.org,* 9 February 2022), <https://legal.un.org/ilc/guide/8_3.shtml> accessed 13 June 2024; Attila Tanzi and Mauricio Arcari, *The United Nations Convention on the Law of International Watercourses: A Framework for Sharing* (Kluwer Law International 2001).

cooperation,[92] prior notification,[93] transboundary groundwater,[94] and ecosystem protection,[95] or focusing on particular basin agreements and countries.[96] An additional body of legal scholarship has explored the normative content of the Water Convention and the Watercourses Convention, or analysed regional agreements relating to transboundary waters.[97]

Non-legal scholars have also sought to bring their disciplinary perspectives to the study of transboundary water agreements. Some of this analysis has sought to consider the general influence of treaties on state conflict and cooperation over transboundary waters. As noted above, Wolf and others, for

---

[92] See Christina Leb, *Cooperation in the Law of Transboundary Water Resources* (CUP 2013).

[93] See Mara Tignino, 'Prior Notification and Water Rights' (2021) 115 AJIL Unbound 189; Alistair Rieu-Clarke, 'Notification and Consultation on Planned Measures Concerning International Watercourses: Learning Lessons from the *Pulp Mills* and *Kishenganga* Cases' (2014) 24(1) Yearbook of International Environmental Law 102.

[94] See Francesco Sindico, *International Law and Transboundary Aquifers* (Edward Elgar 2020); Gabriel Eckstein, *The International Law of Transboundary Groundwater* (Routledge 2017).

[95] See Owen McIntyre, 'The Protection of Freshwater Ecosystems Revisited: Towards a Common Understanding of the 'Ecosystems Approach' to the Protection of Transboundary Water Resources' (2014) 23(1) Review of European, Comparative & International Environmental Law 88; Jing Lee, *Preservation of Ecosystems of International Watercourses and the Integration of Relevant Rules* (Brill 2014).

[96] See Stephen P. Mumme, 'The 1944 Water Treaty and the Incorporation of Environmental Values in US-Mexico Transboundary Water Governance' (2020) 112 Environmental Science & Policy 126; Patricia Wouters, 'The Yin and Yang of International Water Law: China's Transboundary Water Practice and the Changing Contours of State Sovereignty' (2014) 23(1) Review of European, Comparative & International Environmental Law 67; Salman M.A. Salman, 'The Nile Basin Cooperative Framework Agreement – Disentangling the Gordian Knot', in Zeray Yihdego, Alistair Rieu-Clarke and Ana E. Cascão (eds), *The Grand Ethiopian Renaissance Dam and the Nile Basin* (Routledge 2017).

[97] Tanzi and Arcari (n 91); Atilla Tanzi and others (eds), *The UNECE Water Convention on the Protection and Use of Transboundary Watercourses and International Lakes* (Brill 2015); Ruby Moynihan, *Transboundary Freshwater Ecosystems in International Law – The Role and Impact of the UNECE Environmental Regime* (CUP 2021); Gerhard Reichert, *Transboundary Water Cooperation in Europe: A Successful Multi-dimensional Regime?* (Brill 2016); Alistair Rieu-Clarke, 'The Role and Relevance of the UN Convention on Law of the Non-navigational Uses of International Watercourses to the EU and its Member States' (2007) 78(1) British Yearbook of International Law 389.

instance, analysed 'institutional capacity' and concluded that it is likely to reduce water conflict within a basin.[98] Other non-legal scholars have gone further by assessing the influence of specific treaty design features on conflict and cooperation over transboundary waters. Mitchell and Zawahri, for example, suggest that information exchange and enforcement provisions in transboundary water agreements are most effective at preventing conflict.[99] Similarly, Tir and Stinnett's review of 325 treaties vis-à-vis the issues that they sought to address concluded that highly contentious issues generally result in more detailed legal and institutional arrangements.[100]

A further line of (albeit limited) enquiry has considered compliance, or non-compliance, with transboundary water agreements. Much of this body of research has focused on specific basins. Bernauer and Siegfried, for example, assess compliance and performance within the context of the Naryn/Syr Draya Basin.[101] The authors argue that while compliance with the relevant agreement might be high, the limitations of the agreement might mean that it does not necessarily solve the problem it was set out to address.[102] Along similar lines, Zeitoun and others draw upon insights from the Amu Darya, Jordan, Ganges, Tigris, Mekong and Nile rivers to stress the point that compliance with an international agreement might have more to do with the power asymmetries found within a particular river basin than with the design of the agreement itself.[103]

While scholarship has therefore made significant advances in knowledge and understanding relating to transboundary water agreements, there are still major gaps. For instance, while enforcement mechanisms are considered important to address conflict, the type of enforcement mechanisms that are most effective within a transboundary water context remain underexplored.

---

98 Wolf, Stahl and Macomber (n 81); Wolf, Yoffe and Giordano (n 73). See also Paul Hensel and Marit Brochmann, 'Peaceful Management of International River Claims' (2009) 14(2) International Negotiation 293.

99 Sara M. Mitchell and Neda A. Zawahri, 'The Effectiveness of Treaty Design in Addressing Water Disputes' (2015) 52(2) Journal of Peace Research 187. See also Shlomi Dinar, *International Water Treaties – Negotiation and Cooperation along Transboundary Waters* (Routledge 2008).

100 Jaroslav Tir and Douglas M. Stinnett, 'The Institutional Design of Riparian Treaties: The Role of River Issues' (2011) 55(4) Journal of Conflict Resolution 606.

101 Thomas Bernauer and Tobias Siegfried, 'Compliance and Performance in International Water Agreements: the Case of the Naryn/Syr Darya Basin' (2009) 14(4) Global Governance 479.

102 Ibid.

103 Mark Zeitoun and others, 'Transboundary Water Interaction III: Contest and Compliance' (2017) 17 International Environmental Agreements: Politics, Law and Economics 271.

Similarly, in relation to compliance and implementation, scholars have not considered whether there are any particular types of compliance and implementation mechanisms (CIMs) that might prove advantageous in ensuring that transboundary water agreements are implemented both fairly and effectively between states. Despite the importance of transboundary water agreements in preventing and managing conflicts, it is surprising that there has not been more attention on analysing this important design feature of transboundary water agreements.[104]

This lack of focus on treaty implementation and compliance within the context of transboundary waters can be contrasted with other areas of law, such as human rights[105] and environmental protection.[106] Particularly since the 1992 Rio Conference on Environment and Development, a major effort has been undertaken 'to ensure the effective, full and prompt implementation of legally binding instruments'.[107] Scholars from a range of disciplines, including law, political science and economics, responded with vigour to this call through their analysis of the implementation of multilateral environmental agreements (MEAs).[108] In turn, this work has led to advances in our understanding of

---

104 Throughout this book, 'compliance' means 'the fulfilment by the contracting parties of their obligations' under an agreement; whereas, 'implementation' refers to 'all relevant laws, regulations, policies, and other measures and initiatives, that contracting parties adopt and/or take to meet their obligations' (see UNEP, *Manual on Compliance with and Enforcement of Multilateral Environmental Agreements* (UNEP 2006), 59).

105 Helen Watchirs, 'Review of Methodologies Measuring Human Rights Implementation' (2002) 30(4) Journal of Law, Medicine and Ethics 716; Wade M. Cole, 'Mind the Gap: State Capacity and the Implementation of Human Rights Treaties' (2015) 69 International Organisation 405; Christina M. Cerna, 'Universality of Human Rights and Cultural Diversity: Implementation of Human Rights in Different Socio-cultural Contexts' (1994) 16 Human Rights Quarterly 740.

106 Paul Martin and Amanda Kennedy (eds), *Implementing Environmental Law* (Edward Elgar 2015); Alice Palmer, 'National Implementation', in Lavanya Rajamani and Jacqueline Peel (eds), *The Oxford Handbook of International Environmental Law* (2nd edn, OUP 2007).

107 Agenda 21, in 'Report of the United Nations Conference on Environmental and Development' (Rio de Janeiro, 3–14 June 1992), UN Doc A/Conf.151/26/Rev.1, para 39.3(e).

108 See for example, Edith Brown Weiss and Harold K. Jacobson (eds), *Engaging Countries – Strengthening Compliance with International Accords* (The MIT Press 2000); David G. Victor, Kal Raustiala and Eugene B. Skolnikoff (eds), *The Implementation and Effectiveness of International Environmental Commitments* (The MIT Press 1998).

the factors that influence treaty compliance and the types of mechanisms that might be introduced within treaty regimes to secure their compliance.[109] For instance, institutional frameworks, such as meetings or conferences of the parties, secretariats and subsidiary bodies, have become commonplace in most MEAs. Similarly, mechanisms, such as regular reporting, compliance committees, and technical and financial assistance programmes, have been incorporated into MEAs to improve treaty compliance and implementation.[110] This trend shows no sign of slowing down.[111] Such a trend is reflected in the adoption of recent instruments, such as the Paris Agreement,[112] and ongoing negotiations, such as those related to an international legally binding instrument on plastic pollution.[113]

While institutional frameworks for reviewing the implementation of international agreements, such as regular meetings of the parties, secretariats and working groups, are commonplace in transboundary water agreements, there has been little practice of establishing the more specific types of CIMs that can be found in MEAs, such as reporting mechanisms or compliance committees.[114] Out of over 400 transboundary water agreements, one of the few examples is the 2004 Zambezi Agreement, which includes a provision on

---

[109] For example, Brown-Weiss and Jacobson highlight a series of strategies for strengthening compliance, including (i) 'sunshine methods', including monitoring, reporting, on-site inspections, access to information and NGO participation; (ii) positive incentives, such as financial and technical assistance; and (iii) coercive methods, such as penalties, sanctions and membership withdrawal (n 108, 542–552).

[110] Tullio Treves, 'Introduction', in Tullio Treves and others (eds), *Non-compliance Procedures and Mechanisms and the Effectiveness of International Environmental Agreements* (TMC Asser Press 2009).

[111] Malgosia Fitzmaurice, 'The New Generation of Environmental Non-Compliance Procedures and the Question of Legitimacy', in Christina Voigt and Caroline Foster (eds), *International Courts versus Non-Compliance Mechanisms – Comparative Advantages in Strengthening Treaty Implementation* (CUP 2024).

[112] Caroline E. Foster, 'Lessons from the Paris Agreement for International Pandemic Law and Beyond', in Christina Voigt and Caroline Foster (eds), *International Courts versus Non-Compliance Mechanisms – Comparative Advantages in Strengthening Treaty Implementation* (CUP 2024).

[113] UNEP, 'Revised draft text of the international legally binding instrument on plastic pollution, including the marine environment – note by the secretariat', UN Doc UNEP/PP/INC.4/3 (28 December 2023), 48–54.

[114] Chapter 4 provides an in-depth analysis of the way in which implementation and compliance are directly or indirectly incorporated into the text of transboundary water agreements.

non-compliance,[115] and the 2002 Framework Agreement on the Sava River, which requires its parties to establish a methodology for implementing the Agreement.[116] Very few studies have directly considered compliance within the context of transboundary water agreements,[117] and no study has considered whether the design of transboundary water agreements could benefit from the adoption of CIMs.

1.5 AIMS AND OBJECTIVES

The aim of this book is to respond to the need for a greater focus on CIMs within the context of transboundary water agreements. Put simply, the book enquires whether there is a benefit in widespread incorporation of CIMs within transboundary water agreements. The key components of a CIM that will be the focus of study will be institutional frameworks responsible for implementing a treaty, e.g., a river basin organisation, any requirements for reporting on compliance and implementation, any bespoke body established to address issues of treaty implementation or non-compliance, e.g., an implementation, compliance or non-compliance committee, and any provision for financial and technical assistance to address implementation or compliance issues.

In recognising the multitude of differing contexts that exist across the world's transboundary rivers, lakes and aquifers, the book will aim to identify general principles or key elements of a CIM that might enhance transboundary water cooperation irrespective of the cultural, economic, environmental, political, social or other contexts that exist within a basin. An ambition is therefore to provide insights that are applicable across a range of diverse contexts. In terms of assessing benefits, the book aims to ask whether incorporating the key components of a CIM into transboundary water agreements would improve the implementation and effectiveness of existing agreements. It might therefore be asked whether the incorporation of CIMs might lead to a more transparent and systematic implementation of treaty commitments. In other words, within

---

115 Article 20, Agreement on the Establishment of the Zambezi Watercourse Commission (adopted 13 July 2004, entered into force 19 June 2011), <https://www.zambezicommission.org/publication/zamcom-agreement> accessed 13 June 2024.

116 Article 21, Framework Agreement on the Sava River (adopted 3 December 2002, entered into force 29 December 2004), 2366 UNTS 479.

117 The few examples that exist include UNECE, 'Geneva Strategy and Framework for Monitoring Compliance with Agreements on Transboundary Waters' (17 December 1999) MP.WAT/2000/5; Patricia A. Jones, 'Compliance Mechanisms of International Water Agreements: A Case of US-Mexico Boundary Waters' (2000) 25(4) Water International 554.

existing treaty practice, is there a risk that commitments within transboundary water agreements are not being fully implemented? Are parties simply unaware of the extent to which other parties are meeting, or failing to meet, their commitments? Is there a risk that without such transparency, there is a certain inequity between parties in how a treaty is implemented? Might it be the case that a 'free riding' party profits from a transboundary water agreement without meeting their commitments in full?

It might also be asked whether the incorporation of a CIM within transboundary water agreements could assist with conflict avoidance or management. For instance, would the incorporation of CIMs offer a more effective way to solve the types of disputes that arise between countries sharing transboundary waters compared to traditional dispute settlement mechanisms, such as arbitration or adjudication? Where treaties are lacking, could the prospect of introducing a CIM act as an incentive for countries to enter into agreements in the first place? For example, where there is a lack of trust between the countries, would the inclusion of CIMs give countries the necessary confidence to adopt a treaty?

To address these types of questions and explore whether there is a benefit in widespread incorporation of CIMs within transboundary water agreements, the book will seek to fulfil a series of objectives.

Firstly, in order to set a context in which to better understand the successes and failures concerning the implementation of transboundary water agreements, the book will review scholarship from a range of disciplines, including law, political science and economics, to ascertain the factors that drive cooperation and conflict over transboundary waters, and more specifically influence the implementation of, and compliance with, transboundary water agreements.

A second key objective will be to draw upon the experience of CIMs found within MEAs with a view to assessing any lessons that might be learned for their incorporation into transboundary water agreements. In particular, the book will explore three key components of CIMs that are commonly found within MEAs, namely i) regular reporting on compliance and/or implementation; ii) the bodies and processes established to review the results of any reporting; and iii) the measures in place to address any incidences of weak implementation or non-compliance, such as the provision of technical and financial assistance. The primary outcome of this analysis will be to identify the types of mechanisms that could potentially be transferable to the context of transboundary watercourse agreements.

A third objective will be to assess the degree to which existing transboundary water agreements explicitly or implicitly already address compliance and implementation. While it has already been noted that few agreements explicitly contain any elements of a CIM, such as a reporting mechanism or a compliance committee, the research will ask whether there are alternative means by which existing agreements secure their compliance and implementation. The assessment of existing treaties will therefore consider whether compliance and implementation might be implicitly captured in more general commitments found in transboundary water agreements, such as those relating to the mandate of river basin organisations, provisions concerning the exchange of data and information, and general dispute settlement mechanisms. In addition, such an analysis provides an opportunity to survey the current architecture of transboundary water agreements and identify the foundations upon which CIMs might be built. The analysis will seek to draw upon the text of over 400 agreements concluded by two or more states that address the protection and use and transboundary rivers, lakes or aquifers. These agreements include bilateral agreements covering several transboundary waters, basin-wide agreements between two or more states, as well as any sub-basin or tributary agreements that two or more states have adopted. The analysis will also aim to provide a widespread and representative body of agreements encompassing all the regions of the world where transboundary waters are shared. Additionally, it will be possible through this analysis to identify any temporal trends and ask whether provisions on compliance and implementation, or at least elements thereof, are more likely to be found in contemporary practice.

A fourth objective, closely aligned to the third objective, is to examine the extent to which CIMs are incorporated into regional and multilateral treaties concerning the protection and use of transboundary rivers, lakes and aquifers. This analysis will focus on three key instruments: the 1992 Water Convention, the 2000 EU Water Framework Directive[118] and the 2000 Revised SADC Protocol on Shared Watercourses.[119] While all three are relevant given their general focus on transboundary waters, they also warrant special attention given that each instrument deals to a greater or lesser extent with matters related to compliance and implementation. The Water Convention is of importance not only because it now operates at a global level, but also because it has introduced a regular reporting mechanism and an implementation committee as part of its institutional framework.[120] Both the 2000 EU Water Framework Directive and the 2000 Revised SADC Protocol on Shared Watercourses offer interesting and differing perspectives on how compliance and implementation are addressed. While neither of these instruments says much about compliance and implementation within their text, useful insights can be gained by studying

[118] Water Framework Directive (n 57).

[119] 2000 Revised SADC Protocol (n 56).

[120] UNECE, 'Decision VI/1 Support to Implementation and Compliance', UN Doc ECE/MP.WAT/37/Add.2 (30 November 2021).

the bodies and processes established by the EU and SADC to support regular reporting, implementation reviews, and the management of non-compliance.

The study would be incomplete if it did not also consider how transboundary water cooperation is monitored within the SDG framework.[121] Pursuant to SDG indicator 6.5.2, states sharing transboundary waters are asked to regularly report on their progress both in the adoption and implementation of transboundary water agreements.[122] SDG indicator 6.5.2 reporting is not obligatory and has not been established under any treaty framework for transboundary waters. However, a question to be explored is whether this softer type of arrangement might be preferred, or might act as a complement to, the type of binding CIMs found in treaty frameworks.

The second, third and fourth objectives largely focus on treaty commitments and require doctrinal analysis of the text of those treaties. However, such an analysis may not provide a full picture of compliance and implementation. It may be the case that while states do not include provisions on compliance and implementation within the text of their transboundary water agreements, they may still address such issues in other ways. A fifth objective of the work will therefore be to ask whether there are alternative ways in which states address issues of compliance and implementation. While a comprehensive assessment of the practice found in all transboundary rivers, lakes and aquifers would not be feasible, the book will seek to draw generic insights from an analysis of three case studies – the Danube, the Orange-Senqu and the Mekong river basins. Other basins might provide equally useful insights; however, these three basins were chosen for several reasons. Firstly, each basin has a well-established basin-wide agreement in place.[123] These basin-wide agreements not only set out rules and principles by which the parties should protect and use transboundary waters of the basin, but also an institutional framework, including a river basin organisation, that is responsible for overseeing the implementation of the agreement. It will therefore be possible to not only analyse the normative content of the agreement, but also any efforts that the parties have taken to implement and comply with it. Secondly, each of the basins offers a different regional perspective: the Danube Basin sits within a European context and is influenced by both the Water Convention and the EU Water Framework Directive; the Orange-Senqu is situated within the Southern African context and is influenced by the 2000 Revised SADC Protocol; and the Mekong is located within a South East Asian context where no multi-basin

[121] See UNGA Res 66/288 (n 15).

[122] UNGA, 'Work of the Statistical Commission Pertaining to the 2030 Agenda for Sustainable Development', UN Doc A/RES/71/313 (6 July 2017).

[123] In the case of the Mekong, the focus will be on the 1995 Mekong Agreement adopted by the lower Mekong states of Cambodia, Laos, Thailand and Vietnam.

regional legal instruments on transboundary waters exist. Thirdly, sufficient data and information is available on each of the river basins to not only analyse formal arrangements themselves, but also the progress and outcomes of country efforts to implement those arrangements.

By achieving the objectives set out above, this book seeks to ultimately provide a comprehensive and persuasive account of whether there is benefit in the widespread incorporation of CIMs within transboundary water agreements, and if so, what type of CIMs would best suit those agreements. For existing agreements, the insights provided within this book will point to where there may be benefit in existing regimes adopting supplementary bodies or processes to improve their compliance and implementation record. For new agreements, negotiators and other interested parties might use this research to inform the design of those agreements.

Through the analysis of transboundary water agreements, this book also aims to provide useful insights for the evolution of international law generally, and treaty law. The relationship between 'law on paper' vis-à-vis 'law in practice' will be a key theme running throughout the research. A further key theme that runs through much of the analysis is the relationship between different arrangements, particularly the relationship between global, regional and basin-specific legal regimes. The research will explore whether these legal regimes are in conflict or whether they work in a mutually supportive way to strengthen the implementation of and compliance with transboundary water agreements.

The structure of the book closely follows the five objectives set out above. To better understand the context in which transboundary water agreements operate, the next chapter will review scholarship related to transboundary water conflict and cooperation. Chapter 3 will then review CIMs found in MEAs with a view to identifying what lessons might be learned for transboundary water agreements. Chapter 4 will explore the extent to which CIMs, or elements thereof, are found either explicitly or implicitly within existing transboundary water agreements. This analysis will be complemented in Chapter 5 by a study of how CIMs, or elements thereof, have been incorporated into global and regional treaties, i.e., the 1992 Water Convention, the 2000 EU Water Framework Directive and the 2000 Revised SADC Protocol, as well as 'softer' policy frameworks, i.e., the SDG indicator 6.5.2. Chapters 6 to 8 are then dedicated to the Mekong, Orange-Senqu and Danube basin case studies, assessing not only the commitments that the riparian parties have entered into through their basin-wide agreements, but also the extent to which treaty compliance and implementation are addressed in practice within each of the basins. The penultimate chapter, Chapter 9, draws together the key research findings and presents the lessons that can be learned for the possible incorporation of CIMs within transboundary water agreements. The last chapter will then provide a conclusion to the research by summarising the key insights from each of the preceding chapters.

2. Commitment, compliance and transboundary water agreements

2.1 INTRODUCTION

Over four decades ago, Louis Henkin declared that 'almost all nations observe almost all principles of international law and almost all of their obligations almost all of the time'.[1] While this statement might give the optimistic impression that international law has significant influence on state behaviour, it is also a reminder of the importance of examining the wider context in which law operates. Not only is it important to ask whether states comply with their treaty commitments, but it is equally important to ask *why* they do so. Ignoring the latter question may give a false impression of treaty performance. For example, it may be the case that a state commits to a treaty only because its requirements are already in accordance with those commitments. In such circumstances, while compliance is likely to be high, not much can be said about the influence of the treaty itself.[2] Also, what if only the downstream states are party to a transboundary water agreement while much of the practice that the agreement aims to address, such as industrial pollution or hydropower development, takes place upstream? In such a scenario, full compliance with the provisions of the agreement would say little about the ability of that agreement to address the key transboundary challenges within a basin.

[1] Louis Henkin, *How Nations Behave: Law and Foreign Policy* (Columbia University Press 1979), 47.

[2] Ronald Mitchell, for example, suggests that the lack of mining in Antarctica has more to do with economic factors, i.e., the availability of cheaper alternatives, than the influence of international law banning it (see Ronald B. Mitchell, 'Compliance Theory: Compliance, Effectiveness, and Behaviour Change in International Environmental Law', in Daniel Bodansky, Jutta Brunnée and Ellen Hey (eds), *The Oxford Handbook of International Environmental Law* (OUP 2007), 904).

This chapter therefore recognises the importance of exploring the wider context in which transboundary water agreements operate, which is a critical precondition to any study of treaty implementation and compliance. Through a review of different disciplinary perspectives, including law, political science and economics, the chapter seeks to identify the main external factors that are likely to influence a state's decision to comply with its treaty commitments. Three cross-disciplinary strands of scholarship are drawn upon, namely work focused on power relations, incentives and reciprocity, and norms and ideas.

2.2 DOES POWER MOTIVATE STATES TO COOPERATE OVER TRANSBOUNDARY WATERS?

Power is considered by some scholars as the most important factor explaining why states implement and comply with their treaty commitments.[3] A classic realist perspective argues that power is likely to override any influence that treaty commitments may have on a state, and states would rather pursue their own interests based on their capacity and subject to the relative power and interests of others.[4] Power in this context is interpreted as 'the ability of states to use material resources to get others to do what they otherwise would not'.[5] Rather than international law, a realist perspective sees relative military and economic capacity as a key factor in explaining state behaviour.[6]

When viewing the world through a realist perspective, it might be queried why states ever enter into treaty commitments. The realist response would be that states do so when the most powerful state, also known as the hegemon, decides that it is advantageous to do so.[7] Moreover, a realist perspective would suggest that, given their relative power over others, the hegemon may well skew the terms of an agreement to suit their own interests.[8] However, if circumstances change and a legal commitment becomes inconsistent with a significant interest of a hegemon, a realist perspective suggests that the state

---

[3] Hans J. Morgenthau, *Politics Among Nations: The Struggle for Power and Peace* (McGraw-Hill 1993), 4–5. See also Emilie M. Hafner-Burton, David G. Victor and Yonatan Lupu, 'Political Science Research on International Law: The State of the Field' (2012) 106 AJIL 47.

[4] Morgenthau (n 3).

[5] Michael Barnett and Raymond Duvall, 'Power in International Politics' (2005) 59(1) International Organisation 39, 40.

[6] Jack K. Goldsmith and Eric A. Posner, *The Limits of International Law* (OUP 2005); David Armstrong, Theo Farrell and Hélène Lambert, *International Law and International Relations* (CUP 2007), 73.

[7] Morgenthau (n 3).

[8] Ibid.

would readily breach its legal commitments.[9] Similarly, coercion, it is argued, might be used by the most powerful state party to an agreement as the primary means by which to ensure that other states adopt a treaty in the first place and, once adopted, dictate the manner in which commitments are complied with.[10]

Such an interpretation of international relations has proven popular in explaining why states cooperate over transboundary waters.[11] Pursuant to this perspective where the most powerful state sharing a transboundary basin, also known as the 'hydro-hegemon',[12] is upstream, it is suggested that they will have little incentive to enter into cooperative arrangements.[13]

China is offered as an example of a state that is in a position to use its relative power, and its geographic position of being upstream on transboundary rivers shared with its neighbours.[14] China shares transboundary rivers with 14 neighbours (Afghanistan, Bhutan, India, Kazakhstan, Kyrgyzstan, Laos, Mongolia, Myanmar, Nepal, North Korea, Pakistan, Russia, Tajikistan and Vietnam), and most of Asia relies on water flowing from China.[15] On the

---

9 Benedict Kingsbury, 'The Concept of Compliance as a Function of Competing Conceptions of International Law' (1998) 19 Michigan Journal of International Law 345, 351.

10 Christian Reus-Smit, 'Politics and International Legal Obligation' (2003) 9(4) European Journal of International Relations 591, 592.

11 Frederick W. Frey, 'The Political Context of Conflict and Cooperation over International River Basins' (2009) 18(1) Water International 54; Miriam R. Lowi, *Water and Power – The politics of a scarce resource in the Jordan River basin* (CUP 2009), 169. Lowi suggests that weaker states sharing transboundary waters have, 'little alternative but to accept a modus vivendi dictated by the stronger' (ibid).

12 Mark Zeitoun and Jeroen Warner, 'Hydro-hegemony – A Framework for Analysis of Trans-boundary Water Conflicts' (2006) 8 Water Policy 435.

13 Mark Zeitoun and John Anthony Allan, 'Applying hegemony and power theory to transboundary water analysis' (2008) 10 Water Policy 3; John Waterbury, 'Between Unilateralism and Comprehensive Accords: Modest Steps Toward Cooperation in International River Basins' (1997) 13 International Journal of Water Resources and Development 279, 281; Frederick W. Frey and Tomas Naff, 'Water: An Emerging Issue in the Middle East' (1985) 482 The Annals of the American Academy of Political and Social Sciences 65; Thomas Naff, 'A Case for Demand-side Water Management' in Jad Isaac and Hillel Shuval (eds), *Water and Peace in the Middle East* (Elsevier Science 1994), 10.

14 See Patricia Wouters, Huiping Chen, and James E. Nickum (eds), *Transboundary Water Cooperation – Principles, Practice, and Prospects for China and its Neighbours* (Abingdon 2018).

15 Patricia Wouters and Sergei Vinogradov, 'Reframing the Transboundary Water Discourse: Contextualised international law in practice' (2020) 29 Review of European, Comparative and International Environmental Law 285, 286.

Mekong River, China's unilateral development of a cascade of 11 upstream hydropower dams is seen as reflective of asymmetric power within the basin.[16] These unilateral developments upstream have raised concerns downstream.[17] Similar concerns are voiced over Chinese unilateral upstream developments in the Yarlung-Tsangpo/Brahmaputra River Basin, which it shares with India and Bangladesh,[18] the Irrawaddy shared with Myanmar and India, and the Salween shared with Myanmar and Thailand.[19]

However, while a realist perspective would suggest that China has little incentive to enter into cooperative arrangements, the reality is slightly different.[20] China has entered into bilateral agreements with Kazakhstan, Mongolia and Russia.[21] These agreements follow a similar model. They tend to cover

---

16 Akarath Soukhaphon, Ian G. Baird and Zeb S. Hogan, 'The Impacts of Hydropower Dams in the Mekong River: A Review' (2021) 13(1) Water 26; Jim E. Nickum, 'The Upstream Superpower: China's International Rivers', in Olli Varis, Asit K. Biswas and Cecilia Tortajada (eds), *Management of Transboundary Rivers and Lakes* (Springer 2008), 227.

17 Ibid. Brian Eyler, Regan Kwan and Courtney Weatherby, 'How China Turned off the Tap on the Mekong River' (*Stimson,* 13 April 2020) <https://www.stimson.org/2020/new-evidence-how-china-turned-off-the-mekong-tap/> accessed 13 June 2024.

18 Jaideep Saikia, 'The Chinese Threat to Lower Brahmaputra Riparians India and Bangladesh' (*The Diplomat*, 19 February 2022) <https://thediplomat.com/2022/02/the-chinese-threat-to-lower-brahmaputra-riparians-india-and-bangladesh> accessed 13 June 2024.

19 Nicholas Lo, 'Rebellious River: Chinese hydropower development in an illegible landscape' (2019) 38 Tropical Resources <https://tri.yale.edu/tropical-resources/tropical-resources-vol-38/rebellious-river-chinese-hydropower-development> accessed 13 June 2024; Truong-Minh Vu and Maximilian Mayer, 'Hydropower Infrastructure and Regional Order Making in the Sub-Mekong Region' (2018) 61(1) Revista Brasileira de Política Internacional <https://www.scielo.br/j/rbpi/a/qV5R3RLprx43By43MpfPLKv/?format=pdf&lang=en> accessed 13 June 2024, 9.

20 See generally Wouters, Chen and Nickum (n 14).

21 Agreement between the Government of the People's Republic of China and the Government of Mongolia on the Protection and Utilisation of Transboundary Waters (adopted 29 April 1994, entered into force 16 January 1995) (China-Mongolia Agreement) <http://gis.nacse.org/tfdd/tfdddocs/528ENG.pdf> accessed 13 June 2024; Agreement between the Government of the Russian Federation and the Government of the People's Republic of China on Rational Management and Protection of Transboundary Waters (adopted 19 January 2008) (China-Russia Agreement) <https://www.fao.org/faolex/results/details/en/c/LEX-FAOC094367/> accessed 13 June 2024; Agreement between the Government of the Republic of Kazakhstan and the Government of the People's Republic of China on Cooperation

all transboundary waters shared exclusively by the two respective countries, and they set out fundamental principles for the protection and use of transboundary waters. While not particularly detailed and using slightly different formulations, these three bilateral agreements are also consistent with the fundamental customary international law principles of equitable and reasonable utilisation and no significant harm, and, albeit in general terms, seek a balance between the interests of the upstream and downstream state.[22]

The three bilateral agreements also provide for the establishment of bilateral commissions.[23] However, in each of them, very little detail is given on the mandated tasks and activities of these commissions. For example, the China-Mongolia Agreement simply stipulates that the Commission will 'take charge of handling matters related to the implementation of this Agreement'.[24] No specifics are provided on how any issues of weak implementation or non-compliance might be addressed. Each of the agreements simply provides that any disputes will be resolved through consultation between the parties.[25]

China has proven to be reluctant to enter into similar agreements where its transboundary waters are shared with more than one other country. For instance, China is not party to the 1995 Mekong Agreement, and no basin agreement exists for the Yarlung-Tsangpo/Brahmaputra, Irrawaddy or Salween.[26] China is

---

in the Use and Protection of Transboundary Rivers (adopted 12 September 2001) (China-Kazakhstan Agreement) <http://www.cawater-info.net/library/eng/l/kazakhstan_china.pdf> accessed 13 June 2024; see also Agreement between the Government of the Republic of Kazakhstan and the Government of the People's Republic of China on Transboundary Rivers Water Quality Protection (adopted 30 September 2011) <https://adilet.zan.kz/eng/docs/P1100001114> accessed 13 June 2024. See generally Yu Su, 'Contemporary Legal Analysis of China's Transboundary Watercourse Regimes: International Law in Practice' (2013) 39 Water International 705.

22 For further analysis on this point, see Huiping Chen, Alistair Rieu-Clarke and Patricia Wouters, 'Exploring China's Transboundary Water Practice through the Prism of the UN Watercourses Convention' (2013) 38(2) Water International 217.

23 Article 4, China-Russia Agreement (n 21), Articles 10–12, China-Mongolia Agreement (n 21), and Articles 8–10, China-Kazakhstan Agreement (n 21).

24 Article 10, China-Mongolia Agreement (n 21).

25 Article 14, China-Mongolia Agreement (n 21), Article 7, China-Russia Agreement (n 21), and Article 12, China-Kazakhstan Agreement (n 21).

26 Agreement on the Cooperation for the Sustainable Development of the Mekong River Basin (adopted 5 April 1995), 34 ILM 864. On the process of negotiating and adopting the agreement, see Greg Browder, 'An Analysis of the Negotiations for the 1995 Mekong Agreement' (2000) 5 International Negotiation 237.

also not a party to the Convention on the Law of the Non-navigational Uses of International Watercourses (Watercourses Convention),[27] nor the Convention on the Protection and Use of Transboundary Watercourses and International Lakes (Water Convention).[28] In fact, China voted against the Watercourses Convention at the time of its adoption by the UN General Assembly.[29] When doing so, China raised concerns over a lack of reference to territorial sovereignty within the text of the agreement, an 'obvious imbalance' between the rights and obligations of upstream and downstream countries, and a concern over the binding nature of certain dispute settlement procedures.[30]

Despite China's reticence to enter into multilateral agreements concerning transboundary waters, it has since 1996 been a 'dialogue partner' within the institutional framework set up to implement the Mekong Agreement, namely the Mekong River Commission (MRC).[31] This led to a Memorandum of Understanding (MoU) between China and the MRC in October 2002 that calls upon China to provide daily river flow and rainfall data in the wet season.[32] The MoU was extended in 2020 to commit China to provide data all year round.[33] Cooperation between the Mekong countries has also been evidenced through China's release of water from its upstream impoundments to address emergency drought levels in downstream states.[34] Additionally, China has championed its own Mekong basin initiative, i.e., the Lancang-Mekong Cooperation framework, which was adopted by the heads of state of China, Myanmar, Thailand, Cambodia, Laos and Vietnam in 2016.[35] Under this framework, a joint working group on Lancang-Mekong Water Resources

[27] Convention on the Law of the Non-navigational Uses of International Watercourses (adopted 21 May 1997, entered into force 17 August 2014), 2999 UNTS 77 (Watercourses Convention).

[28] Convention on the Protection and Use of Transboundary Watercourses and International Lakes (adopted 17 March 1992, entered into force 6 October 1996), 31 ILM 1312 (Water Convention).

[29] Convention on the Law of the Non-navigational Uses of International Watercourses, UN Doc UNGA Res 51/229 (8 July 1997).

[30] Ibid, at 6–7.

[31] Mekong River Commission, 'Dialogue Partners' (*MRCmekong.org*) <https://www.mrcmekong.org/dialogue-partners/> accessed 13 June 2024.

[32] Ibid.

[33] Ibid.

[34] Tian Fuqiang and Liu Hui, '"China's Water Hegemony in Asia" or "Shared Rivers, Shared Futures": Which?' (*th.china-embassy.gov.cn*, 27 July 2016) <http://th.china-embassy.gov.cn/eng/ztbd/201607/t20160727_10148408.htm> accessed 13 June 2024.

[35] Carl Middleton and Jeremy Allouche, 'Watershed or Powershed? Critical Hydropolitics, China and the Lancang-Mekong Cooperation Framework' (2016) 51(3) The International Spectator 100, 101.

Cooperation has been established with the view to advancing, 'experience sharing, data and information exchange, monitoring, joint assessment and joint research and study, knowledge management and associated capacity building relating to water and related resources development and management so as to jointly promote sustainable social and economic development of the Lancang-Mekong Countries'.[36] An important distinction between the MoU, as well as the broader Lancang-Mekong Cooperation framework, and the 1995 Mekong Agreement is their legal status. While the 1995 Mekong Agreement is legally binding, the Lancang-Mekong arrangements are softer in nature.[37] The MoU even explicitly states that it, 'does not create any rights or legally binding obligations upon both parties and does not constitute a treaty under international law'.[38]

A similar strategy has been adopted by China with Bangladesh and India, where the respective bilateral MoUs are limited to data exchange during flood seasons.[39]

While China may therefore largely fit the classic model of a 'hydro-hegemon', it would appear that such a categorisation does not provide the full picture. Despite its upstream position, China has demonstrated some willingness to cooperate over its transboundary rivers and even described these shared waters as 'ambassadors of peace, cooperation and friendship'.[40] Through bilateral cooperation with Kazakhstan, Mongolia and Russia, China has evidenced a general commitment to embrace fundamental principles of customary inter-

[36] MoU between the Mekong River Commission Secretariat and the Lancang-Mekong Water Resources Cooperation Centre (adopted 17 December 2019) <https://faolex.fao.org/docs/pdf/bi215422.pdf> accessed 28 January 2025.

[37] See David J. Devlaeminck, 'Softness in the Law of the International Watercourses: The (E)merging Normativities of China's Lancang Mekong Cooperation' (2020) 11(2) Transnational Environmental Law 357.

[38] MoU (n 36).

[39] See for example, MoU between the Ministry of Water Resources, the Republic of India, and the Ministry of Water Resources, the People's Republic of China on Strengthening Cooperation on Trans-border Rivers (adopted 23 October 2013), <https://mea.gov.in/bilateral-documents.htm?dtl/22368> accessed 13 June 2024; MoU Concerning the Provision of Hydrological Information of the Brahmaputra/Yaluzangbu River in Flood Season by China to Bangladesh (adopted 16 September 2008), <http://www.mwr.gov.cn/english/news/200809/t20080919_102801.html> accessed 13 June 2024.

[40] Ministry of Water Resources of the People's Republic of China, 'International Cooperation on Integrated Water Resources Management of Transboundary Rivers in China' (SDG indicator 6.5.2 national report), <https://unece.org/sites/default/files/2021-11/China_2ndReporting_SDG652_2020_web.pdf> accessed 13 June 2024.

national law, such as equitable and reasonable utilisation and no significant harm. Given that these principles seek to find a balance between the interests of upstream and downstream states, their adoption by China through its treaty practice is arguably at variance with the strictest account of a hydro-hegemon. However, a realist perspective might claim that this commitment differs from actual practice. Admittedly, the willingness to commit to these general principles may be contrasted with the lack of specifics in terms of how the principles are both implemented and complied with. The bilateral commissions established under each have a very vague and general mandate, and any tasks and activities they might carry out are largely undefined. Similarly, in terms of addressing issues of non-compliance, there is simply a soft requirement that the parties enter into consultations. A realist perspective would therefore argue that there is still plenty of scope for China to skew the implementation of these principles in its favour.[41]

China has also demonstrated a preference to conduct bilateral MoUs on specific issues, e.g., data exchange, or develop non-legally binding arrangements, such as the Lancang-Mekong Cooperation framework. China is less ready to adopt basin-wide legally binding commitments and would likely resist detailed compliance and implementation mechanisms (CIMs).

Another oft-cited example of an upstream riparian state dominating basin dynamics is Turkey within the context of the Tigris-Euphrates River Basin shared with its downstream neighbours – Iraq and Syria.[42] In the 1960s, Turkey unilaterally commenced construction of the Keban Dam on the Euphrates River.[43] At the same time, Syria was unilaterally developing their Tabqa Dam on the Euphrates River.[44] This led to both Iraq and Syria raising

[41] See for example, Justin Brassett, Moldir Akmadi and Troy Sternberg, 'Seeing Beyond Negotiations: The Impacts of the Belt and Road on Sino-Kazakh Transboundary Water Management' (2022) 39(3) International Journal of Water Resources Development 361.

[42] Paul A. Williams, 'Turkish Hydro-Hegemony – The Impact of Dams', in Marcus D. King (ed), *Water and Conflict in the Middle East* (OUP 2020); Ahmet Conker, 'Understanding Turkish Water Nationalism and its Role in the Historical Hydraulic Development of Turkey' (2018) 46(5) Nationalities Papers 877; Behnam Sarkheil, 'Water and Strategy of Turkish Hydro-hegemony in Mesopotamia' (2021) 11(2) International Relations Research Quarterly 97; Jeroen Warner, 'Contested Hydrohegemony: Hydraulic Control and Security in Turkey' (2008) 1(2) Water Alternatives 271.

[43] Gerald E. Gruen, 'Turkish Waters: Source of Regional Conflict or Catalyst for Peace?', in S. Belkin (ed), *Environmental Challenges* (Springer 2000).

[44] Aysegül Kibaroglu and Waltina Scheumann, 'Evolution of Transboundary Politics in the Euphrates-Tigris River System: New perspectives and political challenges' (2013) 19(2) Global Governance 279, 285.

concerns over the amount of water Turkey might impound upstream.[45] Iraq also raised concerns over Syria withholding water.[46] In the 1970s, Turkey's unilateral plans for the Tigris and Euphrates expanded into the South-eastern Anatolia Project (Güneydogu Anadolu Projesi (GAP)), which was originally conceived as a hydropower and irrigation project to exploit the potential of the Tigris and Euphrates basins, but later evolved into a broader regional development initiative to improve socio-economic conditions in the South-eastern Anatolia Region of Turkey.[47] The water resources component of GAP originally comprised 22 dams, 19 hydropower plants, and 17,000 km^2 of irrigated land upstream within the Tigris and Euphrates River Basins. To date, 18 of these dams and 13 hydropower plants have been completed.[48]

While Turkey's unilateral developments on the Tigris and Euphrates River Basins would appear to align squarely with a realist perspective, as in the case of China, the reality exposes certain nuances. Ever since Iraq and Syria raised concerns over Turkey's developments in the 1960s, the three riparian states have entered into negotiations with a view to agreeing a basin-wide treaty.[49] The riparian states sought to achieve this through a series of trilateral meetings. Despite a basin-wide agreement proving to be elusive, these meetings delivered some progress. For instance, Turkey committed to release certain flows to its downstream neighbours during the construction and impoundment of the Keban Dam.[50] Also, when tensions further escalated during the 1980s with Turkey's development of the Atatürk Dam on the Euphrates River, there were renewed calls for cooperation.[51] These calls resulted in the establishment of a Joint Technical Committee (JTC), which also sought to reach agreements on water allocations between the three riparians.[52] While the JTC ultimately proved unsuccessful in delivering a basin-wide agreement, two interim bilateral instruments were adopted: a 1987 bilateral protocol between Turkey and Syria

---

45 Aysegül Kibaroglu and Ramazan C. Sayan, 'Water and "imperfect peace" in the Euphrates-Tigris River Basin' (2021) 97 International Affairs 139, 144.

46 Ibid.

47 Ali I. Bagis, 'Turkey's Hydropolitics of the Euphrates-Tigris Basin' (1997) 13(4) International Journal of Water Resources Development 567, 568.

48 Ministry of Industry and Technology, Southeastern Anatolia Project Regional Development Administration, 'Latest State in GAP' (*gap.gov.tr*) <http://www.gap.gov.tr/en/latest-state-in-gap-page-47.html> accessed 13 June 2024.

49 Kibaroglu and Sayan (n 45), 144.

50 Kibaroglu and Scheumann (n 44), 285.

51 Ibid, 286.

52 Sameh W. Al-Muqdadi and others, 'Dispute Over Water Resources Management – Iraq and Turkey' (2016) 7(8) Journal of Environmental Protection 1096, 1098.

committing Turkey to provide Syria with a flow of up to 500 km^3 per second of the Euphrates River;[53] and joint minutes between Syria and Iraq provisionally setting water shares of the Euphrates River between the two countries.[54] Unfortunately, a failure to agree on any permanent trilateral arrangement, coupled with generally poor relations between the countries, led to the suspension of the JTC in 1993.[55] It was then not until the 2000s that any meaningful cooperation on transboundary waters took place between the riparian states.[56] Following consultations and the establishment of the Turkey-Iraq High Level Strategic Cooperation Council (HSCC) and the Turkey-Syria HSCC in 2008 and 2009 respectively, some progress was made on transboundary water issues, including reconvening the meetings of the JTC. In 2009, this resulted in the Ministry of Environment and Forestry of Turkey and the Ministry of Water Resources of Iraq adopting an MoU. The 2009 MoU avoided the difficult issue of water allocations and instead identified a range of broader water management areas where collaboration could be advanced between both governmental and non-governmental experts from both countries.[57] The Turkey-Syria HSCC resulted in more specific cooperation, including an agreement to build a joint hydropower project on the Orontes River, which was initiated in 2011 but suspended due to the unrest in Syria.[58] In addition, Turkey and Syria signed a protocol whereby it was agreed that Syria had a right to withdraw 1.25 km^3 of water annually from the Tigris River provided that the water flows were within the average.[59] Two additional MoUs between Iraq and Syria addressed technical cooperation in the areas of water efficiency in times of drought and

---

[53] Protocol on Matters Pertaining to Economic Cooperation between the Republic of Turkey and the Syrian Arab Republic (adopted 17 July 1986), 87 UNTS 12171.

[54] 1989 Joint Minutes Concerning the Provisional Division of the Euphrates Waters between the Republic of Iraq and the Arab Republic of Syria (adopted 17 March 1989), <https://www.fao.org/faolex/results/details/fr/c/LEX-FAOC015920/> accessed 15 January 2025.

[55] Kibaroglu and Scheumann (n 44), 286.

[56] Özden Z. Oktav, 'Turkey's Water Policy in the Euphrates-Tigris Basin', in Mohamed Behnassi and Katriona McGlade (eds), *Environmental Change and Human Security in Africa and the Middle East* (Springer 2017).

[57] Kibaroglu and Scheumann (n 44), 292.

[58] Ahmet Conker and Hussam Hussein, 'Hydropolitics and Issue-Linkage Along the Orontes River Basin: An Analysis of the Lebanon-Syria and Syria-Turkey Hydropolitical Relations' (2020) 20 International Environmental Agreements 103, 115–116.

[59] MoU between the Government of the Syrian Arab Republic and the Government of the Republic of Turkey on the Establishment of a Pumping Station in the Territories of the Syrian Arab Republic for Water Withdrawal from the

water quality.[60] This new wave of cooperation led to the reinvigoration of the JTC, which reconvened in May 2007 and resulted in commitments that moved away from rigid insistence on water shares and perceived entitlements and instead tackled innovative ways in which the countries could collaborate to improve water efficiency, address climate change threats and protect ecosystems.[61] As a result of these discussions, Turkey also committed to provide 550 m^3 per second of water from the Euphrates River to Iraq during the dry season.[62] Unfortunately, developing similar arrangements between Turkey and Syria stalled due to the civil war in Syria.

Tensions between Turkey and Iraq heightened during the early 2000s due to Turkey's decision to construct the Ilisu Dam on the Tigris River – the second largest of the dams planned under GAP.[63] Construction of the dam started in 2006 and was completed in early 2018.[64] The filling of the Ilisu reservoir then took place during mid-2019 before the dam was officially opened in November 2021.[65] Iraq raised concerns over this project, which – coupled with a severe drought period – has placed significant pressure on Iraq's water supplies.[66] Concerns have even extended to Iran, which accuses Turkey's Ilisu impound-

Tigris River (adopted 23 December 2009, entered into force 9 June 2011), UNTS 48828.

60 MoU between the Government of the Republic of Turkey and the Government of the Syrian Arab Republic in the Field of Efficient Utilisation of Water Resources and Combatting of Drought (adopted 23 December 2009) <http://www.cawater-info.net/bk/water_law/pdf/syria-turkey-1-2009.pdf> accessed 13 June 2024; MoU between the Government of the Republic of Turkey and the Government of the Syrian Arab Republic in the Field of Remediation of Water Quality (adopted 23 December 2009) <https://www.resmigazete.gov.tr/eskiler/2011/05/20110528M1-15-1.pdf> accessed 13 June 2024.

61 Asysegül Kibaroglu, 'Transboundary Water Governance in the Euphrates Tigris River Basin' (*E-relations,* 22 July 2015) <https://www.e-ir.info/2015/07/22/transboundary-water-governance-in-the-euphrates-tigris-river-basin> accessed 13 June 2024.

62 Ibid.

63 Günes M. Tezcür, Rebecca Schiel and Bruce M. Wilson, 'The Effectiveness of Harnessing Human Rights: The Struggle over the Ilisu Dam in Turkey' (2021) 52(6) Development and Change 1343, 1347.

64 Ibid.

65 Mohammed Al-Sulami, 'Region at Risk Due to Divisive Water Policies' (*Arab News*, 27 June 2022) <https://www.arabnews.com/node/1977746> accessed 13 June 2024.

66 Abdul-Sahib T. Al Madhhachi, Khayyun A. Rahi, and Wafa K. Leabi, 'Hydrological impact of Ilisu Dam on Mosul Dam: the River Tigris' (2020) 10(4) Geosciences 120.

ment of exacerbating dust storms in the region.[67] While Iraq has been able to secure some delays to the filling of the dam from Turkey, no legal safeguards over downstream flows have been achieved.[68]

Another important feature of transboundary relations within the Tigris and Euphrates River Basins is the influence of external factors. For instance, the Cold War heightened tensions over waters, as reflected in Turkey's membership in the North Atlantic Treaty Organisation (NATO), and Iraq and Syria's ties with the Union of Soviet Socialist Republics (USSR).[69] In addition, political support for the Kurdistan Workers Party (PKK) has had an impact on water relations. For example, Turkey's commitment to release 500 m^3 per second of water to Syria in 1987 was tied to Syria's commitment to put an end to its support of the PKK.[70] Furthermore, the civil war in Syria, together with the Iraq war and subsequent regional instability, has added significant complexity to transboundary water issues, and often weakened the capacity of Iraq and Syria to enter into meaningful negotiations.[71] An added dynamic is that armed conflict in the region has resulted in both state and non-state militia groups capturing and destroying water installations, and groups such as the Islamic State of Iraq and Syria (ISIS) exploiting water as a weapon.[72]

As in the case of China, Turkey's transboundary water relations partly fit the mode of a classic upstream hydro-hegemon. It is evident that adopting any type of basin-wide treaty arrangement is a challenge, let alone one that provides for CIMs. However, as in the case of China, there are also nuances. The downstream states have managed to secure some concessions in terms of water allocations, and softer cooperation in the form of knowledge exchange and technical collaboration has been possible.

---

[67] Nima Khorrami, 'Amid Dust Storms and Drought, Turkey and Iran Are at Odds Over Transboundary Water Management' (*Middle East Institute*, 13 June 2022) <https://www.mei.edu/publications/amid-dust-storms-and-drought-turkey-and-iran-are-odds-over-transboundary-water> accessed 13 June 2024.

[68] Tezcür, Schiel and Wildon (n 63), 1363.

[69] Asegül Kibaroglu, 'An Analysis of Turkey's Water Diplomacy and its Evolving Position vis-à-vis International Water Law' (2014) 40(1) Water International 153.

[70] Frederick Lorenz and Edward J. Erickson, *Strategic Water – Iraq and Security Planning in the Euphrates-Tigris Basin* (Marine Corps University Press 2013), 57–58.

[71] Kibaroglu and Sayan (n 45), 147–148.

[72] Ibid, 151.

While both China and Turkey are examples of upstream 'hydro-hegemons', India's relations with Bhutan and Nepal are often used as an example of a downstream 'hydro-hegemon'.[73]

There are more than 6,000 transboundary rivers in Nepal with a combined runoff of around 200 billion m^3.[74] These waters account for 46% of the flow of the Ganges.[75] As a downstream riparian, India relies on these rivers in the dry season (October to May) for water supplies but must also deal with the negative impacts of floods due to high flow rates in the wet season.[76] In the last 50 years or so, floods have taken a devastating toll on communities in both Nepal and India – and, based on current projections, the magnitude and frequency of flood events are set to increase.[77]

India's reliance on the transboundary waters flowing from Nepal has resulted in it adopting a strategy of entering into bilateral transboundary water treaties. In the 1920s, an exchange of letters between Nepal and the British India Government set out plans for the Sarada barrage, which would support irrigation in India.[78] The agreement transferred 4,000 acres of land in Nepal on the eastern banks of the Mahakali River to India so it could build a barrage.[79] Nepal received compensation in the form of 4,000 acres of forested land in India and 50,000 Indian rupees.[80] Additionally, Nepal was entitled to withdraw 460 cusecs of water in the dry season and an additional 1,000 cusecs 'provided the surplus is available' between 15 May and 15 October, i.e., the wet season, and 150 m^3 per second between 15 October and 15 May, i.e., the dry season.[81] Critics in Nepal questioned the fairness of such a water

[73] Dharma R. Bagale, 'Nepal-India Water Cooperation: Consequences of Mutuality or Hegemony' (2020) 22 Water Policy 1098.

[74] Hari Bansh Jha, 'Nepal-India Cooperation in River Water Management' (2013) 37(2) Strategic Analysis 217.

[75] Ibid.

[76] Shaik I. Ahmed and Neetu Gaur, 'India-Nepal Water Cooperation: Issues and Concerns' (2020) 52(2) Journal of Indian Water Works Association 125, 125.

[77] Nishikant Gupta and others, 'Rich Water, Poor People: Potential for Transboundary Flood Management between Nepal and India' (2021) 3 Environmental Sustainability 1, 1.

[78] 1920 Sarada Barrage Project Assessment between British India and Nepal (adopted 23 August 1920) <https://www.yumpu.com/en/document/view/40068817/a-nepal-india-water-treaties-agreements-and-contracts-1920-> accessed 13 June 2024.

[79] Ibid.

[80] Ibid.

[81] Ibid. This figure could be increased to 28.34 m^3 per second where water was available.

allocation, as well as the net value of the land that was exchanged.[82] Another disadvantage claimed by Nepal was that it could only make use of its entitlement of water when the Mahakali Irrigation Project was eventually completed in 1998.[83]

The Mahakali Irrigation Project only proved possible following the adoption of the Mahakali Treaty in 1996. The treaty provided commitments to develop hydropower projects of equal capacity between the two countries as well as irrigation on each side of the Mahakali River, and joint flood control measures.[84] It also took into account India's earlier development of the Tanakpur Barrage, which was developed in the 1980s on Indian territory to replace the then-ageing Sarada Barrage and provide 1.61 million hectares of irrigated land and some hydropower generation.[85] Pursuant to the treaty, Nepal had the right to 1,000 cusecs of water in the wet season and 300 cusecs in the dry season.[86] Nepal also has a right to 70 kWh of energy 'free of cost' from the Tanakpur Power Station in India.[87] In addition, the treaty set out terms for the Pancheshwar Multipurpose Project on the border of India and Nepal.[88] The project comprised the Pancheshwar High Dam and Rupali Gad Re-regulating Dam, which would produce 11,885 GWh of energy.[89] The costs of the project were to, 'be borne by the parties in proportion to the benefits accruing to them'.[90] A portion of Nepal's share of energy was to be sold to India.[91] Much of the detail was left for the parties to finalise through a 'Detailed Project

82 Dipak Gyawali and Ajay Dixit, 'Mahakali Impasse and Indo-Nepal Water Conflict' (1999) 34(9) Economic and Political Weekly 553, 553.

83 Ibid.

84 Treaty between His Majesty's Government of Nepal and the Government of India Concerning the Integrated Development of Mahakali River including Sarada Barrage, Tanakpur Barrage and Pancheshwar Project (1966 Mahakali Treaty) (adopted 12 February 1996, entered into force 5 June 1997) <http://faolex.fao.org/docs/pdf/bi-17432.pdf> accessed 13 June 2024.

85 Bagale (n 73), 1102.

86 Article 2, Mahakali Treaty (n 84).

87 Ibid. Pursuant to Article 2, Nepal also had the right to half of the incremental energy generated from the Tanakpur Power Station, while bearing half of the additional operational costs, and where required, half of any additional capital costs associated with the incremental energy generated.

88 Ibid.

89 WAPCOS Ltd, 'Pancheshwar Multipurpose Project – Detail Project Report. Detail Project Report, Pancheswar Development Authority' (December 2016) <https://savemahakali.files.wordpress.com/2017/10/section-1-executive-summary-final.pdf> accessed 13 June 2024.

90 Article 3, Mahakali Treaty (n 84).

91 Ibid.

Report', which was to be produced six months after entry into force of the treaty.[92] Unfortunately, while the treaty was ratified by both governments, it faced significant opposition within Nepal's Parliament and the countries have yet to agree on the Detailed Project Report.[93] In Nepal, questions remain over the cost-sharing arrangements set out in the treaty, as well as perceptions pertaining to the equality of rights to use the waters of the Mahakali River.[94]

A further example of transboundary water treaty-making between India and Nepal concerns the Koshi/Kosi River, another sub-basin of the Ganges River Basin. In 1954, India and Nepal entered into a treaty primarily concerned with flood control in the Koshi/Kosi River.[95] Pursuant to the agreement, Nepal constructed a barrage to control floods in 1962 and later upgraded the barrage to provide irrigation and hydropower functions in Nepal and India.[96] A 1966 amendment to the original agreement clarified certain matters, including Nepal's right to the full use of the waters of the Kosi River in Nepal; that land used by India for project-related activities was to be leased and therefore to remain under Nepalese sovereignty; and that Nepal was to receive 50% of the total electricity generated by any hydropower installations within a 10 km radius of the site.[97] While the countries have been unable to agree on the development of a high dam on the Koshi/Kosi River, which would bring significant benefits in terms of energy and irrigation to both countries, the construction of the barrage has generated some benefits. Although India incurred the full costs of constructing the Koshi/Kosi barrage, both countries have benefited from improved flood control and irrigation.[98] Nepal also benefited from the royalties paid by India for the construction materials used for the project, and the barrage, which acts as a bridge across the river, has brought economic prosperity to the region by connecting the Eastern and Western regions of Nepal.[99] However, critiques have pointed to the project's inappropriate use of

---

[92] Ibid.

[93] Bagale (n 73), 1102.

[94] Gyawali and Dixit (n 82), 559.

[95] Agreement Between the Government of India and the Government of Nepal on the Kosi Project (adopted 25 April 1954) <https://www.internationalwaterlaw.org/documents/regionaldocs/kosi-river1.html> accessed 13 June 2024.

[96] Jha (n 74).

[97] Amended Agreement Between His Majesty's Government of Nepal and the Government of India concerning the Kosi Project (adopted 19 December 1966) <http://www.cawater-info.net/bk/water_law/pdf/nepal-india-1966.pdf> accessed 13 June 2024.

[98] Jha (n 74).

[99] Ibid. Prior to the barrage, the Koshi/Kosi River formed a natural barrier between the regions.

technology and its inability to control floods in the Koshi/Kosi River, particularly in light of the devastating floods of August 2008 that affected millions in India and Nepal.[100] Some experts go as far as to say that it is misguided to believe that 'engineered methods such as dams and embankments' can control 'powerful rivers such as the Koshi and Gandak'.[101] The fact that there was no compensation for the communities displaced by the project is also a source of contention for Nepal.[102]

A third focus of cooperation between India and Nepal is the Gandak River. In 1959, the countries adopted a bilateral treaty on the Gandak River for the purpose of irrigation, power generation and flood control.[103] However, the treaty proved unpopular in Nepal, particularly because it significantly curtailed irrigation development in Nepal.[104] An amendment to the agreement in 1964 sought to rectify this concern by affirming Nepal's 'right to withdraw for irrigation or any other purpose from the river or its tributaries in Nepal such supplies of water as may be required by them from time to time in the Valley'.[105] However, the amendment avoided the contentious issue of how to deal with trans-valley uses of the Gandak waters in the dry season. Instead, the agreement simply stated that the parties would enter into separate agreements 'for the uses of the months of February to April only'.[106] To date, India and Nepal have not been able to agree on any separate arrangements.[107] The amendment did, however, pave the way for the construction of the Gandak barrage in 1968.[108] This project, the largest in Nepal after the Koshi/Kosi project,

---

[100] Kishor Uprety, 'South Asian Water Treaty Practice: An Overview', in Stephen McCaffrey, Christina Leb and Riley T. Denoon (eds), *Research Handbook on International Water Law* (Edward Elgar 2019), at 441.

[101] Gupta and others (n 77), 4.

[102] Shafqat Kakakhel, 'Agreements and Institutions Related to Shared Rivers within South Asia and Beyond', in Imtiaz Ahmed (ed), *South Asian Rivers – A Framework for Cooperation* (Springer 2018), 57.

[103] Agreement between Nepal and India on the Gandak Irrigation and Power Project (adopted 4 December 1959) <https://mea.gov.in/bilateral-documents.htm?dtl/6239/Agreement+regarding+Gandak+Irrigation+amp+Power+Project> accessed 13 June 2024.

[104] Uprety (n 100), 441.

[105] Article 9, Exchange of Letters between the Government of India and His Majesty's Government of Nepal Regarding Amendment to the Gandak Project Agreement (adopted 30 April 1964) <https://mea.gov.in/bilateral-documents.htm?dtl/6374/Exchange+of+Letters+relating+to+Gandak+Project> accessed 13 June 2024.

[106] Ibid.

[107] Uprety (n 100), 441.

[108] Jha (n 74).

irrigates 63 hectares of agricultural land in Nepal and 1,850,520 hectares of land in India.[109] While Nepal provides virtually no financial investment for the project, it gains through irrigation, flood protection and hydropower production.[110]

The aforementioned projects between India and Nepal demonstrate that both countries have benefited from entering into agreements concerning their transboundary waters, even if certain agreements have been challenging to conclude and implement, and the equitable share of benefits has sometimes been questioned by Nepal. Perhaps one of the biggest challenges in securing mutually beneficial arrangements between India and Nepal is that water issues are not easily separated from the broader political context within the countries.[111] Transboundary water cooperation is highly politicised within Nepal.[112] This broader political context results in a prevailing notion that Nepal, 'has not been treated fairly and the bilateral agreements are favorable to India'.[113] Conversely, it is suggested that for India, 'the major grievance is that Nepal inhibits effective cooperation for domestic political gains while reaping benefits of various agreements without making any investment in project development'.[114] While it can be maintained that India's transboundary water relations with Nepal reflect a realist perspective, as in the case of China and Turkey, there are certain nuances. Not all of the proposed projects that India would like to implement have gone ahead due to opposition from Nepal. This would suggest that Nepal can also influence the shape of negotiations. Also, while there are concerns voiced by Nepal over whether the benefits of these joint projects have been shared equitably between both countries, they have both benefited from the projects. A notable trend that differs from the upstream 'hydro-hegemon' scenario is that there appears to be a greater willingness for India to enter into legally binding commitments with Nepal – although these treaty arrangements tend to be project-specific rather than providing a broader

---

109 Ibid.

110 Ibid. India and Nepal agreed to construct one powerhouse with an installed capacity of 15 MW, which was subsequently constructed and handed over to Nepal in 1981.

111 Ramaswamy R. Iyer, 'Neighborhood Tensions: India's Transboundary Water Relations' (2015) 10(1) Global Asia, <https://globalasia.org/v10no1/cover/neighborhood-tensions-indias-trans-boundary-water-relations_ramaswamy-r-iyer> accessed 13 June 2024.

112 Dharma R. Bagale and Keshab D. Adhikari, 'Mahakali Treaty: Delay in Implementation and Resulting Impacts from Nepal's Perspective' (2020) 22 Water Policy 658, 663.

113 Ahmed (n 76), 125.

114 Ibid.

basin-wide framework for the protection and use of transboundary waters. However, this raises the question of whether there might be more scope for downstream 'hydro-hegemons' to embed CIMs within their treaty arrangements compared to the upstream 'hydro-hegemons', such as China and Turkey.

An analysis of relations with India and Nepal only provides part of the picture. In contrast to Nepal, India's relationship pertaining to the transboundary waters it shares with Bhutan has been described as one of 'political goodwill', and as reflecting 'a robust economic partnership'.[115] India and Bhutan started to cooperate over their transboundary waters on the basis of a 1949 Treaty of Perpetual Peace and Friendship.[116] This led to more specific cooperation on hydropower in 1961 through a commitment to develop hydropower on the Jaldhaka River on the border between Bhutan and India.[117] The Jaldhaka project was completed in 1968 by the construction of a barrage in the territory of Bhutan and a 27,000 kilowatt power plant in West Bengal India.[118] The costs of the project were borne by India, while Bhutan benefited through the provision of 250 kilowatts of electricity free of charge.[119] This initial project paved the way for more ambitious cooperative initiatives. In 1974, an agreement between Bhutan and India was reached on the Chukha Hydro-Electric Project.[120] The project was commissioned in 1988 and has an installed capacity of 336 megawatts.[121] 75% of electricity generation from the project is sold by Bhutan to India at an 'agreed rate'.[122] This rate is revised by the countries every four years to account for operating and maintenance costs, inflation and the market price for energy.[123] India committed to providing both technical and financial

---

115 Medha Bisht, 'Bhutan-India Power Cooperation: Benefits Beyond Bilateralism' (2012) 36(5) Strategic Analysis 787, 787.

116 Treaty of Perpetual Peace and Friendship between the Government of India and the Government of Bhutan (adopted 8 August 1949) <https://mea.gov.in/bilateral-documents.htm?dtl/5242/treaty+or+perpetual+p> accessed 13 June 2024.

117 Valentine J. Belfiglio, 'India's Economic and Political Relations with Bhutan' (1972) 12(8) Asian Survey 676, 678.

118 Cecilia Llamosas and Benjamin K. Sovacool, 'Transboundary Hydropower in Contested Contexts: Energy Security, Capabilities, and Justice in Comparative Perspective' (2021) 37 Energy Strategy Reviews 1, 10.

119 Ibid.

120 Agreement between the Government of India and the Royal Government of Bhutan Regarding the Chukha Hydro-electric Project (adopted 23 March 1974) <https://www.mea.gov.in/bilateral-documents.htm?dtl/6349/Agreement> accessed 13 June 2024.

121 Ibid, Article 8.

122 Ibid.

123 See Debasis Sarkar, 'India accepted restructuring of 336 MW Chukha Hydroproject in Bhutan' (*The Economic Times*, 10 February 2014) <https://

assistance (40% loan and 60% grant) for the project.[124] The Chukha Project was followed by two other projects: the 60 megawatt Kurichu Hypropower project, which was commissioned in 2002, and the 1,020 megawatt Tala hydropower project, which was commissioned in 2007. Similar financing arrangements were set up for the Kurichu and Tala projects, i.e., 40% loan and 60% grant from India, with the surplus energy generated from these projects going to India.[125] Cooperation over hydropower was further expanded through a 2006 Agreement on Cooperation in the Field of Hydroelectric Power.[126] A subsequent protocol to the 2006 Agreement was adopted in 2008 to increase the scale of projects from 5,000 megawatts to 10,000 megawatts, and a 2014 bilateral agreement provides a framework for the development of projects through a joint venture model between public sector undertakings in both countries.[127] To date, this has led to the commissioning of the 720 megawatt Mangdechhu project in August 2019, which is registered as a clean development mechanism project under the UN Framework Convention on Climate Change.[128] Several

---

economictimes.indiatimes.com/industry/energy/power/india-accepted-restructuring-of-336-mw-chukha-hydroproject-in-bhutan/articleshow/30160368.cms?from=mdr> accessed 13 June 2024.

124 Ibid, Article 4.

125 Bisht (n 115), 788.

126 Agreement between the Government of the Republic of India and the Royal Government of Bhutan Concerning Cooperation in the Field of Hydropower (adopted 28 July 2006) <https://www.riverresourcehub.org/wp-content/uploads/files/attached-files/india_bhutan_hydropower_agreement_july_2006.pdf> accessed 13 June 2024.

127 Protocol to the 2006 Agreement between the Government of the Republic of India and the Royal Government of Bhutan Concerning Cooperation in the Field of Hydroelectric Power (adopted 16 March 2009) <https://www.riverresourcehub.org/wp-content/uploads/files/attached-files/india_bhutan_hydropower_protocol_march_2009.pdf> accessed 13 June 2024; Inter-governmental Agreement between the Royal Government of Bhutan and the Government of the Republic of India Concerning the Development of Joint Venture Hydropower Projects through the Public Sector Undertakings of the two Governments (adopted 22 April 2014) <https://www.mea.gov.in/press-releases.htm?dtl/23230/InterGovernmental+Agreement+between+Bhutan+and+India+on+development+of+Joint+Venture+Hydropower+Projects> accessed 13 June 2024.

128 Clean Development Mechanism, 'Project 10473: Mangdechhu Hydroelectric Project Authority' (1 July 2022) <https://cdm.unfccc.int/Projects/DB/BVQI1554122442.49/view> accessed 13 June 2024.

other projects between Bhutan and India are either planned or currently under construction.[129]

As well as satisfying most of Bhutan's domestic energy demands, the sale of hydropower from these projects provides around 40% of Bhutan's total exports and about 20% of the government's total revenue.[130] India also benefits significantly from the supply of relatively cheap electricity. From time to time, the cost that India pays for electricity in Bhutan is raised as a concern in Bhutan.[131] For example, in 2017, the tariff rate for electricity from the Tala hydroelectric project was US$ 0.24 cents per unit, which was much lower than India's domestic market price.[132] However, when the countries have had differences over the unit price, they have managed to reach agreement.[133] The government of Bhutan points to the economic benefits of the projects and their ability to offset 4.4 million tons of carbon dioxide, although opponents question the environmental credentials of Bhutan's hydropower schemes as well as their vulnerability in the face of future climate change impacts.[134]

What is clear from transboundary water relations between Bhutan and India is that both countries have been able to significantly benefit from these projects, and while there may be periodic questions over the tariff rate that India pays for the electricity it imports from Bhutan, any concerns appear to be settled amicably. This experience may therefore be contrasted with the India-Nepal case, which is symptomatic of the broader political context that exists within the countries. Like Nepal, however, the Bhutanese experience

---

129 These projects include the 1200 MW Punatsangchu-I project, the 1020 MW Punatsangchu-II project, the 600 MW Kholongchhu project, the 1080 MW Bunakha project, the 570 MW Wangchu project, and 770 MW Chamkuchu project; see Royal Bhutanese Embassy, New Delhi, India, 'Bhutan-India Hydropower Relations' (*mfa.gov.bt*) <https://www.mfa.gov.bt/rbedelhi/?page_id=28> accessed 13 June 2024.

130 Llamosas and Sovacool (n 118), 10. It is estimated that Bhutan's export of electricity to India provides the country with around US$ 1,575 million annually.

131 Amit Ranjan, *Contested Waters: India's Transboundary Water Disputes in South Asia* (Abingdon 2021), 51.

132 Ibid.

133 Debasis Sarkar, 'India-Bhutan sign Rs 4,500 crore Mangdechhu Hydro project's power tariff protocol' (*The Economic Times,* 26 April 2019) <https://economictimes.indiatimes.com/industry/energy/power/india-bhutan-sign-rs-4500-crore-mangdechhu-hydro-projects-power-tariff-protocol/articleshow/69053103.cms?from=mdr> accessed 13 June 2024.

134 Beth Walker, 'Will Mega Dams Turn Bhutan's Happiness Sour?' (*The Guardian*, 20 May 2015) <https://www.theguardian.com/sustainable-business/2015/may/20/will-mega-dams-turn-bhutans-happiness-sour> accessed 13 June 2024.

also demonstrates the willingness of India to enter into legally binding agreements concerning their transboundary waters – although, as in the case of Nepal, they tend to be project-focused agreements. In the case of Bhutan, these agreements say little about compliance and implementation. For example, the 2006 Agreement Concerning Cooperation in the Field of Hydroelectric Power simply provides that, 'any differences regarding interpretation and application of this Agreement shall be resolved by mutual consultations between the two Governments'.[135] While still minimal, the arrangements between India and Nepal include more detail. For example, the 1966 Mahakali Treaty establishes a river commission comprised of representatives from both parties.[136] The Commission is required to 'co-ordinate and monitor plans of actions' related to the Treaty's implementation, and 'to examine any differences arising between the parties concerning the [Treaty's] interpretation and application'.[137] Additionally, the Treaty provides that any differences that are unresolved by the Commission after three months must be submitted to an arbitration tribunal.[138] Key features of the arbitration procedure are also included in the Treaty.[139]

A further example of a downstream country seeking to control transboundary waters is Egypt within the context of the Nile.[140] The Nile River System is made up of two distinct rivers: the Blue and White Nile.[141] The White Nile, which contributes 14% of the Nile's flow, originates in the equatorial lakes region before flowing through South Sudan, Sudan and finally Egypt. Meanwhile, the Blue Nile, which contributes 86% of the Nile's flow, originates in the highlands of Ethiopia before flowing through Sudan and Egypt.[142] Egypt's precarious position as the furthest downstream riparian to share the

---

[135] Article 10, Agreement between the Government of the Republic of India and the Royal Government of Bhutan Concerning Cooperation in the Field of Hydropower (n 126). See similar wording in Article 13, Agreement between India and Bhutan Regarding the Chukha Hydro-Electric Project (n 120); and Article VI, Protocol to the 2006 Agreement between the Government of the Republic of India and the Royal Government of Bhutan concerning cooperation in the field of hydroelectric power (n 127).

[136] Article 9, 1966 Mahakali Treaty (n 84).

[137] Ibid.

[138] Article 11, ibid.

[139] Ibid.

[140] Alexis Carles, 'Power Asymmetry and Conflict over Water Resources in the Nile River Basin: the Egyptian hydro-hegemony' (Dissertation, King's College London, 2006).

[141] Salman M.A. Salman, 'The Nile Basin Cooperative Framework Agreement: A Peacefully Unfolding African Spring?' 2012 38(1) Water International 17, 17.

[142] Ibid.

Nile has resulted in it adopting a long-term strategy of seeking to control the headwaters of the Nile.[143] A colonial influence on this strategy can be seen through the United Kingdom's attempts to secure treaty commitments from upstream countries. For example, in 1902, a treaty was signed between Ethiopia and the United Kingdom (on behalf of Egypt) that obliged Emperor Menelik II of Ethiopia 'not to construct, or allow to be constructed, any work across the Blue Nile, Lake Tsana, or the Sobat which would arrest the flow of their waters into the Nile, except in agreement with His Britannic Majesty's Government and the Government of Sudan'.[144] Then, in 1929, an Exchange of Notes between the United Kingdom (acting on behalf of its colonies of Kenya, Uganda and Tanganyika, as well as Sudan) and Egypt was adopted on the Use of the Waters of the River Nile for Irrigation Purposes.[145] This Exchange of Notes stipulated that,

> … save with the previous agreement of the Egyptian Government, no irrigation or power works on measures are to be constructed or taken on the River Nile and its branches, or on the lakes from which it flows, so far as all these are in the Sudan or in countries under British administration, which would, in such a manner as to entail any prejudice to the interests of Egypt, either reduce the quantity of water arriving in Egypt, or modify the date of its arrival, or lower its level.[146]

A third treaty adopted in 1959 between Egypt and Sudan noted that, 'the Nile waters Agreement concluded in 1929 provided only for the partial use of the Nile waters and did not extend to include complete control of the River waters'.[147] The agreement also stipulated that the *total flow* of the Nile shall be allocated between both Egypt and Sudan on a ratio of 14.5:7.5 respectively.[148]

---

[143] Mahemud E. Tekuya, 'The Egyptian Hydro-Hegemony in the Nile Basin: The Quest for Changing the Status Quo' (2018) 26(1) Journal of Water Law 10, 10.

[144] Treaties Between the United Kingdom and Ethiopia and Between the United Kingdom, Italy and Ethiopia, Relative to the Frontiers Between the Soudan, Ethiopia, and Eritrea (adopted 15 May 1902) <https://m.marefa.org/images/b/bd/Treaty_of_Addis_Ababa_1902.pdf> accessed 13 June 2024.

[145] Exchange of Notes between His Majesty's Government in the United Kingdom and the Egyptian Government in regard to the Use of the Waters of the River Nile for Irrigation Purposes (adopted 7 May 1929) <https://treaties.fcdo.gov.uk/awweb/pdfopener?md=1&did=64266> accessed 13 June 2024.

[146] Ibid.

[147] Agreement between the Republic of Sudan and the United Arab Republic for the Full Utilisation of the Nile Waters (adopted 8 November 1959), 6519 UNTS 64.

[148] Based on this ratio, the treaty estimated the allocation of water between the two countries to be 18.5 billion cubic metres for Sudan and 55.5 billion cubic metres for Egypt, ibid.

This agreement paved the way for the development of the Aswan High Dam on the Nile River in Egypt, which was primarily designed to regulate the flow of the Nile in order to mitigate floods and droughts, and to generate hydropower; as well as the Roseires Dam in Sudan, which was used for irrigation and hydropower generation purposes.[149]

While these actions by Egypt might fit the classic model of a downstream 'hydro-hegemon', the upstream Nile states have consistently questioned the legal validity of the legal arrangements.[150] The 1902 Nile Treaty has been queried by Ethiopia on the basis that it was concluded under duress, it was not ratified, and there are discrepancies between the English and Amharic language versions.[151] However, Egypt insists that the treaty is binding on Ethiopia and it obliges Ethiopia not to build any project on the Blue Nile without Egypt's prior approval.[152] Upon their independence in the 1960s, Kenya, Tanzania and Uganda have also argued that, based on the Nyerere Doctrine of state succession and the right of newly independent states to choose to reject colonial treaties, they are not bound by the 1929 Nile Agreement.[153] Unsurprisingly, the upper riparians also oppose the 1959 Nile Agreement and its attempt to exclusively allocate the waters of the Nile between the two furthest downstream riparians, and they also complain that they were not involved or even invited to any of the negotiations leading up to the agreement.[154] Such an approach is at variance with the Watercourses Convention, which stipulates that, 'every watercourse state is entitled to participate in the negotiation of and to become a party to any watercourse agreement that applies to the entire international watercourse, as well as to participate in any relevant consultations', and is

---

149 Salman (n 141).

150 See Zeray Yihdego and Alistair Rieu-Clarke, 'International Law Development on the Sharing of Blue Nile Waters – A Fairness Perspective', in Zeray Yihdego, Alistair Rieu-Clarke and Ana Casço (eds), *The Grand Ethiopian Renaissance Dam and the Nile Basin* (Routledge 2017).

151 Gebre T. Degefu, *The Nile – Historical, Legal and Developmental Perspectives* (Trafford Publishing 2003), 98.

152 Degefu suggests that while the English version of the 1902 Nile Treaty obliges Ethiopia to seek agreement from Egypt prior to undertaking any works on the Blue Nile, the Amharic version does not include such a requirement, ibid.

153 Dereje Z. Mekonnen, 'The Nile Basin Cooperative Framework Agreement Negotiations and the Adoption of a 'Water Security' Paradigm: Flight into Obscurity or a Logical Cul-de-Sac?' (2010) 21(2) European Journal of International Law 421, 432–435.

154 Charles O. Okidi, 'History of the Nile and Lake Victoria Basins Through Treaties', in Paul Howell and J. A. (Tony) Allan (eds), *The Nile – Sharing a Scarce Resource* (CUP 1994), 334.

inconsistent with the general customary international law principle of good faith.[155]

While up to this part in the story Egypt's actions would appear to align squarely with a realist perspective, cooperation amongst the Nile riparian states has evolved since the 1960s. Between the 1960s and 1980s, most of the focus was on sharing data and information.[156] In the late 1990s, with support from the World Bank, the UN Development Programme and other development partners, the Nile basin states created the Nile Basin Initiative (NBI).[157] The NBI was set up as a transitional arrangement with the aim of developing a permanent basin-wide cooperative framework.[158] While, through the NBI, the Nile riparians spent over ten years negotiating a draft legal framework, the previous contentious issues within the Nile have proven difficult to overcome within the text of the final agreement – the 2010 Agreement on the Nile River Basin Cooperative Framework (CFA).[159] Throughout the negotiations, Egypt and Sudan insisted that their existing and historic rights to the waters of the Nile be safeguarded, whereas the other Nile riparian states demanded that there should be no reference to existing or historic rights within the Agreement.[160] While no consensus was reached, in April 2010, seven of the Nile riparian countries agreed to open the CFA for signature, a decision that was opposed by Egypt and Sudan.[161] Cascão and Nicol suggest this step was symbolic in challenging Egypt's dominance over transboundary water relations.[162] To date, six countries have ratified the agreement – Burundi (23 August 2024), Ethiopia (13 June 2013), Rwanda (28 August 2013), Tanzania (26 March 2015), South

[155] Article 4, Watercourses Convention (n 27). See also Yidhego and Rieu-Clarke (n 150).

[156] Salman (n 141).

[157] Ibid.

[158] Ibid.

[159] Agreement on the Nile River Basin Cooperative Framework (adopted 14 May 2010) <https://nilebasin.org/about-us/cooperative-framework-agreement> accessed 13 June 2024 (CFA). See Salman M.A. Salman, 'The Nile Basin Cooperative Framework Agreement – Disentangling the Gordian Knot', in Zeray Yihdego, Alistair Rieu-Clarke and Ana Elisa Cascão (eds), *The Grand Ethiopian Renaissance Dam and the Nile Basin* (Routledge 2017).

[160] Salman, ibid.

[161] Nile Basin Initiative, 'Cooperative Framework Agreement' (*nilebasin.org*) <https://nilebasin.org/about-us/cooperative-framework-agreement> accessed 13 June 2024

[162] Ana Elisa Casão and Alan Nicol, 'Changing cooperation dynamics in the Nile Basin and the role of the GERD', in Zeray Yihdego, Alistair Rieu-Clarke and Ana Elisa Cascão (eds), *The Grand Ethiopian Renaissance Dam and the Nile Basin* (Routledge 2017), at 95–96.

Sudan (8 July 2024) and Uganda (15 August 2019).[163] South Sudan's ratification of the CFA on 8 July 2024 paves the way for the agreement to enter into force.[164]

The text of the CFA only provides general provisions related to implementation and compliance. The Nile River Basin Commission, which is to be established pursuant to the Agreement, has an overarching role to 'promote and facilitate' the implementation of the Agreement.[165] The CFA also provides general provisions related to dispute settlement, which encourage the parties to reach a solution through negotiation, mediation, conciliation or good offices through the Nile River Basin Commission or a third party, or submit the dispute to arbitration or the International Court of Justice.[166] Similar to the Watercourses Convention, there is also the requirement to submit the dispute to a fact-finding commission if the dispute is unresolved after six months.[167]

A shift in transboundary water relations was further reflected just after the CFA was adopted when Ethiopia announced its plans to build a dam on the Blue Nile (the Grand Ethiopian Renaissance Dam (GERD)), 40 km from the border with Sudan.[168] The timing of this announcement coincided with the governmental crisis in Egypt and the fall of Egyptian President Hosni Mubarak in February 2011.[169] However, despite their differences, cooperation between Egypt, Ethiopia and Sudan did continue. In September 2011, the countries agreed to establish an international panel of experts to study the impact of the dam on Egypt and Sudan, and in July 2012, the Egyptian President Mohamed Morsi visited the dam site – the first visit of an Egyptian president to Ethiopia since 1995.[170] While Ethiopia continued to construct the GERD, the international panel of experts produced several recommendations, including a call

---

[163] Ibid.

[164] Article 43 of the CFA (n 159) provides that the agreement, 'shall enter into force on the sixtieth day following the date of the deposit of the sixth instrument of ratification or accession with the African Union'. See Mahemud Takuya, 'Entry into force of the Nile Basin Cooperative Framework Agreement: Challenges and Prospects' (*EJIL:Talk!,* 2 August 2024) <https://www.ejiltalk.org/entry-into-force-of-the-nile-basin-cooperative-framework-agreement-challenges-and-prospects/> accessed 8 August 2024.

[165] Article 16, ibid.

[166] Article 34(1)(a), ibid.

[167] Article 34(1(b), ibid. Further details on the fact-finding commission are provided in Annex 1 of the agreement.

[168] Ibid.

[169] Hala Nasr and Andreas Neef, 'Ethiopia's Challenge to Egyptian Hegemony in the Nile River Basin: The Case of the Grand Ethiopian Renaissance Dam' (2016) 21(4) Geopolitics 969, 970.

[170] Ibid, 976.

in May 2013 to conduct further studies.[171] In September 2014, a tripartite national committee was established to oversee the completion of the studies.[172] A significant step was also achieved through the signing of an Agreement on Declaration of Principles between Egypt, Ethiopia and Sudan on the Grand Ethiopian Renaissance Dam Project on 23 March 2015.[173] The Declaration of Principles is significant in its reference to the two key substantive principles of equitable and reasonable utilisation and no significant harm and the absence of any reference to existing or historic rights.[174] In addition, the Declaration of Principles set out principles for the first filling and operation of the dam.[175] However, the Declaration says little about compliance and implementation. The only direct reference is in the final Articles, which obliges the countries to settle disputes through consultation and negotiation.[176] Where consultation and negotiation fail, the parties 'may' refer the matter to their respective Heads of State, as well as conciliation or mediation.[177] The Declaration of Principles paved the way for additional studies to assess the impact of the dam, and in September 2016, contracts were signed with two French consultancy firms to conduct those studies.[178] Unfortunately, while Egypt accepted the preliminary reports by the consultants, Sudan and Ethiopia expressed concerns over the baseline used by the companies to assess GERD's impact.[179] This marked a

---

[171] International Panel of Experts on Grand Ethiopian Renaissance Dam Project, 'Final Report' (31 May 2013) <https://www.scidev.net/wp-content/uploads/site_assets/docs/international_panel_of_experts_for_ethiopian_renaissance_dam-_final_report.pdf> accessed 13 June 2024.

[172] Nasr and Neef (n 169).

[173] Agreement on Declaration of Principles Between the Arab Republic of Egypt, the Federal Democratic Republic of Ethiopia and the Republic of Sudan on the Grand Ethiopian Renaissance Dam Project (GERDP) (adopted 23 March 2015) <https://www.internationalwaterlaw.org/documents/regionaldocs/Final_Nile_Agreement_23_March_2015.pdf> accessed 13 June 2024.

[174] Salman M.A. Salman, 'Agreement on declaration of principles on the GERD – Levelling the Nile Basin playing field', in Zeray Yihdego, Alistair Rieu-Clarke and Ana Elisa Cascão (eds), *The Grand Ethiopian Renaissance Dam and the Nile Basin* (Routledge 2017), 53.

[175] Principle V, Declaration of Principles (n 173).

[176] Principle X, ibid.

[177] Ibid.

[178] 'Egypt, Ethiopia, Sudan sign final contracts on Nile dam studies' (*Ahram Online*, 20 September 2016) <https://english.ahram.org.eg/NewsContent/1/64/244290/-.aspx> accessed 13 June 2024.

[179] 'Regional ministers fail to reach agreement on Ethiopian dam studies' (*Ahram Online*, 13 November 2017) <https://english.ahram.org.eg/News/281392.aspx> accessed 13 June 2024.

clear shift in allegiance for Sudan, which gradually began to appreciate the benefits that GERD might offer in terms of limiting sedimentation flows to Sudanese dams, regulating flow and reducing recurrent flooding, and providing a relatively cheap supply of electricity.[180] Tripartite meetings on the filling of the dam and its operation continued, but by 2019 Egypt declared that they had reached a deadlock and there was a need for international mediation.[181] Despite the involvement of the UN Security Council, the African Union, the United States and others, negotiations between the countries have failed to make any meaningful progress, and Ethiopia began to fill the dam in 2020.[182]

These events on the Nile show that Egypt's relations with its upstream neighbours have clearly evolved over time. While it is unlikely that Egypt will commit to the CFA in its current form, at least in the Blue Nile context the states have managed to agree on a declaration that aligns with the core principle of international water law. Agreement on the GERD's future remains uncertain. The case of the Nile, therefore, shows both the willingness of states to negotiate with a view to concluding legal arrangements and the challenge of reaching any consensus.

More generally, the examples of transboundary relations between China, Turkey, India, Egypt and their respective neighbours illustrate some of the difficulties of solely relying on a realist perspective in explaining state relations over transboundary waters. Admittedly, both the examples of China and Turkey show a dominance of the hydro-hegemon to develop upstream projects on transboundary rivers unilaterally. Both cases show how the countries have implemented major hydropower projects upstream with little consultation with their downstream riparians. However, the picture is somewhat blurred by the willingness of China and Turkey to progress other forms of cooperation with their downstream neighbours. In the case of China, despite its power asymmetry in relations vis-à-vis the downstream states of the Mekong, it has cooperated through the exchange of data and information, joint monitoring and capacity building initiatives, the release of water during periods of low

---

180 Salman M.A. Salman, 'The Grand Ethiopian Renaissance Dam: the road to the declaration of principles and the Khartoum document' (2016) 41(4) Water International 512, 517.

181 Khalid Abdelaziz and Mahmoud Mourad, 'Egypt says talks over Ethiopia's Nile dam deadlocked, calls for mediation' (*Reuters*, 5 October 2019) <https://www.reuters.com/article/us-ethiopia-dam-egypt-idUSKCN1WK0IE> accessed 13 June 2024.

182 Mohamed Saied, 'Ethiopia Courts Two Downstream Countries Before Third Filling of Nile Dam' (*Al-Monitor*, 22 May 2022) <https://www.al-monitor.com/originals/2022/05/ethiopia-courts-two-downstream-countries-third-filling-nile-dam> accessed 13 June 2024.

water flow, and the adoption of cooperative mechanisms such as the Lancang-Mekong Cooperation framework, and the various MoUs it has agreed upon. It has also adopted bilateral legally binding treaties with Kazakhstan, Mongolia and Russia. Similarly, Turkey has cooperated with Iraq and Syria through the interim guarantees of downstream flows, the exchange of data and information, joint monitoring and capacity building initiatives. Turkey has also been willing to enter into bilateral arrangements and to foster cooperation through bilateral and trilateral institutional arrangements such as the JTC. Experience from China and Turkey would therefore suggest that, while the upstream hydro-hegemon may dominate developments within a transboundary basin, the less powerful states are not completely powerless, and there appear to be opportunities for those states to gain certain concessions. Any claim that the upstream hydro-hegemon simply acts without due regard to downstream interests can therefore be questioned.

Similarly, where the hydro-hegemon is downstream, the cases reviewed reveal that it is not always easy for them to exert their full control over transboundary waters. In the case of India, there is a marked difference between relations with Bhutan and Nepal. Within the Bhutanese context, the countries have managed to enter into mutually beneficial relations. India has gained through the supply of hydropower from Bhutan in addition to flood control. Bhutan has benefited largely through the revenue gained from the export of electricity to India. Also, where there have been differences of opinion, the countries have managed to reach a mutually agreeable solution, such as in the negotiation of the electricity tariff. Bhutan and India's transboundary water relations therefore appear to illustrate a reciprocal relationship, rather than the hegemon dominating relations. The relations between India and Nepal are different. While it has been possible to implement some joint projects, they have not reached the level enjoyed between Bhutan and India. This therefore points to the importance of considering the domestic context when determining whether or not states might be willing to enter into cooperative arrangements. In the context of Nepal, domestic politics would appear to inhibit the opportunities to develop joint projects. Also, the limited joint projects that have been implemented still raise questions over whether or not Nepal achieved a fair deal.

Lastly, the experience of Egypt on the Nile waters also questions whether a realist perspective can fully account for transboundary water relations. While Egypt has certainly sought to control the waters of the Nile, the upstream states have managed to challenge Egypt's actions. This is particularly evident in Ethiopia's development of the GERD. However, in parallel, the Nile countries have demonstrated a willingness to cooperate in order to seek compromises, such as through the Nile Basin Initiative, and more recently through the negotiations over the Grand Ethiopian Renaissance Dam. The Nile case also illustrates how cooperation evolves over time.

What, then, can the above cases and a realist perspective say about a state's willingness to adopt legally binding treaties relating to their transboundary waters and incorporate CIMs into those arrangements? As already noted, it would appear that upstream 'hydro-hegemons' are less likely to enter into legally binding arrangements, especially at the basin level. The selected cases would suggest that any arrangements are likely to be bilateral and will probably simply set out general principles of cooperation. The likelihood of detailed provisions for systematically reviewing progress in the implementation of a treaty and addressing incidences of non-compliance is likely to be low. However, downstream 'hydro-hegemons' appear to demonstrate a greater willingness to enter into legally binding arrangements on their shared waters. The cases cited above suggest that these arrangements are likely to be focused on implementing projects that can provide mutual benefits rather than agreements that encompass wider aspects of water management. The question of whether CIMs are likely to be part of these arrangements appears to be one that is not easy to answer. While none of the cases demonstrate a practice of adopting CIMs, there is some practice in affording joint commissions with a general role in overseeing implementation and a willingness to adopt procedures for addressing disputes. It is also interesting to note that India has more detailed procedures with Nepal compared to Bhutan. This would suggest that there is not always a 'one-size-fits-all' approach to the development of legal arrangements within the context of power asymmetric relationships. A realist perspective does not therefore offer a full account of whether or not states will adopt CIMs. The question of what other factors may influence the decision of states to incorporate CIMs into their transboundary water agreements therefore remains to be answered.

Finally, another shortcoming of relying solely on a realist account of transboundary water relations is that it is not always easy to categorise states into upstream or downstream countries. The Colorado River, for example, flows from the United States into Mexico, but several rivers flow from Mexico to the United States.[183] Similarly, Vietnam is upstream of Cambodia on several tributaries of the Mekong River but is also the furthest downstream state within the basin. Rivers may also cross borders or form borders. In the case of border-forming rivers, opportunities for hegemons to exert their control on the water resource itself will be much more difficult than in the case of an

[183] Albert Utton, 'Problems and Successes of International Water Agreements: The Example of the United States and Mexico', in John E. Carol (ed), *International Environmental Diplomacy* (CUP 1988).

upstream-downstream scenario, given that they are unable to exclusively control the source. These examples therefore beg the question of whether there are alternative accounts that can help explain the conditions under which states might firstly be willing to enter into legally binding agreements concerning their transboundary waters, and secondly, incorporate CIMs into those treaties.

2.3 INCENTIVES AND RECIPROCITY

An alternative perspective on international relations argues that incentives and reciprocity shape behaviour, and institutions have an important role to play in structuring that behaviour.[184] Such a perspective suggests that states will commit to legally binding arrangements when they are able to gain more than what would be available to them if they acted unilaterally.[185]

To some extent, this perspective does not contradict a realist perspective. As illustrated in the examples above, power asymmetric relationships, like the one that India has with its upstream riparians, offer incentives to cooperation that are structured through the use of legally binding arrangements.

Another example of a reciprocal relationship is the Columbia River shared between the Canada and the United States.[186] The two countries started to discuss a range of options to develop the basin in the 1940s.[187] In 1948, greater impetus on joint action was provided by devastating spring floods, which destroyed the town of Vanport in Oregon and led to the loss of 30,000 people's homes and 50 fatalities.[188] A treaty focused on flood control and hydropower development was subsequently adopted in 1961 and ratified by Canada and

---

184 Arthur A. Stein, *Why Nations Cooperate: Circumstances and Choice in International Relations* (Cornell University Press 1990), 39.

185 Ibid.

186 Barbara Cosens, 'The Columbia River Treaty: An Opportunity for Modernization of Basin Governance' (2016) 27(1) Colorado Natural Resources, Energy and Environmental Law Review 27, 30; Taylor Henshaw, Richard K. Paisley and Glen Hearns, 'Building Climate Change and Ecosystem-Based Function Considerations into a Modernized Columbia River Treaty: A Commentary' (2021) 57 Idaho Law Review 151; Dan A. Tarlock and P. Wouters, 'Are Shared Benefits of International Waters and Equitable Apportionment?' 18 Colorado Journal of International Environmental Law and Policy 523 (2007).

187 US Army Corps of Engineers and Bonneville Power Administration, 'Columbia River Treaty – History and 2014/2024 Review', <https://usace.contentdm.oclc.org/digital/collection/p16021coll7/id/8409/> accessed 13 June 2024.

188 Matthew J. McKinney, Richard K. Paisley and Molly S. Stenovec, 'A Sacred Responsibility: Governing the Use of Water and Related Resources in the International Columbia Basin Through the Prism of Tribes and First Nations' (2016) 37 Public Land and Resources Law Review 157, 175.

the United States in 1964.[189] Through the construction of the Duncan, Hugh Keenleyside (also known as Arrow), and Mica Dams, the Treaty committed Canada to provide 15.5 million acre-feet of storage in the upper reaches of the Columbia River.[190] The United States was also provided with the option to build the Libby Dam on the Kootenai River, a tributary of the Columbia River, the reservoir of which (Lake Koocanusa) extended 42 miles back into Canada.[191] By the early 1970s, all these projects had been completed.[192] These developments doubled the storage capacity of the Columbia River Basin and allowed the countries to provide a more consistent streamflow throughout the year.[193] In return for Canada's development of dams upstream, it receives the so-called 'Canadian Entitlement', which consists of half of the downstream power benefits created by the storage of water in Canada.[194] Additionally, Canada is entitled to receive 50% of the estimated value of flood damages prevented due to the development of the upstream dams.[195] While the arrangement between Canada and the United States has generated benefits for both countries, those benefits do not come without costs. Indigenous and tribal groups were absent from the negotiations of the Columbia River Treaty.[196] However, the projects had a devastating toll on their livelihoods, including the blocking of salmon migration, as well as the loss of lands and cultural sites

---

189 Treaty between Canada and the United States of America Relating to Cooperative Development of the Water Resources of the Columbia River Basin (adopted 17 January 1961, entered into force 16 September 1964) <https://www.canada.ca/content/dam/eccc/documents/pdf/international-affairs/compendium/2022/b-12/canada-united-states-columbia-river.pdf> accessed 8 August 2024 (Columbia River Treaty).

190 Article II, ibid.

191 Article XII, ibid.

192 US Army Corps of Engineers and Bonneville Power Administration (n 187), 4–5.

193 Matthew McKinney and others, 'Managing Transboundary Natural Resources – An Assessment of the Need to Revise and Update the Columbia River Treaty' (2010) 16(2) Hastings Environmental Law Journal 308, 310.

194 Article V, 1961 Columbia River Treaty (n 189). The first 30 years of this entitlement was sold to a group of utilities for US$ 254 million to pay for the development of the upstream dams (McKinney and others (n 193), 310).

195 Article VI, 1961 Columbia River Treaty (n 189). Canada elected to receive a lump sum payment totalling US$ 64 million for flood control benefits from the date when the dams were operational to 2024 (US Army Corps of Engineers and Bonneville Power Administration (n 187), 6).

196 Alice Cohen and Emma S. Norman, 'Renegotiating the Columbia River Treaty: Transboundary Governance and Indigenous Rights' (2018) 18(4) Global Environmental Politics 4, 15.

through the flooding of their lands.[197] Cohen and Norman maintain that, 'the decision of the United States and Canadian governments to prioritise hydropower, flood control, and large engineering projects over maintaining ecological diversity was also a decision to knowingly adulterate and compromise an Indigenous way of life'.[198]

The requirement to better account for the needs and interests of Indigenous and tribal groups, as well as the Columbia River's ecosystem, has been raised in recent years through calls to renegotiate the Columbia River Treaty.[199] While the Treaty does not have an expiration date, it does stipulate that from September 2024 onwards either party can unilaterally terminate the treaty if it gives the other party ten years written notice of its intention to do so.[200] As a result of this provision, Canada and the United States started to discuss how the Columbia River Treaty might be renegotiated in May 2018.[201] At the forefront of these discussions are calls to better balance ecosystem needs with flood protection and power generation, to improve the equitable sharing of benefits among stakeholders and communities within the basin, to return salmon to the Canadian part of the Basin, to account for climate change impacts within the Basin, and to meaningfully address the lack of Indigenous voices in the negotiation of the original treaty.[202]

The 1964 Columbia Treaty follows a similar style to those established by India with Bhutan and Nepal, in that it is primarily focused on providing details of the project to be implemented rather than setting out a broader regime for the protection and use of the shared river basin. Pursuant to the Treaty, a Permanent Engineering Board is charged with making annual reports 'of the results being achieved under the Treaty'.[203] Dispute settlement procedures are also provided for in the Treaty, whereby disputes are firstly considered by the International Joint Commission – a body established by Canada and the United States to cover all its transboundary waters – and failing resolution by the Commission, submitted to arbitration.[204]

---

197 Ibid.

198 Ibid, 15.

199 See Cosens (n 186).

200 Article XIX, 1961 Columbia River Treaty (n 189).

201 US Department of State, 'On the Opening of Negotiations to Modernize the Columbia River Treaty Regime' (30 May 2018) <https://2017-2021.state.gov/on-the-opening-of-negotiations-to-modernize-the-columbia-river-treaty-regime/index.html> accessed 13 June 2024.

202 Henshaw, Paisley and Hearns (n 186), 152.

203 Article XV, 1961 Columbia River Treaty (n 189).

204 Article XVI, ibid.

A further example of countries benefiting from joint action on transboundary waters is the case of the Senegal River Basin shared between Guinea, Mali, Mauritania and Senegal. As early as 1963, through the adoption of the Bamako Convention, the riparians made their intentions for joint action clear by declaring the Senegal River as international.[205] The international nature of the Senegal River was enhanced through the procedural and institutional requirement that all water-related projects within the basin be agreed on the basis of consensus amongst all four riparians.[206] To facilitate such approvals, the riparian states established an inter-state committee.[207] As Mbengue observes, 'the Bamako Convention paved the way for a joint management system of the Senegal River and left almost no room for unilateral actions by the riparian states in the exploitation of the resources of the Senegal'.[208] Joint action in the Senegal River took a major step forward in 1972 through the adoption of the Convention on the Statute of the Senegal River and the Convention creating the Organisation for the Development of the Senegal River – albeit initially with only three of the riparian states (Mali, Mauritania and Senegal).[209] The 1972 Convention on the Statute of the Senegal River enhanced the common approach to basin management originally set out in the 1963 Bamako Convention by stipulating that:

> No project which is likely to bring about serious modifications on the characteristics of the river's regime, on its navigation conditions, the agricultural and industrial exploitation of the river, the sanitary state of the waters, the biological characteristics of its fauna and its flora, as well as its water level, will be implemented without the prior approval of the contracting states.[210]

---

205 Article 13, Convention Relating to the General Development of the Senegal River Basin (adopted 26 July 1963), (1965) 21(2) Revue Juridique et Politique (Paris) 299.

206 Article 8, ibid.

207 Article 1, ibid.

208 Makane M. Mbengue, 'The Senegal River Legal Regime and its Contribution to the Development of the Law of International Watercourses in Africa', in Laurence Boisson de Chazournes, Christina Leb and Mara Tignino (eds), *International Law and Freshwater: The Multiple Challenges* (Edward Elgar 2012), 221.

209 Convention on the Status of the Senegal River (adopted 11 March 1972) <https://iea.uoregon.edu/treaty-text/2804> accessed 13 June 2024; Convention Creating the Organisation for the Development of the Senegal River (adopted 11 March 1971) <http://www.cawater-info.net/bk/water_law/pdf/senegal_1972.pdf> accessed 13 June 2024. Guinea later acceded in 2006.

210 Article 4, ibid.

This joint action approach was further safeguarded by a requirement that only the Organisation for the Development of the Senegal River (OMVS) could decide whether a planned activity was, 'likely to bring about serious modifications' to the Senegal river regime.[211] The 1972 conventions provided the legal basis by which Mali, Mauritania and Senegal developed two further agreements related to common projects – the 1978 Convention Concerning the Legal Status of Common Works[212] and the 1982 Convention Regarding Financing Arrangements for Common Works.[213] Pursuant to the 1978 Convention, Mali, Mauritania and Senegal declared that common works were to be the 'joint and indivisible property' of the three countries.[214] Vick observes that in so doing, the countries went far beyond what 'would be expected under the most cooperative theories of basin management or good neighbourliness'.[215] These legal instruments led to the development of the Diama and Manantali Dams, as well as port facilities. The Diama Dam, located near the delta of the Senegal River, was completed in 1986 to control floods, prevent saltwater intrusion, provide 120 hectares of irrigated land, and satisfy the needs of urban and rural populations.[216] The Manantali Dam provides irrigation for over 3,750 km^2 of land, improved navigation, and 800 million kilowatt hours per year of electricity.[217]

These projects were financed through loans from twelve international development partners to the sum of US$ 620 million.[218] An additional sum of US$ 445 million was secured to develop the power generation facilities, which were completed in 2002.[219] Through the 'Clé de Répartition', the Council of Ministers of the Organisation for the Development of the Senegal River

[211] Article 1, ibid.

[212] Convention Concerning the Legal Status of Common Works (adopted 21 December 1978) <https://iea.uoregon.edu/treaty-text/2891> accessed 13 June 2024.

[213] Convention Regarding the Financing Arrangements for Common Works (adopted 12 May 1982) <https://iea.uoregon.edu/treaty-text/4464> accessed 17 June 2024.

[214] Article 2, Convention Concerning the Legal Status of Common Works (n 212).

[215] Margaret J. Vick, 'The Senegal River Basin: A Retrospective and Prospective Look at the Legal Regime' (2006) 46(1) Natural Resources Journal 211, 216.

[216] Mara Tignino, 'Joint Infrastructure and the Sharing of Benefits in the Senegal and Niger Watersheds' (2016) 41(6) Water International 835, 839.

[217] Ibid.

[218] Winston Yu, *Benefit Sharing in International Rivers: Findings from the Senegal River Basin, the Columbia River Basin, and the Lesotho Highlands Water Project* (World Bank Group 2008), 15.

[219] Ibid.

agreed on a cost-sharing arrangement for the common works which sets out percentage shares of project costs and benefits between the three countries.[220] While these projects have demonstrated the value of cooperation in achieving joint benefits, they were not without significant social and environmental impacts, including deforestation, the resettlement of 12,000 people, a reduction in fisheries and an increase in occurrences of water-borne diseases.[221] These concerns led to the development of the 2002 Water Charter of the Senegal River, which supplements the existing treaties while also recognizing the importance of sustainable management and public participation within the basin.[222] Additionally, the Charter provided the impetus to include Guinea in the membership of OMVS.[223] Cooperation over the Senegal River Basin takes one step further than the previously cited examples in that a legally binding agreement exists, i.e., the 2002 Water Charter, which covers the protection and use of transboundary waters at a basin level. However, the Charter provides only very general provisions concerning the monitoring of its implementation and in relation to how any issues of non-compliance will be addressed.[224]

While not international, another example where downstream payments to upstream users have incentivised cooperation is the case of the Catskills watershed and New York City. The Safe Drinking Water Act was passed by the United States Congress in 1974 in order to provide a common set of standards for drinking water quality and ensure that those standards were monitored and enforced.[225] The Safe Drinking Water Act was then amended in 1986 to include the Surface Water Treatment Rule, which required municipalities to either put in place chemical filtration facilities to remove pollutants or to maintain the ecosystem function of drinking water source watersheds as a natural means of preventing and filtering pollutants.[226] New York City is reliant upon

---

220 Ibid, 19.

221 Oliver Hensengerth, Innes Dombrowsky and Waltina Scheumann, 'Benefit-sharing in dam projects on shared waters' (*Deutsches Institut für Entwicklungspolitik (DIE), Discussion Paper No. 6/20212*) <http://hdl.handle.net/10419/199375> accessed 17 June 2024, 13.

222 Water Charter of the Senegal River (adopted 28 May 2002) <https://whatconvention.org/en/convention/1668> accessed 17 June 2024.

223 Mbengue (n 208), 232.

224 See for example, Articles 19–23 and 30, 2002 Water Charter (n 222). Pursuant to Article 30, the parties must first seek to resolve any differences by mediation or conciliation. Article 30 goes on to stipulate that if mediation or conciliation fails, they are required to submit the dispute to the African Union, or if that proves unsuccessful, the International Court of Justice.

225 Safe Drinking Water Act 1974 (US).

226 Safe Drinking Water Act Amendments of 1986 (US).

watersheds that are located north of the City for its water supply: the Croton River watershed supplies 10% of New York's water needs, and the Catskill-Delaware watershed system supplies 90% of New York's water needs.[227] However, Appleton observes that, 'by the end of the 1980s, an environmentally destructive pattern of land use was replacing the traditional agricultural and land use patterns that had been compatible with the drinking water needs of the City'.[228] Faced with the requirements of the Surface Water Treatment Rule, New York City had the choice to build a new water filtration plant or develop a cooperative arrangement with Catskill and Delaware municipalities to restore the ecosystem function of the Catskills watershed.[229] The capital cost of a new water filtration plant was estimated to be US$ 6–8 billion, in addition to the US$ 300 million annual operating costs.[230] Safeguarding natural capital investments in the Catskills watershed in order to comply with the Surface Water Treatment Rule was estimated at US$ 1–1.5 billion.[231] A clear economic incentive for downstream New York to invest in the upstream Catskills watershed therefore existed. Appleton summed up the choice as follows:

> Initial calculations showed that a comprehensive program of watershed protection would cost far less than filtration, would maintain water quality even more effectively, and would produce numerous other benefits as well, both for New York City and also for the Catskills, whereas a filtration system would protect water quality but also be a black hole for money that would do nothing for the Catskills.[232]

In order to implement the Catskills arrangement, New York City negotiated a Memorandum of Agreement (MoA) as a basic framework by which to govern the relationship with the Catskills Watershed.[233] The MoA created an institutional

---

[227] Albert F. Appleton, 'How New York City Used an Ecosystem Services Strategy Carried out Through an Urban-Rural Partnership to Preserve the Pristine Quality of its Drinking Water and Save Billions of Dollars' (Forest Trends conference, Tokyo, 5 November 2002) <https://freshwater.issuelab.org/resources/23434/23434.pdf>, 2.

[228] Ibid, 3.

[229] Jeff W. Hanlon, 'Watershed Protection to Secure Ecosystems Services – the New York City Watershed Governance Arrangement' (2017) 1 Case Studies in the Environment 1, 3.

[230] Graciela Chichilnisky and Geoffrey Heal, 'Economic Returns from the Biosphere' (1998) 391 Nature 629, 629.

[231] Ibid.

[232] Appleton (n 227), 5.

[233] New York City Watershed Memorandum of Agreement (adopted 1 January 1997) <https://dos.ny.gov/system/files/documents/2020/08/nyc_watershed_moa_1997.pdf> accessed 17 June 2024.

structure to bring together elected representatives of the watershed communities, appointed representatives of New York City, the State Department of Environmental Conservation, and environmental advocacy groups; and the Catskill Watershed Corporation was established to develop programmes and allocate funds to public and private watershed users.[234] New York City committed to funding a range of projects in the Catskills watershed, including wastewater treatment plants, septic systems, farm consultations, as well as land acquisition and restoration.[235] A particular challenge for New York City was to address non-point source pollution from privately owned farms.[236] This was only achieved by working in partnership with the farming communities to find win-win solutions, which protected the economic and social prosperity of the farming community while also reducing non-point source pollution and preserving the full environmental functioning of the watershed.[237] Through the Whole Farm programme, funded by New York City, the farmers received bespoke assistance to support them in adopting pollution control measures that were advantageous both from a business and environmental point of view.[238]

The Catskills experience presents a compelling case for supporting green infrastructure over grey infrastructure. From a transboundary perspective, it demonstrates the value and incentives for upstream-downstream cooperation and the incentives that can be put in place to prevent upstream pollution. The case also demonstrates the importance of a strong governance framework that engages with key stakeholders within the basin and ensures that any programmes are co-produced with those stakeholders in a way that delivers win-win solutions for upstream and downstream users. [239]

Taken together, the cases of the Columbia River, the Senegal River, and the Catskills watershed demonstrate that there are significant benefits to countries cooperating over their transboundary waters. Both within power asymmetric relationships and elsewhere, states have shown that cooperation can lead to greater benefits in terms of *inter alia* energy production, flood control, water quality protection and supply, and ecosystem protection. Power relationships may, therefore, not be the only factor that influences cooperation. The cases of the Columbia and Senegal Rivers demonstrate that countries resort to legally binding arrangements as a means by which to set out the terms and conditions of their cooperation. These examples also demonstrate that countries see the value of establishing institutions, such as joint commissions, that have

---

[234] Article IV, ibid.
[235] Article V, ibid.
[236] Appleton (n 227), 5.
[237] Ibid.
[238] Ibid.
[239] Hanlon (n 229), 5–6.

responsibility for supporting the implementation of their treaty arrangements. In addition, the examples show that in terms of monitoring implementation and addressing issues of non-compliance, the treaty arrangements that are established tend to be quite general. Specific measures for monitoring implementation are not contained in these treaties, and non-compliance is usually only considered through general dispute settlement procedures. It might be that the incentives to cooperate are so compelling that implementation does not need to be monitored and any non-compliance is unlikely. Whether this is indeed the case will be considered in subsequent chapters.

2.4 TREATIES AND THEIR INSTITUTIONS MATTER

A common feature of many of the examples of cooperation above is the central role that treaties and their institutions, such as river basin commissions, play in fostering cooperation.[240] A number of key functions of legal and institutional arrangements have been identified. Firstly, legal and institutional arrangements set out rights and obligations between states. In so doing, they have the capacity to, 'establish stable mutual expectations about others' patterns of behaviour', and all countries to, 'develop working relationships that will allow the parties to adapt their practices to new situations'.[241] Frank maintains that the ability of those rights and obligations to exert a 'compliance pull' is enhanced through their 'textual determinacy', or in other words, 'the ability of the text to convey a clear message', and 'to appear transparent in the sense that one can see through the language to the meaning'.[242] Secondly, legal and institutional arrangements reduce 'transaction costs' due to their capacity to cluster several

---

[240] See generally Robert O. Keohane, *International Institutions and State Power* (Routledge 2018), 1–20; Kenneth A. Oye (ed), *Cooperation under Anarchy* (Princeton University Press 1986); Robert O. Keohane, *After Hegemony – Cooperation and Discord in the World Political Economy* (Princeton University Press 1984); David G. Victor, Kal Raustiala and Eugene B. Skolnikoff (eds), *The Implementation and Effectiveness of International Environmental Commitments – Theory and Practice* (The MIT Press 1998); Oran Young (ed), *The Effectiveness of International Environmental Regimes – Causal Connections and Behavioural Mechanisms* (The MIT Press 1999); Edward L. Miles and others (eds), *Environmental Regime Effectiveness – Confronting Theory with Evidence* (The MIT Press 2002); Helmut Breitmeier, Oran R. Young and Michael Zürn, *Analysing International Environmental Regimes – From Case Study to Database* (The MIT Press 2006).

[241] Keohane (n 240), 89.

[242] Thomas M. Franck, 'Legitimacy in the International System' (1998) 82(4) The American Journal of International Law 705, 713–725.

issues under the same umbrella.[243] Legal arrangements and their institutions can also play an important role in providing information that is otherwise unavailable or only available at a high cost.[244] Furthermore, Underdal highlights the role that institutions can play as collective learning forums.[245] Through the exchange of information, and joint technical and scientific programmes, these legal and institutional arrangements can evolve to develop a better understanding of the problems for which they were created.[246] While asymmetries in knowledge and information between countries may act as a barrier to the adoption of any meaningful agreement, data exchange can help build trust and confidence in any joint institution.[247] Secretariats often play an important role in providing unbiased information that can aid decision-makers in making joint decisions on the implementation of agreements.[248] Ultimately, while both power asymmetries between countries and the identification of mutual benefits potentially influence water cooperation, legal and institutional arrangements may also have an influence on transboundary relations between states.

The example of cooperation between Canada and the United States concerning the Columbia River Basin takes place within a broader legal and institutional arrangement that has evolved significantly over time. The basis of this legal and institutional arrangement is set out in the 1909 Boundary Waters Treaty and its International Joint Commission (IJC).[249] The original focus of the Boundary Waters Treaty was on granting equal navigation access to shared waters between Canada and the United States and certain provisions concerning water diversions and changes in water levels, though the Treaty did also contain a provision concerning the prevention of transboundary pollution.[250]

---

243 Keohane (n 240), 89–92.

244 Marc A. Levy, Oran R. Young and Michael Zürn, 'The Study of International Regimes' (1995) 1(3) European Journal of International Relations 267, 288.

245 A. Underdal, 'Conclusions: Patterns of Regime Effectiveness' in Miles and others (n 240), 440.

246 Ibid, 467–468; Oran R. Young, 'Regime Effectiveness: Taking Stock' (n 240), 249.

247 Jonathan L. Chenoweth and Eran Feitelson, 'Analysis of Factors Influencing Data and Information Exchange in International River Basins' (2001) 26(4) Water International 499, 299; Oran R. Young, 'Regime Effectiveness: Taking Stock' (n 240), 249; Keohane (n 240), 93.

248 Patience Mukuyu and others, 'The devil's in the details: data exchange in transboundary waters' (2020) 45 Water International 884, 885.

249 Boundary Waters Treaty – Treaty Relating to Boundary Waters, and Questions Arising between the United States and Canada, Washington (adopted 11 January 1909), [1910] British Treaty Series 3 (Boundary Waters Treaty).

250 Ibid, Article IV.

Pursuant to the Treaty, the IJC was afforded a number of functions, including approving any subsequent uses, obstructions and diversions of boundary waters,[251] as well as changes to water levels.[252] The IJC was also given the power to examine and report on 'questions or matters of differences' between the parties, the outcome of which was to be recommendatory in nature and 'in no way have the character of an arbitral award'.[253] However, following the consent of both parties, questions or matters of difference could also be explicitly referred to the IJC for a binding decision.[254] The six member IJC is made up of three representatives from each party.[255] While constrained by the interests of the two federal governments, the IJC has addressed a wide range of transboundary water issues.[256] Up until the 1950s, most of the matters that came before the IJC dealt with applications for specific works. However, since then, most of the IJC's work has been investigative.[257] Through these investigations, the IJC has developed recommendations addressing both air and water pollution, settled disputes over water diversions, promoted joint infrastructure schemes for energy production and flood control, and tackled water quality in the Great Lakes.[258] In relation to the latter, an agreement on the Water Quality of the Great Lakes was adopted in 1972 and updated in 2012 to better protect the chemical, physical and biological integrity of these shared lakes.[259] These activities, which find their legal basis within the 1909 Boundary Waters Treaty

---

251 Ibid, Article III.

252 Ibid, Article IV.

253 Ibid, Article IX.

254 Ibid, Article X.

255 Ibid, Article VII.

256 Noah D. Hall, 'The Centennial of the Boundary Waters Treaty: A Century of United States-Canadian Transboundary Water Management' (2008) 54(4) The Wayne Law Review 1418.

257 Murray Clamen and Daniel Macfarlane, 'Introduction' in Daniel Macfarlane and Murray Clamen (eds), *The First Century of the International Joint Commission* (University of Calgary Press 2018).

258 Noah D. Hall, Dan A. Tarlock and Marcia Valiante, 'The Boundary Waters Treaty, the International Joint Commission and the Evolution of Transboundary Environmental Law and Governance', in Daniel Macfarlane and Murray Clamen (eds), *The First Century of the International Joint Commission* (University of Calgary Press 2018).

259 Protocol Amending the Agreement Between Canada and the United States of America on Great Lakes Water Quality, 1978, as Amended on October 16, 1983, and on November 18, 1987 (adopted 7 September 2012, entered into force 12 February 2013) <https://www.ijc.org/sites/default/files/2018-07/GLWQA_2012.pdf> accessed 8 August 2024.

and build on the efforts of the IJC, demonstrate the value of such arrangements in progressing cooperation.

Within the South Asian context, another example of a legal and institutional arrangement that has stood the test of time is the 1960 Indus Waters Treaty and its Commission. In 1947, British partitioning divided the province of Punjab between India and Pakistan, which in turn meant that water infrastructure in the Indus River was split.[260] This split meant that India controlled the upstream infrastructure that Pakistan relied upon to safeguard the flow of water through a canal system used for irrigational purposes.[261] Following over ten years of extensive negotiations mediated by the World Bank, India and Pakistan sought to address the sharing of Indus waters through the adoption of the 1960 Indus Waters Treaty.[262] The Indus Waters Treaty stipulates that all the waters of the eastern tributaries of the Indus (Sutlej, Beas and Ravi) were to be allocated to India, and Pakistan was allocated the western tributaries (Indus, Jhelum and Chenab).[263] In addition to allocating the waters of the Indus River between the countries, the 1960 Indus Waters Treaty also established the Permanent Indus Commission.[264] The Commission, made up of one commissioner from each country, provides an important forum by which the parties exchange data and information relating to matters under the Indus Waters Treaty.[265] Additionally, the Commission is tasked with examining 'any question which arises between the parties concerning the interpretation or application' of the Indus Waters Treaty.[266] Where the Commission is unable to find a solution, they are obliged to either refer the question to the Governments to negotiate a settlement, to a neutral expert, or to a Court of Arbitration.[267]

The Indus Waters Treaty, and its dispute settlement procedures, have been highlighted as an important means by which the states have prevented or

[260] Undala Z. Alam, 'Questioning the water wars rationale: a case study of the Indus Waters Treaty' (2002) 168(4) The Geographical Journal 241, 342.

[261] Neda A. Zawahri, 'India, Pakistan and cooperation along the Indus River System' (2009) 11 Water Policy 1, 4.

[262] See Asit K. Biswas, 'Indus Water Treaty: the Negotiating Process' (1992) 17 Water International 201.

[263] Article II and III, Indus Waters Treaty (adopted 19 September 1960), 419 UNTS 125.

[264] Ibid, Article VIII.

[265] Ibid.

[266] Ibid, Article IX.

[267] Ibid. In accordance with Article IX of the Indus Water Treaty, the choice of procedure will depend on the nature of the dispute.

resolved their water conflicts and advanced cooperation.[268] The Treaty and its Commission have survived political tensions between the countries, including two wars.[269]

Several water disputes between the countries have been resolved through recourse to the Treaty's dispute settlement procedures. In 2005, India and Pakistan agreed to follow the procedures for establishing a neutral expert in relation to India's plan to construct the Baglihar hydropower plant on the Chenab River.[270] While Pakistan was allocated the Chenab River under the Indus Waters Treaty, India is permitted certain uses of the river, including installing run-of-river hydropower plants within its part of the river.[271] Pakistan questioned whether the design of the Baglihar dam was consistent with the strict requirements for run-of-river hydropower plants that were set in Annex D of the Indus Waters Treaty.[272] Following the appointment of the neutral expert, Mr Raymond Lafitte, a highly qualified Swiss engineer, proceedings took place through 2006, and a final determination was made by Mr Lafitte on 12 February 2007.[273] Mr Lafitte's determination addressed several contentious design issues related to the Baglihar hydropower plant, including the maximum amount of water that can arrive at the dam; whether the spillway should be gated; the level of the spillway gates; the artificial raising of the water level; the maximum pondage volume; and the level of the power intake.[274] In his determination, Mr Lafitte agreed with India's proposed maximum amount of water that can arrive at the dam, i.e., 16,500 m^3 per second, its proposal to include spillway gates, which were considered as common practice

---

268 Salman M.A. Salman and Kishor Uprety, *Cooperation and Conflict on South Asia's International Rivers* (The World Bank 2001); Neda Zawahri and David Michel, 'Assessing the Indus Water Treaty from a comparative perspective' (2018) 43(5) Water International 696; Saleem H. Ali, 'Water Politics in South Asia: Technocratic Cooperation and Lasting Security in the Indus Basin and Beyond' (2008) 61(1) Journal of International Affairs 167; Mary Miner and others, 'Water Sharing Between India and Pakistan: a critical evaluation of the Indus Water Treaty' (2009) 34(2) Water International 204.

269 Zawahri (n 261), at 1.

270 Raymond Lafitte, 'Baglihar Hydroelectric Plant – Expert Determination on points of difference referred by the Government of Pakistan under the provisions of the Indus Water Treaty' (12 February 2007) <https://mowr.gov.pk/SiteImage/Misc/files/Baglihar%20Expert%20Determination%20(PDF).pdf> accessed 17 June 2024.

271 Article III(3) and Annex D, Indus Water Treaty (n 263).

272 Ibid.

273 Salman M.A. Salman, 'The Baglihar difference and its resolution process – a triumph for the Indus Water Treaty?' (2008) 10 Water Policy 105, 113.

274 Lafitte (n 270).

in the design of such projects, and the levels of the spillway gates. However, he agreed with Pakistan that the artificial raising of the water level and the maximum pondage volume should be lower than India had proposed, and that the level of power intake should be higher.[275] Both parties accepted the determination, which has been considered an important reflection of the strength of the Indus Waters Treaty.[276]

Soon after the Baglihar difference, the dispute settlement procedures were once again invoked in relation to India's construction of the Kishenganga Dam, which was designed to divert water from the Kishenganga/Neelum River to the Jhelum River for the purpose of hydropower generation.[277] The Kishenganga dispute fell under the remit of Article IX(5) and Annexure G of the Indus Waters Treaty, which required it to be referred to a Court of Arbitration. Concerned with the downstream impacts of the project, Pakistan requested that the dispute be addressed by a Court of Arbitration in May 2010, and the Court was constituted in December 2010.[278] Following site visits and oral hearings, the Court issued a partial award in February 2013, which agreed with India's interpretation of the project as a run-of-river project in accordance with the Treaty.[279] However, the Court stipulated that the project must be implemented in such a way as to maintain a minimum flow of water in the Kishenganga/Neelum River, and India was not permitted to reduce water levels below the 'Dead Storage Level' except in an unforeseen emergency.[280] The Court then requested the parties to submit to the Court their determination of an appropriate minimum flow of water.[281] Following the submission of the parties' proposals, the Court issued its final award on 20 December 2013.[282]

275 Ibid.

276 Salman (n 273), 116.

277 See Kishor Uprety, 'The Kishenganga Arbitration: Reviving the Indus Waters Treaty and Managing Transboundary Hydropolitics' (2005) 14(3) Chinese Journal of International Law 497.

278 Shashank P. Kumar, 'The Indus Waters Kishenganga Arbitration (Pakistan v India) (2013) 17(13) American Society of International Law Insights, <https://papers.ssrn.com/sol3/papers.cfm?abstract_id=2264464> accessed 17 June 2024.

279 *In the Matter of the Indus Waters Kishenganga Arbitration (Pakistan/India) – Partial Award* (18 February 2013) <https://pcacases.com/web/sendAttach/1681> accessed 17 June 2024, 201.

280 Ibid. India had argued that it should be permitted to lower water levels in order to flush sediment from the reservoir, but the Court decided that this did not fall within the meaning of an unforeseen emergency under the Indus Waters Treaty.

281 Ibid.

282 *In the Matter of the Indus Waters Kishenganga Arbitration (Pakistan/India) – Final Award* (20 December 2013) <https://pcacases.com/web/sendAttach

The Court's final award obliged India to release a minimum flow of 9 m^3 per second into the Kishenganga/Neelum River and gave each party the right to review the flow levels seven years after the final award was issued.[283]

More recently, disputes over the design of two hydropower plants, the Kishenganga Project (as noted above) and the Ratle Project, have resulted in the countries relying once again on the dispute settlement procedures of the Indus Waters Treaty.[284] Proceedings before another neutral expert and the Permanent Court of Arbitration have been initiated by the countries with a view to resolving disagreement.[285]

These disagreements between India and Pakistan illustrate how legal and institutional arrangements can endure despite the contentious issues that co-riparians might experience. While it could not be said that cooperation between India and Pakistan has evolved to encompass broader water management issues,[286] the case does illustrate how the legal and institutional arrangements themselves can play a role in influencing cooperation – and can even do so where relations between the countries concerned are strained. An important conclusion of this section is therefore to recognise that legal and institutional arrangements do appear to have some influence on state behaviour.

2.5 THE POWER OF IDEAS

A further feature of India and Pakistan water relations illustrated by both the Baghlihar difference and the Kishenganga arbitration is how treaty interpretation evolves over time. In the Baglihar difference, the neutral expert referred to the need to account for potential climate change impacts when determining the maximum amount of water levels that can arrive at the dam.[287] In the Kishenganga arbitration, the Court expressly recognized that, 'it is …

/48> accessed 17 June 2024.

283 Ibid.

284 The World Bank, 'World Bank Holds Hand-Over Meetings with the Neutral Expert and the Chairman of the Court of Arbitration under the Indus Waters Treaty' (Press Release, 21 November 2022) <https://www.worldbank.org/en/news/press-release/2022/11/21/world-bank-holds-handover-meetings-under-indus-waters-treaty> accessed 17 June 2024.

285 Ibid.

286 The Treaty even faces criticism for not covering broader river basin management concerns, such as accounting for transboundary aquifers and groundwater management, water quality, pollution and environmental concerns (see Hamid Sarfraz, 'Revisiting the 1960 Indus Water Treaty' (2013) 38(2) Water International 204).

287 Lafitte (n 270), 89.

incumbent upon this Court to interpret and apply this 1960 Treaty in light of the customary international principles for the protection of the environment in force today'.[288] This interpretation gave the Court impetus to request that the countries consider environmental needs through an agreement on a minimum flow of the Indus waters. Neither environmental protection nor climate change were explicitly mentioned by the drafters of the Indus Waters Treaty in the 1960s.[289] This raises the question of whether ideas can themselves shape state behaviour.[290]

Snyder maintains that 'debates about ideas are the fundamental building blocks of international life', and that 'individuals and groups become powerful if they can convince others to adopt their ideas'.[291] Similarly, Wendt suggests that, 'international life is determined by the beliefs and expectations that states have about each other, and these are constructed largely by social rather than material structure'.[292] Within a transboundary context, Zeitoun and Cascão recognise the notion of 'ideational power', namely 'the capacity to impose and legitimize particular ideas and narratives'.[293] In other words, it is argued that norms and ideas have the ability to 'constrain, enable and constitute actors in their choices, and thus help to shape world politics'.[294]

---

[288] Kishenganga Arbitration (n 279), para 452.

[289] Kishenganga Arbitration final award (n 282), para 87.

[290] See generally, Martha Finnemore, *International Organizations as Teachers of Norms: The United Nations Educational, Scientific, and Cultural Organization and Science Policy* (1993) 47 International Organisation 565. See also Martha Finnemore, *National Interests in International Society* (Cornell University Press 1996); Peter J. Katzenstein (ed), *The Culture of National Security: Norms and Identity* (Columbia University Press 1996).

[291] Jack Snyder, 'One World, Rival Theories' (2004) 83(6) Foreign Policy 52.

[292] Alexander Wendt, *Social Theory of International Politics* (CUP 1999).

[293] Ana Cascão and Mark Zeitoun, 'Power, Hegemony and Critical Hydropolitics', in Anton Earle, Anders Jägerskög and Joakim Öjendal (eds), *Transboundary Water Management – Principles and Practice* (Earthscan 2010), 30. See also Steven Lukes, *Power: A Radical View* (2nd edn, Red Globe Press 2005); Michael Barnett and Raymond Duvall, 'Power in International Politics' (2005) 59 International Organisation 39; Jeroen Warner and Mark Zeitoun, 'International Relations Theory and Water Do Mix: A response to Furlong's troubled waters, hydro-hegemony and international water relations' (2008) 27 Political Geography 802 (2008).

[294] John G. Ruggie, 'What Makes the World Hang Together? Neo-utilitarianism and the Social Constructivist Challenge' (1998) 52(4) International Organisation 855. See also Jutta Brunée and Stephen J. Toope, 'Constructivist Approaches to International Law', in Jeffrey L. Dunoff and Mark A. Pollack (eds),

More specific to the transboundary water context, Brunnée and Toope analyse the influence of legal norms on shaping state behaviour within the Nile River Basin.[295] They suggest that customary international law principles and global legal instruments, such as the Watercourses Convention, have shaped the behaviour of states in the Nile basin by determining what counts as persuasive argument.[296] By tracing negotiations between Nile Basin states, the authors show how differing views on the relationship between key international water law principles, namely equitable and reasonable utilisation and no significant harm, had the effect of entrenching diverging ideas on transboundary water sharing between the states.[297] However, the authors show how the adoption of the Watercourses Convention, and the way in which it reconciled the principles of equitable and reasonable utilisation and no significant harm, had a positive influence on transboundary water negotiations in the Nile.[298] Brunnée and Toope go further to suggest that this positive development in part influenced the decision of the Nile Basin states, with the support of the World Bank, to review the Nile River Basin Action Plan in 1997 and establish the NBI in 1999.[299] The shared vision of the NBI certainly aligns with the text of the Watercourses Convention in its desire for 'sustainable socio-economic development through the equitable utilization of, and benefit from, the common Nile Basin water resources'.[300] As noted earlier, the similarity between the Watercourses Convention provisions related to equitable and reasonable utilisation and no significant harm, and the provisions of the GERD Declaration of Principles also reflects international law's influence on cooperation amongst Nile states. Furthermore, the CFA shares much with the text of the Watercourses Convention.

Another example of the influence of the Watercourses Convention relates to transboundary waters within the Southern African region. Jacobs' empirical analysis of transboundary water cooperation in Southern Africa shows how Southern African states revised their 1995 Protocol on Shared Watercourses System through the adoption of the 2000 Revised SADC Protocol in order to

---

Interdisciplinary Perspectives on International Law and International Relations: The State of the Art (CUP 2012).

[295] Jutta Brunnée and Stephen J. Toope, 'The Changing Nile Basin Regime: Does Law Matter?' (2002) 43(1) Harvard International Law Journal 105, 144.

[296] Ibid, 148–153.

[297] Ibid.

[298] Bunnée and Toope (n 295), 151.

[299] Ibid.

[300] Ibid

ensure that it was aligned with the Watercourses Convention.[301] Jacobs goes on to show how SADC states sharing transboundary waters have aligned their domestic policies with that of the Revised SADC Protocol.[302] Both Brunnée and Toope, and Jacobs, highlight the importance of interaction in the generation and maintenance of a common acceptance and understanding of certain norms and ideas.[303] Brunnée and Toope also stress the importance of 'communities of practice', which 'provide the settings in which the knowledge or norms that shape actors' understandings of the world are generated and practices evolve'.[304] According to Brunnée and Toope, it is not sufficient to adopt a particular treaty in order to invoke commitment and compliance, rather actors must 'participate in its ongoing application, clarification and adjustment'.[305]

Other scholars have highlighted how these norms and ideas can be used by less powerful states to strengthen their position. Daoudy, for example, shows how Turkey 'has … been careful not to completely disregard International Water Law, but offered its own interpretation of the principles of equitable and reasonable utilization and harm avoidance'.[306] She goes on to suggest that, 'as a source of bargaining power, international principles increase downstream riparians' legitimacy and enhance their bargaining position in the negotiation process'.[307] Along similar lines, Cascão demonstrates how the upstream states on the Nile River basin, as a collective unit, have been able to influence multilateral negotiations and regional agendas, and in turn, pressurize downstream states on legal issues.[308] In so doing, reputation is arguably a key influence. Daoudy, for instance, alludes to the idea that Turkey would not be keen to be seen in breach of international law.[309] Zeitoun and Jägerskog also suggest that

---

301 Inga Jacobs, 'Norms and Transboundary Co-operation in Africa: the Cases of the Orange-Senqu and Nile Rivers' (PhD Thesis, University of St Andrews 2010) <https://research-repository.st-andrews.ac.uk/bitstream/handle/10023/2139/IngaJacobsPhDThesis.pdf?sequence=7&isAllowed=y> accessed 17 June 2024, 146.

302 Ibid.

303 See also Emanuel Adler and Vincent Pouliot (eds), *International Practices* (CUP 2011); John G. Ruggie, *Constructing the World Polity* (Routledge 1998).

304 Bunnée and Toope (n 295), 63.

305 Ibid, 73.

306 Marwa Daoudy, 'Asymmetric Power: Negotiating Water in the Euphrates and Tigris' (2009) 14 International Negotiation 361.

307 Ibid, 363.

308 Ana Cascão, 'Changing Power Relations in the Nile River Basin: Unilateralism vs Cooperation?' (2009) 2 Water Alternatives 245; Ana Cascão, 'Ethiopia – Challenges to Egyptian Hegemony in the Nile Basin' (2008) 10 Water Policy 13.

309 Daoudy (n 306).

'basin bullies can be susceptible to the powers of persuasion, and may be less likely to force an arrangement if they are held accountable to an objective standard, or risk being "named and shamed"'.[310]

If it is accepted that transboundary water cooperation is influenced by norms and ideas, then two key trends should be considered within the context of treaty compliance and implementation. Firstly, there has been a growing trend to recognise the importance of managing waters at the basin level. In 1992, Agenda 21 noted that, 'integrated water resources management is based on the perception of water as an integral part of the ecosystem, a natural resource and a socio and economic good, whose quantity and quality determine the nature of its utilisation'.[311] It goes on to suggest that, 'integrated water resources management, including the integration of land- and water-related aspects, should be carried out at the level of the catchment basin or sub-basin'.[312] More recently, integrated water resources management (IWRM) has been incorporated into the SDG framework, through SDG target 6.5, which calls for the implementation of IWRM at all levels, including through transboundary cooperation where appropriate, by 2030.[313] Since the adoption of Agenda 21 in 1992, the influence of IWRM at the transboundary level is evident in the text of contemporary transboundary water agreements. Agreements such as the 1994 Danube Convention,[314] the 1995 Mekong Agreement,[315] the

---

310 Mark Zeitoun and Anders Jägerskog, 'Confronting Power: strategies to support less powerful states', in Anders Jägerskog and Mark Zeitoun (eds), *Getting Transboundary Water Right: Theory and Practice for Effective Cooperation* (Stockholm International Water Institute 2009).

311 Agenda 21, in 'Report of the United Nations Conference on Environmental and Development' (Rio de Janeiro, 3–14 June 1992), UN Doc A/Conf.151/26/Rev.1, para 18.8.

312 Ibid, para 18.9. See also, International Hydrological Programme (IHP) and Network of Asian River Basin Organisation, *Introduction to the IWRM Guidelines at River Basin Level* (UNESCO 2009).

313 Transforming our World: the 2030 Agenda for Sustainable Development, UNGA Res 70/1 (21 October 2015).

314 Convention on the Protection and Sustainable Use of the Danube River (adopted 29 June 1994) <http://www.icpdr.org/main/icpdr/danube-river-protection-convention> accessed 17 June 2024 (Danube Convention). Article 2(1) of the Danube Convention states one of its objectives as being to 'strive at achieving the goals of a sustainable and equitable water management, including the conservation, improvement and the rational use of surface waters and groundwater *in the catchment area* as far as possible' [emphasis added].

315 Agreement on the Cooperation for the Sustainable Development of the Mekong River Basin (adopted 5 April 1995), 34 ILM 864 (Mekong Agreement). Article 1 of the Mekong Agreement calls upon its parties 'to cooperate in all fields

1999 Rhine Convention[316] and the 2000 ORASECOM Agreement[317] offer just a few examples where countries sharing a particular basin have recognised the need to advance IWRM at the basin level.

More generally, it can be argued that there has been a growing recognition of the need to develop legal and institutional arrangements for transboundary rivers, lakes and aquifers. For instance, both the Watercourses Convention and the Water Convention recognise the importance of having legal and institutional arrangements in place at the basin level.[318] In the case of the Water Convention, it is even an explicit requirement that riparian parties enter into bilateral or multilateral agreements or other arrangements for their shared waters and establish 'joint bodies' to support the implementation of those arrangements.[319] The importance of legal and institutional arrangements for transboundary waters is also reflected within the SDG framework. Under the aforementioned SDG target 6.5, indicator 6.5.1 asks countries to monitor the degree of IWRM implementation, including any arrangements and/or organisational frameworks that have been established for transboundary water management.[320] This is complemented by indicator 6.5.2, which asks states sharing transboundary waters to monitor the proportion of their basin area (river, lakes and aquifers) covered by an operational arrangement for transboundary water cooperation.[321] While the monitoring framework for the SDGs will be considered in more detail in Chapter 5, it is important to note here the potential of these global policy developments to influence basin-level cooperation.

---

of sustainable development, utilization, management and conservation of the water and related resources of the Mekong River Basin'.

316 Article 3(1) of the Convention on the Protection of the Rhine (adopted 22 January 1998) <https://www.iksr.org/en/icpr/legal-basis/convention> accessed 8 July 2024 (1998 Rhine Convention), calls upon its parties to, *inter alia* pursue the aim of the 'sustainable development of the Rhine ecosystem'.

317 Agreement Between the Governments of the Republic of Botswana, the Kingdom of Lesotho, the Republic of Namibia and the Republic of South Africa on the Establishment of the Orange-Senqu River Commission (adopted 3 November 2000) <https://faolex.fao.org/docs/pdf/mul215151.pdf> accessed 17 June 2024 (ORASECOM Agreement). The preamble of the ORASECOM Agreement recognises, 'that collaboration between the parties with regard to the development of the River System as a water source of common interest could significantly contribute towards the mutual benefit, peace, security, welfare and prosperity of their people'.

318 See Articles 3, 4 and 8 of the Watercourses Convention (n 27); and Article 9 of the Water Convention (n 28).

319 Ibid.

320 UNEP, 'Country Survey Instrument for SDG Indicator 6.5.1' (2020) <https://iwrmdataportal.unepdhi.org/> accessed 17 June 2024.

321 Transforming our World (n 313), 11.

This is particularly pertinent given the call upon states within the UN system to submit data on all SDG indicators and annually report on their collective progress towards the SDG targets. The collective value of this reporting is reflected in some of the key policy outcomes of the SDG global monitoring process, such as the Ministerial Declaration of the high-level political forum on sustainable development, which stipulates that, 'we, the ministers and high representatives … commit to improving cooperation across borders, in transboundary waters'.[322] Another example can be seen in the United Nations' concept paper on Water for Cooperation, which was produced in preparation of the UN Midterm Comprehensive Review of the Objectives of the International Decade for Action, 'Water for Sustainable Development' 2018–2028.[323] The paper notes that, 'at the transboundary level, the adoption of arrangements for transboundary water cooperation, based on established principles of international law, is a key feature of any multilevel governance system', and 'at the transboundary level, where operational arrangements are lacking or not adaptable or resilient enough to meet contemporary challenges, governance should take responsibility, in partnership with non-governmental actors and with support from the international community, for establishing such arrangements'.[324]

While there remains a significant challenge in ensuring that all transboundary waters are covered by legal and institutional arrangements, these developments illustrate the influence of global ideas at the basin level.

2.6 CONCLUSION

While generally highlighting the complexities of transboundary water cooperation, this chapter has demonstrated that there is no single factor that can explain why states cooperate or fail to cooperate over their transboundary waters. Rather, existing scholarship and state practice would suggest that a complex web of factors influence transboundary relations to varying degrees and context is important.

---

322 UN Economic and Social Council, 'Ministerial Declaration of the 2018 High-level Political Forum on Sustainable Development, convened under the auspices of the Economic and Social Council, on the theme "Transformation towards sustainable and resilient societies"', UN Doc E/HLS/2018/1 (1 August 2018).

323 UN, 'Interactive Dialogue 4: Water for Cooperation: transboundary and international water cooperation, cross-sectoral cooperation, including scientific cooperation, and water across the 2030 Agenda for Sustainable Development (Sustainable Development Goal targets 6.5 and 6.b and Goals 16 and 17', UN Doc A/CONF.240/2023/7 (31 January 2023).

324 Ibid, paras 36 and 40(r).

Power, as a realist scholar would posit, is certainly an important factor in explaining whether or not states cooperate over their transboundary waters, and in explaining the structure that cooperation might take. This is particularly the case for acutely power-asymmetric relationships between upstream and downstream countries. As the chapter illustrates, China's relations with its neighbours largely fit this explanatory model. In the case of Kazakhstan, Mongolia and Russia, this has led to China adopting bilateral legal and institutional arrangements that only set out broad principles of cooperation. In relation to Bangladesh and India, China's cooperation has also been at the bilateral level, but even more focused, i.e., on data exchange. There would therefore appear to be little appetite to develop holistic basin-wide legally binding agreements for rivers such as the Indus or the Ganges-Brahmaputra-Meghna River basins. A slightly different approach exists for the Mekong, where China has proven reluctant to join a legally binding basin-wide arrangement, i.e., the 1995 Mekong Agreement, but has progressed expressly non-legally binding political commitments in the form of the Lancang-Mekong Cooperation framework. A reticence to enter into legally binding holistic water management is also reflective of Turkey's transboundary relations. As in the case of China, Turkey has however still cooperated with its downstream neighbours. While attempts to develop a basin-wide legally binding framework for the Tigris-Euphrates have largely failed, trilateral meetings and the establishment of the Joint Technical Committee are positive signs of cooperation. In addition, some concessions have been achieved on water flow allocations through bilateral treaties, as well as softer commitments concerning technical cooperation. These cases ultimately demonstrate that CIMs would likely not find a home in any negotiations between upstream hegemons, such as China and Turkey.

In the case of a power asymmetric relationship where the hegemon is downstream, such as in the examples of India, transboundary relations appear to take a different course. While China and Turkey have been able to utilise their geographic advantage to unilaterally develop hydropower projects on upstream rivers, India has instead entered into legally binding commitments with its upstream neighbours in order to secure benefits from transboundary waters, which include hydropower generation and flood control. India offers an interesting case where cooperation with Bhutan has proven more fruitful than cooperation with Nepal. This suggests that domestic contexts and broader political relations between the countries are likely to influence cooperation. This would also suggest that 'hydro-hegemons' do not have it all their own way. Certainly, while the equity of how transboundary waters are shared might be questioned in all incidences, in the cases of the neighbours of China, Turkey and India some concessions have been achieved. Another common feature of the downstream hegemons is that there is a tendency for any legally binding arrangements to be project-focused, rather than addressing broader water management issues within a basin. Also, in terms of implementation, while joint institutions are often established, their mandate tends to be focused on implementation of the project. Any provisions related to implementation and non-compliance tend to have a narrow remit, i.e., mostly requiring states to consult and utilise arbitration proceedings where disputes are unresolved at the bilateral level. However, there may be scope to introduce CIMs into such arrangements. This potential will be explored in subsequent chapters.

The case of the Nile shares some similarities with the power asymmetric relationships described above. Certainly, there has been a reluctance in downstream Egypt to enter into basin-wide legally binding arrangements, although their willingness to sign the 2015 Declaration of Principles suggests a softening of their position towards upstream states. However, it is perhaps too early to assess what will happen at the basin level. As things currently stand, although a basin-wide treaty framework has been developed, Egypt does not appear willing to ratify it in its current form.

What then can power tell us about a country's willingness to enter into legally binding treaty arrangements at the basin level, and for those arrangements to contain CIMs? Ultimately, the analysis would suggest that hydro-hegemons are reluctant to develop basin-wide legally binding arrangements. Rather, they have a tendency to set out very general principles for transboundary water cooperation or legal binding arrangements focused solely on a specific project. The same can be said of the institutions that are established to support the implementation of these arrangements. These institutions tend to have a very specific mandate. More broader issues, if part of any cooperation between the countries, tend to be expressed in softer political arrangements that are not legally binding.

However, while this may therefore mean that the likelihood of developing CIMs within the context of power asymmetric relationships is low, the chapter has shown that power is not the only factor that shapes transboundary water cooperation. The Catskills, Columbia and Senegal experiences demonstrate that a shared interest in the utilisation and protection of transboundary waters can be a compelling driver of cooperation irrespective of the power dynamics within a basin. As was demonstrated in the case of the IJC between Canada and the United States, cooperation can evolve and expand over time to take a more holistic approach to water management. Evolving cooperation is also reflective of the Senegal experience, where cooperation based on infrastructure development has progressed, most notably through the adoption of the 2002 Water Charter, to cover a broad range of water management issues. There are two key conclusions from this analysis. Firstly, states that have a shared interest in the protection and use of a transboundary river, lake or aquifer, are likely to develop legally binding arrangements to advance their cooperation. Secondly, these legal and institutional arrangements may in turn evolve to take a more holistic approach to water management. An issue that will be returned to is, therefore, whether there might be windows of opportunity to include CIMs in the evolution of treaties.

Before concluding this chapter, it is also important to recognise the reasons why treaties evolve over time. As scholars such as Brunnée and Toope and Daoudy have identified through their empirical analysis, cooperation between countries within a particular basin may be influenced by developments at regional and global level.[325] The development of global legal instruments, such as the Watercourses Convention and the Water Convention, appears to shape, at least in part, the practice of states at the basin level. Similarly, concepts such as IWRM, while not legal terms, may shape what happens at a basin level due to their widespread acceptance at the global level. Through the SDG framework, both IWRM and legal and institutional arrangements for transboundary water cooperation appear to have reached such a global status and therefore may influence the practice of states at the basin level. The extent of the influence of such global and regional processes will be further explored in Chapter 5. In particular, it will be asked whether a focus on compliance and implementation might be developing within these global and regional frameworks related to transboundary water cooperation.

325 Daoudy (n 306) and Brunnée and Toope (n 295).

3. The practice of compliance and implementation in multilateral environmental agreements

3.1 INTRODUCTION

The international community has expended a considerable amount of effort negotiating multilateral environmental agreements (MEAs). More than 500 MEAs are now believed to be in force.[1] These MEAs cover a host of issues, including loss of biological diversity, transboundary pollution, ocean degradation and desertification. Environmental treaty-making dates back to the 19th century.[2] However, it is only in recent decades that serious questions have been raised over the extent to which MEAs actually make a difference.[3] In reflecting on this phenomenon, Gillespie suggests that, 'the gap between the burgeoning hundreds of international environmental laws and the actual condition of the environment – [is] perhaps one of the largest contradictions of our time'.[4]

---

1 See UNEP, 'Register of International Treaties and other Agreements in the Field of Environment', UN Doc UNEP/ENV.Law/2005/3 (30 December 2005).

2 Edith Brown Weiss, 'The Evolution of International Environmental Law' (2011) 54 Japanese Yearbook of International Law 1.

3 Edith Brown Weiss, 'International Environmental Law: Contemporary issues and the emergence of a new world order' (1992) 81 Georgetown Law Journal 675; Philippe Sands and Jacqueline Peel, *Principles of International Environmental Law* (4th edn, CUP 2018), 25–69; Benedikt Heid and Laura Márquez-Ramos, 'International environmental agreements and imperfect enforcement: Evidence from CITES' (2023) 118 Journal of Environmental Economics and Management 102784; Kannan Ambalam, 'Challenges of Compliance with Multilateral Environmental Agreements: the case of the United Nations Convention to Combat Desertification in Africa' (2014) 5(2) Journal of Sustainable Development Studies 145.

4 Alexander Gillespie, 'International Environmental Law and Policy', in Klaus Bosselmann and David Grinlinton (eds), *Environmental Law for a Sustainable Society* (New Zealand Centre for Environmental Law 2002).

Concerns over the weak implementation of MEAs existed during the 1992 Rio Conference on the Environment and Development. At that time, Agenda 21 encouraged states 'to ensure the effective, full and prompt implementation of legally binding instruments'.[5] A major response to the need to address the 'impact gap' was to incorporate compliance and implementation mechanisms (CIMs) into the institutional framework of MEAs.[6] This practice was inspired by the 1987 Protocol on Substantives that Deplete the Ozone Layer (Montreal Protocol), which was considered the 'best practice' in the use of CIMs.[7] Article 8 of the protocol calls upon parties to 'approve procedures and institutional mechanisms for determining non-compliance with the provisions of this Protocol and for treatment of parties found to be in non-compliance'.[8] Other MEAs followed the practice of the Montreal Protocol, resulting in a proliferation of CIMs. This proliferation has led some commentators to suggest that CIMs have now 'become a sort of "must" within the institutional regimes established by multilateral environmental agreements'.[9]

---

[5] Agenda 21, in 'Report of the United Nations Conference on Environmental and Development' (Rio de Janeiro, 3–14 June 1992), UN Doc A/Conf.151/26/Rev.1.

[6] Hugh Adsett and others, 'Compliance Committees and Recent Multilateral Environmental Agreements: The Canadian Experience with Their Negotiation and Operation' (2004) 42 Canadian Yearbook of International Law 91; Malgosia Fitzmaurice, 'Compliance with Multilateral Environmental Agreements' (2008) 20 Hague Yearbook of International Law 19.

[7] Protocol on Substantives that Deplete the Ozone Layer (adopted 16 September 1987, entered into force 1 January 1989), 26 ILM 1550 (1987) (Montreal Protocol); Ruth Greenspan Bell, 'Developing a Culture of Compliance in the International Environmental Regime' (1997) 27 Environmental Law Reporting 10402; Winfried Lang, 'Compliance Control in International Environmental Law: Institutional Necessities' (1996) 56(3) Zeitschrift für Ausländishches Recht und Völkerrecht 685.

[8] Ibid. The non-compliance procedure under the Montreal Protocol was subsequently established by Decision IV/5, during the Fourth Meeting of the parties to the Protocol, see 'Report of the Fourth Meeting of the parties, Annex V', UN Doc UNEP/OzL.Pro.4/5 (25 November 1992).

[9] Attila Tanzi and Cesare Pitea, 'Non-Compliance Mechanisms: Lessons Learned and the Way Forward', in Tulio Treves and others (eds), *Non-compliance Procedures and Mechanisms and the Effectiveness of International Environmental Agreements* (TMC Asser Press 2009), 569. See also Malgosia Fitzmaurice and Catherine Redgwell, 'Environmental Non-compliance Procedures and International Law' (2000) 31 Netherlands Yearbook of International Law 35, 42.

Several perceived benefits of CIMs have no doubt caused this proliferation. Firstly, in the field of environmental protection, CIMs are considered to be a better option than traditional dispute settlement mechanisms. The law of state responsibility is designed to allow a state to seek reparation for harm caused by injurious acts of another, or to suspend their performance under a treaty due to another state's failure to comply with their treaty commitments.[10] However, many MEAs address 'global or regional commons', such as the atmosphere, oceans or biological diversity, where it is extremely difficult or even impossible to trace a causal link between any harm suffered by one state and the specific act of non-compliance by another state.[11]

The issue of causality raises the question of whether CIMs are better suited to multilateral, as opposed to bilateral, agreements.[12] It could be argued that the law of state responsibility is better suited to bilateral agreements where a direct detrimental impact on an individual state can be readily discerned. However, it might still be maintained that there are benefits to incorporating CIMs within a bilateral treaty setting. For instance, in both a multilateral and bilateral context, the remedies of restitution or compensation found under the law of state responsibility may be inadequate in the realm of environmental protection, where significant emphasis is placed on preventing irreversible harm.[13] Furthermore, the difficulty in reversing environmental harm may lead states to avoid traditional dispute settlement institutions, such as the

---

10 See for example, Draft Articles on Responsibility of States for International Wrongful Acts with commentaries in 'Report of the International Law Commission on the Work of its 53rd Session', UN Doc A/63/10 (23 April – 3 June, and 2 July – 10 August), 31–143. See also Xueman Wang and Glen Wiser, 'The Implementation and Compliance Regimes under the Climate Change Convention and its Kyoto Protocol' (2002) 11 Review of European Community and International Environmental Law 181.

11 Teall E. Crossen, 'Multilateral Environmental Agreements and the Compliance Continuum' (2003–4) 16 Georgetown International Environmental Law Review 473, 480–481.

12 Haroldo Machado Filho, 'Looking for Adequate Tools for the Enforcement of Multilateral Environmental Agreements: Compliance Procedures and Mechanisms' (ESIL Research Forum, International Law: contemporary problems, Geneva, May 2005) <https://esil-sedi.eu/pre-2009-conference-papers> accessed 21 June 2024, 5. See also Ulrich Beyerlin, Peter-Tobias Stoll and Rüdiger Wolfrum, 'Conclusions drawn from the Conference on Ensuring Compliance with MEAs', in Ulrich Beyerlin, Peter-Tobias Stoll and Rüdiger Wolfrum (eds), *Ensuring Compliance with Multilateral Environmental Agreements: A Dialogue between Practitioners and Academia* (Martinus Nijhoff 2006).

13 Fitzmaurice and Redgwell (n 9).

International Court of Justice, given the time-consuming nature of proceedings and their adversarial nature.[14]

Another argument relating to the limits of the law of state responsibility is that some norms of international environmental law have not been fully or universally recognised, or their 'soft' nature means that a discernible breach will prove elusive to find.[15] Additionally, where the root causes of non-compliance are of a technical nature or due to weak capacity, the effectiveness of the law of state responsibility may be limited if a state does not have the means by which to rectify the issue.

Secondly, CIMs have proven to constitute an important means by which to foster learning and knowledge exchange when addressing 'wicked' problems, such as environmental protection.[16] Haas, for example, demonstrates the value of 'learning by persuasion', whereby epistemic communities are able to advance and agree upon the technological knowledge required to address a particular problem.[17] More generally, by reviewing compliance and implementation practices, states, as well as non-state actors, can work collaboratively to exchange 'best practice' in implementing treaty commitments and overcome any perceived barriers to implementation.[18]

Thirdly, CIMs have offered a means by which to enhance transparency and trust-building amongst the parties to a particular treaty.[19] An effective report-

---

[14] Wang and Wiser (n 10). See also Beyerlin, Stoll and Wolfrum (n 12). While international courts and tribunals do have the possibility to adopt provisional measures to prevent environmental harm prior to a case being decided, they have proven reticent to use such measures (see Alistair Rieu-Clarke, 'Notification and Consultation on Planned Measures Concerning International Watercourses: Learning Lessons from the *Pulp Mills* and *Kishenganga* Cases' (2013) 24(1) Yearbook of International Environmental Law 102). In the *Pulp Mills* Case, the dissenting opinion by Judge Awn Al-Khasawneh and Judge Bruno Simma criticised the International Court of Justice's reticence to adopt provisional measures by arguing that the Court should, 'embrace a preventative rather than compensatory logic when determining what the risk might entail' (*Case Concerning Pulp Mills on the River Uruguay (Argentina v. Uruguay)* (Joint Dissenting Opinion of Judges Al-Khasawneh and Simma) (20 April 2010) ICJ Reports 14, 118).

[15] Filho (n 12). See also Beyerlin, Stoll and Wolfrum (n 12).

[16] Helen L. Well, 'Wicked problems and a "wicked" solution' (2018) 14 Globalisation and Health 34.

[17] Peter M. Haas, 'Introduction: Epistemic Communities and International Policy Coordination' (1992) 46(1) Knowledge, Power and International Policy Coordination 1.

[18] Kal Raustiala, *Reporting and Review Institutions in 10 Multilateral Environmental Agreements* (UNEP 2001), 10.

[19] Lang (n 7).

ing procedure may reduce misperceptions over whether or not states are in compliance with their treaty commitments. In turn, the information gathered and exchanged can increase the confidence of states that they are collectively working towards the same goal.[20] Moreover, states may be more willing to implement their commitments if they know that others are doing the same and are not 'free-riding'.[21]

Finally, and closely associated with the benefits of transparency, CIMs have the potential to redistribute power to domestic actors that favour full implementation and compliance.[22] These actors, such as non-governmental organisations (NGOs) and user groups, may be able to take advantage of CIMs and information on their state's record of compliance and implementation to strengthen their position in domestic policy debates. Engaging domestic actors in the reporting process may also secure their 'buy-in' and thus enhance the process of implementing treaty commitments at a domestic level.

While the benefits of incorporating CIMs into MEAs may appear compelling, they are not without their limitations. Even if CIMs are able to secure compliance, i.e., adherence to the provisions of the agreement, they may still fall short of guaranteeing the effectiveness of an international agreement, i.e., solving 'the underlying problem'.[23] Similarly, it may be difficult to isolate the individual contribution of an MEA in addressing a particular problem. Other social, political or environmental factors may have a significant bearing on an issue. For instance, it has been argued that the dramatic reduction in economic activity in Russia during the 1990s contributed more to ensuring conformity with environmental treaty commitments than the influence of any treaty *per se*.[24]

However, despite these limitations, if approached cautiously, 'compliance can provide a valuable proxy for effectiveness'.[25] Understanding why and how

---

[20] Thilo Marauhn, 'Towards a Procedural Law of Compliance Control in International Environmental Relations' (1996) 56(3) Zeitschrift für Ausländishches Recht und Völkerrecht 696.

[21] Raustialia (n 18).

[22] Ibid.

[23] Kal Raustialia, 'Compliance and Effectiveness in International Regulatory Cooperation' (2000) 32 Case W. Res. J. Int'l 387, 393.

[24] David G. Victor, Kal Raustiala and Eugene B. Skolnikoff, 'Introduction and Overview', in David G. Victor, Kal Raustiala and Eugene B. Skolnikoff (eds), *The Implementation and Effectiveness of International Environmental Commitments – Theory and Practice* (The MIT Press 1998), 26.

[25] Ronald B. Mitchell, 'Compliance Theory: An Overview', in James Cameron and others (eds), *Improving Compliance with International Environmental Law* 3 (Routledge 1996), 25.

states comply with their treaty commitments can maximise the potential of a particular instrument.[26] More generally, while it may not be *the* solution, an agreement's inability to ensure compliance will significantly weaken its value. Put succinctly, 'without compliance, the rule of law has no meaning' within the context of MEAs.[27]

In recognition of both their value and widespread usage, this chapter will examine the practice of adopting CIMs within MEAs. While there is significant variation in the design of CIMs across MEAs, a number of common elements can be identified and compared. Firstly, the chapter will analyse the monitoring and reporting requirements under various MEAs designed to assess the methods and practices by which states and other actors evidence their implementation and compliance records. Secondly, the chapter will examine the institutional arrangements by which various MEAs raise and address issues of weak implementation or non-compliance. Such an examination will encompass the membership, institutional framework and mandate of compliance and implementation committees, as well as the 'triggering mechanisms' by which incidences of alleged weak implementation or non-compliance can be brought before a committee. Finally, the chapter will assess the strategies that are in place to address compliance and implementation issues, such as the provision of financial and technical assistance or the issuing of cautions.

By identifying the types of approaches to compliance and implementation adopted by MEAs, the chapter will set the foundation upon which to examine the extent to which these key elements are reflected in transboundary water agreements in the following chapter.

3.2 REPORTING AND VERIFICATION

Without evidence, compliance and implementation cannot be measured. Reporting, therefore, offers an important basis upon which a state's record of treaty compliance and implementation can be assessed. Particularly where environmental treaty commitments are of a technical nature, reporting can also serve to assess 'facts on the ground'.[28] Additionally, and indirectly, reporting requirements can foster a dialogue between the body assessing the reports

---

[26] Crossen (n 11), 480–481

[27] Durwood Zaelke, Matthew Stilwell and Oran Young, 'What reason demands: making law work for sustainable development', in Durwood Zaelke, Donald Kaniaru and Eva Kruzikovo (eds), *Making Law Work for Environmental Compliance and Sustainable Development* (Cameron 2005).

[28] Jesse H. Ausubel and David G. Victor, 'Verification of International Environmental Agreements' (1992) 17(1) Annual Review of Energy and the Environment 1.

and the reporting state(s), which in turn may facilitate further compliance and implementation.[29] Similarly, at the domestic level, the production of reports by a state may foster a dialogue across several government agencies, as well as civil society groups in any particular country.[30] Reporting may also play a persuasive role in treaty compliance and implementation. In other words, states may feel more compelled to comply with their treaty commitments if they know that they have to periodically report on their performance before an international body and other parties.

The majority of reporting mechanisms require the parties themselves to submit reports on their performance, i.e., self-reporting.[31] Such an approach has the benefit that parties are likely to provide information in an engaged and cooperative manner, while avoiding any risks or concerns associated with third-party data gathering.[32] In some instances, guidance and financial support may be provided to parties to support their reporting obligations.[33]

A common approach found in MEAs is to oblige parties to submit reports to every conference of the parties. Article 21 of the 2013 Minamata Convention on Mercury, for example, provides that 'each party shall report to the conference of the parties, through the secretariat, on the measures it has taken to implement the provisions of this Convention on the effectiveness of such measures and the possible challenges in meeting the objectives of the Convention'.[34] It is also usually up to the conference of the parties to decide on the prescribed format for the national reports.[35] These national reports may require parties to provide quantitative data, qualitative data, or a combination of both. For example, under the Convention on International Trade in Endangered Species of Wild Fauna and Flora (CITES), parties must provide a summary of permits and annual trade in listed species, as well as biennial reports on the legislative, regulatory and administrative measures taken to enforce the provisions of

---

29 Beyerlin, Stoll and Wolfrum (n 12).

30 Bell (n 7).

31 Beyerlin, Stoll and Wolfrum (n 12).

32 Glenn M. Wiser, *Compliance Systems under Multilateral Agreements – A Survey for the Benefit of Kyoto Protocol Policy Makers* (CIEL 1999), 3.

33 The Montreal Protocol, for example, provides a Multilateral Fund which *inter alia* supports developing country focal points on data reporting (see UNEP, 'Multilateral Fund for the Implementation of the Montreal Protocol' (*multilateralfund.org*) <https://www.multilateralfund.org/> accessed 21 June 2024).

34 Minamata Convention on Mercury (adopted 10 October 2013, entered into force 16 August 2017) <https://mercuryconvention.org/sites/default/files/2021-06/Minamata-Convention-booklet-Sep2019-EN.pdf> accessed 21 June 2024.

35 See for example, Article 21(3), Minamata Convention, ibid.

the Convention.[36] Through its 'transparency framework', the Paris Agreement places parties under a range of differentiated reporting requirements.[37] Following prescribed formats, all parties must provide both quantitative and qualitative data on national greenhouse gas emissions, information necessary to track progress made in implementing and achieving its nationally determined contributions, and provide information on measures adopted to strengthen resilience and reduce vulnerability to climate change.[38] Developed country parties, and other countries that provide support, should also provide information on the financial, technical transfer and capacity-building support they provide to developing country parties; whereas developing country parties should provide information on the financial, technology transfer and capacity-building support needed and received.[39]

In some cases, there are opportunities for inter-governmental organisations and NGOs to play a role in reporting. Non-state actors may perform two broad functions in this regard. They may support the reporting requirements of states at a national level. NGOs may be included in the process of preparing national reports. In the case of the Convention on Access to Information, Public Participation in Decision-making and Access to Justice in Environmental Matters (Aarhus Convention), for example, public consultations during the preparation of national reports are considered to be critical to the reporting process.[40] The Convention encourages parties to establish 'multi-stakeholder working groups' as 'one of the best ways of ensuring comprehensiveness of information', and encourages opportunities for the public to comment on various draft reports that the group may produce.[41] NGOs may also provide supplementary information to any national reports that are produced by the states. In the case of the Aarhus Convention, the parties adopted Decision

---

36 Article VIII(7), Convention on International Trade in Endangered Species of Wild Fauna and Flora (CITES) (adopted 3 March 1973, entered into force 1 July 1975) 993 UNTS 243.

37 Article 13, Paris Agreement (adopted 12 December 2015, entered into force 4 November 2016) 3156 UNTS 79.

38 Article 13(7) and (8), Paris Agreement, ibid. Article 4 of the Paris Agreement obliges parties to prepare, communicate and maintain successive nationally determined contributions that support the overarching aims of the Agreement as set out in Article 2.

39 Article 13(9) and (10), Paris Agreement, ibid.

40 Convention on Access to Information, Public Participation in Decision-making and Access to Justice in Environmental Matters (adopted 25 June 1988, entered into force 30 October 2001) 2161 UNTS 447 (Aarhus Convention); Compliance Committee of the Aarhus Convention, 'Guidance on Reporting Requirements', UN Doc ECE/MP.PP/WG.1/2007/L.4 (20 February 2007), para 9.

41 Ibid, paras 11–12.

I/8 during the first meeting of the parties in October 2002, which *inter alia* invites, 'international, regional and NGOs engaged in programmes or activities providing support to parties and/or other states in the implementation of the Convention to provide the secretariat with reports on their programmes or activities and lessons learned'.[42] This function has at times been used to provide supplementary information to a party's official report,[43] or for NGOs to provide an alternative or 'shadow' report to the official report.[44] Along similar lines, Decision I/3 of the first meeting of the parties to the Nagoya Protocol on Access to Genetic Resources and the Fair and Equitable Sharing of Benefits Arising from their Utilisation to the Convention on Biological Diversity (Nagoya Protocol) in 2014 invited parties to submit national reports on the implementation of the Protocol and encouraged, 'submissions of relevant information by non-parties'.[45]

The effectiveness of any reporting mechanism will be heavily dependent on both the uniformity and quality of reports that are produced. However, the quality of reporting across MEAs varies considerably.[46] Concern over the poor quality of reporting in many MEAs has led to efforts to enhance reporting through the provision of technical and financial assistance, the development of guidance material, clarifying and simplifying requirements, and placing greater attention and priority on reporting processes.[47] For example, a common trend has been to develop electronic reporting systems to make it easier for parties to submit their national reports.[48] Another effort to improve report-

---

[42] UNECE, 'Report of the First Meeting of the parties – Decision I/8, Reporting Requirements', UN Doc ECE/MP.pp/2/Add.9 (2 April 1994), para 7.

[43] See Danielyan and others, 'Supplement to the national implementation report submitted by Armenia' (2005) <https://unece.org/DAM/env/pp/documents/mop2%20informal/NGOSupp.Stat.Armenia.e.pdf> accessed 21 June 2024.

[44] Arnika and others, 'Environmental democracy in Bosnia and Herzegovina – Aarhus Convention shadow implementation report' (2021) <https://arnika.org/en/publications/environmental-democracy-in-bosnia-and-herzegovina> accessed 21 June 2024.

[45] Nagoya Protocol on Access to Genetic Resources and the Fair and Equitable Sharing of Benefits Arising from their Utilisation to the Convention on Biological Diversity (adopted 29 October 2010, entered into force 12 October 2014) 3008 UNTS 3 (Nagoya Protocol); UNEP, 'NP-1/3 – Monitoring and reporting (Article 29)', UN Doc UNEP/CBD/NP/COP-MLP/DEC/I/3 (20 October 2014).

[46] Raustialia (n 23).

[47] See, for instance, CITES Secretariat, 'Guidelines for the preparation and submission of CITES annual reports', <https://cites.org/sites/default/files/notifications/E-Notif-2021-044-A1.pdf> accessed 15 January 2025.

[48] See UNEP and WCMC, 'Online Reporting System', <https://ors.ngo/> accessed 8 August 2024.

ing is the 'Data Reporting Tool for MEAs (DART)' which has been developed by UNEP to support data and knowledge management needs across biodiversity-related MEAs.[49]

A range of formal and informal mechanisms have also adopted verification measures to assess the quality of reports. Verification, in its strictest sense, is aimed at assessing the factual accuracy of the data and information provided within national reports, rather than providing any opinion on whether or not a party is in compliance with its treaty commitments.[50] Compliance and implementation committees may play a role in the verification of national reports.[51] Under the Kyoto Protocol to the United Nations Framework Convention on Climate Change (Kyoto Protocol), for example, the enforcement branch of the Compliance Committee is responsible for determining whether a party is not in compliance with its reporting requirements pursuant to the Protocol.[52] Secretariat's may also play a verification role. For CITES, the secretariat plays an important role in reviewing national reports submitted by parties.[53] The secretariat is supported in this task by several external institutions. For example, the World Conservation Monitoring Centre maintains a database of data from the parties' national reports that allows the secretariat to compare import and export records with a party's export quotas.[54] More generally, national reporting under CITES is supported by the Trade Records Analysis of Flora and Fauna in Commerce (TRAFFIC) network, which was established in 1976 by the International Union for Conservation of Nature (IUCN) and the World Wide Fund for Nature (WWF).[55] TRAFFIC monitors the illegal trade in flora and fauna through its global network of experts and partners

---

[49] UNEP and others, 'Handbook for the DaRT Data Reporting Tool for MEAs' (June 2020) <https://dart.informea.org/sites/default/files/inline-files/DaRT_Handbook_200626_1.pdf> accessed 21 June 2024.

[50] Clare Breidenich and Daniel Bodansky, 'Measurement, Reporting and Verification in a Post-2012 Climate Agreement' (April 2009) <http://www.indiaenvironmentportal.org.in/files/mrv-report.pdf> accessed 21 June 2024, 6–7.

[51] Wiser (n 32), 5–9.

[52] Kyoto Protocol to the United Nations Framework Convention on Climate Change (adopted 11 December 1997, 16 February 2005) (Kyoto Protocol); Decision 27/CMP.1, Procedures and mechanisms relating to compliance under the Kyoto Protocol, UN Doc FCC/KP/CMP/2005/8/Add.3 (9–10 December 2005).

[53] Article XII of CITES (n 36) stipulates that the secretariat shall, 'study the reports of parties and ... request from parties such further information with respect thereto as it deems necessary to ensure implementation of the present Convention'.

[54] Rosalind Reeve, 'Verification mechanisms in CITES', Trevor Findlay and Oliver Meier (eds), *Verification Yearbook 2001* (Vertic 2001), 140.

[55] See Taskforce on Nature Markets, 'Legal and sustainable wild species trade – learnings and implications for nature market governance' (June 2023) <https://

and informs the CITES secretariat directly of any issues of non-compliance.[56] While more prevalent within human rights instruments, verification for the implementation of an MEA may also be provided by an independent expert group.[57] Through its measurement, reporting and verification system, the UN Framework Convention on Climate Change (UNFCCC) has adopted detailed arrangements for the assessment of national reports.[58] For instance, since 2015, the biennial update reports submitted by certain parties to the UNFCCC containing updates of national Greenhouse Gas inventories are reviewed by a technical team of independent experts.[59]

3.3 INSTITUTIONAL ARRANGEMENTS

Whilst there is considerable variation in their design, most MEAs establish a committee that has the mandate to review compliance and/or implementation.[60] These committees can be established through a variety of means. In some instances, an 'enabling clause' can be found within the agreement itself, and the committee is then developed and agreed upon through a decision of the meeting of the parties. For example, Article 8 of the 1987 Montreal Protocol provides that, 'the parties, at their first meeting, shall consider and approve procedures and institutional mechanisms for determining non-compliance

www.traffic.org/site/assets/files/21932/legalandsustainablewildspeciestrade.pdf> accessed 21 June 2024.

56 Memorandum of Understanding (MOU) Concluded between Traffic International, on behalf of the traffic network, 2019C, Huntingdon Road, Cambridge, CB3 ODL, United Kingdom and the United Nations Environment Programme, secretariat of the Convention on International Trade in Endangered Species of Wild Fauna and Flora (The CITES secretariat), 15, Chemin Des Anémones, 1219 Châtelaine, Geneva, Switzerland (adopted 1 November 1999) <https://cites.org/sites/default/files/common/disc/sec/CITES-TRAFFIC.pdf> accessed 21 June 2024.

57 See Breidenich and Bodansky (n 50).

58 Article 12 of UNFCCC obliges parties to communicate certain information related to the implementation of the Convention. See also, Decision 1/CP.13, Bali Action Plan, in UNFCCC, 'Report of the Conference of the Parties on its thirteenth session', UN Doc FCCC/CP/2007/6/Add (14 March 2008).

59 Decision 17/CP.18, Composition, modalities and procedures of the team of technical experts under international consultations and analysis, in UNFCCC, 'Report of the Conference of the parties on its eighteenth session', UN Doc FCCC/CP/2012/8/Add.2 (28 February 2013).

60 See Jan Klabbers, 'Compliance Procedures', in Daniel Bodansky, Jutta Brunnée and Ellen Hey (eds) *The Oxford Handbook of International Environmental Law* (OUP 2007), 995–1009.

with the provisions of this Protocol and for treatment of parties found to be in non-compliance'.[61] The first meeting of the parties to the Montreal Protocol in May 1989 then decided to establish an *ad hoc* Working Group of Legal Experts to develop a proposal on non-compliance procedures, which was eventually approved at the fourth meeting of the parties in November 1992.[62]

In other cases, there may not be an explicit provision in the MEA itself, but the more general provisions of an agreement may form the basis upon which a decision is made by the meeting of the parties. For example, under the 1989 Basel Convention, the conference of the parties is given the responsibility to keep the effective implementation of the Convention, 'under continuous review and evaluation', and is provided with a mandate to, 'establish such subsidiary bodies as are deemed necessary for the implementation of the Convention'.[63] This Article provided the basis upon which the parties adopted a 'Mechanism for Promoting Implementation and Compliance' at the sixth meeting of the parties in December 2002.[64]

Fodella suggests that the legal status of the Convention on the Control of Transboundary Movements of Hazardous Wastes and Their Disposal (Basel Convention) compliance committee is 'somewhat controversial' given that

---

61 Montreal Protocol (n 8).

62 See Decision I/8: Non-compliance (First Meeting of the Parties, Helsinki, 2–5 May 1989) <https://ozone.unep.org/treaties/montreal-protocol/meetings/first-meeting-parties/decisions/decision-i8-non-compliance> accessed 24 June 2024; Decision II/5: Non-compliance (Second Meeting of the Parties, London, 27–29 June 1990) <https://ozone.unep.org/treaties/montreal-protocol/meetings/second-meeting-parties> accessed 24 June 2024; Decision III/2: Non-compliance (Third Meeting of the Parties, Nairobi, 19–21 June 1991) <https://ozone.unep.org/treaties/montreal-protocol/meetings/third-meeting-parties/decisions/decision-iii2-non-compliance-procedure> accessed 24 June 2024; Decision IV/5: Non-compliance (Fourth Meeting of the Parties, Copenhagen, 23–25 November 1992) <https://ozone.unep.org/treaties/montreal-protocol/meetings/fourth-meeting-parties> accessed 24 June 2024.

63 Article 15(5), Convention on the Control of Transboundary Movements of Hazardous Wastes and Their Disposal (adopted 22 March 1989, entered into force 5 May 1992) (Basel Convention).

64 Decision VI/12, Establishment of a mechanism for promoting implementation and compliance, in UNEP, 'Report of the Conference of the parties to the Basel Convention on the Control of Transboundary Movements of Hazardous Wastes and Their Disposal', UN Doc UNEP/CHW.6/40 (10 February 2003). See also Decision V/16, Monitoring the implementation of and compliance with the obligations set out by the Basel Convention, in 'Report of the Fifth Meeting of the Conference of the parties to the Basel Convention', UN Doc UNEP/CHW.5/29 (10 December 1999).

the conference of the parties is only afforded general powers to review the Convention's implementation and decisions of the conference of the parties are likely to be non-binding in nature.[65] This issue has raised wider questions over the legal nature of treaty bodies, such as compliance or implementation committees.[66] However, it can be argued that parties are best placed to navigate the course between legally binding and non-binding commitments and normative evolution, whether through decisions taken during their plenary meetings or in the authority they delegate to subsidiary bodies.[67] In the case of the Rotterdam Convention, a different approach was adopted, whereby the text of the Convention was amended to include an additional annex on procedures and mechanisms on compliance.[68] However, amendments can take considerable time and effort to enter into force.

The composition of a compliance or implementation committee has an important bearing on the nature of both its mandate and outputs. Where a committee is composed of state representatives, it is likely to be more political in nature, with a focus on negotiation and compromise.[69] However, some MEAs do explicitly stress the importance of state representatives serving on committees, 'objectively and in the best interest of the Convention'.[70] Beyerlin, Stoll and Wolfrum remain sceptical, thus suggesting that 'representative organs, composed of politically acting persons, do not meet the required standards of expertise and impartiality'.[71] Conversely, it has been argued that a body composed of state representatives, 'may even authoritatively take politically bold

[65] Alessandro Fodella, 'Mechanism for Promoting Implementation and Compliance with the 1989 Basel Convention on the Transboundary Movements of Hazardous Wastes and Their Disposal', in Tullio Treves and others (eds), *Non-Compliance Procedures and Mechanisms and the Effectiveness of International Environmental Agreements* (TMC Asser Press 2009), 35.

[66] See Robin R. Churchill and Geir Ulfstein, 'Autonomous Institutional Arrangements in Multilateral Environmental Agreements: A little-noticed phenomenon in international law' (2000) 94(4) American Journal of International Law 623; René Lefeber, 'Creative Legal Engineering' (2000) 13(1) Leiden Journal of International Law 13.

[67] Malgosia Fitzmaurice, 'Compliance with Multilateral Environmental Agreements' (2008) 20 Hague Yearbook of International Law 19.

[68] Annex VII, Procedures and Mechanisms on Compliance with the Rotterdam Convention, Rotterdam Convention on the Prior Informed Consent Procedures for Certain Hazardous Chemicals and Pesticides in International Trade (adopted 10 September 1998, entered into force 24 February 2004, amended 6 November 2020).

[69] Tanzi and Pitea (n 9), 573.

[70] Decision VI/12 (n 64).

[71] Beyerlin, Stoll and Wolfrum (n 12).

stands that a body of experts could not take'.[72] While Jendrośka observes that the political nature of the Convention on Environmental Impact Assessment in a Transboundary Context (Espoo Convention)'s implementation committee has not appeared to compromise its objectivity, he does identify continuity as an inherent challenge of having state representatives as members.[73] A related issue is that state representatives, especially where there is a lot of changes in membership, may not have the best skills and experience required to serve on a committee.[74]

An alternative is for members of a compliance or implementation committee to serve in their personal capacity.[75] However, the use of independent experts serving in their personal capacity tends to be less common given the sensitivity governments may have over the external scrutiny of their compliance with treaty obligations.[76] Under the Cartagena Protocol on Biosafety to the Convention on Biological Diversity (Cartagena Protocol), for example, a 15 member committee has been established.[77] The procedures establishing the compliance committee under the Protocol stipulate that, 'Members of the Committee shall have recognised competence in the field of biosafety and other relevant fields, including legal or technical expertise, and serve objectively and in a personal capacity'.[78] Members are nominated by parties and elected by the conference of the parties on the basis of three members from

---

72 Tanzi and Pitea (n 9).

73 Convention on Environmental Impact Assessment in a Transboundary Context (adopted 25 February 1991, entered into force 10 September 1997), (1991) 30 ILM 802 (Espoo Convention); Jerzy Jendrośka, 'Practice and Relevant Cases that Emerged in the Context of the Espoo Convention Implementation Committee', in in Tulio Treves and others (eds), *Non-compliance Procedures and Mechanisms and the Effectiveness of International Environmental Agreements* (TMC Asser Press 2009), 326–327. See also UNECE, 'Report of the Second Meeting of the Implementation Committee', UN Doc MP.EIA/WG.1/2003/3 (13 December 2002), para 3.

74 Jendrośka (n 73).

75 Cartagena Protocol on Biosafety to the Convention on Biological Diversity (adopted 29 January 2000, entered into force 11 September 2003) 226 UNTS 208 (Cartagena Protocol).

76 Convention on Biological Diversity, Intergovernmental Committee for the Cartagena Protocol on Biosafety, 'Compliance (Article 34), Development of compliance procedures and mechanisms under the Cartagena Protocol on Biosafety', UN Doc UNEP/CBD/ICCP/1/7 (19 September 2000), para 40.

77 See Article 34, Cartagena Protocol (n 75); Cartagena Protocol, 'Decision BS-I/7, Establishment of procedures and mechanisms on compliance under the Cartagena Protocol on Biosafety', UN Doc BS-I/7 (23–27 February 2004).

78 Ibid.

each of the five regional groups of the United Nations.[79] The compliance committee under the Aarhus Convention also requires that its members serve in their personal capacity, but goes slightly further than the Cartagena Protocol in allowing nominations to not only come from parties and signatories but also NGOs.[80]

Requisite expertise is another issue that must be carefully considered when establishing compliance or implementation committees. Experts may have a range of expertise. Under the Basel Convention, for example, it is simply stated that members of the compliance committee should 'have expertise relating to the subject matter of the Convention in areas including scientific, technical, socio-economic and/or legal fields'.[81]

Another consideration in the design of compliance and implementation procedures is the question of who may initiate or 'trigger' the procedure.[82] Several options are present within the procedures of MEAs.[83] One possibility is for a party to trigger the procedure itself due to a difficulty it is facing in complying with its treaty commitments. This option to 'self-incriminate' reflects the facilitative nature of these procedures.[84] Another option is the 'party-on-

---

[79] Ibid.

[80] Decision I/7, Review of Compliance in 'Report of the Meeting of the parties to the Convention on Access to Information, Public Participation in Decision-making and Access to Justice in Environmental Matters', UN Doc ECE/MP.PP/2/Add.8 (2 April 2004).

[81] Decision VI/12 (n 64).

[82] Adsett and others (n 6), 106–111.

[83] For example, pursuant to the review mechanism under the Convention on Migratory Species (Establishment of a Review Mechanism and a National Legislation Programme, in 'Report of the Conference of the Parties to the Convention on Migratory Species', UN Doc UNEP/CMS/Resolution 12.9 (October 2017)), a review may be initiated on the basis of:

1. The Triennial review of National Reports by the secretariat; or
2. Information submitted to the secretariat, when an implementation matter arises, by:

a. Self-reporting by party
b. Party-on-party reporting
c. Thesecretariat
d. The Standing Committee
e. Anybody or agency technically qualified in protection, conservation and management of migratory species, which is either:

    1. An international non-governmental agency or body; or
    2. An accredited national non-governmental agency or body.

[84] Beyerlin, Stoll and Wolfrum (n 12), 369. See, for example the submissions by the Central African Republic and Togo pursuant to the compliance procedure

party' option, where one party initiates a procedure on the basis of another party's alleged failure to comply with their treaty commitments. This option may provide that any party can initiate the procedure,[85] or a party may have to demonstrate some direct interest. Under the Basel Convention's compliance procedure, for example, a party must show that 'it is directly involved' with the other party that it claims is failing to comply with and/or implement the Convention.[86] Similarly, the Cartagena Protocol's compliance procedure permits submissions from any party, which is affected or likely to be affected by another party's failure to comply with its treaty commitments.[87]

The secretariat of a Convention may also be given the possibility of triggering proceedings. Under the Convention on Long-range Transboundary Air Pollution, for example, when the secretariat becomes aware of possible non-compliance by a party, either through its own review of national reports, or 'on receipt of information from a technical body or centre under the Convention', it shall raise the matter with the party in question and request any necessary information on the matter.[88]

Where the secretariat does not receive a response or the matter is not resolved after three months, or 'such longer period as the circumstances of the matter may require', the secretariat is obliged to bring the matter to the attention of the implementation committee under the Convention.[89] Affording this role to a secretariat may raise concerns over its impartiality, however, such concerns must be weighed against the recognition that the secretariat is often in a central position to monitor compliance and implementation, especially where it also has the mandate to review national reports.

A further possibility is that the committee itself has the ability to trigger an implementation or compliance procedure. For example, under the Espoo

---

under the Basel Convention (Basel Convention, 'Current submissions', <https://www.basel.int/Implementation/LegalMatters/Compliance/SpecificSubmissionsActivities/Currentsubmissions/tabid/2310/Default.aspx> accessed 24 June 2024.

85 Under the Montreal Protocol non-compliance procedure, for example, it is simply stated that, 'if one or more parties have reservations regarding another party's implementation of its obligations under the Protocol, those concerns may be addressed in writing to the secretariat' (see Decision IV/5, n 62).

86 Decision VI/12 (n 64).

87 Decision BS-I/7 (n 77).

88 Convention on Long-range Transboundary Air Pollution (adopted 13 November 1979, entered into force 16 March 1983), 1302 UNTS 217; Decision, 2012/25, On improving the functioning of the Implementation Committee, UN Doc ECE/EB.AIR/113/Add.1, <https://unece.org/fileadmin/DAM/env/documents/2012/EB/Decision_2012_25.pdf> 24 June 2012.

89 Ibid.

Convention the compliance committee may request information from a party when it 'becomes aware of possible non-compliance by a party with its obligations'.[90] How the committee might become aware of possible incidences of non-compliance is left open.

As well as triggering specific incidences of non-compliance, a committee may be given a mandate to address systemic compliance and implementation issues.[91] For instance, when reviewing national reports of the parties, a committee may become aware of a common trend in those reports that might be addressed by the committee.

While not common practice, a further option is that a procedure may be triggered by a non-state actor. Under the Aarhus Convention, for example, the compliance committee may receive 'communications from the public' concerning a party's compliance with the Convention.[92] However, Adsett and others maintain that such an option is unlikely to gain widespread acceptance given that, 'there may be little appetite to provide non-state actors that have been unsuccessful domestically with an avenue to continue the challenge before an international body'.[93]

Other considerations in the establishment of a compliance or implementation committee include the size of the committee, which usually ranges from 10 to 25 persons; the period of office, which tends to be around two to three years, with the option to extend for a second term; the geographical representation of members; the frequency of meetings, which is usually once or twice per year;[94] and, whether meetings are closed or open. On the latter issue, practice varies, with some committee meetings being closed to the public, others being open, and others being closed for certain issues and open for less sensitive matters.[95]

The function of compliance and implementation committees may vary, with some promoting compliance and/or implementation in general, others dealing with individual cases of non-compliance, and others covering both functions. For example, the Cartagena Protocol's compliance mechanism has the function to 'promote compliance with the provisions of the Protocol, to address

---

[90] Decision II/4, Review of Compliance, in 'Report of the Second Session of the Meeting of the parties to the Convention on Environmental Impact Assessment in a Transboundary Context', UN Doc ECE/MP.EIA/4 (7 August 2001), 74.

[91] See for example Decision VI/12 (n 64).

[92] Decision I/7 (n 80).

[93] Adsett and others (n 6), 110–111.

[94] See Convention on Biological Diversity (n 75).

[95] The meetings of the Implementation Committee under the Basel Convention, for example, 'is open to other parties or the public, unless the Committee and the party whose compliance is in question agree otherwise' (Decision VI/12 (n 64)).

cases of non-compliance by parties, and to provide advice or assistance, where appropriate'.[96] By contrast, the Review Mechanism under the Convention on the Conservation of Migratory Species of Wild Animals has a more specific function to review specific implementation matters of parties.[97]

In order to perform these general tasks, Lang identifies several specific functions that compliance and implementation committees may be given.[98] Either on general or specific compliance issues, committees may be afforded a *data-collection* function, the focus of which is normally the submission of national reports on implementation.[99] Data gathering is usually complemented by a committee being given a *review* function, which may simply be to assess the completeness of the reports, or may extend to evaluating, on the strength of the information provided, whether the commitments of the Convention in question are being met.[100] Committees may also be provided with an *investigative* function, whereby they supplement national reports with data and information gathered from other sources, such as publicly available data, interviews with government representatives, government responses to specific written questions, or onsite inspections.[101] On-site inspections or fact-finding missions are a common feature of treaty arrangements related to disarmament and arms control, but less common in MEAs.[102] Exceptions include the in-country technical reviews pursuant to the Paris Agreement,[103] information gathering under the implementation and compliance committee of the Basel Committee,[104] and the Convention on Wetlands of International Importance especially as Waterfowl Habitat (Ramsar Convention)'s Advisory Missions.[105]

---

[96] Decision BS-I/7 (n 77).

[97] Convention on Migratory Species (n 83).

[98] Lang (n 7), 688.

[99] Ibid.

[100] Ibid.

[101] Ibid.

[102] See Eleni Methymaki, 'Thinking Beyond International Adjudication: Inspections as Instruments of Order Production in the International System' (2022) 21 The Law and Practice of International Courts and Tribunals 520.

[103] Decision 18/CMA.1, Modalities, procedures and guidelines for the transparency framework for action and support referred to in Article 13 of the Parties Agreement, in 'Report to the Conference of the Parties serving as the Meeting of the Parties to the Paris Agreement on the third part of its session', UN Doc FCCC/PA/CMA/2018/3/Add.2 (19 March 2019), 45.

[104] Decision VI/12 (n 64).

[105] Convention on Wetlands of International Importance especially as Waterfowl Habitat (adopted 2 February 1971, entered into force 21 December 1975) (Ramsar Convention) <https://www.ramsar.org/sites/default/files/documents/library/current_convention_text_e.pdf> accessed 8 August 2024; Convention

While the aforementioned functions focus on gathering and evaluating information related to treaty compliance and implementation, committees may also play a role in addressing compliance and implementation issues. Such a function may raise questions about the relationship between compliance and implementation committees and traditional dispute settlement procedures. MEAs often seek to make a clear distinction between the two procedures by describing compliance and implementation committees as being non-adversarial, non-judicial, transparent and facilitative.[106] Some MEAs even go further and explicitly state that their compliance and/or implementation procedures are separate and without prejudice to any dispute settlement procedures.[107] A distinction can also be made between a compliance and implementation committee's focus on identifying and addressing the root causes of weak implementation or non-compliance in a facilitative and collaborative way, vis-à-vis a dispute settlement procedure being adversarial in nature and having a stronger focus on providing a remedy for past breaches.[108] Such a distinction is also reflected in the fact that decisions of courts and tribunals are binding on the parties in question, whereas the decisions of compliance or implementation committees tend to be recommendatory in nature.[109] These recommendations

on Wetlands, 'Recommendation 4.7: Mechanisms for improved application of the Ramsar Convention' (June 1990) <https://www.ramsar.org/sites/default/files/documents/library/key_rec_4.07e.pdf> accessed 24 June 2024; Resolution XIII.11, Ramsar Advisory Missions', in 'Report of the Thirteenth Meeting of the Conference of the Contracting parties to the Ramsar Convention on Wetlands' (Dubai, October 2018) <https://www.ramsar.org/sites/default/files/documents/library/xiii.11_ramsar_advisory_missions_e.pdf> accessed 24 June 2024.

106 See for example Decision SC-4/33, Procedures and mechanisms on compliance with the Stockholm Convention, <https://chm.pops.int/TheConvention/ComplianceCommittee/Decisions/tabid/9587/Default.aspx> accessed 8 August 2024.

107 For example, Article 30 of the Nagoya Protocol (n 45), explicitly states that 'procedures and mechanisms to promote compliance with this protocol', shall be separate from, and without prejudice to the dispute settlement procedures and mechanisms under Article 27 of the Convention.

108 Jane Bulmer, 'Compliance Regimes in MEAs', in Jutta Brunnée, Meinhard Doelle and Lavanya Rajamani (eds), *Promoting Compliance in an Evolving Climate Regime* (CUP 2012), 73. However, it is also important to recognise that dispute settlement procedures may act to deter potential breaches of treaty obligations (see Fitzmaurice and Redgwell (n 9), 43–44). Additionally, while they have proven reluctant to do so in environmental cases, courts and tribunals may also play a role in preventing environmental harm through the issuance of provisional measures (see Rieu-Clarke (n 14)).

109 Fitzmaurice and Redgwell (n 9), 43–44.

may be directed specifically at the country or countries in question or to the political body of the Convention, i.e., the conference or meeting of the parties, who will then decide what action to take. It is therefore normally for the main political body of the respective MEA, such as the conference of the parties to take a decision on what punitive or assistive measures to take to address any issues of weak implementation or non-compliance rather than the committee itself.[110]

While there are therefore differences between dispute settlement procedures and the functions of a compliance or implementation committee, the lines between both may at times become blurred. For example, while rare, a committee may possess powers akin to that of a court or tribunal. For example, where a party is found to be in breach of certain commitments under the Kyoto Protocol, the enforcement branch of its compliance committee may suspend a party's eligibility to make emission transfers.[111] More generally, Beyerlin, Stoll and Wolfrum argue that 'due to the expertise involved and the compliance control committee's legitimacy, any measure recommended or taken in a non-compliance procedure is likely to have so much weight and persuasiveness that it will have to be respected in any subsequent dispute settlement proceedings'.[112] This observation also raises questions over the timing and priority of procedures. What, for example, would happen if a compliance procedure and dispute settlement procedure were triggered at the same time? Klabbers raises a series of related questions:

> ... if a state has developed a plan to improve its environmental compliance procedure, does this intention immunize it against more formal action? If an aggrieved state has participated in a non-compliance procedure, will it be estopped from claiming individual compensation under a formal procedure? And what does 'participated' mean in this case? Does it matter whether it was represented in the Implementation Committee or whether it did not block a consensus within the COP or MOP? Can a victim state (or any other party, for that matter) ask for interim measures of protection?[113]

Fortunately, these types of questions have tended to remain conceptual in nature, given that, while most MEAs include dispute settlement provisions, they do not tend to provide for compulsory third-party dispute settlement and

110 Beyerlin, Stoll and Wolfrum (n 12), 369.

111 Section XV, Decision 27/CMP.1 (n 52).

112 Beyerlin, Stoll and Wolfrum (n 12), 369.

113 Klabbers (n 60), 1006. See also Günter Handl, 'Compliance Control Mechanisms and International Environmental Obligations' (1997) 5 Tulane Journal of International and Comparative Law 29, 46–48.

their uptake by parties is rare.[114] Their relevance within the context of transboundary water issues will be returned to in Chapter 9.

3.4 RESPONSES TO WEAK IMPLEMENTATION AND/OR NON-COMPLIANCE

Measures to respond to incidences of weak implementation or non-compliance may fall into two broad categories of incentives (i.e., 'carrots') and sanctions (i.e., 'sticks'). Most compliance procedures, given their focus on being non-confrontational and supportive, tend to be orientated towards inducing compliance through incentives.[115] Even where committees are provided with the option of recommending or issuing sanctions on a non-complying state, such as under the 1987 Montreal Protocol, they tend to be used sparingly in practice.[116]

A focus on incentives presumes that the underlying issues affecting compliance and/or implementation relate not to a reticence to commit but to a lack of capacity.[117] However, there are inherent risks in adopting such an approach. Providing incentives may be perceived as countries receiving rewards for their failure to implement and/or comply with their treaty obligations.[118] As Bradford and Ben-Shahar suggest, 'while no country wants to have sanctions imposed on it, many countries would be eager to be targets of an enforcement action based on rewards'.[119] Van Aaken and Simsek suggest that this risk can be overcome by, for example, 'the joint financing of activities ... that also creates burdens for the target, stepwise cooperation, the use of hostages (in the political sense, not literally), and the option of senders to withdraw rewards when moral hazard is suspected'.[120] However, other scholars question

---

114 Fitzmaurice and Redgwell (n 9), 43–44.

115 Convention on Biological Diversity (n 76), para 45.

116 Ibid. An indicative list of measures that might be taken by a meeting of the parties in respect to non-compliance includes appropriate assistance, issuing cautions, and suspension (see Protocol on Substantives that Deplete the Ozone Layer (n 8)).

117 Harold K. Jacobson and Edith Brown Weiss, 'Assessing the Record and Designing Strategies to Engage Countries', in Edith Brown Weiss and Harold K Jacobson (eds), *Engaging Countries – Strengthening compliance with international environmental accords* (MIT Press 2000), 547.

118 Adsett and others (n 6), 112.

119 Omri Ben-Hahar and Anu Bradford, 'Efficient Enforcement in International Law' (2012) 12 Chicago Journal of International Law 375, 423.

120 Anne van Aaken and Betül Simsek, 'Rewarding in International Law' (2021) 115(2) American Journal of International Law 195, 236.

the underlying rationale for providing incentives in the first place – thus asking: 'Shouldn't states just comply with the legal obligation? Otherwise, what's the point of having a legal rule in the first place?'[121] Irrespective of scholarly opinion, most MEAs do seek to manage implementation and compliance through the provision of incentives as well as sanctions. In so doing, there is a general recognition of the significant scientific, technical, bureaucratic and financial resources required to implement treaty commitments, and the challenges that many countries face in providing those resources.[122] Also, environmental issues may not receive priority on the agendas of governments with limited resources, which are allocated to national concerns that are seen as more pressing.[123]

A range of measures may be adopted within compliance and implementation procedures to address issues.

A common measure is the provision of technical and/or financial assistance. Technical and financial assistance may support activities such as the introduction of new technologies, the reform of national governance systems, capacity development, and support to improve data collection, monitoring and analysis, as well as reporting requirements.[124] While committees may themselves provide advice, such as guidance on the establishment or strengthening of domestic regulatory regimes, it is more likely that assistance will come from an external body. This therefore raises the question of how any recommended technical and/or financial assistance might be resourced.

In certain scenarios, MEAs may have specific technical and financial programmes dedicated to addressing issues of non-compliance and implementation. For example, a Multilateral Fund to support the implementation of the Montreal Protocol was established pursuant to a decision taken by the parties at the second meeting of the parties in 1990.[125] A direct link exists between the

---

[121] Daniel Peat, 'Rewarding Compliance – on normative implications of rewarding in international law' (*Völkerrechtsblog*, 6 June 2021) <https://voelkerrechtsblog.org/rewarding-compliance-on-normative-implications-of-rewarding-in-international-law/> accessed 24 June 2024.

[122] Abram Chayes and Antonia Handler Chayes, *The New Sovereignty – Compliance with international regulatory agreements* (Harvard University Press 1995), 14–15.

[123] Jacobson and Brown Weiss (n 117), 546.

[124] See generally, Laurence Boisson de Chazournes, 'Technical and Financial Assistance', in Daniel Bodansky, Jutta Brunnée and Ellen Hey (eds), *The Oxford Handbook of International Environmental Law* (OUP 2007), 948–973.

[125] Decision II/8, Financial Mechanism, in 'Report of the Second Meeting of the parties to the Montreal Protocol on Substances that Deplete the Ozone Layer', UN Doc UNEP/OzL.Pro.2/3 (29 June 1990).

implementation committee of the Protocol and the Multilateral Fund, whereby the former is obliged to work with the latter prior to making any recommendations regarding technical and/or financial assistance.[126] In other instances, a committee's role may be limited. The implementation and compliance committee under the Basel Convention, for example, is simply tasked with providing advice on the 'facilitation of assistance ... including on how to access financial and technical support, including technology transfer and capacity-building'.[127] Where MEAs have access to funds to support implementation, either directly or indirectly, a recommendation from a committee can be an important means by which to leverage such funds.[128] However, Bulmer cautions that this facilitatory role is 'possibly a weakness, as the committee is unable to direct funding directly to a non-compliant party in a focused and timely manner'.[129]

Another option provided to compliance and implementation committees is to request a non-compliant party to develop a 'compliance plan'.[130] For example, the compliance committee under the Cartagena Protocol has the option to 'request or assist' a party in developing a 'compliance action plan' and also invite the party in question to provide progress reports on its efforts to address any compliance issues.[131] Similarly, the compliance mechanism under the Basel Convention provides the possibility for the committee to work with the party or parties facing compliance problems to elaborate a voluntary action plan and review its implementation.[132] The soft nature of these mechanisms is evident in that the compliance committee under the Cartagena Protocol can merely request such a plan, and under the Basel Convention, such plans are voluntary. The enforcement branch under the Kyoto Protocol's compliance procedure adopts a stronger approach by stipulating that where a party is not in compliance with the applicable commitments, it must submit a compliance action plan, as well as annual progress reports on the implementation of plan.[133] The action plan must also contain an analysis of the causes of non-

126 Decision IV/5 (n 85), para 7(f).

127 Decision VI/12 (n 64), para 19.

128 See Laurence Boisson de Chazournes, 'Technical and Financial Assistance and Compliance: the Interplay', in Ulrich Beyerlin, Peter-Tobias Stoll and Rüdiger Wolfrum (eds), *Ensuring Compliance with Multilateral Environmental Agreements: Academic Analysis and Views from Practice* (Koninklijke Brill NV 2006), 273.

129 Bulmer (n 108), 71.

130 Beyerlin, Stoll and Wolfrum (n 12), 369.

131 Decision BS-I/7 (n 77).

132 Decision VI/12 (n 64), para 19(c).

133 Section XV, Decision 27/CMP.1 (n 52).

compliance, the actions that the party intends to take to address non-compliance, and a timetable for implementing that action.[134]

While technical and financial assistance might be seen as positive incentives for promoting compliance, compliance procedures may also encompass negative incentives, such as the issuance of cautions or suspension.[135] The latter rely on reputational impact being a significant factor that would induce a party to comply with its treaty commitments.[136] Under the Minamata Convention's compliance procedure, for example, the Committee has the option to recommend to the conference of the parties that the latter issue a statement regarding compliance.[137] Similarly, the Basel Convention's compliance procedure provides the option for the conference of the parties to issue 'a cautionary statement'.[138] Under CITES, the Standing Committee is provided with a variety of similar options, including issuing a written caution, sending a public notification of a compliance matter via the secretariat to all parties, and issuing a warning to the party concerned that it is in non-compliance.[139] However, these three procedures all envisage that such measures would only be issued where there is a persistent failure to comply, and the aforementioned options, e.g., technical and financial assistance, have been exhausted. Brack observes that the issuance of such cautions can have both positive and negative impacts.[140] Within the context of the Montreal Protocol he notes the following:

> Whether or not non-complying parties really feel threatened by these measures is, perhaps, questionable, but it is clear that they do not like being identified in MOP decisions, often saying so openly in the meeting. Conversely officials from non-complying parties have sometimes found it useful for their country to be listed,

---

[134] Ibid.

[135] Adsett and others (n 6), 113.

[136] See generally, Andrew T. Guzman, 'Reputation and International Law' (2006) 34 Georgia Journal of International and Comparative Law 379; George W. Downs, 'Reputation, Compliance and International Law' (2002) 31 Journal of Legal Studies 95; Rachel Brewster, 'Unpacking the State's Reputation' (2009) 50(2) Harvard International Law Journal 231.

[137] Decision MC-9, Implementation and Compliance Committee: terms of reference and template for written submissions from parties with respect to their own compliance, in 'Report of the Third Meeting of the Conference of the Parties to the Minamata Convention on Mercury', UN Doc UNEP/MC/COP.3/Dec.9 (7 January 2020), para 24.

[138] Decision VI/12 (n 64), para 20(a).

[139] Resolution Conf. 14.3 (*CITES Compliance Procedures*, 2007) <https://cites.org/eng/prog/compliance> accessed 24 June 2024.

[140] Duncan Brack, 'Monitoring the Montreal Protocol', *Verification Yearbook 2003* (Vertic 2003), 218.

> helping them to argue with colleagues at home the need for greater urgency in dealing with the issue.

Bulmer also recognises the positive impact of such measures, especially where they have been accompanied by deadlines, which, if not met, trigger stronger measures.[141]

Stronger measures that might be available include the withdrawal of rights and privileges enjoyed through membership of a Convention. Specific options, while not common in MEAs, may include the right to vote or to serve on one of the Convention's bodies.[142] The CITES, the Montreal Protocol and the Kyoto Protocol include some form of trade sanctions.[143] In the case of CITES, the Standing Committee may 'recommend the suspension of commercial or all trade in specimens of one or more CITES-listed species ... in cases where a party's compliance matter is unresolved and persistent, and the party is showing no intention to achieve compliance'.[144] While Voigt and Scanlon note that the use of CITES suspensions has not achieved universal compliance, they suggest that the threat of sanctions has at least in part helped advance compliance 'much faster than would otherwise have been the case'.[145] Under the World Heritage Convention, sites afforded world heritage status have been removed from the list, such as the Liverpool Maritime Mercantile City in the UK, the Arabian Oryx Sanctuary in Oman, and the Elbe Valley in Dresden.[146]

Adsett and others caution that measures related to the suspension of rights and privileges are likely to be limited to those that are available at the discretion of a COP, such as the receipt of financial and technical assistance, the hosting of meetings or participation on the bureau, rather than broader options that might be envisaged pursuant to Article 60 of the Vienna Convention

---

141 Bulmer (n 108), 71.

142 Decision VI/12 (n 64), Annex V.

143 The use of trade sanctions to solicit compliance with MEAs has been questioned over their compatibility with GATT/WTO rules (see Robert K. Omura, 'Chasing Hamlet's Ghost: State Responsibility and the Use of Countermeasures to Compel Compliance with Multilateral Environmental Agreements' (2010) 15 Appeal: Review of Current Law and Law Reform 86, 110–112).

144 CITES Compliance Procedures (n 139), para 30.

145 Christina Voigt and John Scanlon, 'Does CITES really have 'teeth'? CITES and Compliance' (*IISD*, 18 January 2023) <http://sdg.iisd.org/commentary/guest-articles/does-cites-really-have-teeth-cites-and-compliance/#:~:text=CITES%20compliance%20procedures%20are%20set,for%20more%20support%20than%20sanctions> (24 June 2024).

146 UNESCO World Heritage Convention, 'World Heritage Convention deletes Liverpool – Maritime Mercantile City from UNESCO's World Heritage List' (21 June 2021) <https://whc.unesco.org/en/news/2314> accessed 24 June 2024.

on the Law of Treaties.[147] While such an approach still raises lots of issues over the relationship between the law of state responsibility and compliance procedures,[148] the practical realities seem clear. As Goeteyn and Maes note, 'compliance mechanisms ... respond to an existing demand for collective action by parties in the event of non-compliance by one party with its international obligations'.[149] However, they do so in a way that recognises some of the particularities of MEAs, such as the notion that many parties join MEAs based on the expectation that financial and technical assistance will be made available to facilitate their compliance and implementation of their commitments.[150] Inevitably, this means that there is a need for a 'softer approach' to state responsibility and liability that recognises that, 'compliance control usually is about "less" and "more", than it is, about degrees of conformity';[151] and that in relation to MEAs and international environmental issues, 'the main traditional answers to non-compliance and dispute resolution are not a viable solution'.[152]

3.5 CONCLUSION

The types of CIMs found in MEAs differ depending on the nature of the issue that they aim to address and the political context in which they operate. This has led Beyerlin, Stoll and Wolfrum to conclude that 'any attempt to develop an ideal model of compliance control that suits a wide range of MEAs is doomed to failure'.[153] However, while there might not be a 'one-size-fits-all' model, an analysis of a range of CIMs found in MEAs demonstrates a number of similarities. Most of the CIMs that exist within MEAs contain, to varying degrees, three key elements that can be classified under reporting, assessment and response.

In terms of reporting, the most common approach is to invite or oblige parties to submit regular national reports. However, there are also examples, such as the Aarhus Convention, whereby non-state actors may contribute to national reports, or even submit reports, either as a supplement or alternative

[147] Adsett and others (n 6), 115–116. See also Omura (n 143).

[148] See generally, Fitzmaurice and Redgwell (n 9), 59–62.

[149] Nils Goeteyn and Frank Maes, 'Compliance Mechanisms in Multilateral Environmental Agreements: An effective way to improve compliance?' (2011) 10 Chinese Journal of International Law 791, 826.

[150] Omura (n 143), 112.

[151] Lang (n 7), 695.

[152] Goeteyn and Maes (n 149).

[153] Beyerlin, Stoll and Wolfrum (n 12), 369.

to an official report. National reports may also be complemented by alternative sources of data and information in certain circumstances.

An effective means by which national reports are assessed is essential to any CIM. Committees are usually tasked with assessing national reports. However, secretariats, sometimes assisted by external bodies, may also play such a role. At a basic level, this role may involve assessing the completeness of national reports, but it may also extend to more extensive analysis of reports, such as those envisaged under the UNFCCC and its use of a technical team of experts. Another common trend has been for MEAs to focus efforts on supporting reporting processes and building the capacity of parties to improve the quality of reports.

Committees are central to addressing any incidences of non-compliance. These committees are formed in a variety of ways, including through an enabling provision within the MEA in question or through a decision of the meeting of the parties. Membership tends to rest in a representative body of the parties to an MEA, although there are some examples of a committee's membership resting with independent experts.

A key question for any of these committees is how incidences of weak implementation or non-compliance come to their attention. Again, there may be variations within MEAs, including parties themselves raising concerns, i.e., self-reporting; other parties raising a concern, i.e., party-on-party; the secretariat raising a concern; the committee itself becoming aware of an issue; or a non-party raising a concern. States have proven reticent to provide non-parties, such as NGOs, with the ability to trigger non-compliance procedures, but examples, such as under the Aarhus Convention, do exist.

There are also significant similarities concerning the function of committees, which essentially break down into two key features: to review individual cases of non-compliance and to review general issues of non-compliance. Irrespective of whether a compliance committee performs one or both functions, they tend to be restricted in that function to providing recommendations either directly to the party or parties in question or to the conference of the parties. Rarely are committees given the mandate to adopt binding decisions themselves, although some examples do exist, such as under the Kyoto Protocol. The non-binding nature of decisions of compliance and implementation committees helps to distinguish them from any dispute settlement procedures that may apply.

There are notable similarities among the types of measures that compliance and implementation committees and/or conference of the parties may adopt. Most common is for committees to be afforded the option to recommend direct measures, such as law and policy reforms or technical and financial assistance. Another defining feature is that it is unusual for the committee itself to have technical and financial resources at its disposal to address incidences of non-compliance. Rather, the committee plays a role in leveraging any necessary resources. More punitive measures, such as sanctions or the suspension of rights and privileges, are sometimes available. CIMs tend to be restricted to proposing decisions that may then be adopted by their respective conference of the parties. While CITES and the Kyoto Protocol offer exceptions, they also raise questions over their compatibility with the law of state responsibility.

Ultimately, a review of CIMs shows that there is a significant body of MEA practice that has evolved in a way where common trends can be identified across MEAs. The subsequent chapters will consider the extent to which these common trends are either implicitly or explicitly contained within transboundary water agreements and whether there is any scope for transboundary water agreements to learn lessons from MEA practice.

4. Treaty practice related to transboundary waters

4.1 INTRODUCTION

There is considerable diversity in the types of transboundary water agreements that states have entered into. Diversity exists in relation to the number of parties to a particular agreement. Not surprisingly, the instruments operating at a global and regional level have the most parties: the Convention on the Protection and Use of Transboundary Watercourses and International Lakes (Water Convention) has 55 parties,[1] and the Convention on the Law of the Non-navigational Uses of International Watercourses (Watercourses Convention) has 40 parties.[2] Of the treaties that focus on specific transboundary rivers, the Convention on the Protection and Sustainable Use of the Danube River (1994 Danube Convention) has the most parties at 15.[3] However, despite calls for basin-wide approaches to the management of water resources, the general

[1] Convention on the Protection and Use of Transboundary Watercourses and International Lakes (adopted 17 March 1992, entered into force 6 October 1996), 1936 UNTS 269. For an up-to-date list of parties see UN Treaty Collection, <https://treaties.un.org/Pages/ViewDetails.aspx?src=TREATY&mtdsg_no=XXVII-5&chapter=27&clang=_en> accessed 5 July 2024 (Water Convention).

[2] Convention on the Law of the Non-navigational Uses of International Watercourses (adopted 21 May 1997, entered into force 17 August 2014), 2999 UNTS (Watercourses Convention). For an up-to-date list of parties see UN Treaty Collection, <https://treaties.un.org/Pages/ViewDetails.aspx?src=TREATY&mtdsg_no=XXVII-12&chapter=27&clang=_en> accessed 5 July 2024.

[3] Convention on the Protection and Sustainable Use of the Danube River (adopted 29 June 1994, entered into force 22 October 1998) <https://www.icpdr.org/sites/default/files/DRPC%20English%20ver.pdf> 5 July 2024 (1994 Danube Convention).

preference of states has been to enter into bilateral agreements irrespective of the number of countries sharing a particular river, lake or aquifer.[4]

There is also diversity in the geographic coverage of treaties. A common approach has been for two states to enter into cooperative arrangements that cover all their shared waters.[5] Another well-used approach has been for states to conclude agreements on specific transboundary rivers, lakes and aquifers.[6]

---

4 Neda A. Zawahri and Sara McLaughlin Mitchell, 'Fragmented Governance in International Rivers: Negotiating Bilateral versus Multilateral Treaties' (2011) 55 International Studies Quarterly 835.

5 See for example Agreement on Cooperation for the Protection and Sustainable Use of the Waters of the Spanish-Portuguese Hydrographic Basins (adopted 30 November 1998, entered into force 2 February 2000), 2099 UNTS 2016 (1998 Albufeira Convention); Treaty Relating to Boundary Waters, and Questions Arising between the United States and Canada (adopted 11 January 1909), 1910(3) British Treaty Series (1909 Boundary Waters Treaty); Agreement on the Protection and Utilization of Transboundary Waters Concluded between China and Mongolia (adopted 29 April 1994) <https://faolex.fao.org/docs/pdf/bi-17921.pdf> accessed 15 January 2025 (1994 China-Mongolia Agreement); Treaty Concerning Regulation of Water Management Questions Relating to Frontier Waters between Austria and Czechoslovakia (adopted 7 December 1967), 728 UNTS 313 (1967 Austria-Czechoslovakia Treaty); Agreement between the Government of Estonia and the Government of the Russian Federation on the Protection and Rational Use of Transboundary Waters (adopted 20 August 1997) <https://faolex.fao.org/docs/pdf/bi-32669.pdf> accessed 15 January 2025 (1997 Estonia-Russia Agreement); Agreement Between the Federal Republic of Nigeria and the Republic of Niger Concerning the Equitable Sharing in the Development, Conservation and Use of their Common Water Resources (adopted 18 July 1990) <http://gis.nacse.org/tfdd/tfdddocs/483ENG.pdf> accessed 5 July 2024 (1990 Nigeria-Niger Agreement).

6 See for example Indus Waters Treaty (adopted 19 September 1960, entered into force 12 January 1961), 419 UNTS 125; Agreement Between Lebanon and Syria on the Distribution of Water of Al-Asi River Rising in Lebanon (adopted 20 September 1994) <http://gis.nacse.org/tfdd/tfdddocs/537ARA.pdf> accessed 5 July 2024 (1994 Syria-Lebanon Agreement); Agreement for Cooperation between Uruguay and Brazil for the Improvement of Natural Resources and the Development of the Cuareim River Basin (adopted 11 March 1991) <http://gis.nacse.org/tfdd/treaties.php?page=full&origin=river&tn=493> accessed 5 July 2024; Agreement between the Government of the Hashemite Kingdom of Jordan and the Government of the Kingdom of Saudi Arabia for the Management and Utilisation of the Ground Waters in the Al-Sag/ Al-Disi Layer (adopted 30 April 2015) <http://www.internationalwaterlaw.org/documents/regionaldocs/Disi_Aquifer_Agreement-English2015.pdf> accessed 5 July 2024 (2015 Disi Aquifer Agreement); Treaty between the Government of the Republic of Moldova and the

Here, diversity exists in the types of water bodies covered, with the majority focusing on rivers, and a smaller number focused on lakes and aquifers.[7] Other transboundary water agreements have sought to cover only part of a particular water system, such as a transboundary tributary or lagoon,[8] or focus on a particular project.[9] Another approach has been to include transboundary waters

---

Cabinet of Ministers of Ukraine on Cooperation in the Field of Protection and Sustainable Development of the Dniester River Basin (adopted 29 November 2012) <http://www.unece.org/fileadmin/DAM/env/water/activities/Dniester/Dniester-treaty-final-EN-29Nov2012_web.pdf> accessed 5 July 2024 (2012 Dniester Convention).

[7] See for example, Convention on the Sustainable Management of Lake Tanganyika (adopted 12 June 2003) <https://faolex.fao.org/docs/pdf/mul45450.pdf> accessed 15 January 2025 (2003 Lake Tanganyika Convention); Agreement Between the Council of Ministers of the Republic of Albania and the Government of the Republic of Macedonia for the Protection and Sustainable Development of Lake Ohrid and its Watershed (adopted 17 June 2004) <http://faolex.fao.org/docs/pdf/bi-69075E.pdf> accessed 5 July 2024; Guarani Aquifer Agreement (adopted 2 August 2010) <http://faolex.fao.org/docs/pdf/mul-143888English.pdf> accessed 5 July 2024; Programme for the Development of a Regional Strategy for the Utilisation of the Nubian Sandstone Aquifer System (NSAS) (adopted 5 October 2000) <http://faolex.fao.org/docs/pdf/int39094E.pdf> accessed 5 July 2024.

[8] Framework Agreement on the Sava River (adopted 3 December 2002, entered into force 29 December 2004), 2366 UNTS 479 (2002 Sava Agreement); Treaty on Cooperation for the Utilization of the Natural Resources and the Development of the Mirim Lagoon Basin (adopted 7 July 1977), 1079 UNTS 375.

[9] See for example, Agreement Between the Government of the Republic of Austria and the Government of the Federal Republic of Germany and of the Free state of Bavaria concerning the Donaukraftwerk-Jochenstein-Aktiengesellschaft (Danube Power-Plant and Jochenstein Joint-Stock Company), (adopted 13 February 1952) <http://www.internationalwaterlaw.org/documents/regionaldocs/danube-austria-germany.html> accessed 5 July 2024; Agreement Between the Government of the Socialist Republic of Romania and the Government of the Union of the Soviet Socialist Republics on the Joint Construction of the Stinca-Costesti Hydraulic Engineering Scheme on the River Prut and the Establishment of the Conditions for its Operation (with Protocol) (adopted 16 December 1971) <http://gis.nacse.org/tfdd/tfdddocs/341ENG.pdf> accessed 5 July 2024 (Romania-USSR Agreement 1971); Agreement Between His Majesty's Government of Nepal and the Government of India on the Gandak Irrigation and Power Project (adopted 4 December 1959) <https://www.moewri.gov.np/storage/listies/May2020/aggrement-on-nepal-and-india-gandak-river-1959.pdf> accessed 5 July 2024.

within wider cooperative arrangements, such as peace treaties,[10] treaties covering border areas,[11] or mountain landscapes.[12]

Considerable diversity is also evident in the types of activities covered by transboundary water agreements. Some agreements focus on a specific task, such as carrying out a joint study.[13] Other agreements focus on certain uses,

---

[10] See for example, Article 6 and Annex II of the Treaty of Peace Between the State of Israel and the Hashemite Kingdom of Jordan (adopted 26 October 1994) <https://peacemaker.un.org/sites/default/files/document/files/2024/05/il20jo941026peacetreatyisraeljordan.pdf> accessed 15 January 2025 (1994 Israel-Jordan Peace Treaty); and Annex III, Article 40, Israeli-Palestinian Interim Agreement on the West Bank and Gaza Strip (adopted 28 September 1995) <https://www.un.org/unispal/document/auto-insert-185434/> accessed 15 January 2024.

[11] See for example Agreement Between the Government of Belarus and the Government of the Latvian Republic on Cooperation in the Area of Environmental Protection (adopted 21 February 1994) <https://faolex.fao.org/docs/pdf/bi-63058.pdf> accessed 15 January 2025; and Article 3, Agreement Between Guatemala and Mexico on the Protection and Improvement of the Environment in the Border Area, Guatemala City (adopted 10 April 1987) <http://faolex.fao.org/docs/pdf/bi-16748.pdf> accessed 8 July 2024.

[12] Article 6 of the Framework Convention on the Protection and Sustainable Development of the Carpathians (adopted 22 May 2003) <http://www.carpathianconvention.org/tl_files/carpathiancon/Downloads/01%20The%20Convention/1.1.1.1_CarpathianConvention.pdf> accessed 8 July 2024 (2003 Carpathians Convention).

[13] See for example, Agreement Between Bolivia and Peru Concerning a Preliminary Economic Study of the Joint Utilisation of the Waters of Lake Titicaca (adopted 19 February 1957) <https://gis.nacse.org/tfdd/tfdddocs/206ENG.pdf> accessed 8 July 2024; and Agreement Between the Union of Soviet Socialist Republics and the People's Republic of China on Joint Research Operations to Determine the Natural Resources of the Amur River Basin and the Prospects for Development of its Productive Potentialities and on Planning and Survey Operations to Prepare a Scheme for the Multi-Purpose Exploitation of the Argun River and the Upper Amur River (adopted 1956) <http://www.internationalwaterlaw.org/documents/regionaldocs/ussr-china.html> accessed 8 July 2024 (USSR-China Agreement 1956).

such as fisheries,[14] water allocation,[15] water supply,[16] monitoring,[17] flood

---

[14] See for example, Convention Concerning Fishing in the Waters of the Danube, Bucharest (adopted 29 January 1958), 339 UNTS 23; Preliminary Convention Between Bolivia and Peru for the Exploitation of Fisheries in Lake Titicaca (adopted 17 July 1935) <https://gis.nacse.org/tfdd/tfdddocs/archiveApril2010/342ENG.htm> accessed 8 July 2024; and Treaty Between the Government of the Republic of Estonia and the Government of the Russian Federation on the Conservation and Use of Fishing Stocks in Lake Peipsi, Lake Lammi and Lake Pihkva (adopted 4 May 1994) <https://faolex.fao.org/docs/pdf/bi-42741.pdf> accessed 8 July 2024.

[15] See for example Indus Waters Treaty (n 6); Treaty between the Government of the Republic of India and the Government of the People's Republic of Bangladesh on sharing of the Ganga/Ganges waters at Farakka (adopted 12 December 1996), 1066 UNTS 16.

[16] Agreement Between the Government of the French Republic and the Spanish Government Relating to Lake Lannoux (adopted 12 July 1958) <https://www.internationalwaterlaw.org/documents/regionaldocs/lake-lanoux.html> accessed 8 July 2024 (1958 Lake Lannoux Agreement).

[17] Agreement between Chad, Egypt, Libya and Sudan concerning the monitoring and exchange of groundwater information of the Nubian Sandstone Aquifer System (adopted 5 October 2000) <http://faolex.fao.org/docs/pdf/int39094E.pdf> accessed 8 July 2024.

control,[18] water quality and pollution,[19] hydropower[20] or irrigation.[21] More

---

[18] See for example, Convention between the Government of the Union of Soviet Socialist Republics and the Government of the Romanian People's Republic concerning measures to prevent floods and to regulate the water regime of the River Prut (adopted 25 December 1952) <http://gis.nacse.org/tfdd/tfdddocs/168ENG.pdf> accessed 8 July 2024; Agreement Between the Government of Canada and the Government of the United States of America for Water Supply and Flood Control in the Souris River Basin (adopted 26 October 1989) <http://www.treaty-accord.gc.ca/text-texte.aspx?id=100475> accessed 8 July 2024 (1989 Souris Agreement); Agreement Between the Government of the French Republic, the Government of the Federal Republic of Germany, and the Government of the Duchy of Luxembourg on Flood Warning for the Catchment Basin of the Moselle (adopted 1 October 1987), 1506 UNTS 98 (1987 Moselle Agreement).

[19] See for example, Convention Concerning the Protection of Italo-Swiss Waters Against Pollution (adopted 20 April 1972) <https://www.fao.org/faolex/results/details/en/c/LEX-FAOC031925/> accessed 8 July 2024; Cooperation Agreement Between the Republic of Argentina and the Oriental Republic of Uruguay to Prevent and Fight Against Pollution Incidents of the Aquatic Environment Produced by Hydrocarbons and Other Noxious Substances (adopted 16 September 1987) <https://gis.nacse.org/tfdd/treaties.php?page=full&origin=river&tn=459> accessed 8 July 2024.

[20] See for example, Treaty Relating to Cooperative Development of the Water Resources of the Columbia River Basin (adopted 17 January 1961) <https://faolex.fao.org/docs/pdf/bi-145062.pdf> accessed 8 July 2024; Treaty Between the Federative Republic of Brazil and the Republic of Paraguay Concerning the Hydroelectric Utilization of the Water Resources of the Parana River Owned in Condominium by the Two Countries, from and including the Salto Grande de Sete Quedas or Salto del Guaira, to the Mouth of the Iguassu River (adopted 26 April 1973), 923 UNTS 92; Agreement Between the Governments of the Republic of Portugal, the People's Republic of Mozambique and the Republic of South Africa Relative to the Cohora Bassa Project (adopted 2 May 1984) <http://www.fao.org/docrep/w7414b/w7414b0i.htm> accessed 8 July 2024.

[21] Agreement on the Vioolsdrift and Noordoewer Joint Irrigation Scheme Between the Government of the Republic of South Africa and the Government of the Republic of Namibia (adopted 14 September 1992) <https://www.fao.org/3/w7414b/w7414b0y.htm> accessed 8 July 2024; Agreement Between His Majesty's Government, Nepal and the Government of India on 'The Renovation and Extension of Chandra Canal, Pumped Canal and Distribution System of the Western Kosi Canal in Nepal' (adopted 7 April 1978) <https://indiawris.gov.in/wiki/doku.php?id=volume-iv> accessed 8 July 2024 (1978 Kosi Canal Agreement); Agreement Between Iran and the Soviet Union for the Joint Utilisation of the Frontier Part of the Rivers Aras and Atrak for Irrigation and Power Generation Teheran (adopted 11 August 1957), 163 British and Foreign State Papers 426 (USSR-Iran 1957 Agreement).

recently, and as a result of the aforementioned call for basin-wide approaches, transboundary water agreements have sought to adopt a holistic approach with the aim of fostering the broader goal of sustainable development throughout an entire basin.[22] These types of agreements tend to be framework agreements and provide space for cooperation to develop through subsequent protocols and soft law instruments.[23]

Another area where there is considerable diversity within transboundary water agreements concerns structure. Some agreements simply lay out broad principles to guide state conduct on transboundary waters.[24] Others are of a highly technical nature and include considerable detail on a particular project or sharing arrangement.[25] Another common approach is for transboundary water agreements to only briefly set out basic rules and principles, and focus more on the creation of a joint institution, such as a river basin organisation, that has the mandate to develop more details as the cooperation between the countries evolves.[26] Other agreements adopt a more comprehensive approach

---

22 See for example Agreement on the Cooperation for the Sustainable Development of the Mekong River Basin (adopted 5 April 1995), 34 ILM 864 (1995 Mekong Agreement); 1994 Danube Convention (n 5); 2012 Dniester Convention (n 6); Tripartite Interim Agreement Between Mozambique, South Africa and Swaziland for Cooperation on the Protection and Sustainable Utilisation of the Water Resources of the Incomati and Maputo Watercourses (adopted 29 August 2002) <https://faolex.fao.org/docs/pdf/mul34943.pdf> (2002 IncoMaputo Agreement); Convention on the Protection of the Rhine (adopted 22 January 1998) <https://www.iksr.org/en/icpr/legal-basis/convention> accessed 8 July 2024 (1998 Rhine Convention); and Lake Tanganyika Convention (n 7).

23 See generally, Nele Matz-Lück, 'Framework Conventions as Regulatory Tools' (2009) 1(3) Goettingen Journal of International Law 439.

24 See for example, 1994 China-Mongolia Agreement (n 5); Agreement Between the Government of the Republic of Kazakhstan and the Government of the People's Republic of China on Cooperation in the Use and Protection of Transboundary Rivers (adopted 12 September 2001) <https://faolex.fao.org/docs/pdf/bi-65815e.pdf>; and Agreement Between the Government of the People's Republic of China and the Government of the Russian Federation on the Management and Protection of Transboundary Waters (adopted 29 January 2008) <https://www.fao.org/faolex/results/details/en/c/LEX-FAOC094367/> accessed 8 July 2024.

25 See for example, Treaty on the Lesotho Highlands Water Project Between the Government of the Kingdom of Lesotho and the Government of the Republic of South Africa (adopted 24 October 1986) <https://faolex.fao.org/docs/pdf/bi-15909.pdf> accessed 8 July 2024 (1986 Lesotho Highlands Treaty); and Indus Water Treaty (n 6).

26 See for example, Agreement for the Development of the Binational Puyango-Tumbes and Catamayo-Chira Basins by Peru and Ecuador (adopted 27 September

by setting out relatively detailed substantive and procedural provisions, whilst also establishing a joint institution to oversee the agreement's implementation and development.[27]

Whilst such diversity in the design of transboundary water agreements makes analysing provisions related to compliance and implementation challenging, it is possible to identify three key aspects of these agreements that can be compared, namely provisions related to monitoring and reporting, provisions related to reviewing implementation, and provisions focused on addressing incidences of weak implementation or non-compliance. For each of these key aspects, the chapter asks a series of questions designed to assess the extent to which transboundary water agreements either explicitly or implicitly incorporate the types of elements found in compliance and implementation mechanisms (CIMs).

Firstly, the chapter will seek to identify provisions within transboundary water agreements that concern monitoring and reporting. Key questions to consider in identifying such provisions include: Are states obliged to exchange data and information, and if so, what data and information are they obliged to exchange? Similarly, are states obliged to conduct any joint monitoring? For example, are there any general requirements to monitor water conditions and uses? Are there specific requirements for states to periodically report on their progress in implementing the agreement? Are states or a joint institution required to share data and information on the implementation of an agreement with non-state actors, such as the general public? Also, is there an obligation on the parties or a joint institution to adopt plans to support the implementation

1971), 1259 UNTS 141; Convention on the International Commission for the Protection of the Elbe (adopted 8 October 1990) <https://www.ecolex.org/details/treaty/convention-on-the-international-commission-for-the-protection-of-the-elbe-tre-001110/> accessed 8 July 2024; Statute of the Indo-Bangladesh Joint Rivers Commission (adopted 24 November 1972) <https://www.fao.org/fileadmin/user_upload/legal/docs/ls55-ef.pdf> accessed 8 July 2024; Agreement Between the Government of the Republic of South Africa, the Government of the Kingdom of Swaziland and the Government of the People's Republic of Mozambique Relative to the Establishment of a Tripartite Permanent Technical Committee (adopted 17 February 1983) <http://faolex.fao.org/docs/pdf/mul15880.pdf> accessed 8 July 2024 (1983 Swaziland-Mozambique-South Africa Agreement); Agreement on the Establishment of the Zambezi Watercourse Commission (adopted 13 July 2004) <https://www.fao.org/faolex/results/details/en/c/LEX-FAOC180628/> accessed 8 July 2024 (2004 Zambezi Agreement); and Convention Creating the Senegal River Development Organisation (adopted 11 March 1972) <https://www.fao.org/faolex/results/details/en/c/LEX-FAOC091150/> accessed 8 July 2024 (1972 Senegal Convention).

[27] See agreements referred to at n 22.

of their treaty commitments, such as a joint or co-ordinated basin management plan?

The second aspect of transboundary water agreements that will be considered relates to the tasks and mandate of a joint institution, such as a river basin organisation. Key questions to consider in this area include: Is there a requirement to establish a joint institution? If a joint institution is provided for, what are its decision-making powers, i.e., autonomous, by consensus of the parties, or by majority of the parties? Is the joint institution explicitly tasked with periodically reviewing implementation and/or compliance, or does it have a more general mandate to monitor the implementation of the agreement? Also, are the public entitled to participate in the decision-making of a joint institution, both generally and specifically in relation to issues related to compliance and/or implementation?

The third key aspect that will be considered concerns how any incidences of weak implementation or non-compliance are addressed. This aspect examines whether agreements contain any specific provisions to address incidences of weak implementation and non-compliance, and whether any institution is provided with a mandate to address such matters. As it is assumed that transboundary water agreements include few provisions that specifically address weak implementation and non-compliance, more traditional provisions contained in agreements that address dispute settlement will be the focus of the analysis.

At the outset, it is important to note that while the chapter will seek to analyse a diverse range of treaty practices, the study will not be comprehensive. There are several databases of transboundary water agreements, but gaps remain in these collections.[28] Rather, the chapter will aim to provide an indication of the types of provisions that are included within transboundary water agreements and highlight the diversity in approaches adopted in such agreements.

A further caveat to the analysis in this chapter is that it will not examine *actual* implementation practices. To conduct such empirical analysis for all transboundary rivers, lakes and aquifers with agreements would not be possible within the confines of the research. However, it is envisaged that the

---

[28] Oregon State University's International Freshwater Treaties Database offers the fullest collection with more than 400 treaties covering the years 1820 to 2007, see <https://transboundarywaters.science.oregonstate.edu/content/international-freshwater-treaties-database> accessed 8 July 2024. Other collections include the FAO's FAOLEX <http://faolex.fao.org/faolex/index.htm> accessed 8 July 2024; the International Water Law Project <http://www.internationalwaterlaw.org> accessed 8 July 2024; and the Interstate Commission for Water Coordination of Central Asia <http://www.icwc-aral.uz/> accessed 8 July 2024.

subsequent case study chapters will go further by assessing specific experiences in the implementation of transboundary water agreements.

4.2 MONITORING AND REPORTING

At the basin or aquifer level, while no transboundary water agreements include a CIM explicitly, they may include more general provisions relating to monitoring and reporting. Such provisions can offer an important foundation upon which to assess the compliance and implementation record of the parties.

At a basic level, obligations on states to exchange data and information can assist in assessing existing knowledge and current data gaps.[29] More advanced cooperation provides for monitoring, either by the parties individually or jointly through an institutional arrangement. Monitoring can offer a more advanced means by which to build upon existing knowledge, address any data gaps, assess progress, and foster trust amongst the parties.[30] A further means by which to support monitoring and reporting is the use of joint action plans or programmes that can potentially provide a more deliberate process by which to implement a transboundary water agreement.[31] If the parties to an agreement are then required to periodically report on the implementation of those plans or programmes, it will be possible to build up a picture of the extent to which a transboundary water agreement has been implemented. Finally, non-state actors can play an important role in monitoring compliance and implementation given that they are often directly affected by the actions of the parties to an agreement.[32] However, such a role will only be possible if non-state actors have access to sufficient data and information concerning treaty implementation and compliance.

---

[29] See Patience Mukuyu and others, 'The devil's in the details: data exchange in transboundary waters' (2020) 45 Water International 884.

[30] See UNECE, *Updated Strategies for Monitoring and Assessment of Transboundary Rivers, Lakes and Groundwaters,* UN Doc ECE/MP.WAT/70 (2023).

[31] See UNECE, 'Guide to reporting under the Water Convention and as a contribution to SDG indicator 6.5.2', UN Doc ECE/MP.WAT/60 (January 2020), 33–35.

[32] Mara Tignino and Komlan Sangbana (eds), *Public Participation and Water Resources Management – Where Do We Stand in International Law?* (UNESCO 2015).

4.2.1 Exchange of Data and Information

It is widely accepted that there is a customary law requirement upon states to share data and information relating to their transboundary waters.[33] Such a requirement is set out in the Watercourses Convention, where it is stipulated that, 'states shall on a regular basis exchange readily available data and information on the condition of the watercourse, in particular that of a hydrological, meteorological, hydrogeological and ecological nature and related to the water quality as well as related forecasts'.[34] While the Revised Protocol on Shared Watercourses in the Southern African Development Community (Revised SADC Protocol) follows similar wording to the Watercourses Convention,[35] the Water Convention adds additional requirements to exchange data and information regarding, *inter alia*, 'experience gained in the application and operation of best available technology and results of research and development', 'emission and monitoring data', 'measures taken and planned to be taken to prevent, control and reduce transboundary impact', 'permits or regulations for waste-water discharges issued by the competent authority or appropriate body' and national regulations pertaining to emission limits.[36] The Water Convention therefore goes further than the other two instruments by explicitly requiring its riparian parties to share information on the measures taken but all instruments fall short of explicitly requiring countries to periodically share data on their progress in complying with and implementing their transboundary water agreements.

At the basin or aquifer level, provisions in transboundary water agreements differ in relation to data and information exchange. Some agreements simply set out general principles for the exchange of data and information on the conditions of transboundary waters.[37] Other agreements require states

---

[33] Stephen C. McCaffrey, *The Law of International Watercourses* (2nd edn, OUP 2007), 478–479.

[34] Article 9, Watercourses Convention (n 2).

[35] See Article 3(6), Revised Protocol on Shared Watercourses in the Southern African Development Community (adopted 7 August 2000, entered into force 22 September 2003), 40 ILM 321 (SADC Revised Protocol).

[36] Article 13, Water Convention (n 1).

[37] See for example, Article 14 USSR-Iran 1957 Agreement (n 21); Article 19, Treaty Between the Government of the Union of Soviet Socialist Republics and the Government of the Hungarian People's Republic Concerning the Regime of the Soviet-Hungarian State Frontier and Final Protocol (adopted 24 February 1950) <http://gis.nacse.org/tfdd/tfdddocs/146ENG.pdf> accessed 8 July 2024; Article 7, Treaty for Amazonian Cooperation (adopted 3 July 1978) <https://otca.org/en/project/amazon-cooperation-treaty/> accessed 8 July 2024 (1978 Amazon

to exchange information on specific matters, including any studies pertaining to the transboundary watercourse,[38] existing and planned activities,[39] likely sources of pollution,[40] and relevant national laws, policies and programmes.[41]

Treaty); Article 19, Treaty Concerning the Regime of the Soviet-Romanian State Frontier and Final Protocol (adopted 25 November 1949) <http://gis.nacse.org/tfdd/tfdddocs/144ENG.pdf> accessed 8 July 2024; Article 6, Indus Waters Treaty (n 6); Article VI, Israel-Jordan Peace Treaty (n 10); Article 3, Agreement Between the People's Republic of Bulgaria and the Republic of Turkey Concerning Co-operation in the Use of the Waters of Rivers Flowing Through the Territory of Both Countries (Maritsa/Marica, Tundzha, Veleka, Rezovska Rivers) (adopted 23 October 1968) <https://www.internationalwaterlaw.org/documents/regionaldocs/bulg_and_turk.html> accessed 8 July 2024 (1968 Bulgaria-Turkey Agreement); Article 7(4), Agreement Between the Governments of the Republic of Botswana, the Kingdom of Lesotho, the Republic of Namibia and the Republic of South Africa on the Establishment of the Orange-Senqu River Commission (adopted 3 November 2000) <https://orasecom.org/wp-content/uploads/2020/09/ORASECOM_Agreement_Reprint-August-2012.pdf> accessed 8 July 2024 (2000 ORASECOM Agreement); Article 8, Protocol Amending the Agreement Between Canada and the United States of America on Great Lakes Water Quality, 1978, as Amended on October 16, 1983, and on November 18, 1987 (adopted 7 September 2012) <https://publications.gc.ca/site/eng/9.822800/publication.html> accessed 8 July 2024 (2012 Great Lakes Protocol); Article 8, Agreement Between Poland and the Union of Soviet Socialist Republics Concerning the Use of Water Resources in Frontier Waters (adopted 17 July 1964), 552 UNTS 175; Article 18, 2012 Dniester Convention (n 6).

[38] See for example, Article 5, USSR-China Agreement 1956 (n 13); and Article 4, 2002 Sava Agreement (n 8).

[39] See for example, Article 12, 2002 IncoMaputo Agreement (n 22); Article 5, 1998 Albufeira Convention (n 5); Articles 8 and 9, Guarani Aquifer Agreement (n 7); Lake Tanganyika Convention (n 7); Article 1(2)(f), Agreement Between the Federal Germany and the European Economic Community, on the one hand, and the Republic of Austria, on the other, on Cooperation on Management of Water Resources in the Danube Basin (adopted 1 December 1987) <http://eur-lex.europa.eu/legal-content/EN/TXT/?uri=CELEX:21990A0405(01)> accessed 8 July 2024 (Germany-EEC-Austria Agreement).

[40] See for example, Article 6, United States – Mexico Agreement on the Environment in the Border Area (adopted 14 August 1983), 22 ILM 1025.

[41] See for example, Article 5, 1998 Albufeira Convention (n 5); Article 20(1), Lake Tanganyika Convention (n 7); Article 1(2)(b), Germany-EEC-Austria Agreement (n 39); Article 4, Sava Agreement (n 8); and Article 4, Treaty Between Czech Republic and Slovak Republic on Mutual Relations and Principles of Cooperation in Agriculture, Food Industry, Forestry, and Water Economy under the Conditions of the Customs Union (adopted 23 November 1992) <https://www

In addition to the requirement to exchange available data and information, various agreements stipulate that the parties should use their best efforts to comply with requests from other parties to provide additional information.[42] What constitutes 'best efforts' is open to interpretation, but it would be reasonable to assume that a request to receive data and information on matters pertaining to the implementation of the agreement would be covered by this provision.[43] However, no agreement explicitly requires parties to exchange data and information on their progress in complying with and implementing an agreement's provisions.

4.2.2 Monitoring

The requirement to monitor the conditions of transboundary waters is a common feature of transboundary water agreements.[44] Some agreements include a soft requirement relating to monitoring. The 1994 China-Mongolia Agreement, for instance, simply provides that the parties *may* conduct 'monitoring of the quality, dynamics and resources of the transboundary waters and changes of the boundary rivers and lake and their basins'.[45] Other agreements provide a stronger, albeit general, obligation to monitor. The 1997 Estonia-Russia Agreement, for example, provides that, 'monitoring shall be carried out on both sides to get regular information about the state of the transboundary waters'.[46]

Some agreements go further by requiring co-ordinated or joint monitoring. The 2003 Lake Victoria Protocol, for instance, requires that each party within its own jurisdiction 'monitor activities and natural phenomena with a view to determining the potential risk they pose to the resources of the Basin and its

---

.fao.org/faolex/results/details/ar/c/LEX-FAOC023131/> accessed 8 July 2024 (1992 Czech-Slovak Agreement).

[42] See for example, Article 13(3), Water Convention (n 1); Article 2, Watercourses Convention (n 2); Article 12(5), 2002 IncoMaputo Agreement (n 22); Article 5(3), 1998 Albufeira Convention (n 5); Article 20(2), Lake Tanganyika Convention (n 7); and Article 18(2), 2012 Dniester Convention (n 6).

[43] For an explanation of 'best efforts', International Law Commission, 'Report of the International Law Commission on the Work of its 46th Session' (2 May – 22 July 1994), UN Doc A/CN.4/SER.A/1994/Add1 (Part 2), 109.

[44] UNECE (n 30), 11.

[45] Article 3, 1994 China-Mongolia Agreement (n 5). See also Article 8, Agreement between the United Mexican States and the Republic of Guatemala on the Protection and Improvement of the Environment in the Border Area (adopted 10 April 1987), 1509 UNTS 182.

[46] 1997 Estonia-Russia Agreement (n 5); see also Article 3, 2012 Great Lakes Protocol (n 37).

people'; and requires the states to 'adopt standardized equipment and methods of monitoring'.[47]

Other treaties go further by requiring states to jointly monitor the conditions of transboundary waters through a harmonised system.[48] In some instances, a joint institution, such as a river basin organisation, is specifically tasked with establishing joint monitoring arrangements.[49]

The only agreement that explicitly requires its parties to monitor its implementation is the 2002 Sava Agreement.[50] Pursuant to Article 21(1) of the Agreement, the parties are obliged to establish a 'methodology of permanent monitoring of implementation of the Agreement'.[51] The methodology for monitoring the implementation of the Sava Agreement was adopted at the first meeting of the parties to the International Sava River Basin Commission.[52] Parties are required, in advance of each meeting of the parties, to submit a report on the implementation of the Sava Agreement within their national jurisdiction.[53]

---

47 Protocol for Sustainable Development of Lake Victoria Basin (adopted 29 November 2003) <https://www.fao.org/faolex/results/details/en/c/LEX-FAOC041042/> accessed 8 July 2024 (2003 Lake Victoria Protocol). See also Article 16, 2012 Dniester Convention (n 6); Article 2, Agreement of the Republic of Kazakhstan, Republic of Kyrgyzstan, Republic of Tajikistan, Turkmenistan, and Republic of Uzbekistan on Joint Activities in Addressing the Aral Sea (adopted 26 March 1993) <http://www.internationalwaterlaw.org/documents/regionaldocs/aral-sea.html> accessed 8 July 2024.

48 See for example, Article 12, 2003 Carpathians Convention (n 12); Article 9, 1994 Danube Convention (n 3); 1989 Souris Agreement (n 18); Article 11, Water Convention (n 1).

49 See for example, Articles 9(j) and 12(d), Treaty Between the United States of America and Mexico Concerning the Utilization of Waters of the Colorado and Tijuana Rivers and of the Rio Grande (adopted 3 February 1944) <https://www.ibwc.gov/wp-content/uploads/2022/11/1944Treaty.pdf> accessed 8 July 2024; Article 3 and Annex II, 1994 Israel-Jordan Peace Treaty (n 10); Article 5, 1998 Rhine Convention (n 22).

50 2002 Sava Agreement (n 8).

51 Article 21(1), 2002 Sava Agreement (n 8). See also, International Sava River Basin Commission, 'Strategy on Implementation of the Framework Agreement on the Sava River Basin', April 2011, <https://www.savacommission.org/UserDocsImages/05_documents_publications/basic_documents/strategy_on_implementation_of_the_fasrb_2011.pdf> accessed 8 July 2024.

52 International Sava River Basin Commission, 'Strategy on Implementation of the Framework on the Sava River Basin', ibid, 33.

53 Ibid.

4.2.3 Joint Strategies, Plans and Programmes

The development of joint strategies, plans and programmes offers an important means by which parties to an agreement can set out specific details as to how a transboundary water agreement is to be implemented.[54]

The importance of such strategies, plans and programmes is recognised in the Watercourses Convention, which encourages states to establish 'joint management mechanisms', including 'planning the sustainable development of an international watercourse and providing for the implementation of any plans adopted'.[55] A general obligation is also provided in the Water Convention for riparian parties 'to develop harmonised policies, programmes and strategies covering the relevant catchment areas, or parts thereof'.[56]

Some transboundary water agreements require states to adopt, or at least co-ordinate, basin management plans, and also require that those plans be periodically reviewed. The 2002 Dniester Treaty, for instance, sets out a general obligation on parties to 'develop and implement joint and co-ordinated Dniester basin management plans, projects and measures for the utilisation, protection and rehabilitation of water and other natural resources and ecosystems of the Dniester River basin'.[57] Along similar lines, the 2003 Lake Tanganyika Convention requires that state parties 'collaborate in the implementation of a strategic action program to give effect to the measures set out in this Convention'.[58] Pursuant to the Convention, the strategic action programme must 'include specific aims directed at achieving the objective of this Convention, strategies for achieving these aims, specific measures to be taken

---

[54] Susanne Schmeier and Birgit Vogel, 'Ensuring long-term cooperation over transboundary water resources through joint river basin management', in Stefan Schmutz and Jan Sendzimir (eds), *Riverine Ecosystem Management – Science for Governing Towards a Sustainable Future* (Springer 2018), 358–361.

[55] Article 24, Watercourses Convention (n 2).

[56] Article 2(6), Water Convention (n 1).

[57] Article 5(a), 2012 Dniester Convention (n 6). See also Article 12, 2002 Sava Agreement (n 8); Article 5(2), 1989 Souris Agreement (n 18); Article 4(1)(B), Revised Convention on Establishment of the Niger Basin Authority (adopted 29 October 1987) <http://www.abn.ne/images/documents/Convention/revised_convention.pdf> accessed 8 July 2024 (1987 Niger Basin Convention); Article 1, Convention for the Establishment of the Lake Victoria Fisheries Organisation (adopted 30 June 1994) <http://www.fao.org/docrep/w7414b/w7414b0l.htm> accessed 8 July 2024; Article 1 and 4, Agreement on the Action Plan for the Environmentally Sound Management of the Common Zambezi River System (adopted 28 May 1987) <http://www.fao.org/docrep/w7414b/w7414b0j.htm> accessed 8 July 2024.

[58] Article 13(1), 2003 Lake Tanganyika Convention (n 7).

by the contracting states separately or jointly to achieve these aims and details of the means to be used to monitor progress toward the achievement of these aims'.[59] As well as establishing the action plan, state parties are under a commitment to monitor the effectiveness of the plan and revise it if necessary.[60]

Other transboundary water agreements provide for a more targeted assessment of certain commitments contained therein. In its focus on water pollution, the 1994 Danube Convention, for instance, requires its parties to first establish inventories of relevant point and non-point sources, and list prevention and abatement measures that have already been taken; second, establish a list of additional prevention and abatement measures to be taken in order to achieve the objectives of the Convention; and third, monitor the progress made in the implementation of joint action programmes.[61]

A more general requirement to assign national agencies with the task of developing a package of implementation measures, without stipulating the type of measures to be adopted, is provided for in the 1997 Agreement between Kazakhstan, the Kyrgyz Republic and Uzbekistan.[62]

4.2.4 Reporting Requirements

As well as providing the requirement that parties establish and monitor the implementation of strategies, plans and programmes, some treaties require parties to individually report on their efforts to implement their commitments.

As noted above, the Sava Agreement provides an explicit requirement for parties to report periodically as part of a commitment to monitor the

---

59 Article 13(2), ibid.

60 Article 13(3), ibid.

61 Article 8, 1994 Danube Convention (n 3). See also, Article 2, Agreement Between the Government of Finland and Norway on the Transfer from the Course of the Näätämo (Neiden) River to the Course of the Gandvik River of Water from the Garsjoen, Kjerringvatan and Forstevannene Lakes (adopted 25 April 1951) <http://gis.nacse.org/tfdd/tfdddocs/160ENG.pdf> accessed 8 July 2024, which relates to the movement of fish.

62 Article 8, Agreement Between the Government of the Republic of Kazakhstan, the Government of the Kyrgyz Republic and the Government of the Republic of Uzbekistan on Cooperation in the Area of Environment and Rational Nature Use (adopted 17 March 1998) <https://faolex.fao.org/docs/pdf/mul-54532.pdf> accessed 8 July 2024. See also Exchange of Notes Constituting an Agreement Between the United States of America and Canada Relating to a Study to be made by the International Joint Commission with Respect to the Upper Columbia River Basin (adopted 25 February 1944) <http://gis.nacse.org/tfdd/tfdddocs/126ENG.pdf> accessed 8 July 2024 (1944 Upper Columbia Basin Agreement).

implementation of the agreement.[63] Other agreements provide a more general requirement to report. For example, under the 1998 Albufeira Convention, the parties agree that, through the Commission for the Implementation and Development of the Albufeira Convention (CADC), they will report annually on 'the procedures for the national implementation of actions established under the terms of the Convention'; and 'draft an annual report … on the development of matters governed by the Convention and on the implementation at national level of actions'.[64] More specifically, such measures might include information on the national laws, policies and administrative arrangements adopted in support of treaty implementation;[65] the environmental conditions of the transboundary waters within their national jurisdiction;[66] and any existing and planned activities related to treaty objectives.[67]

As well as reporting on the measures adopted, some transboundary water agreements also stipulate that the parties should report on the effectiveness of those measures.[68] Other transboundary water agreements simply provide a more general obligation on parties to inform each other of the measures carried out in support of the implementation of a particular agreement.[69]

The only explicit reference to reporting incidences of non-compliance within basin-specific treaties appears in the 2004 Zambezi Agreement. Pursuant to Article 20, the Zambezi Agreement provides a self-reporting mechanism whereby member states are obliged to inform the secretariat of the Zambezi Commission of the reasons for failing to comply with the Agreement, and identify any measures taken to remedy the failure.[70] Upon receiving notice of non-compliance, the secretariat is then required to enter into consultation with the member state with a view to assisting where necessary to address non-compliance.[71] If after six months of consultations the issue is not resolved,

---

[63] International Sava River Basin Commission (n 52).

[64] Article 7(1)(b) and (2), 1998 Albufeira (n 5). See also Article 83, Lake Chad Charter (adopted 30 April 2012) <https://www.fao.org/faolex/results/details/en/c/LEX-FAOC203691> accessed 6 February 2025.

[65] Article 22(1)(a) and (b), 2003 Lake Tanganyika Convention (n 7); Article 10(b)–(e), 1994 Danube Convention (n 3).

[66] Article 22(1)(c), 2003 Lake Tanganyika Convention (n 7).

[67] Article 22(1)(d), ibid; Article 10(b)–(f), 1994 Danube Convention (n 3).

[68] Article 22(1)(d), 2003 Lake Tanganyika Convention (n 7).

[69] See for example, Article 5, 1998 Rhine Convention (n 22); Article 3, Agreement Between the Federal Republic of Nigeria and the Republic of Niger Concerning the Equitable Sharing in the Development, Conservation and Use of their Common Water Resources (adopted 18 July 1990) <http://faolex.fao.org/docs/pdf/bi-16750.pdf> accessed 8 July 2024.

[70] Article 20(1), 2004 Zambezi Agreement (n 26).

[71] Article 20(2), ibid.

the secretariat is obliged to refer the matter to the Council for a decision.[72] Decisions of the Council are to be reached by consensus.[73]

4.2.5 Public Information

Some transboundary water agreements include a general requirement that information relating to activities under the agreement be made publicly available. The 1998 Albufeira Convention, for example, provides a broad requirement that, in accordance with EU legislation,[74] parties must provide the necessary conditions by which to respond to any reasonable request for 'information on matters covered by the Convention'.[75] Similarly, the 2003 Lake Tanganyika Convention requires that 'adequate information is made available to the public concerning the state of the Lake Basin, planned development activities, measures taken or planned to be taken to prevent, control and reduce adverse impacts, and the effectiveness of those measures'.[76] Such information, according to the 2003 Lake Tanganyika Convention, should be made available to the public at all reasonable times free of charge.[77] Along similar lines, the 2002 Inco-Maputo Agreement stipulates that 'the parties shall create the necessary conditions to ensure that, in conformity with applicable domestic law or International Law, information on matters covered by this Agreement is available to whoever makes a reasonable request'.[78]

Over and above the requirement to make information publicly available, some transboundary water agreements call upon their parties to proactively inform the public of activities related to the agreement and the results thereof. Under the 2012 Dniester Convention, for example, the parties are obliged to 'inform the public on the status of water and other natural resources and ecosystems of the Dniester River Basin, measures taken or planned to prevent, control or reduce any transboundary impact, as well as involve the public in resolving matters to which the present Treaty relate'.[79] Similarly, parties to the 2003 Lake Victoria Protocol are required to 'promote and encourage

---

72 Article 20(3), ibid.

73 Article 7(4), ibid.

74 Directive 2003/4/EC of 28 January 2003 on Public Access to Environmental Information [2003] OJ L 41/26; Directive 2003/35/EC of 26 May 2004 Providing Public Participation in Respect of the Drawing Up of Certain Plans and Programmes Relating to the Environment [2003] OJ L 156/17.

75 Article 6, 1998 Luso-Spanish Convention (n 5).

76 Article 19(1), 2003 Lake Tanganyika Convention (n 7).

77 Article 19(2), ibid; See also Article 16, Water Convention (n 1).

78 Article 12(8), 2002 IncoMaputo Agreement (n 22).

79 Article 21, 2012 Dniester Convention (n 6).

awareness of the importance of, and the measures required for, the sustainable development of the basin'.[80]

Some transboundary water agreements also stipulate that any reporting required under the agreement should be made available to the public. In the case of the Sava Agreement, for instance, the parties commit to 'include timely provision of information to stakeholders and the general authorities' as part of the monitoring methodology.[81] Similarly, pursuant to the 2012 Great Lakes Protocol, parties are obligated to 'publicly report' on the progress in achieving the objectives of the treaty.[82]

4.3 REVIEWING TREATY IMPLEMENTATION AND COMPLIANCE

4.3.1 Joint Institutions

While provisions relating to monitoring and reporting offer an important foundation upon which to assess treaty implementation and compliance, there must also be a mechanism by which to review that data and information. Within the context of transboundary water agreements, the most likely mechanism that could perform this role is a joint institution, such as a river basin organisation. Provisions related to the establishment of joint institutions are a common feature of transboundary watercourse agreements.[83] These institutions can be

[80] Article 21, 2003 Lake Victoria Protocol (n 47). See also Article 12, 1997 Estonia-Russia Agreement (n 5); Article 13(1), 2003 Carpathians Convention (n 12).

[81] Article 21(2), 2002 Sava Agreement (n 8).

[82] Article 4, 2012 Great Lakes Protocol (n 37).

[83] See Dante A. Caponera, 'Administration of International Water Resources', in Slavko Bogdanović (ed), *International Law of Water Resources – Contribution of the International Law Association* (Kluwer Law International 2001), 245–268.

referred to by different names, including Commission,[84] Authority,[85] Council,[86] Committee,[87] Conference,[88] Board,[89] Administration[90] and Organisation.[91]

---

[84] Article 18, 1994 Danube Convention (n 3); Article 8, Indus Waters Treaty (n 6); Article 9(1), Treaty Between His Majesty's Government of Nepal and the Government of India Concerning the Integrated Development of the Mahakali River Including Sarada Barrage, Tanakpur Barrage and Pancheshwar Project (adopted 12 February 1996) <http://faolex.fao.org/docs/pdf/bi-17432.pdf> accessed 8 July 2024 (1996 Mahakali River Treaty); Article 11, 1990 Nigeria-Niger Agreement (n 5); Article 33(1), 2003 Lake Victoria Protocol (n 47); Article 4, Convention Between France and Switzerland Respecting the Chatelot Falls Concession on the Doubs, Paris, 19 November 1930, 133 British and Foreign State Papers 487 (1930 Swiss-French Convention); Article 8 and Annex 2, Agreement Between Finland and Sweden Concerning Transboundary Waters (adopted 11 November 2009) <https://www.fsgk.se/en/finsk-svenska-gransalvskommisionen-english/> accessed 8 July 2024 (2009 Finland-Sweden Agreement); Article 2, Agreement Between Greece and Yugoslavia Concerning the Hydro-Economic Questions (adopted 18 June 1959), 363 UNTS 135 (1959 Greece-Yugoslavia Agreement); Article 4, Convention on the Emosson Hydroelectric Project (adopted 23 August 1963), XXXVI Revue Générale de Droit International Public 571; Article 4, International Agreement on the River Meuse (adopted 3 December 2002) <https://faolex.fao.org/docs/pdf/mul216204.pdf> accessed 8 July 2024 (2002 Meuse Agreement).

[85] See for example, Article 23, Lake Tanganyika Convention (n 7).

[86] Article 21, 1978 Amazon Treaty (n 37); Article 4, Agreement Between the Republic of Zimbabwe and the Republic of Zambia Concerning the Utilization of the Zambezi River, Harare, 28 July 1987 <http://www.fao.org/docrep/w7414b/w7414b17.htm> accessed 8 July 2024 (1987 Zimbabwe-Zambia Agreement).

[87] Article 11, 1994 China-Mongolia Agreement (n 6); Article 7, 1994 Syria-Lebanon Agreement (n 6); Article 3, 2015 Disi Aquifer Agreement (n 6); Article 2, Agreement on the Establishment of the Tumen River Area Development Coordination Committee (adopted 1 January 1994) <http://nautilus.org/aprenet/agreement-on-the-establishment-of-the-tumen-river-area-development-coordination-committee-1994> accessed 8 July 2024 (1994 Tumen River Agreement).

[88] Article 14, 2003 Carpathians Convention (n 12).

[89] Article 8, 2012 Great Lakes Protocol (n 37); Article 3, Agreement Between Canada and the United States of America to Regulate the Level of Lake of the Woods (adopted 24 February 1925) <http://www.internationalwaterlaw.org/documents/regionaldocs/lake-woods.html> adopted 8 July 2024 (1925 Lake of Woods Agreement).

[90] Article 1, Agreement Between the Government of the Czechoslovak Socialist Republic and the Government of the Hungarian People's Republic Concerning the Establishment of a River Administration in the Rajka-Gönyü Sector of the Danube (adopted 27 February 1968) <http://gis.nacse.org/tfdd/tfdd-docs/306ENG.pdf> accessed 8 July 2024.

[91] Article 1, 1972 Senegal Convention (n 26).

Transboundary water agreements vary in the level of detail they include on the establishment of joint institutions. Some agreements simply provide a general provision establishing the joint arrangement, while other agreements provide detailed provisions on the legal mandate, structure, decision-making powers,[92] function and objectives of a joint institution.[93]

There is also considerable variety in the types of structures established through transboundary water agreements. A common approach is to establish a series of sub-institutional arrangements. At the highest level, there may be a Council or Conference of Ministers that is the ultimate decision-making body of the institution.[94] Technical committees or working groups might then be established to carry out supplementary roles, such as the development of guidelines and recommendations, or the implementation of joint monitoring arrangements.[95] Finally, a secretariat might be established to support the activities of the Council or Conference of Ministers and any technical committees or working groups.[96] Other transboundary water agreements adopt a lighter institutional structure, such as arrangements whereby a plenipotentiary from each country meets on a regular basis.[97] A further feature of several joint institutions is to establish national committees that are responsible for co-ordinating the implementation of the agreement at both national and sub-national levels.[98]

---

92 See for example, 1994 China-Mongolia Agreement (n 6).

93 See for example, the 2009 Finland-Sweden Agreement (n 84).

94 See for example, Articles 3–6, 1972 Senegal Convention (n 26).

95 See for example, Article 9, 2004 Zambezi Agreement (n 26).

96 See for example, Article 23, Lake Tanganyika Convention (n 7); Article 18, 1995 Mekong Agreement (n 22); Annex IV, 1994 Danube Convention (n 3); Articles 33–42, 2003 Lake Victoria Protocol (n 47); Articles 17–19, Water Convention, note 1; Article 15, 2002 Sava Agreement (n 8).

97 See for example, Article 8(1) and (3), 1960 Indus Waters Treaty (n 6); Article 5, Agreement Between the Government of the Republic of Finland and the Government of the Union of Soviet Socialist Republics Concerning the Protection of Electric Power in the Part of the Vuoksi River Bounded by the Imatra and Svetogorsk Hydroelectric Station (adopted 12 July 1972) <http://gis.nacse.org/tfdd/tfdddocs/349ENG.pdf> accessed 8 July 2024 (1972 Finland-USSR Agreement); Article 6, 1992 Czech-Slovak Agreement (n 41); Article 9, Agreement Between the Government of the Czechoslovak Republic and the Government of the Polish People's Republic Concerning the Use of the Water Resources in Frontier Waters (adopted 21 March 1958) <http://www.internationalwaterlaw.org/documents/regionaldocs/czech-pol-frontier.html> accessed 8 July 2024 (1958 Czech-Poland Agreement); Article 10, 1994 China-Mongolia Agreement (n 6).

98 See for example, 1995 Mekong Agreement (n 22); and the 1978 Amazon Treaty (n 37).

Irrespective of the structure chosen, the decision-making authority provided for in transboundary water agreements invariably rests with state parties. Normally, major decisions are taken by state parties within a Conference or Council.[99] Alternatively, a joint institution might be given the power to make proposals or recommendations that are then considered by the state parties.[100] Decision-making authority is further constrained by a common requirement found in transboundary water agreements that decisions must be made by consensus.[101] It is therefore rare for any joint institution to enjoy supranational authority over state parties, which has implications for the extent to which such an institution can address issues of weak implementation or non-compliance. This aspect of joint institutions will be considered further in section 4.4 below.

Transboundary water agreements set out a large array of functions that joint institutions may perform. Some institutions are assigned specific tasks, such as carrying out joint studies,[102] or overseeing the construction of joint works.[103]

---

[99] See for example, 1995 Mekong Agreement (n 22); Article 2, 2004 Zambezi Agreement (n 26).

[100] See for example, Article 18(1), 1994 Danube Convention (n 3); Article 11, 1994 China-Mongolia Agreement (n 6); Article 1, Agreement Between the Government of the Republic of Namibia and the Government of the Republic of South Africa on the Establishment of a Permanent Water Commission (adopted 14 September 1992) <http://www.fao.org/docrep/w7414b/w7414b0y.htm> accessed 8 July 2024; Article 1(2), Agreement Between the Governments of the Republic of Angola, the Republic of Botswana, and the Republic of Namibia on the Establishment of a Permanent Okavango River Basin Water Commission (OKACOM) (adopted 16 September 1994) <http://www.fao.org/docrep/w7414b/w7414b0m.htm> accessed 8 July 2024 (1994 OKACOM Agreement); Article 9, 1958 Czech-Poland Agreement (n 97); Article 5, 1983 Swaziland-Mozambique-South Africa Agreement (n 26).

[101] See for example, Article 17, 2003 Carpathians Convention (n 12); Article 7, 2004 Zambezi Agreement (n 26); Article 4, 1987 Zimbabwe-Zambia Agreement (n 86); Article 2, 1994 Tumen River Agreement (n 87); Article IV, Convention Between Italy and Switzerland Concerning the Regulation of Lake Lugano (adopted 17 September 1955) <https://faolex.fao.org/docs/pdf/bi-32513.pdf> accessed 8 July 2024 (1955 Lake Lugano Convention); Article 1, 2000 ORASECOM Agreement (n 37).

[102] See for example, Article 2, 1959 Greece-Yugoslavia Agreement (n 84); Article 5, Act Regarding Navigation and Economic Co-operation Between the States of the Niger Basin (adopted 26 October 1963) <http://www.fao.org/docrep/w7414b/w7414b04.htm> accessed 8 July 2024 (1963 Niger Basin Act).

[103] See for example, the Treaty between the Swiss Confederation and the Republic of Austria for the regulation of the Rhine from the mouth of the Ill to Lake Constance (adopted 10 April 1954), 1003 UNTS 62 (1954 Lake Constance Treaty).

Other transboundary water agreements place more general requirements on a joint institution, for example, to advise on 'matters relating to the conservation, development and utilisation of water resources of common interest to the Contracting parties'.[104]

Some transboundary water agreements explicitly stipulate that the function of a joint institution is to implement the agreement.[105] Under the 1995 Mekong Agreement, for example, the Council is given the responsibility to 'make decisions necessary to successfully implement' the Mekong Agreement.[106] Similarly, the function of the Lake Tanganyika Authority is simply stated as being 'to co-ordinate the implementation of the present Convention'.[107]

Over and above a general responsibility to implement transboundary water agreements, some joint institutions are specifically tasked with the responsibility to *review* implementation.[108] Along similar lines, the International

---

[104] Article 1(2), 1994 OKACOM Agreement (n 100).

[105] See for example, Article 1, 1972 Senegal Convention (n 26); Article 5, 1972 Finland-USSR Agreement (n 97); Article 5(i), 2004 Zambezi Agreement (n 26); Article 4(2), 2002 Meuse Agreement (n 84); Article 66, Treaty Between the Kingdom of the Netherlands and the Federal Republic of Germany Concerning the Course of the Common Frontier, the Boundary Waters, Real Property Situated Near the Frontier, Traffic Crossing the Frontier on Land and via Inland Waters, and Other Frontier Questions (adopted 8 April 1960) <http://gis.nacse.org/tfdd/tfdddocs/241ENG.pdf> accessed 8 July 2024 (1960 Netherlands-Germany Treaty); Article 6, 1997 Estonia-Russia Agreement (n 5); Article 7, Israel-Jordan Peace Treaty (n 10); Article 10, 1994 China-Mongolia Agreement (n 6); Convention Relating to the Creation of the Gambia River Basin Development Organisation (adopted 30 June 1978) <http://www.fao.org/docrep/w7414b/w7414b0c.htm> accessed 8 July 2024 (1978 Gambia Convention); Article 15(1), 2002 Sava Agreement (n 8).

[106] Article 18(B), 1995 Mekong Agreement (n 22).

[107] Article 23, Lake Tanganyika Convention (n 7).

[108] See for example, Article 11, 1990 Nigeria-Niger Agreement (n 5); Article 33, Lake Victoria Protocol (n 47); Article 4, 1930 Swiss-French Convention (n 84); Article 8, 1998 Rhine Convention (n 22); Article 5(2)(a)(i), SADC Revised Protocol (n 35); Article 17(2), Water Convention (n 1); Article 5, 1997 Estonia-Russia Agreement (n 5); Article 6, 1989 Souris Agreement (n 18); Article 10, Agreement Between the Republic of Syria and the Hashemite Kingdom of Jordan Concerning the Utilization of the Yarmuk Waters (adopted 4 June 1953) <http://www.internationalwaterlaw.org/documents/regionaldocs/syria-jordan-1953.html> accessed 8 July 2024; Article 4, Protocol Agreement Between the Republic of Guinea and the Republic of Guinea-Bissau for the Management of the Kaliba-Korubal River (adopted 21 October 1978) <https://www.fao.org/faolex/results/details/en/c/LEX-FAOC108857/> accessed 8 July 2024 (1978 Kaliba-Korubal River Agreement); Article 10, 2009 Finland-Sweden Agreement (n 84).

Commission for the Protection of the Danube River is required to 'review experience acquired implementing [the] Convention'.[109]

As well as reviewing whether a particular transboundary water agreement is implemented, an albeit limited number of treaties call upon the parties to review effectiveness. The 1998 Albufeira Convention, for instance, stipulates that the parties must 'promote actions to increase the effectiveness of the Convention'.[110] More specifically, the 2012 Dniester Treaty requires the Dniester Commission to conduct a 'review of the effectiveness of measures taken on the national and interstate level and the appropriateness of additional measures'.[111] Along similar lines, the Rhine Commission is tasked both with the obligation to elaborate proposals for different measures and programmes of measures in support of the implementation of the 1998 Rhine Convention, and 'to evaluate the effectiveness of the measures decided upon'.[112] Similarly, within the 2012 Great Lakes Protocol, the International Joint Commission is given the responsibility to advise and recommend to the parties, 'approaches and options that the parties may consider to improve effectiveness in achieving the purpose and objectives of [the] Agreement'.[113]

Only a few transboundary water agreements go so far as tasking the parties and/or a joint institution with identifying incidences of non-compliance. In general terms, the 1978 Amazon Treaty stipulates that one of the tasks of the Amazon Authority is to 'ensure that the aims and objectives of the Treaty are complied with'.[114] The 1998 Albufeira Convention stipulates that the parties must 'promote actions to review the compliance with the Convention'.[115] Along similar lines, the Lake Victoria Basin Commission is given the tasks of 'monitoring, evaluation and compliance with policies and agreed actions'.[116] A slightly different requirement is provided for under the 1975 Uruguay Statute, where the Commission is provided with the function to 'co-ordinate between the competent authorities of the parties activities for the presentation and prosecution of unlawful acts'.[117] While it is not clear what might fall under the scope of unlawful acts, it could be argued that this provision opens up the possibility

109 Article 18(5), 1994 Danube Convention (n 3).

110 Article (10)(1)(l), 1998 Albufeira Convention (n 5).

111 Article 27(1), 2012 Dniester Convention (n 6).

112 Article (8), 1998 Rhine Convention (n 22).

113 Article 7, 2012 Great Lakes Protocol (n 37).

114 Article 21, 1978 Amazon Treaty (n 37);

115 Article (10)(1)(k), 1998 Albufeira Convention (n 5).

116 Article 33(3)(g), 2003 Lake Victoria Protocol (n 47).

117 Article 56(d), Statute of the Uruguay River (adopted 26 February 1975), 295 UNTS 340 (1975 Uruguay Statute).

for the bilateral commission to address incidences of non-compliance that concern the actions of non-state actors via national enforcement agencies.

4.3.2 Rights of Public to Participate in the Decision-making of Joint Institutions

Affording the public the right to participate in the decision-making procedures of any joint institution can provide another useful means by which to monitor implementation and compliance.[118]

However, states have proven reluctant to incorporate such a right within transboundary water agreements. Exceptions include the 2003 Lake Tanganyika Convention, which requires its parties to 'adopt and implement legal, administrative and other appropriate measures to ensure that the public, and in particular those individuals and communities living within the Lake Basin … have the right to participate at the appropriate level, in decision-making processes that affect the Lake Basin or their livelihoods, including participation in the procedure for assessing the environmental impacts of projects or activities that are likely to result in adverse impacts'; and the public 'are given the opportunity to make oral or written representations before a final decision is taken'.[119] The Lake Tanganyika Convention goes on to provide that each party must 'ensure that appeal or review procedures exist in respect of any decision by a public body to authorise an activity that is likely to give rise to an adverse impact'.[120] While the 2003 Lake Tanganyika Convention, therefore, falls short of guaranteeing non-state actors joint decision-making rights, it does at least go some way to ensuring that the interests of non-state actors are taken into account when decisions concerning the implementation of the Convention are being made.

The 2003 Lake Victoria Protocol is more general in its provisions related to non-state actors. It obliges its parties to 'create an environment conducive for stakeholders' views to influence governmental decisions on project formulation and implementation'.[121] The Protocol does specifically recognise the importance of gender issues in the implementation of transboundary water agreements by stipulating that the Partners must 'promote community involvement and mainstreaming of gender concerns at all levels of socio-economic

[118] Nadia Seqat, 'The principle of public participation in transboundary water resources management: a case study of transboundary basin organisations' (2022) 2 Revue Internationale de Droit Économique 55.

[119] Article 17(1), Lake Tanganyika Convention (n 7).

[120] Article 17(2), ibid.

[121] Article 22, 2003 Lake Victoria Protocol (n 47).

development, especially with regard to decision-making, policy formulation and implementation of projects and programmes'.[122]

Non-state actors are also recognised in the 2012 Dniester Treaty. The parties are required to 'involve the public in resolving matters to which the present Treaty relates',[123] and to 'facilitate public participation in activities related to implementation of the present Treaty'.[124] The parties are then more specifically tasked with informing the potentially affected public in an adequate, timely and effective manner of any proposed activities at 'the earliest stage of the decision-making procedure'.[125] The Treaty goes on to stipulate that the public should be given an opportunity to submit 'comments, information, analysis or opinions' on any proposed activities, and due account must be taken of the outcome of the public participation in the relevant decision-making process.[126]

More specific provisions are provided for in the 2012 Great Lakes Protocol, which requires that the parties establish a 'Great Lakes Public Forum'.[127] The forum, pursuant to the Protocol, provides an opportunity for 'the parties to discuss and receive Public comments on the state of the lakes and binational priorities for science and action to inform future priorities and actions'; and 'the Commission to discuss and receive Public input on the Progress Report of the parties'.[128]

4.4 PROVISIONS ADDRESSING INCIDENCES OF WEAK IMPLEMENTATION AND NON-COMPLIANCE

Monitoring and reporting can provide a baseline by which to assess the implementation and compliance record of the parties to a transboundary water agreement. Joint institutions can then offer a means to review and evaluate that record. Another important consideration is to assess what might be done to address any incidences of weak implementation or non-compliance with a transboundary water agreement. The most common approach found in transboundary water agreements is to resort to traditional dispute settlement mechanisms.[129] Some treaties simply contain a very basic provision on dispute

---

[122] Article 23, ibid.

[123] Article 5(h), 2012 Dniester Convention (n 6).

[124] Article 21(3), ibid.

[125] Article 21(2), ibid.

[126] Article 21(2), ibid.

[127] Article 5(1), 2012 Great Lakes Protocol (n 37).

[128] Article 5(1)(a) and (b), ibid.

[129] Such an approach follows the general obligation on states to settle their disputes in a peaceful manner, see Article 33 of the Charter of the United Nations

settlement, such as the 1994 China-Mongolia Agreement, which stipulates that 'the two contracting parties shall resolve the problems in the implementation of this agreement through friendly consultation'.[130]

Another option is to refer disputes to a joint institution. The 2012 Dniester Treaty, for example, gives the parties the option to bring 'collisions or disputes arising from the use and protection of water and other natural and ecosystems of the Dniester River basin' before the Dniester Commission.[131] The Dniester Commission then has the responsibility to study the facts and circumstances of the case, and submit its findings and recommendations to the parties.

Joint institutions are often afforded the power to make decisions by consensus. In the case of the 1898 Convention between the US and Mexico, for example, it is provided that 'if both Commissioners shall agree to a decision, their judgement shall be considered binding upon both Governments'.[132] Under the

---

(adopted 26 June 1945), 1 UNTS XVI.

[130] Article 14, 1994 China-Mongolia Agreement (n 6); Article 7, 1959 Greece-Yugoslavia Agreement (n 84); Article 8, 2002 Meuse Agreement (n 84); Article 7(4), 1994 OKACOM Agreement (n 100); Article 20, 1987 Niger Basin Convention (n 57); Article 9, Agreement Between the Government of the People's Republic of Bangladesh and the Government of the Republic of India on Sharing of the Ganges Waters at Farakka and on Augmenting its Flows (adopted 5 November 1977) <http://gis.nacse.org/tfdd/tfdddocs/394ENG.pdf> accessed 8 July 2024; Article 20, 2003 Carpathians Convention (n 12); Article 8, 1978 Kaliba-Korubal River Agreement (n 108); Article 30, 2009 Finland-Sweden Agreement (n 84).

[131] Article 25(1), 2012 Dniester Convention (n 6). See also Article 21(2), 2004 Zambezi Agreement (n 26); Article 6, 1925 Lake of Woods Agreement (n 89); Article 7, Agreement Between Finland and the Soviet Union Concerning Frontier Watercourses (with Exchange of Letters) (adopted 24 April 1964), 537 UNTS 252; Article 17(1), 1990 Nigeria-Niger Agreement (n 5); Article 12, 1989 Souris Agreement (n 18); Article 8, 1968 Bulgaria-Turkey Agreement (n 37); Article 13, Agreement for the Multiple Uses of the Resources of the Upper Basin of the Bermejo River and the Grande de Tarija River (adopted 9 June 1995), 3445 UNTS 2; Article 58(1), 1975 Uruguay Statute (n 117); Article 9(1), Indus Waters Treaty (n 6); Article 38, Convention Instituting the Definitive Statute of the Danube (adopted 23 July 1921) <http://www.forost.ungarisches-institut.de/pdf/19210723-1.pdf> accessed 8 July 2024; Articles 17 and 18, Guarani Aquifer Agreement (n 7); Article 24, 1994 Danube Convention (n 3); Article 34, 1995 Mekong Agreement (n 22), Article IX, 1909 Boundary Waters Treaty (n 5).

[132] Article VIII, Convention Between the United States of America and the United States of Mexico, to Facilitate the Carrying out of the Principles Contained in the Treaty of November 12, 1884, and to Avoid the Difficulty Occasioned by Reason of the Changes which Take Place in the Beds of the Rio Grande and Rio Colorado (adopted 2 December 1898) <https://faolex.fao.org/docs/pdf/bi-51880.pdf> accessed 8 July 2024.

1998 Albufeira Convention, both parties must agree to any resolutions by the joint commission.[133] A slight variation to this model can be seen in the Danube Convention whereby, in adopting recommendations or decisions, the conference of the parties shall make every effort to reach consensus, but where that is not possible, decisions may be made by a four-fifths majority.[134] However, any decisions will not be binding on those parties that did not vote in favour of it.[135]

Another common means by which to resolve disputes is to require states to enter into negotiations and consultations. In the case of some transboundary water agreements, the requirement to enter into negotiations and consultations is established as the first means of dispute settlement, whereas in others, the requirement may come after a joint institution has issued its recommendations.[136]

Some transboundary water agreements provide that, where negotiation and/or consultation fail, the parties can request third-party intervention. Various modes of third-party intervention have been included within transboundary water agreements. Under the 1975 Iran-Iraq Treaty, for example, the parties are required to 'have recourse, within a three-month period, to the good offices of a friendly third state'.[137] Other transboundary water agreements stipulate that if negotiation and consultation are unsuccessful after a certain period, the parties should establish a fact-finding committee. In the case of the 2002 Sava Agreement, for example, the parties agree that if a dispute is not resolved within six months, they will establish a 'Fact-finding Expert Committee'.[138] The Committee is then tasked with developing recommendations as to how the dispute might be resolved. In carrying out its work, the Committee is entitled to receive relevant information from the parties and to enter into the terri-

133 Article 23(4), 1998 Albufeira Convention (n 5).

134 Article 22(4), 1994 Danube Convention (n 3).

135 Article 22(5), ibid.

136 See for example, Article 21, 2004 Zambezi Agreement (n 26); Article 6(2), Treaty Concerning the State Frontier and Neighbourly Relationships Between Iran and Iraq (adopted 6 March 1975) <http://www.internationalwaterlaw.org/documents/regionaldocs/iran-iraq.html> accessed 8 July 2024 (1975 Iran-Iraq Treaty); Article 24, 1972 Senegal Convention (n 26); Article 8, 2000 ORASECOM Agreement (n 37); Article 15, 2002 IncoMaputo Agreement (n 22); Article 2, 1978 Gambia Convention (n 105); Article 9, Agreement Between the Governments of the Republic of Kazakhstan, the Kyrgyz Republic, and the Republic of Uzbekistan on the Use of Water and Energy Resources of the Syr Darya Basin (adopted 17 March 1998) <https://www.fao.org/faolex/results/details/en/c/LEX-FAOC054530/> accessed 8 July 2024 (1998 Syr Darya Agreement); Article 16, Guarani Aquifer Agreement (n 7); Article 26, 1998 Luso-Spanish Convention (n 5).

137 Article 6, 1975 Iran-Iraq Treaty (n 136).

138 Article 22(3), 2002 Sava Agreement (n 8).

tory of the parties in order to 'inspect locations, installations and equipment necessary to its work'.[139] Along similar lines, the 1998 Albufeira Convention requires disputes 'of a predominantly technical nature' to be submitted to an 'inquiry commission'.[140] Under the 1960 Indus Waters Treaty, any difference that falls within a specified scope of the Treaty, i.e., technical in nature, shall be referred to a 'Neutral Expert', who should be an engineer.[141] Decisions of the neutral expert are to be 'final and binding'.[142]

Many transboundary water agreements provide for the option that if disputes are not resolved through negotiation and consultation, or through third-party intervention, then they should be submitted to arbitration or adjudication. In some incidences, the requirement to submit a dispute to arbitration or adjudication only requires the decision of one of the parties. The 1975 Iran-Iraq Treaty, for instance, stipulates that 'should one of the two parties refuse to have recourse to the good offices or should the good-offices procedure fail, the dispute shall be settled by arbitration within a period of no more than one month after the date of such refusal or failure'.[143] Similarly, the 1967 France-Italian Convention requires that 'any disputes relating to the interpretation and application of this Convention which cannot be settled through the diplomatic channel *shall* be submitted for arbitration at the request of *either* party' [emphasis added].[144]

---

139 Article 24, 2002 Sava Agreement (n 8). See also, Article 33, Watercourses Convention (n 2); Article 29(2)(b), Lake Tanganyika Convention (n 7).

140 Article 26, 1998 Albufeira Convention (n 5).

141 Article 9(2), and Annexure F, Indus Water Treaty (n 6).

142 Annexure F, Part 2, para 11, Indus Water Treaty (n 6). See also Raymond Lafitte, 'Expert determination on points of difference referred by the Government of Pakistan under the provisions of the Indus Waters Treaty' (Lausanne, 12 February 2007) <https://mowr.gov.pk/SiteImage/Misc/files/Baglihar%20Expert%20Determination%20(PDF).pdf> accessed 8 July 2024.

143 Article 6(4), 1975 Iran-Iraq Treaty (n 136).

144 Article 13, Franco-Italian Convention Concerning the Supply of Water to the Commune of Menton, Paris, 28 September 1967, 940 UNTS 205. See also, Article 46, 2003 Lake Victoria Protocol (n 47); Article 15, 2002 IncoMaputo Agreement (n 22); Article 12(1), 1959 Nepal-India Agreement (n 9); Article 45, Convention Regarding the Regime of Navigation on the Danube (adopted 18 August 1948) <http://www.danubecommission.org/uploads/doc/convention-en.pdf> accessed 8 July 2024; Article 16, 1998 Rhine Convention (n 22); Article 19, 1967 Austria-Czechoslovakia Treaty (n 5); Article 25, Agreement Between the Government of the Republic of Austria and the Government of the Federal Republic of Germany and of the Free state of Bavaria Concerning the Donaukraft werk-Jochenstein-Aktiengesellschaft (Danube Power-Plant and Jochenstein Joint-Stock Company), (adopted 13 February 1952) <http://gis.nacse.org/tfdd/tfdddocs

Other transboundary water agreements simply stipulate that if a dispute is not resolved after a certain period, it must be submitted to arbitration or adjudication.[145] A further approach is for agreements to simply provide states with the option of submitting their dispute to arbitration or adjudication without making it compulsory. For instance, the 1955 Lake Lugano Convention simply provides that 'any dispute concerning the interpretation or application of this Convention, which could not be settled by negotiation, may be submitted, at the request of either Government, to the International Court of Justice'.[146]

In terms of the appropriate forums for arbitration and adjudication, transboundary water agreements offer a range of options, including *ad hoc* courts of arbitration (with their procedures usually set out within the treaty itself),[147]

/164ENG.pdf> accessed 8 July 2024; Article 15, 1944 Upper Columbia Basin Agreement (n 62).

[145] See for example 1986 Lesotho Highlands Treaty (n 25); Article 17, 1978 Kosi Canal Agreement (n 21); Article 69, 1960 Netherlands-Germany Treaty (n 105); Article 12, 1930 Swiss-French Convention (n 84); Article 13, Agreement Between Italy and Switzerland on the Reno di Lei Hydraulic Concession (adopted 18 June 1949), *Legislative Texts and Treaty Provisions Concerning the Utilisation of International Rivers for Other Purposes Than Navigation* (UN, New York 1968); Article 24, 1972 Senegal Convention (n 26); Article 11, State Treaty Between the Grand Duchy of Luxembourg and the Land Rhineland-Palatinate in the Federal Republic of Germany Concerning the Construction of Hydroelectric Power-Installations on the Our (adopted 10 July 1958) <http://gis.nacse.org/tfdd/tfdddocs/224ENG.pdf> accessed 8 July 2024; Article 33, 1954 Lake Constance Treaty (n 103); Article 22, State Treaty Between the Grand Duchy of Luxembourg and the *Land* Rhineland-Palatinate in the Federal Republic of Germany Concerning the Construction of a Hydro-Electric Powerplant on the Sauer (Sure) at Rosport/Ralingen (adopted 25 April 1950) <http://gis.nacse.org/tfdd/tfdddocs/1011ENG.pdf> accessed 8 July 2024; Article 8, 2000 ORASECOM Agreement (n 37); Article 17, 1990 Nigeria-Niger Agreement (n 5); Article 12, 1989 Souris Agreement (n 18); Article 9, Indus Waters Treaty (n 6); Article 7, 1958 Lake Lannoux Agreement (n 16); Article 11, 1996 Mahakali River Treaty (n 84); Article 23, 1978 Gambia Convention (n 105); Article 9, 1987 Moselle Agreement (n 18); Article 9, 1998 Syr Darya Agreement (n 136); Article 29, Lake Tanganyika Convention (n 7); Article 19, Guarani Aquifer Agreement (n 7); Article 26, 1998 Luso-Spanish Convention (n 5); Article 7, 1963 Niger Basin Act (n 102); Article 24, 1994 Danube Convention (n 3).

[146] Article 11, 1955 Lake Lugano Convention (n 101). See also Article 60, 1975 Uruguay Statute (n 117).

[147] See for example, Article 19, 1967 Austria-Czechoslovakia Treaty (n 5); Article 15, 1944 Upper Columbia Basin Agreement (n 62); Article 12, 1989 Souris Agreement (n 18); Article 9, Indus Waters Treaty (n 6); Article 7, 1958 Lake Lannoux Agreement (n 16); Article 11, 1996 Mahakali River Treaty (n 84).

the International Court of Justice,[148] the Commission of Conciliation and Arbitration of the Organisation of African Unity,[149] the SADC Tribunal,[150] and the East African Court of Justice.[151]

4.5 CONCLUSION

An analysis of the provisions of transboundary water agreements reveals that they do not contain CIMs, and only a few have explicit provisions related to the monitoring and review of implementation and compliance. In that respect, they can be contrasted with the general practice of MEAs, which tend to, at a minimum, provide an enabling provision establishing CIMs. The closest references to such mechanisms can be found in the Sava Agreement and its call to establish a methodology for permanently monitoring the implementation of the agreement, and the provision in the 2004 Zambezi Agreement that allows parties to self-report incidences of non-compliance.[152] However, these provisions only provide elements of a CIM.

While explicit CIMs are therefore not found within transboundary water agreements, it is evident that some of their key features, i.e., monitoring and reporting, reviewing implementation and compliance, and addressing incidences of weak implementation or non-compliance, are at least indirectly and/or partially covered within the provisions of transboundary water agreements.

In relation to monitoring and reporting, treaty practice clearly demonstrates a commitment by states to exchange data and information on transboundary waters. However, there is significant variation in the type of data and information that states might be obliged to exchange. These commitments tend to fall short of explicitly requiring states to systematically share data and information on their progress in implementing and/or complying with the provisions of a transboundary water agreement. Rather, the obligation to exchange data and information tends to focus on the conditions of the waters and plans and activities that may affect those conditions. A question that can therefore be asked is whether states should more systematically report on the implementation of key provisions of a transboundary water agreement.

---

148 See for example, Article 11, 1955 Lake Lugano Convention (n 101). See also Article 60, 1975 Uruguay Statute (n 117).

149 See for example, Article 7, Convention and Statute Relating to the Development of the Chad Basin (adopted 22 May 1964) <https://faolex.fao.org/docs/pdf/cmr1076.pdf> accessed 8 July 2024; Article 23, Gambia Convention (n 105); Article 17, 1990 Nigeria-Niger Agreement (n 5).

150 Article 7(2), SADC Revised Protocol (n 35).

151 Article 46, 2003 Lake Victoria Protocol (n 47).

152 Article 20(1), ibid.

Along similar lines, monitoring obligations within transboundary water agreements tend not to focus on monitoring progress in implementing the agreement *per se* or ensuring the parties are in compliance with their commitments. With exceptions such as the Sava Agreement, most provisions relating to monitoring tend to focus on monitoring the conditions of the waters.

The development of joint strategies, plans and programmes can offer an important means by which to support the implementation of any agreement and to demonstrate commitment by the parties beyond the adoption of the agreement itself. While limited, the recognition of the importance of such strategies, plans and programmes is evident in the provisions of some transboundary water agreements, such as the 2003 Lake Tanganyika Convention, which clearly demonstrates a commitment to adopt a programme of measures to support the implementation of the Convention and to monitor the progress of such activities.

As noted above, transboundary water agreements tend to fall short of requiring their parties to systematically share data and information on progress in implementing treaty commitments. However, some exceptions do exist, such as the commitment under the 1998 Albufeira Convention to report annually on actions established to implement the Convention, and their effectiveness. While this commitment clearly calls for regular reporting, it is still limited in that the parties are not required to systematically report on the implementation of all key provisions of the Convention, but rather on the actions that they have chosen to adopt.

The provision of public information also provides an important means by which non-state actors can monitor treaty implementation and compliance. A review of treaty practice demonstrates a trend towards public access to information, which also aligns with broader commitments that countries have entered into to support public participation in environmental matters.[153] However, these requirements tend to be couched in broad terms, i.e., providing the public with information on the conditions of the waters or measures adopted. Specific requirements to provide information to the public on progress in implementing and complying with the provisions of a transboundary water agreements tend to be limited. One exception is the 2012 Great Lakes Protocol, which obliges the parties to report on progress in achieving the objectives of the treaty. However, this is still a relatively broad commitment

---

[153] See for example, the Convention on Access to Information, Public Participation in Decision-making and Access to Justice in Environmental Matters (adopted 25 June 1998, entered into force 30 October 2001), 2161 UNTS 447; and the Regional Agreement on Access to Information, Public Participation and Justice in Environmental Matters in Latin America and the Caribbean (adopted 4 March 2018, entered into force 22 April 2021), 3397 UNTS.

compared to reporting on progress in implementing and complying with key provisions of an agreement.

Joint institutions, such as river basin organisations, are clearly central to any process by which treaty compliance and implementation might be reviewed. It is also evident from a review of transboundary water agreements that the establishment of such institutions is common practice. The text of transboundary water agreements illustrates that there is considerable variation in the structure, mandate and tasks of these joint institutions. However, a key common feature is that decision-making ultimately rests with the parties to the agreement. This has important implications in terms of reviewing implementation and compliance, given that the parties themselves are ultimately responsible for reviewing their own practice. While some transboundary water agreements provide their respective joint institutions with a mandate to support the implementation of the agreement, only a few agreements provide an explicit requirement for the joint institution to periodically review implementation and compliance. This finding is not surprising given that, as noted above and unlike the experience of MEAs, there is not a common practice of parties systematically and periodically reporting to a joint institution on progress in implementing the key provisions of a transboundary water agreement.

Along similar lines, while there is an emerging trend to provide non-state actors with a right to participate in the decision-making processes of joint institutions, few agreements provide specific opportunities for the public to engage in the review of treaty implementation and compliance.

Finally, in relation to addressing incidences of weak implementation and non-compliance, most transboundary water agreements rely on more traditional approaches to dispute settlement, including provisions concerning negotiation and consultation, third-party fact-finding, arbitration and adjudication. At the same time, joint institutions often play a central role in managing any incidences of weak implementation or non-compliance. However, as these institutions ultimately represent the consensus opinion of parties, they may be limited in what they can do. Here, the 2004 Zambezi Agreement, with its provision that a party can self-report an incidence of non-compliance, offers an interesting exception to the general approach of transboundary water agreements.

Ultimately, a review of transboundary water agreements shows that while certain features of CIMs can be found within the treaty practice of states, this practice falls well short of that of MEAs, where such mechanisms are commonplace. This raises the question of whether some of the basic provisions contained within transboundary water agreements are sufficient to promote implementation and compliance, such as obligations to exchange data and information, to establish a joint institution, and to settle disputes by peaceful means. Alternatively, could the implementation of transboundary water agreements be enhanced through the inclusion of more specific provisions that oblige their parties to periodically and systematically report on progress in implementing key provisions, provide a joint institution with a specific mandate to review those periodic reports, and include opportunities to address incidences of weak implementation and non-compliance in a collaborative, transparent and non-adversarial manner? A related question that might be considered is whether such mechanisms need to be included within the text of a transboundary water agreement, or whether the parties could develop mechanisms through subsequent decisions of their decision-making body. This latter approach would be similar to the practice of MEAs, where the details of any CIMs tend to be elaborated by the parties through decisions taken within the meeting of the parties.

Finding an answer to these types of questions requires analysis that goes beyond the transboundary water agreements themselves and considers how they are implemented in practice. Following the review of global and regional approaches to treaty compliance and implementation in the next chapter, these questions will therefore be revisited through a study of practice in the Danube, the lower Mekong and the Orange-Senqu river basins.

5. Global and regional approaches to treaty implementation and compliance

5.1 INTRODUCTION

As noted in the previous chapter, much of the law applicable to the protection and use of transboundary waters has been developed through the practice of states entering into bilateral, basin and sub-basin agreements. At the global level, there have however been notable attempts to develop a set of widely accepted rules and principles applicable to transboundary waters. The adoption of the Convention on the Law of the Non-navigational Uses of International Watercourses (Watercourses Convention) and the amendment of the Convention on the Protection and Use of Transboundary Watercourses and International Lakes (Water Convention) are the most significant milestones in the attempt to develop widely accepted rules and principles applicable to the world's transboundary rivers, lakes and aquifers.[1] In addition to these instruments operating at a global level, important legal developments have also taken place at the regional level, such as through the adoption of the European Union (EU) Directive 2000/60/EC establishing a framework for Community action in the field of water policy (EU Water Framework Directive) and the Southern African Development Community (SADC) Revised Protocol on Shared Watercourses in the Southern African Development Community (Revised SADC Protocol).[2] While the Watercourses Convention does not possess an

[1] Convention on the Law of the Non-navigational Uses of International Watercourses (adopted 21 May 1997, entry into force 17 August 2014), 36 ILM 700; Convention on the Protection and Use of Transboundary Watercourses and International Lakes (adopted 17 March 1992, entered into force 6 October 1996), 1936 UNTS 269 (Water Convention).

[2] Directive 2000/60/EC of 23 October 2000 establishing a framework for Community action in the field of water policy [2000] OJ L 327/1 (EU Water Framework Directive); and Revised Protocol on Shared Watercourses in the Southern African Development Community (adopted 7 August 2000, entered into force 22 September 2003), 40 ILM 321 (Revised SADC Protocol).

institutional framework, such as regular sessions of a meeting of the parties or a secretariat, the other instruments are hosted in institutions, such as the EU, SADC and UN Economic Commission for Europe (UNECE), which to a greater or lesser extent monitor compliance and implementation.

The aim of this chapter is therefore to explore these institutions in greater detail. In so doing, the chapter will focus on two levels. Firstly, it will consider how these institutions monitor and support their respective agreements, i.e., the EU Water Framework Directive, the Revised SADC Protocol, and the Water Convention; and secondly, the chapter will consider how these institutions support compliance and implementation of bilateral, basin and sub-basin water agreements. In exploring both these levels, the chapter will consider the extent to which the respective institutions contain elements of compliance and implementation mechanisms (CIMs) either explicitly or implicitly.

Such an analysis would be incomplete without also considering the Sustainable Development Goals (SDGs) and the introduction of SDG indicator 6.5.2 on the proportion of transboundary basin area covered by operational arrangements.[3] While states have no legal obligation to report on the attainment of the SDGs, there is a system in place for periodic reporting, and indicator 6.5.2 specifically calls upon states to report on their transboundary water agreements. Prior to considering the Water Convention, the EU Water Framework Directive and the Revised SADC Protocol, this chapter will therefore examine the role of the SDGs in supporting the implementation of and compliance with transboundary water agreements.

5.2 THE SDGS AND TRANSBOUNDARY WATER AGREEMENTS

The UN General Assembly adopted the 2030 Agenda for Sustainable Development on 25 September 2015.[4] Through its 17 SDGs, the 2030 Agenda sets forth a transformative agenda for people, planet, prosperity and partnership.[5] Both in terms of scale and level of ambition, the SDGs go beyond previ-

---

[3] See UNECE and UNESCO, Integrated Monitoring Guide for SDG 6 – Step-by-Step Monitoring Methodology for Indicator 6.5.2 on Transboundary Cooperation (Version 11 January 2017) <https://www.unwater.org/app/uploads/2017/05/Step-by-step-methodology-6-5-2_Revision-2017-01-11_Final-1.pdf> accessed 9 July 2024.

[4] Transforming our World: the 2030 Agenda for Sustainable Development, UNGA Res 70/1 (21 October 2015).

[5] Ibid, 2. See also Barbara Adams, 'Commentary on Special Issue: Knowledge and Politics in Setting and Measuring SDGs Numbers and Norms' (2019) 10 Global Policy 157.

ous global commitments related to sustainable development, such as Agenda 21 and the Millennium Development Goals.[6]

In addition to the SDGs themselves, the UN General Assembly adopted a series of targets to guide progress in achieving the goals.[7] The SDG water-related targets reflect the general level of ambition of the SDGs, i.e., to be holistic in not only encompassing the provision of safe drinking water and adequate sanitation, but also broader sustainable water management challenges, including the need for integrated water resources management (IWRM), water-related ecosystems protection, water-use efficiency, pollution prevention, capacity building and local community participation.[8]

Another important step in the evolution of the SDG framework was to develop a set of indicators to accompany these targets. Overall co-ordination for this task fell to the UN Statistical Commission, which at its 46th session on 6 March 2015 created the Inter-Agency and Expert Group on the Sustainable Development Goals (IAEG-SDGs) to oversee the development and implementation of such a framework.[9]

The most pertinent SDG target related to transboundary water cooperation is SDG target 6.5, which calls upon countries to 'by 2030, implement integrated water resources management at all levels, including through transboundary cooperation as appropriate'.[10] In 2015, UN-Water, the co-ordination mechanism of UN entities and international organisations working on water and sanitation issues, proposed an indicator on the 'percentage of transboundary basin area with an operational arrangement for water cooperation'.[11] An arrangement

---

[6] Agenda 21, in 'Report of the United Nations Conference on Environmental and Development' (Rio de Janeiro, 3–14 June 1992), UN Doc A/Conf.151/26/Rev.1; United Nations Millennium Declaration, UNGA Res 55/2 (18 September 2000).

[7] Work of the Statistical Commission pertaining to the 2030 Agenda for Sustainable Development, UNGA Res 71/313 (10 July 2017).

[8] Ibid.

[9] UN Statistical Commission, 'Report on the Forty-Sixth Session' (3–6 March 2015), UN Doc E/2015/24-E/CN.3/2015/40, 12. See also United Nations, Economic and Social Council, 'Report of the Friends of the Chair Group on Broader Measures of Progress', UN Doc E/CN.3/2015/2 (16 September 2014); UN Statistical Commission, 'Report of the Forty-sixth session' (3–6 March 2015), UN Doc E/2015/24-E/CN.3/2015/40. The IAEG-SDGs was comprised of 27 representatives from national statistical offices, the Chair of the Statistical Commission as *ex officio* member, as well as several groups of observers, including representatives of UN agencies and regional commissions.

[10] See (n 4), 18.

[11] See UN Statistical Division, 'Inputs from agencies and other entities on indicator proposals and metadata (as of 15 June 2015)', <https://unstats.un.org/

was to be considered 'operational' if four criteria could be satisfied, namely that a joint institutional structure exists, such as a river basin organisation; the countries in question, on average, exchange data and information at least once a year; the countries in question meet, on average, once a year; and the countries in question have adopted joint or co-ordinated management plans or objectives.[12] This indicator, which became SDG indicator 6.5.2, was approved in 2017 by UN General Assembly Resolution 71/31.[13]

Two UN agencies (UN Educational, Scientific and Cultural Organization (UNESCO) and UNECE) were tasked with developing the indicator and its underlying methodology.[14] As part of this process, they tested the indicator in five countries (Jordan, the Netherlands, Peru, Senegal and Uganda).[15] The indicator was also subject to expert review by all UN-Water members and partners, as well as a public consultation process.[16] Following this testing phase and subsequent refinement of the indicator methodology, UNECE and UNESCO invited countries in early 2017 to report on their basin areas covered by operational arrangements.[17] A total of 107 out of the 153 UN member states sharing transboundary waters engaged in the first exercise.[18] As no similar exercise had been carried out by UN member states at a global level, receiving responses from over two-thirds of countries sharing transboundary waters can be seen as a significant milestone in the global monitoring of transboundary water cooperation.

---

sdgs/meetings/iaeg-sdgs-meeting-01/> accessed 9 July 2024. UN-Water argued that such an indicator 'constituted a significant increase in the aspiration regarding water management compared to previous international commitment', see UN-Water, 'Statement to the 2nd IAEG-SDG meeting in Bangkok' (26–28 October 2015) <https://unstats.un.org/sdgs/files/meetings/iaeg-sdgs-meeting-02/Statements/UNSSO%20statement_Goal%206%20-%20Oct%202015.pdf> accessed 9 July 2024, 2.

12 See UNECE and UNESCO (n 3).

13 See (n 7). See also UN Statistical Commission, 'Report of the Inter-Agency and Expert Group on Sustainable Development Goal Indicators', UN Doc E/CN.3/2016/2/Rev. 1 (19 February 2016), 46.

14 UN-Water, 'A Post-2015 Global Goal for Water' (January 2014) <https://www.unwater.org/sites/default/files/app/uploads/2017/05/UNWater_technical_advice_post_2015_global_goal_ES_final_highres.pdf> accessed 15 January 2025.

15 Ibid.

16 Ibid. See also Alistair Rieu-Clarke and others, 'Advances in monitoring transboundary water cooperation? Reflecting on the development and implementation of SDG indicator 6.5.2' (2022) 47(3) Water International 438, 440–442.

17 UNECE and UNESCO, 'Progress on Transboundary Water Cooperation – Global baseline for SDG Indicator 6.5.2', UN Doc ECE/MP.WAT/57 (2018), 23.

18 Ibid.

In the initial exercise, UNECE and UNESCO invited countries to complete a reporting template.[19] There were four main sections to the template. The first section asked countries for the basic information to calculate the SDG 6.5.2 indicator value, including the name of any transboundary basins (rivers, lakes and aquifers) that they share, the surface area of those basins, and whether or not any operational arrangement covers the basin.[20] Countries then substantiated their calculation of any basin area covered by an operational arrangement in section II of the template.[21] In section II, countries described what arrangements apply to their basins and also provided information on the subjects or topics covered by those arrangements. Additionally, if countries had established joint bodies to support the implementation of their arrangements, they were able to provide information on those joint bodies, including their structure, tasks and activities, and the frequency of their meetings. Section II of the template also asked a series of questions designed to assess the degree to which any arrangements are implemented, including whether and how frequently data and information is exchanged, whether any system is in place for the joint monitoring and assessment of transboundary waters, whether any joint or co-ordinated management plans or objectives have been set, and whether countries had implemented measures related to water quality standards, accidental pollution, extreme weather events and critical situations, and public participation.[22] The third section of the template then asks countries to report on the national laws and policies that supported the implementation of their transboundary arrangements.[23] Finally, the fourth section of the template asks countries more general questions on the main challenges and achievements they faced in progressing transboundary water cooperation.[24]

Out of the 107 countries that responded to the first monitoring exercise, only eight countries failed to complete the full reporting template.[25] In most instances, the reason for not completing the template was because the country's share of any transboundary basin area was considered insignificant, i.e., Brunei, Kuwait, Qatar, Morocco and Monaco, or they had not adopted arrangements with their neighbours, i.e., Chile and the Republic of Korea.[26] In the case of Canada, rather than providing a completed template, the first

19 Ibid, 59–71.
20 Ibid, 59–60.
21 Ibid, 61–67.
22 Ibid.
23 Ibid, 68–70.
24 Ibid, 71.
25 See Rieu-Clarke and others (n 16), 451.
26 Ibid.

section was completed and a letter was submitted to UNECE and UNESCO that described the current coverage of operational arrangements.[27]

In terms of outcomes, the first monitoring exercise suggested that only 17 countries had operational arrangements in place for all their transboundary basins.[28] However, while 107 countries responded to the first monitoring exercise, the custodian agencies were only able to calculate the overall SDG indicator value for 62 of those countries.[29] The average indicator value for those 62 countries was 59%. In other words, on average, operational arrangements covered 59% of the transboundary basin area in each of those 62 countries.[30]

In some respects, the first monitoring exercise could be seen as a success. The response was high, and the figure of 59% broadly aligned with other global estimates of the coverage of arrangements for transboundary water cooperation.[31] However, the exercise also revealed major data gaps, particularly in relation to transboundary aquifers.[32] Lack of data on transboundary aquifers was a common reason why countries did not report on the full SDG indicator

---

[27] Ibid. In its letter, Canada suggested that the full template was not completed because Canada, 'is not a member of the United Nations Economic Commission for Europe's Convention on the Protection and Use of Transboundary Water Courses and International Lakes, and the United Nations Convention on the Law of the Non-Navigational Uses of International Watercourses', see Letter from Honourable Catherine McKenna, Minister of Environmental and Climate Change (20 June 2017) <https://unece.org/fileadmin/DAM/env/water/activities/Reporting_convention/All_countries/CANADA_Reporting_SDG652_final_20.06.2017.pdf> accessed 9 July 2024. However, this reflects a misunderstanding of the reporting process, given that states were invited to complete the questionnaire irrespective of being party or not to the Watercourses Convention or the Water Convention. In the second reporting cycle, Canada completed all four sections of the reporting template, see 'Template of the second cycle for reporting, Canada', <https://unece.org/sites/default/files/2021-11/Canada_2ndReporting_SDG652_2020_web.pdf> accessed 9 July 2024.

[28] UNECE and UNESCO (n 17), 9.

[29] Ibid.

[30] Ibid.

[31] For example, UNEP, Oregon State University, and FAO estimate that 60% of the world's 263 river and lake basins lack any type of cooperative management framework (see UNEP, Oregon State University, and FAO, *Atlas of International Freshwater Agreements* (UNEP 2002), 7). However, the latter study does not account for transboundary aquifers, and only assesses the existing of agreements rather than operationality. See also Transboundary Water Assessment Programme, *Transboundary River Basins – Status and Trends (Volume 3: River Basins)* (UNEP 2016).

[32] UNECE and UNESCO (n 17), 26.

6.5.2 value.[33] Another challenge related to geographic representation. The majority of the 62 countries where a full indicator value was available were situated in the SDG regions of Northern America and Europe, Latin America and the Caribbean, and sub-Saharan Africa.[34] For the first exercise, the SDG indicator value was only available for 33% of countries in Northern Africa and Western Asia, 28% of countries in Central and Southern Asia, and 8% for Eastern and South-Eastern Asia.[35] Asia was therefore particularly under-represented in the first exercise.

Countries were invited to provide feedback on the first monitoring exercise.[36] A general message from countries was that, while improvements could be made, the methodological approach of the monitoring exercise should be kept.[37] Only minor changes were therefore made to the reporting template.[38] These amendments focused primarily on improving the clarity of the questions and providing countries with more opportunities to comment on their responses.[39] The overall method for calculating the SDG 6.5.2 indicator value remained the same.

A further proposal designed to improve the monitoring exercise was to develop a guide to reporting.[40] The drafting group, made up of around 40

---

33 In the first exercise, only 61 countries were able to report on their transboundary aquifers, while 84 countries were able to report on their transboundary river and lake basins, ibid.

34 Ibid.

35 Ibid.

36 Country feedback was sought during a workshop held by the custodian agencies in Budapest, January 2018; see UNECE and UNESCO, 'Technical Meeting on the Template for Reporting on SDG Indicator 6.5.2 and Under the Water Convention – Report', <https://www.unece.org/fileadmin/DAM/env/documents/2018/WAT/01Jan_16-17_Budapest/Report_template_meeting_Budapest.pdf> accessed 9 July 2024. The custodian agencies also invited countries to provide written feedback in the latter part of 2017. By October 2017, feedback had been received from 16 reporting countries, see UNECE, 'Overview of Comments Received on the Template for Reporting under SDG indicator 6.5.2 and the Water Convention' (2018) <https://www.unece.org/fileadmin/DAM/env/documents/2018/WAT/01Jan_16-17_Budapest/Inf4_Comments_template.pdf> accessed 9 July 2024.

37 Ibid.

38 Decision VIII/1, Reporting under the Convention, in UNECE, 'Report of the Meeting of the parties on its Eighth Session', UN Doc ECE/MP.WAT/54/Add.2 (20 January 2019).

39 Ibid.

40 UNECE, 'Report of the Meeting of the parties on its Eighth Session', UN Doc ECE/MP.WAT/54/Add.2 (20 January 2019).

country representatives from different parts of the world, developed the guide over the course of 2019, and in advance of the second monitoring exercise.[41] In addition to the guide to reporting, the custodian agencies updated the step-by-step methodology for calculating the SDG indicator 6.5.2 based on feedback from countries during the first monitoring exercise.[42] These two guidance documents, and the guide in particular, captured the experience of countries in reporting on transboundary water cooperation during the first monitoring exercise.

Another important means by which to share experience in monitoring transboundary water cooperation was a series of online and face-to-face workshops conducted by the custodian agencies. Regional workshops for Central Africa, Central America, Europe and Central Asia, and the Middle East and North Africa were held over the course of 2019 and 2020.[43] These workshops were supplemented by online events in English, French, Spanish and Russian in the latter part of 2020.[44] Over 400 representatives from more than 70 countries participated in the workshops.[45]

The workshops acted as a precursor to the second monitoring exercise, which commenced at the beginning of 2020, and had a deadline for submission of national reports of 30 June 2020.[46] Building on strong engagement in the first exercise and the aforementioned workshops, there was a significant increase in the number of countries submitting national reports to the second exercise – from 107 during the first to 135.[47] This meant that over 80% of countries sharing transboundary basins responded to the second exercise. The second exercise also saw an increase in the number of countries where it was

41 UNECE, 'Guide to Reporting under the Water Convention and as a Contribution to SDG indicator 6.5.2', UN Doc ECE/MP.WAT/60 (February 2020).

42 UN-Water, 'Integrated Monitoring Guide for SDG 6, Step-by-Step monitoring methodology for SDG indicator 6.5.2 version "2020"', <https://www.unwater.org/sites/default/files/app/uploads/2020/02/SDG_652_Step-by-step_methodology_2020_ENG.pdf> accessed 9 July 2024.

43 See UNECE, 'Guidance materials and information for countries', <https://unece.org/guidance-materials-and-information-countries> accessed 9 July 2024.

44 Ibid.

45 See UNECE, 'Second reporting exercise, 2020/21, on SDG indicator 6.5.2', <https://unece.org/second-reporting-exercise-202021-sdg-indicator-652> accessed 9 July 2024.

46 Ibid.

47 UNECE and UNESCO, 'Progress on Transboundary Water Cooperation – Global Status of SDG indicator 6.5.2 and Acceleration Needs 2021', UN Doc ECE/MP.WAT/65 (2021), 10.

possible to calculate the full SDG indicator value, with the indicator available for 101 countries compared to 67 in the first exercise.[48]

The increase in the number of countries submitting national reports resulted in an increase in the global coverage of the indicator. Most notably, more countries from across Asia submitted reports. The indicator value was available for ten countries within Central, Eastern, Southern and South-Eastern Asia compared to only two countries during the first exercise.[49] However, this still only represents 40% of all countries sharing transboundary basins within the region.

The second monitoring exercise re-emphasised the findings of the first exercise by showing that only a minority of countries had all their transboundary basins covered by operational arrangements, namely 24 countries. The average indicator value also remained almost unchanged from 59% in 2017 to 58% in 2020.[50] The 1% fall was attributed to improvements in the quality of data rather than a decline in the coverage of operational arrangements.[51] A key message coming out of the second monitoring exercise was that a major effort was still needed to increase the coverage of operational arrangements across transboundary rivers, lakes and aquifers.[52]

The third monitoring exercise took place in 2023 and received 129 responses, which included responses from seven countries that submitted reports for the first time.[53] There was also an improvement in the quality of data submitted to the third monitoring exercise, with the SDG indicator 6.5.2 value being available for 117 countries in 2023 compared to 101 in 2020.[54] The average SDG indicator value in 2023 was calculated at 59%, which means that it did not change significantly from 2020.[55] Similarly, the number of countries with all their transboundary waters covered by operational arrangements did not change much between the second and third exercise, i.e., from 24 to 26 countries.[56]

A positive message from the SDG indicator 6.5.2 monitoring exercise was the recognition that in some instances the exercise itself had triggered

48 Ibid.

49 Ibid.

50 Ibid.

51 Ibid, 14.

52 Ibid, xv.

53 UNECE, UNESCO and UN-Water, 'Progress on Transboundary Water Cooperation: Mid-term status of SDG indicator 6.5.2 – with a special focus on Climate Change', UN Doc ECE/MP.WAT/76 (2024), 13.

54 Ibid.

55 Ibid, 21.

56 Ibid, 68–74.

cooperation between countries.[57] While countries are ultimately responsible for submitting their own national reports, there were examples of countries entering into a dialogue with their neighbours in order to improve the quality of their reports.[58] In addition, the SDG indicator 6.5.2 monitoring exercise had revealed critical data gaps, especially in relation to transboundary aquifers. States had then used the monitoring exercise as a means by which to secure additional funding and technical support to address those gaps.[59]

A key challenge that was revealed in both the first and second monitoring exercises related to the compatibility of data. An analysis of SDG indicator 6.5.2 data at the basin level revealed that countries are not always consistent in their assessment of whether a basin is operational or not, or they may rely on different data to make their determination. For example, in the case of the Nile Basin, Egypt declared that the part of the basin within its territory is operational based on the agreement it adopted with Sudan in 1959.[60] In contrast, Uganda relies on the interim arrangements establishing the Nile Basin Initiative in 1999 to claim that the part of the Nile Basin within Ugandan territory is covered by an operational arrangement.[61] In some instances, countries even questioned the states that share a particular basin. For example, in the case of the Okavango Basin, Zimbabwe claims that 21,891 km^2 of the basin is situated within its territory and there is no operational arrangement in place.[62] However, the reports of Angola, Botswana and Namibia do not list Zimbabwe as a country sharing the Okavango Basin, and claim that an operational arrangement is in place, namely the 1994 OKACOM Agreement.[63]

---

57 UNECE and UNESCO (n 47), 31–32.

58 Ibid.

59 Ibid, 39–44.

60 Agreement between the Republic of Sudan and the United Arab Republic for the Full Utilization of the Nile Waters (adopted 8 November 1959), 6519 UNTS 64. See also, 'Template for the second cycle for reporting, Egypt' (29 January 2021) <https://unece.org/national-country-reports-sdg-indicator-652> accessed 9 July 2024.

61 See 'Template for the second cycle for reporting, Uganda' (30 June 2020) <https://unece.org/national-country-reports-sdg-indicator-652> accessed 9 July 2024.

62 See 'Template for the second cycle for reporting, Zimbabwe' (5 June 2020) <https://unece.org/national-country-reports-sdg-indicator-652> accessed 9 July 2024.

63 Agreement between the Governments of Angola, the Republic of Botswana and the Republic of Namibia on the establishment of a Permanent Okavango River Basin Water Commission (adopted 15 September 1994) <https://faolex.fao.org/docs/pdf/mul17435.pdf> accessed 9 July 2024; see also, 'Template for the second cycle for reporting, Angola' (13 July 2020) <https://unece.org/national-country

While these types of discrepancies exist, the reports also show that some countries, usually through their joint institutions, made efforts to co-ordinate their reports and ensure a consistent picture was presented at the basin level. In the case of Hungary, for example, drafts of their report were shared with neighbouring states via their bilateral commissions.[64] The need to improve the co-ordination of national reports at the basin level is also something that UNECE and UNESCO, as custodian agencies for SDG indicator 6.5.2, stressed during the third reporting exercise.[65]

The introduction of SDG indicator 6.5.2 on the coverage of operational arrangements for transboundary water cooperation, and its evolution through the three monitoring exercises, demonstrates a significant development at the global level. From a political standpoint, the inclusion of SDG target 6.5 and SDG indicator 6.5.2 within the SDG framework was already an important milestone in recognising the critical value of transboundary water cooperation at the global level. The fact that so many countries sharing transboundary waters have engaged in the monitoring cycles demonstrates a strong, and almost universal, commitment to the exercise. Such strong engagement has also meant that the results of the exercise are able to feed into decision-making processes. For example, SDG indicator 6.5.2 data feeds into the annual *Sustainable Development Goals Report*, which is the only UN official report to monitor global progress on the 2030 Agenda,[66] and informs the discussions and outcomes of the annual UN High-Level Political Forum on Sustainable Development, which is the central platform by which the UN reviews SDG progress.[67] SDG indicator 6.5.2 data has also informed discussions during the UN Water Conference 2023 and is reflected in subsequent calls to accelerate

-reports-sdg-indicator-652> accessed 9 July 2024; 'Template for the second cycle for reporting, Botswana' (26 June 2020) <https://unece.org/national-country-reports-sdg-indicator-652> accessed 9 July 2024; and 'Template for the second cycle for reporting, Namibia' (30 June 2020) <https://unece.org/national-country-reports-sdg-indicator-652> accessed 9 July 2024.

64 See UNECE (n 41), 7.

65 See UNECE and UNESCO, 'Opportunities to Coordinate with Neighbouring Countries When Completing the SDG Indicator 6.5.2 National Report', <https://unece.org/sites/default/files/2023-03/Coordination_document_SDG_Indicator_652_EN.pdf> accessed 9 July 2024.

66 See for example, UN, *The Sustainable Development Goals Report 2023* (UN 2023).

67 Format and organisational aspects of the high-level political forum on sustainable development, UNGA Res 67/290 (23 August 2013).

progress in the adoption of agreements and other arrangements for transboundary water cooperation.[68]

To some extent, SDG indicator 6.5.2 shares some similarities with CIMs. Countries sharing transboundary waters are asked to periodically submit national data related to their transboundary basins and the arrangements that they have in place. The format of the reports is also set out in the reporting template. Moreover, as noted above, this template not only asks countries to set out the basins they share and the arrangements they have adopted but also invites countries to share information on both the content of those arrangements and the progress in their implementation.[69] In addition, countries are invited to report on the main difficulties and challenges they face in implementing their arrangements.[70] In theory, along the lines of reporting mechanisms found in multilateral environmental agreements (MEAs), the SDG indicator 6.5.2 template therefore provides the basic means upon which progress in the implementation of, and compliance with, agreements for transboundary water cooperation could be reported and monitored. This is no coincidence given that, as will be discussed further below, the template is based on the reporting requirements of the Water Convention. However, while parties to an agreement are usually under a binding obligation to report on progress in implementing and complying with an agreement, this is not the case for the SDGs. The SDGs themselves are not a legally binding commitment, and while countries are *urged* to submit data in support of the SDG indicators, they are not under a legal obligation to do so.[71] It might even be questioned whether the

---

68 Midterm comprehensive review of the implementation of the International Decade for Action, 'Water for Sustainable Development' (2018–2029, Report of the Secretary-General), UN Doc A/77/249 (29 July 2022); President of the General Assembly, United Nations Conference on the Mid-term Comprehensive Review of the Implementation of the Objectives of the International Decade for Action 'Water for Sustainable Development', 2018–2028, <https://sdgs.un.org/sites/default/files/2023-05/FINAL%20EDITED%20-%20PGA77%20Summary%20for%20Water%20Conference%202023.pdf> accessed 9 July 2024, 11; and UN, 'Interactive dialogue 4: Water for cooperation: transboundary and international water cooperation, cross-sectoral cooperation, including scientific cooperation, and water across the 2030 Agenda for Sustainable Development (Sustainable Development Goal targets 6.5 and 6.b and Goals 16 and 17)' (Concept paper prepared by the secretariat), UN Doc A/CONF.240/2023/7 (31 January 2023).

69 UNECE and UNESCO (n 17).

70 Question 2(e) of the questionnaire asks countries, 'what are the main difficulties and challenges that your country faces with the agreement or arrangement and its implementation, if any?'. Ibid, 63.

71 See UN General Assembly Resolution 71/313 (n 7), and Stephen Schwebel, 'The Effect of Resolutions of the UN General Assembly on Customary

SDG indicator 6.5.2 monitoring exercise would have been so successful if the requirement to report at the global level had been legally binding. The 'soft' nature of the reporting requirement might therefore be seen as an advantage in ensuring that the majority, i.e., over 80%, of countries sharing transboundary waters engage in the exercise.

There are also similarities and differences in the way in which SDG indicator 6.5.2 data is reviewed and the way in which CIMs review data. As with most CIMs, the review of national reports is centralised. UNECE and UNESCO take overall responsibility as designated custodian agencies for the indicator. Through the three-yearly progress reports, these agencies review all nationally submitted data. They then provide a synthesis report that analyses national data. The custodian agencies' reports also highlight general thematic issues, such as data gaps related to transboundary aquifers or the need to strengthen financing for transboundary water cooperation.[72] While this practice may be similar to some CIMs and the task that a body such as a Convention secretariat might carry out, any recommendations included in these reports are of a general nature. In contrast, CIMs are likely to afford a review body more specific tasks of identifying individual incidences of weak implementation or non-compliance. Such a body may also have a mandate to ask any party in question to provide additional data and information related to the issue. UNECE and UNESCO have limited scope to request additional information from countries and do not have the mandate to critically review the data submitted by countries.[73] However, the fact that all national reports are published on the UNECE's website promotes transparency and offers an incentive for countries to submit accurate data.[74] Additionally, the agencies expend considerable effort working with countries to enhance the quality of data submitted, address any data gaps, and rectify any inconsistencies.[75]

Along similar lines, while it is noted above that UNECE and UNESCO feed their analysis into global policy processes, such as the High-Level Political Forum on Sustainable Development, there is no specific mandate for this forum or any other inter-governmental platform to address specific

International Law' (1979) 73 Proceedings of the Annual Meeting (American Society of International Law) 301.

[72] See for example UNECE and UNESCO (n 17), 31–50.

[73] The only exception to this would be where UNECE and UNESCO might notice discrepancies within the national report or that key data to calculate the SDG indicator 6.5.2 value is missing. However, it is up to the country's discretion to respond to any such request (see UNECE and UNESCO (n 17), 23).

[74] See UNECE, 'National country reports on SDG indicator 6.5.2', <https://unece.org/national-country-reports-sdg-indicator-652> accessed 9 July 2024.

[75] UNECE, UNESCO and UN-Water (n 53), 10–17.

incidences of weak implementation or non-compliance. Indirectly, technical and financial assistance might be provided by UN agencies and others to support a country's efforts in implementing and complying with its treaty commitments. This does, however, differ markedly from a CIM where a specific body is usually afforded a mandate to address specific incidences of weak implementation or non-compliance. Other SDG indicators have a stronger link to the provision of financial and technical assistance. For example, an 'SDG IWRM Support Programme' has been developed by Global Water Partnership, UN Environment Programme, Cap-Net and UNEP-DHI Centre on Water and Environment in order to assist governments in designing and implementing country-led responses aimed at improving their IWRM implementation, which is monitored by SDG indicator 6.5.1.[76]

In sum, the SDG indicator 6.5.2 clearly has some similarities with CIMs but also some clear differences. At this stage in its evolution, it cannot therefore claim to serve an implementation and compliance function. However, given the similarities and its notable support among countries, a question that can be asked is whether it could either develop a stronger implementation and review component, or whether it could work alongside other initiatives to support implementation and compliance. This question is further explored in the concluding part of the chapter.

5.3 THE 1992 WATER CONVENTION

5.3.1 Evolution and Normative Content

The Convention on the Protection and Use of Transboundary Watercourses and International Lakes (Water Convention) was adopted on 17 March 1992, and entered into force on 6 October 1996.[77] The text of the Convention builds upon cooperation between member states of the UNECE that dates back to the 1940s.[78] Following a series of declarations, recommendations and decisions related to water management issues, UNECE member states took the decision

---

76 See Global Water Partnership, 'IWRM Support' (*gwp.org*) <https://www.gwp.org/en/sdg6support/> accessed 9 July 2024.

77 Water Convention (n 1).

78 See generally, Alistair Rieu-Clarke, 'Remarks on the Drafting History of the Convention', in Attila Tanzi and others (eds), *The UNECE Convention on the Protection and Use of Transboundary Watercourses and International Lakes – Its contribution to international water cooperation* (Brill 2015).

to elaborate a Water Convention in 1989.[79] Drafting meetings took place in 1990 and 1991, prior to the Convention's adoption in 1992.[80]

As a framework instrument, the Water Convention supplements and supports cooperation between countries sharing transboundary waters.[81] Central to this aim is the requirement in Article 9 for parties to enter into agreements or other arrangements for the transboundary waters that they share, and to establish joint bodies to support the implementation of those arrangements.[82]

In addition, the Water Convention commits its parties to a series of substantive and procedural rights and obligations. The main substantive obligation of the Water Convention is an obligation on parties to 'take all appropriate measures to prevent, control and reduce any transboundary impact'.[83] In complying with this obligation, parties must, *inter alia*, 'ensure that transboundary waters are used with the aim of ecologically sound and rational water management, conservation of water resources and environmental protection'; 'ensure that transboundary waters are used in a reasonable and equitable way'; and 'ensure conservation and, where necessary, restoration of ecosystems'.[84] This substantive obligation shares a lot in common with the Watercourses Convention and its commitments related to equitable and reasonable utilisation, the duty to take all appropriate measures to prevent significant harm, and the protection of ecosystems of international watercourses.[85]

The Water Convention's procedural requirements oblige its parties to *inter alia* set limits for wastewater discharges, apply environmental impact assessment (EIA) and other means of assessment, adopt contingency planning,

---

[79] OSCE, 'Report on Conclusions and Recommendations of the Meeting on the Protection of the Environment of the Conference on Security and Co-operation in Europe' (5 November 1990) <https://www.osce.org/eea/14075> accessed 9 July 2024.

[80] See Rieu-Clarke (n 78).

[81] The preamble to the convention (n 1) emphasises 'that cooperation between member countries in regard to the protection and use of transboundary waters shall be implemented primarily through the elaboration of agreements between countries bordering the same waters, especially where no such agreements have yet been reached'. 'Transboundary waters' are defined within Article 1(1) of the Convention as including, 'any surface or ground waters which mark, cross or are located on boundaries between two or more states.'

[82] Article 9 of the Water Convention (n 1).

[83] Article 2(1), ibid.

[84] Article 2(2), ibid.

[85] See UNECE, 'The Economic Commission for Europe Water Convention and the United Nations Watercourses Convention – An analysis of their harmonised contribution to international water law' (Water Series No 6, Attila Tanzi), UN Doc ECE/MP.WAT/42 (2015).

elaborate joint monitoring programmes, provide for the widest exchange of information, elaborate joint water-quality objectives and criteria, develop concerted action programmes for the reduction of pollution loads, establish early warning and alarm procedures, undertake research and development activities, and ensure that information on the conditions of transboundary waters is shared.[86] In addition, parties to the Water Convention are obliged to settle their disputes 'by negotiation or by any other means of dispute settlement acceptable to the parties to the dispute'.[87]

A notable distinction between the Water Convention and the Watercourses Convention is the former's institutional framework. During the drafting and negotiation of the Watercourses Convention, an institutional framework was proposed.[88] However, when debated by the International Law Commission, there was general feeling that the Article was 'very ambitious', and that the parties should be left with the option to decide whether an institutional framework was warranted upon entry into force of the instrument.[89] With the subsequent opening of the Water Convention, the significant overlap in membership of both Conventions, and the similarities between both instruments, it is unlikely that the parties to the Watercourses Convention would establish such an institutional framework.[90]

The institutional framework of the Water Convention is set out within the text itself. Pursuant to Article 17 of the Convention, the parties commit to holding a meeting of the parties every three years.[91] Through these meetings, the parties commit to keeping the implementation of the Convention under continuous review.[92] In addition, the Water Convention commits the Executive Secretary of UNECE with certain secretariat functions, including convening and preparing meetings of the parties.[93]

---

86 Articles 3–13 of the Water Convention (n 1).

87 Article 22(1), ibid.

88 See, for instance Sixth Report on the Law of the Non-navigational Uses of International Watercourses by Stephen C. McCaffrey, Special Rapporteur, in ILC, 'Report of the International Law Commission on the Work of its 42nd Session' (23 February and 7 June 1990), UN Doc A/CN.4/SER.A/1990/Add.1f (Part 1), 64.

89 ILC, 'Summary Records of the Meetings of the 42nd Session' (1 May – 20 July), UN Doc A/CN.4/SER.A/1990, 84–115.

90 Alistair Rieu-Clarke and Rémy Kinna, 'Can two global UN Water Conventions effectively co-exist? Making the case for a 'package approach' to support institutional coordination' (2014) 23(1) Review of European, Comparative & International Environmental Law 15.

91 Article 17, ibid.

92 Article 17(2), ibid.

93 Article 19, ibid.

Since its creation, this institutional framework, including the secretariat, has proved highly productive in supporting the development and implementation of the Convention.[94] Two additional protocols have been developed: the Protocol on Water and Health, which entered into force in 2005,[95] and the Protocol on Civil Liability, which is yet to enter into force.[96] As well as the secretariat and the meeting of the parties, several bodies support the implementation of the Water Convention, including its Bureau, Working Groups on Integrated Water Resources Management, Monitoring and Assessment, Task Forces on Water and Climate and the Water-Food-Energy-Ecosystem nexus, a Joint Expert Group on Water and Industrial Accidents and an Implementation committee.[97] The parties, mainly through these subsidiary bodies and in accordance with the Convention's programme of work,[98] have developed many guidelines, recommendations, strategies, model provisions, and assessments designed to support the parties in their implementation of the Convention.[99]

---

[94] See Ruby Moynihan, *Transboundary Freshwater Ecosystems in International Law – The Role and Impact of the UNECE Environmental Regime* (CUP 2012).

[95] Protocol on Water and Health to the 1992 Convention on the Protection and Use of Transboundary Watercourses and International Lakes (adopted 17 June 1999, entered into force 4 August 2005), 2331 UNTS 202.

[96] Protocol on Civil Liability and Compensation for Damage Caused by the Transboundary Effects of Industrial Accidents on Transboundary Waters to the 1992 Convention on the Protection and Use of Transboundary Watercourses and International Lakes and the 1992 Convention on the Transboundary Effects of Industrial Accidents (adopted 21 May 2003). The Protocol requires 16 countries to ratify, accept, approve or accede to it before it will enter into force. So far, only Hungary has ratified the instrument.

[97] See Francesca Bernardini, 'The Normative and Institutional Evolution of the Convention', in Attila Tanzi and others (eds), *The UNECE Convention on the Protection and Use of Transboundary Watercourses and International Lakes – Its contribution to international water cooperation* (Brill 2015).

[98] See infra section 5.3.4.

[99] See for example UNECE, 'Updated Strategies for Monitoring and Assessment of Transboundary Rivers, Lakes and Groundwaters', UN Doc ECE/MP.WAT/70 (2023); UNECE, 'Handbook on Water Allocation in a Transboundary Context', UN Doc ECE/MP.WAT/64 (2021); UNECE, 'A Practical Guide for the Development of Agreements or Other Arrangements for Transboundary Water Cooperation', UN Doc ECE/MP.WAT/68 (2021); UNECE, 'Guide to Reporting under the Water Convention and as a Contribution to SDG indicator 6.5.2', UN Doc ECE/MP.WAT/60 (2020); UNECE, 'Principles for Effective Joint Bodies for Transboundary Water Cooperation', UN Doc ECE/MP.WAT/50 (2018); UNECE, 'Model Provisions on Transboundary Groundwaters', UN Doc ECE/MP.WAT/40

A major milestone in the evolution of the Water Convention was the decision taken at the third session of the meeting of the parties in November 2003 to amend the Convention to allow all UN member states to become a party to it.[100] This formal amendment to the Convention became operational in 2016.[101] Since 2016, the opening of the Water Convention has gained significant momentum with Chad and Senegal as the first non-UNECE states to accede in 2018, followed by Ghana in 2020; Guinea-Bissau and Togo in 2021; Cameroon in 2022; Gambia, Iraq, Namibia, Nigeria and Panama in 2023; and the Ivory Coast, Zambia and Zimbabwe in 2024.[102] Through a strategy of engaging with countries from outside the ECE region and involving them in the activities under the Water Convention, the Convention has also gained significant interest from other countries that are at various stages of acceding to it.[103]

5.3.2 Reporting Under the Water Convention

While a reporting mechanism was not envisaged in the original text of the Convention, one was introduced by a decision of the seventh session of the meeting of the parties in November 2015.[104] Through this decision, the parties agreed to conduct a pilot reporting exercise in 2016–2017 in order to test the reporting process, whilst also leaving sufficient time to make any necessary revisions prior to the eighth session of the meeting of the parties in 2018.[105]

The requirement for parties to report under the Water Convention coincided with the SDG indicator 6.5.2 monitoring exercise. Through the use of the same reporting template, the parties to the Water Convention were therefore asked to report on the area of their territory within transboundary basins and the

(2014); and UNECE, 'Guide to Implementing the Water Convention', UN Doc ECE/MP.WAT/39 (2013).

[100] UNECE, 'Amendment to Articles 25 and 26 of the Convention', UN Doc ECE/MP.WAT/14 (2004).

[101] The amendment became effective 90 days after the last ratification by all the parties that had adopted the amendment in 2003 (see UNECE, 'The Global Opening of the Water Convention', UN Doc ECE/WAT/43/Rev.1 (March 2016), 5).

[102] See UN Treaty Collection, '5. Convention on the Protection and Use of Transboundary Watercourses and International Lakes', <https://treaties.un.org/Pages/ViewDetails.aspx?src=treaty&mtdsg_no=xxvii-5&chapter=27&clang=_en> accessed 9 July 2024.

[103] See Strategy for the implementation of the Convention at the global level, in UNECE, 'Report of the Meeting of the parties on its eighth session', UN Doc ECE/MP.WAT/54/Add.2 (30 January 2019).

[104] UNECE, 'Report of the Meeting of the parties on its Seventh Session', UN Doc ECE/MP.WAT/49/Add.2 (7 July 2017).

[105] Ibid.

extent to which that territory was covered by operational arrangements.[106] The parties were also asked to provide further details on the arrangement and joint bodies in place and the degree to which certain provisions of the Water Convention have been implemented.[107] During the first exercise, the template for parties to report on the Water Convention and SDG indicator 6.5.2 differed slightly from the template sent to all countries to report on under SDG indicator 6.5.2.[108] However, the reporting template was subsequently revised into one version used for all countries to report on SDG indicator 6.5.2, and for the parties of the Water Convention to report on both SDG indicator 6.5.2 and the implementation of the Water Convention.[109] The pilot reporting exercise under the Water Convention resulted in 38 out of 40 parties[110] submitting national reports.[111] A second reporting exercise under the Water Convention was subsequently conducted in parallel with the SDG indicator 6.5.2 monitoring exercise during the period 2017–2020, and a third exercise was undertaken in 2023–2024. During the second and third exercises, all parties, except the EU,[112] submitted national reports.[113]

5.3.3 Implementation and Compliance Review

As well as requesting the secretariat to make all national reports available via its website, a decision was taken at the eighth session of the meeting of the

---

[106] Decision VII/2 – Reporting under the Convention, in UNECE, 'Report of the Meeting of the Parties to the Seventh Session', UN Doc ECE/MP.WAT/49/Add.2 (7 July 2016).

[107] Ibid.

[108] The key distinction between the templates was the ordering of the sections.

[109] See Decision VIII/1 (n 38).

[110] While the EU is party to the Convention, only state parties are required to submit reports.

[111] UNECE, 'Report on implementation of the Convention on the Protection and Use of Transboundary Watercourses and International Lakes', UN Doc ECE/MP.WAT/51 (2018), 3.

[112] See n 110.

[113] See UNECE, 'Second Report on Implementation of the Convention on the Protection and Use of Transboundary Watercourses and International Lakes, 2017–2020', UN Doc ECE/MP.WAT/67 (2021); UNECE, 'Third Report on Implementation of the Convention on the Protection and Use of Transboundary Watercourses and International Lakes, 2020–2023', UN Doc ECE/MP.WAT/77 (2024).

parties to request the secretariat to review the national reports and to prepare a synthesis report on the basis of the national reports submitted by the parties.[114]

The subsequent analyses of the national reports by the secretariat during the first three reporting exercises showed that the parties had made considerable progress in the implementation of the Water Convention.[115] Pursuant to Article 9 of the Convention, most transboundary waters shared between parties had arrangements and associated joint bodies in place.[116] The main topics of cooperation covered by the Convention were considered to be well referenced in those arrangements.[117] Progress in implementing arrangements for transboundary waters was also considered to be well advanced, particularly in relation to the development of joint or co-ordinated water management plans, measures to protect ecosystems, the exchange of data and information, and joint monitoring and assessment.[118] However, the synthesis reports by the secretariat also identified certain issues. For instance, the second report observed that:

> Most of the 144 reported transboundary river and lake basins are covered by agreements or arrangements in force, either wholly or partly. However, there are at least 16 river and lake basins and 15 river and lake sub-basins which are not covered by any agreement or arrangement, either wholly or partly.[119]

As noted above, the absence of agreements or arrangements between riparian parties runs contrary to Article 9 of the Water Convention, which obliges parties to enter into 'bilateral or multilateral agreements or other arrangements, where these do not exist … in order to define their mutual relations and conduct regarding the prevention, control and reduction of transboundary impact'.[120] Of the 16 river and lake basins lacking arrangements, four are shared with

---

114 Decision VIII/1 of the eighth session of the Meeting of the Parties tasked the secretariat with the preparation of 'regular reports for future session of the Meeting of the Parties on the implementation of the Convention' (n 38), 35.

115 UNECE (n 111 and 113).

116 UNECE (n 111).

117 Ibid 24–27.

118 Ibid 39–50.

119 UNECE (n 113), 17.

120 Water Convention (n 1).

non-parties;[121] and four of the river basins[122] are of minor transboundary significance due to their size and remoteness. In these cases, parties would not be obliged, pursuant to Article 9, to enter into agreements. However, in the other eight cases,[123] it could be argued that the riparian parties have an obligation to enter into agreements.

The parties provided the secretariat with the mandate to prepare regular synthesis reports 'on the implementation of the Convention', which would be presented at future sessions of the meetings of the parties. This mandate falls short of addressing specific issues where a party's actions may be at variance with its commitments, such as the case of entering into agreements pursuant to Article 9.[124] It is therefore left to the meeting of the parties to decide what to do with the findings of the secretariat's reports.

There is, however, another body of the Water Convention that plays a role in monitoring compliance and implementation, namely the implementation committee. The implementation committee of the Water Convention was established by a decision of the sixth meeting of the parties in 2012.[125] The committee consists of nine members, who are elected by the meeting of the parties, serve in their personal capacity, and represent legal, scientific and/or technical expertise.[126]

Matters may be brought to the attention of the committee by a variety of means. Through an advisory procedure, a party, or parties jointly, may request advice from the committee about any difficulties it is, or they are, facing in the implementation of the convention.[127] Such difficulties may be solely as a result of that party's own capacity, or a party may seek advice concerning a challenge it faces implementing the Convention due to the actions or inactions of another party or of a non-party.[128]

---

[121] Jandari Lake Basin (Azerbaijan and Georgia (non-party)); Astara Chay River Basin (Azerbaijan and Iran (non-party)); Maroni/Marowijne River Basin (France and Suriname (non-party)); and Oipoque/Oyupock/Oyapock River Basin (Brazil (non-party) and France), see UNECE (n 113), 17.

[122] These are the Alta, Reisa, Sandneselva and Skibotn River Basins between Finland and Norway, ibid.

[123] These are the Adige River Basin (Italy and Switzerland); the Banowka, Pregel, and Prohladnaja/Swieza River Basins (Poland and Russian Federation); the Don and Azov Sea Basins (Russian Federation and Ukraine); Elv fra Svartakslvatnet and Karpelva River Basins (Norway and Russian Federation), ibid.

[124] See Decision VIII/1 (n 38).

[125] UNECE (n 113).

[126] Ibid.

[127] Ibid.

[128] Ibid.

Another means of raising an issue, known as a 'self-submission', is where a party considers that despite its best endeavours, it is or will be unable to comply fully with the Convention.[129] Other parties that are, or may be, affected by another party's difficulties in implementing the convention may also make a submission before the implementation committee. This option is known as a 'party-to-party' submission.[130]

In addition, 'where the Committee becomes aware of possible difficulties in the implementation by a party, or the possible non-compliance by a party with the Convention, including from information received from the public, it may request the party concerned to provide the necessary information on the matter'.[131] The party will then have three months to respond,[132] before the committee, based on the response, considers the matter.

During its work, the committee has a range of information-gathering and consultation functions, which include requesting further information, gathering information in the territory of a party, inviting parties and non-parties to attend meetings, seeking services of experts and advisers, and seeking advice from the meeting of the parties or consulting other bodies of the Convention.[133] As can be shown in the cases considered by the committee,[134] having a neutral body in place to establish the facts of a case, and a neutral forum by which to exchange views, can go a long way.

As illustrated above, the reporting mechanism provides an opportunity by which the implementation committee might identify compliance and implementation issues. While the parties did not provide the committee with a formal mandate to review national reports, at its seventh and eighth meetings in 2017 and 2018 the committee reviewed all national reports submitted to the first reporting exercise and came to the conclusion that, 'parties appear to face some difficulties in the implementation of certain provisions of the Convention and there are problems and gaps within specific basins'.[135] An accompanying decision of the eighth meeting of the parties to the Convention noted, 'with concern that certain common challenges to implementation and compliance remain and that some parties appear to face specific challenges

129 Ibid.

130 Ibid.

131 Ibid.

132 Where circumstances dictate, this period can be extended, but must be no later than six months, ibid, 6.

133 Ibid.

134 See *infra* section 5.3.4.

135 UNECE, 'Report of the Implementation Committee to the Meeting of the parties and draft decision on implementation', UN Doc ECE/MP.WAT/2018/8 (30 July 2018), 11.

in implementation and compliance'.[136] The committee went on to encourage 'parties and other stakeholders to seek the Committee's assistance, support and facilitation to address difficulties in implementing and complying with the Convention, so as to ensure that the object and purpose of the Convention are advanced and to prevent water-related disputes'.[137]

During the second and third reporting exercises, the implementation committee chose not to review all national reports but rather relied on the synthesis report produced by the secretariat.[138] Having reviewed the secretariat's second report, the Committee concluded that,

> … the information presented to it did not justify the Committee engaging, at the current stage, in a Committee initiative in accordance with section VII of annex I to decision VI/1 and that it remained open to receiving requests for assistance or submissions from parties facing difficulties in implementing and/or complying with the Convention.[139]

Along similar lines to the aforementioned decision taken at the eighth session of the meeting of the parties, a decision was taken at the ninth session of the meeting of the parties that expressed 'concern that certain common challenges to implementation and compliance remain and that some parties appear to face specific challenges in implementation and compliance'.[140] The committee therefore encouraged 'parties to seek the Committee's assistance, support and facilitation to address difficulties in implementing and complying with the Convention, so as to ensure that the object and the purpose of the Convention are advanced, and to prevent water-related disputes'.[141]

The Committee has therefore appeared to exercise its mandate conservatively. It has not used any data or information that has resulted from the reporting exercises to embark on a 'committee initiative', such as requesting parties to elaborate on the information they provide in their national reports concerning the difficulties they face in implementing the Water Convention.

---

136 UNECE, 'Report of the Implementation Committee to the Meeting of the parties and draft decision on implementation – Addendum', UN Doc ECE/MP.WAT/54/Add.1 (30 January 2019), 58.

137 Ibid.

138 UNECE, 'Report of the Implementation Committee to the Meeting of the parties and Draft Decision on General Issues of Implementation', UN Doc ECE/MP.WAT/2021/5 (6 July 2021), para 34.

139 Ibid, para 36.

140 Decision IX/1 – General issues of implementation, in UNECE (n 114), 6.

141 Ibid.

5.3.4 Addressing Incidences of Non-compliance or Weak Implementation

While the committee has not utilised its 'committee initiative' function to investigate specific issues of compliance or implementation that have been identified through the reporting exercise, it has tackled several specific cases.

In 2013, ECOSOS, an environmental non-governmental organisation (NGO) based in Astana, requested the committee to examine issues relating to the Irtysh River Basin (shared between Russia, Kazakhstan, China and Mongolia) and the Ili River Basin (shared between China and Kazakhstan).[142] In response, the committee wrote to the parties concerned, i.e., Kazakhstan and the Russian Federation, with a request for further information.[143] Having only received a partial response from the Russian Federation, the committee then wrote to both countries asking for more specific information, as well as to the Russian Federation-Kazakhstan Commission on the Joint Use and Protection of Transboundary Waters, and the Kazakhstan-China Joint Commission on the Use and Protection of Transboundary Rivers.[144] By 2016, the committee had only received partial responses to its questions from the Russian Federation and had received no response from Kazakhstan. It therefore decided to gather information from other sources, including the environmental NGO that had first raised the issue.[145] Based on information received by 2017, including from World Wide Fund for Nature (WWF), the Russian Federation, a member of the Irtysh Basin Council, and the Kazakhstan Agency of Environmental Experts, the committee concluded that there were no grounds for further action.[146] At

---

[142] UNECE, 'Report of the Implementation Committee on its second meeting', UN Doc ECE/MP.WAT/IC/2013/4 (13 January 2014), para 4.

[143] Ibid para 5. The Committee asked the Governments to provide information on (a) the technical characteristics of the development activity carried out in the upstream part of the relevant basins; (b) the related monitoring activities and results addressing water quality, water quantity and ecosystems; (c) the impact, if any, of the development activity on the socioeconomic conditions of the local population in the relevant basins; (d) the contribution of the related bilateral agreements to addressing the possible impact of the development activity in question; and (e) the related mitigation measures, taken or planned, as appropriate (UNECE, 'Report of the Implementation Committee on its third meeting', ECE/MP.WAT/IC/2014/2 (18 June 2014), para 8).

[144] UNECE, 'Report of the Implementation Committee on its fourth meeting', UN Doc ECE/MP.WAT/IC/2014/4 (20 January 2015), para 9.

[145] UNECE, 'Report of the Implementation Committee on its sixth meeting', UN Doc ECE/MP.WAT/IC/2016/2 (14 October 2016), para 16.

[146] UNECE, 'Report of the Implementation Committee on its seventh meeting', UN Doc ECE/MP.WAT/IC/2016/4 (11 May 2017), para 14.

the same time, the committee noted the difficulty it had experienced in receiving information from the parties.[147]

The implementation committee received its first country request in November 2019, which was a request from Montenegro concerning the construction of additional small hydropower plants on the Cijevna/Cem River in Albania.[148] At its tenth session in December 2019, the Committee decided to treat the letter as a request for advice purusant to its advisory procedure.[149] Albania subsequently agreed to participate in the procedure.[150] As an advisory procedure, the Committee was keen to stress that its main function was to facilitate the implementation and application of the Convention rather than allege non-compliance by either or both parties.[151]

Initially, the implementation committee gathered information through direct requests to the parties and two separate 'information-gathering and consultation sessions'.[152] The committee then issued its legal and technical advice to both parties, which highlighted the need to set up a joint or co-ordinated monitoring assessment framework for the Cijevna/Cem River Basin.[153] Additionally, the committee consulted both countries to identify how the committee could best support them in setting up such a framework.[154]

With support from the committee, a joint technical working group on monitoring and assessment was established within the bilateral commission that Albania and Montenegro had in place for their transboundary waters.[155] Through this joint technical working group, Albania and Montenegro have advanced their cooperation by, *inter alia* seeking to develop joint groundwater monitoring projects, the exchange of EIA documents for the planned hydropower projects in Albania, and the development of a draft protocol for cooperation in the exchange of hydrological and meteorological data and information

---

147 Ibid, para 15.

148 UNECE, 'Report of the Implementation Committee on its tenth meeting', UN Doc ECE/MP.WAT/IC/2019/2 (27 May 2020), para 5.

149 Ibid, para 7.

150 UNECE, 'Preparatory meeting of the eleventh meeting of the Implementation Committee' (19 May 2020) <https://unece.org/fileadmin/DAM/env/documents/2020/WATER/03May_15_19thCC/Report_Prep11Mtg.pdf≥ accessed 9 July 2024, para 7.

151 Ibid, para 8.

152 Ibid, para 9.

153 Ibid.

154 Ibid, para 11.

155 UNECE, 'Report of the Implementation Committee on its twelfth meeting', UN Doc ECE/MP.WAT/IC/2021/1 (18 March 2021), para 15. The bilateral commission was established pursuant to a 2018 Framework Agreement on Mutual Relations in the Field of Management of Transboundary Waters (see ibid).

on the Cijevna/Cem River Basin.[156] The implementation committee has facilitated these activities through regular meetings with representatives of both countries, by members of the committee attending a meeting of the joint technical working group, and by conducting a field visit to the Cijevna/Cem River Basin.[157]

Another request received by the implementation committee came in December 2022 from several NGOs involved in the conservation of transboundary waters between Spain and Portugal.[158] The NGOs requested the implementation committee assess whether Spain and Portugal's cooperation under the 1998 Agreement on Cooperation for the Protection and Sustainable Use of the Waters of the Spanish-Portuguese Hydrographic Basins (Albufeira Convention)[159] was in line with the requirements of the Water Convention.[160] In response to this request, the implementation committee sent letters to Portugal and Spain requesting their views and any relevant information, and received replies from both countries in February 2023.[161] Based on the countries' responses, the committee wrote to both countries with a request for additional information on several specific questions related to the implementation of the Water Convention within Portugal and Spain,[162] and subsequently received responses from both countries in June and July respectively, as well as comments on both responses from the NGOs that had originally raised the issue in November 2023.[163] Both countries and the NGOs concerned were then invited

156 UNECE, 'Report of the Implementation Committee on its seventeenth meeting', UN Doc ECE/MP.WAT/IC/2024/2 (25 June 2024) <https://unece.org/sites/default/files/2024-07/ECE_MP.WAT_IC_2024_2_report_ENG.pdf> accessed 12 August 2024, paras 5–12.

157 Focal points for the Water Convention briefed the Committee on progress during subsequent sessions of the Implementation Committee (see, for example, UNECE, 'Report of the Implementation Committee on its seventeenth meeting', UN Doc ECE/MP.WAT/IC/2024/2 (25 June 2024), paras 5–12).

158 Letter from Organisations cooperating in the project "Reconnecting Iberian Rivers" to the Implementation Committee (12 December 2022) <https://unece.org/sites/default/files/2023-12/1_UNECE%20Letter.pdf> accessed 12 August 2024.

159 Agreement on Cooperation for the Protection and Sustainable Use of the Waters of the Spanish-Portuguese Hydrographic Basins (adopted 30 November 1998, entered into force 2 February 2000), 2099 UNTS 2016 (1998 Albufeira Convention).

160 Ibid.

161 UNECE, 'Report of the Implementation Committee on its fifteenth meeting', UN Doc ECE/MP.WAT/IC/2022/4, para 10.

162 Ibid, para 14.

163 UNECE, 'Report of the Implementation Committee on its sixteenth meeting', UN Doc ECE/MP.WAT/IC/2023/2, para 18.

to exchange their views separately on the matter at the seventeenth meeting of the implementation committee on 7 and 8 March 2024.[164] Following these discussions, the implementation committee concluded its information-gathering exercise and formulated a series of 'conclusions' targeted at Portugal and Spain, which recommended enhancing the engagement of stakeholders within their cooperation and the implementation of the Albufeira Convention.[165] In addition, the countries were invited by the implementation committee to report on any measures taken pursuant to their recommendations by June 2025.[166]

These cases show that since its establishment in 2012, the workload of the implementation committee has been light. While it has kept busy reviewing the first national reports pursuant to the reporting exercise, participating in activities under the Water Convention, and answering specific questions that prospective parties to the Convention have had, the only specific request for assistance has come from Montenegro – with the only additional requests focusing on the committee using its information-gathering powers. While the Albania and Montenegro proceedings demonstrate how the committee can support countries in a collaborative and non-adversarial way, the question of whether the committee can play a stronger role in supporting compliance and implementation remains unanswered.

In terms of responding to incidences of weak implementation or non-compliance, the committee has a range of options available to it. As noted above, in the case of advisory procedures, such as the one involving Albania and Montenegro, it will seek to facilitate the application and implementation of the Water Convention, rather than call out non-compliance.[167] In other cases, such as a committee initiative or submission by a party, while its primary aim would also be to provide legal and technical assistance, the committee could also recommend that the meetings of the parties issue a statement of concern, a declaration of non-compliance or caution, or suspend the special rights and privileges accorded to a party under the Convention.[168]

However, while these 'harder' options are available, the parties to the Water Convention have demonstrated a preference to tackle issues related to compliance and implementation through its Programme of Work, which is adopted

164 UNECE (n 156).

165 Letter from Implementation Committee to NGOs (22 July 2024) <https://unece.org/sites/default/files/2024-08/20_Ltr_Chair_MsMiranda_22072024.pdf> accessed 12 August 2024.

166 Ibid.

167 UNECE (n 114).

168 Ibid.

every three years at the meeting of the parties.[169] Each Programme of Work is developed through a collaborative process, which involves both parties and non-parties, as well as non-state actors, such as UN agencies and other intergovernmental organisations, and non-governmental organisations.[170] The three-yearly reporting mechanism and the synthesis reports by the secretariat also provide an important means by which to assess challenges and gaps, and identify what priority actions should be included within the Programme of Work.

Through the implementation of these three yearly Programmes of Work, a range of activities are conducted to support the implementation of the Water Convention, including developing guidance documents, exchanging experiences and capacity-building, policy dialogue at regional and global levels, preparation of reports and publications, and projects 'on the ground'.[171] Key areas that are covered in the Programme of Work for 2022–2024 include 'increasing awareness of and accession to the Convention and application of its principles', 'supporting monitoring, assessment and information-sharing in transboundary basins', 'promoting an integrated and intersectoral approach to water resources management at all levels', 'adapting to climate change in transboundary basins', 'facilitating funding and financing of transboundary water cooperation and basin development', and 'reporting on Sustainable Development Goal indicator 6.5.2 and under the Convention'.[172]

While less specific than the types of cases that might come before an implementation committee, these work areas offer a significant means by which to support the Parties in the implementation of their commitments under the Water Convention. For instance, in relation to the development of agreements, as required by Article 9 of the Water Convention, activities have included developing a *Practical Guide for the Development of Agreements and Other Arrangements for Transboundary Water Convention* and several global and regional workshops on the topic.[173] The Water Convention has also provided

---

[169] See for example, Programme of work for 2022–2024, in UNECE, 'Report of the Meeting of the Parties on its ninth session', UN Doc ECE/MP.WAT/63/Add.1 (8 March 2022).

[170] Ibid, para 14.

[171] Ibid, para 18.

[172] Ibid.

[173] UNECE, 'Practical Guide for the Development of Agreements or Other Arrangements for Transboundary Water Cooperation', UN Doc ECE/MP.WAT/86 (2021). See also UNECE, 'Global Workshop on the Development of Transboundary Water Cooperation Agreements or other Arrangements' (7–8 November 2023, Budapest, Hungary) <https://unece.org/water-global-workshop-2023-budapest> accessed 9 July 2024; and UNECE, 'Workshop on

direct assistance to countries in support of the development of transboundary water agreements.[174]

5.4 THE EUROPEAN UNION WATER FRAMEWORK DIRECTIVE

5.4.1 Evolution and Normative Content

The EU has a long tradition in the development of water-related legislation dating back to the 1970s.[175] Early water policy tended to adopt a piecemeal approach, including legislation that focused on setting water quality objectives for specific water uses or limiting the discharge of certain pollutants.[176] The limitations of this piecemeal approach were recognised in the 1990s when the European Council requested the European Commission to propose a new policy that promoted the integrated management of water resources across the EU region.[177] After a lengthy negotiation process, this initiative resulted in the adoption of Directive 2000/60/EC of the European Parliament and of the Council establishing a Framework for Community Action in the Field of Water Policy (EU Water Framework Directive) on 23 October 2000.[178]

Transboundary Water Allocation, WEFE Nexus and Development of Agreements and other Arrangements: Supporting exchanges of lessons learned, good practices & practical tools' (15–16 April, Zambia 2024) <https://unece.org/environment/event/water-allocation-zambia-2024> accessed 21 August 2024.

[174] Bo Libert, 'The UNECE Water Convention and the development of transboundary cooperation in the Chu-Talas, Kura, Drin and Dniester River basins' (2014) 40(1) Water International 168; UNECE, 'Water Convention facilitates negotiations between Democratic Republic of Congo and Zambia on the establishment of the Luapula River and Lake Mweru Authority' (29 April 2024) <https://unece.org/media/Environment/news/390489> accessed 21 August 2024.

[175] See Giorgos Kallis and Peter Nijkamp, 'Evolution of EU water policy: A critical assessment and a hopeful perspective' (Research Memorandum 1999-27) <https://ideas.repec.org/p/vua/wpaper/1999-27.html> accessed 9 July 2024.

[176] See for example, Council Directive 75/440/EEC of 16 June 1975 concerning the quality required of surface water intended for the abstraction of drinking water in the member states [1975] OJ L 194/26.

[177] See Communication from the Commission on the European Community Water Policy (COM (96), 21 February 1996).

[178] Directive 2000/60/EC of 23 October 2000 establishing a framework for Community action in the field of water policy [2000] OJ L 327/1 (EU Water Framework Directive).

The EU Water Framework Directive applies to all inland surface waters, transitional waters, coastal waters, and groundwaters within the EU region.[179] Both national and transboundary waters therefore fall within the remit of the directive.

The overarching substantive requirement of the EU Water Framework Directive is for member states to protect, enhance, and restore all surface and groundwater bodies with the aim of achieving 'good water status'.[180] What constitutes 'good water status', as well as certain exceptions to the requirement, are set out in the Directive. The EU Water Framework Directive also introduces a set of obligations to support its implementation. Member states must identify individual river basin districts.[181] In the case of transboundary basins, international river basin districts must be identified.[182] EU member states have identified 75 international river basin districts.[183] A 'competent authority' must be identified for each of these river basin districts. Although in the case of transboundary basins, member states have the choice to only identify a component authority for the portion of the basin within their territory and then co-ordinate with the competent authorities that are designated for other parts of the basin.[184] In the majority of cases, these competent authorities are government ministries or agencies operating at the national level.[185]

Another key requirement supporting the implementation of the Water Framework Directive is the obligation on member states to produce river basin management plans and programmes of measures for each river basin district.[186] For transboundary basins, member states are obliged to aim towards a single international river basin management plan (RBMP), but where that does not prove possible they must at least provide a plan covering their part of an international river basin district.[187] The RBMPs must, *inter alia*, include

---

179 Ibid, Article 1 and 2.

180 Ibid, Article 4 and Annex V.

181 Ibid, Article 3(1).

182 Ibid, Article 3(3).

183 European Commission, 'International Cooperation under the Water Framework Directive (2000/60/EC) – Factsheets for International River Basins' (26 February 2019) <https://eur-lex.europa.eu/resource.html?uri=cellar:6cfb451c-39d3-11e9-8d04-01aa75ed71a1.0001.02/DOC_1&format=PDF> accessed 9 July 2024.

184 Article 3(3), EU Water Framework Directive (n 178).

185 European Commission, 'European Overview – River Basin Management Plans' (26 February 2019) <https://eur-lex.europa.eu/LexUriServ/LexUriServ.do?uri=SWD:2019:0030:FIN:EN:PDF>, 34.

186 Articles 11 and 13, EU Water Framework Directive (n 178).

187 Ibid, Article 13(2).

a summary of measures taken to achieve the environmental objectives of the water framework directive, i.e., good water status.[188] Once published, RBMPs are required to be updated every six years.[189]

5.4.2 Reporting Under the EU Water Framework Directive

Member states are obliged to periodically report on the implementation of the EU Water Framework Directive.[190] These reporting requirements align with key dates for the implementation of commitments under the Directive. Member states are therefore obliged to report on their RBMPs and subsequent updates, submit summary reports of the analysis required under Article 5 of the Directive,[191] and the monitoring programme designated under Article 8.[192] Additionally, member states are obliged to submit interim reports that describe progress in the implementation of their programme of measures.[193] In terms of timeframe, member states were required to submit Article 5 Reports in 2004, details of their monitoring programme by 2007, first RBMPs and programmes of measures by 2009, and then every six years thereafter. Article 18 of the Water Framework Directive then gives the European Commission the responsibility to publish periodic reports on progress concerning the implementation of the Directive.[194]

An extensive process has been developed by the Commission in consultation with member states to support the reporting process.[195] Through an electronic system, i.e., Water Information System for Europe (WISE), member states submit data in predefined formats, as well as any supporting background documents.[196] A significant body of guidance has also been developed

---

188 Ibid, Annex VII.

189 Ibid, Article 13(7).

190 Ibid, Article 15.

191 Article 5 obliges member states to '[e]nsure that for each river basin district or for the portion of an international river basin district falling within its territory; an analysis of its characteristics, a review of the impact of human activity on the status of surface waters and on ground, and an economic analysis of water use is undertaken', ibid.

192 Ibid.

193 Ibid, Article 15.

194 Ibid, Article 18.

195 See Common Implementation Strategy for the Water Framework Directive and the Floods Directives – WFD Reporting Guidance 2016 (final version 6.0.6, 26 April 2016) <https://circabc.europa.eu/sd/a/5b969dc0-6863-4f75-b5d8-8561cec91693/Guidance%20No%2035%20-%20WFD%20Reporting%20Guidance.pdf> accessed 9 July 2024.

196 Ibid, at 5.

to support this reporting process by the European Commission and member states through their *Common Implementation Strategy*.[197]

5.4.3 Implementation and Compliance Review

To date, the Commission has produced six reports that have assessed overall progress in the implementation of the Water Framework Directive.[198] In addition to these overarching implementation reports, country-specific assessments of progress are produced by the Commission.[199] Generally, the Commission's assessment reports demonstrate that significant progress has been made in the implementation of the EU Water Framework Directive.[200] By and large, countries have developed the necessary legal, policy, institutional and technical infrastructure. However, major challenges remain in ensuring that all waters achieve good water status. For instance, member states report difficulties in implementing their programmes of measures, with a lack of adequate finance highlighted as a key constraint.[201]

The Commission's country-specific assessment reports are an important mechanism by which it can highlight any areas where a member state may be in non-compliance with its commitments under the EU Water Framework Directive. These reports both highlight areas of non-compliance and include recommendations on how member states should rectify them.[202] Issues of non-compliance may also be brought to the attention of the Commission through complaints submitted by citizens, non-governmental organisations, and other

[197] Ibid.

[198] See European Commission, 'Implementation Reports', <https://environment.ec.europa.eu/topics/water/water-framework-directive/implementation-reports_en>.

[199] Ibid.

[200] See for example European Commission, Report on the implementation of the Water Framework Directive (2000/60/EC), the Environmental Quality Standards Directive (2008/105/EC amended by Directive 2013/39/EU) and the Floods Directive (2007/60/EC), COM(2021) 970 final (15 December 2021) <https://eur-lex.europa.eu/legal-content/EN/TXT/?uri=COM:2021:0970:FIN> accessed 9 July 2024.

[201] Ibid.

[202] See for example European Commission, 'Assessment of member states' progress in Programmes of Measures during the second planning cycle of the Water Framework Directive – Greece' (December 2021) <https://op.europa.eu/en/publication-detail/-/publication/e639cc79-6d0e-11ec-9136-01aa75ed71a1/language-en/format-PDF/source-250304332> accessed 9 July 2024.

non-state actors.[203] It is then up to the Commission to decide whether, after consulting with the member state(s) concerned, to take forward any formal enforcement action.[204]

5.4.4 Addressing Incidence of Weak Implementation or Non-compliance

Where member states fail to address any non-compliance issues raised by the Commission, the Commission has the option to initiate legal proceedings through the European Court of Justice.[205] Since its adoption, the Commission has initiated over 15 cases related to the implementation of the EU Water Framework Directive. Early cases focused on issues where a member state failed to comply with the timetable for implementing the EU Water Framework Directive, including a failure to designate competent authorities and river basin districts,[206] to submit Article 5 reports,[207] to establish monitoring networks,[208] and to adopt RBMPs[209] or subsequent updates.[210] A further set of cases relate to the inadequate transposition of the EU Water Framework Directive into national legislation.[211] More recent cases have related to specific breaches of the EU Water Framework Directive's substantive commitments, such as those

---

203 See Annex, European Commission, 'EU law: Better results through better application' 2017/C (19 January 2017) <https://eur-lex.europa.eu/legal-content/EN/TXT/PDF/?uri=CELEX:52017XC0119(01)&from=EN> accessed 9 July 2024.

204 Ibid.

205 Article 258, Consolidated Version of the Treaty on the Functioning of the European Union, [2016] OJ C 202/160 (6 July 2016) <https://eur-lex.europa.eu/legal-content/EN/TXT/?uri=celex%3A12016E258> accessed 9 July 2024.

206 *Commission v Spain* (Case C-516/07, 7 May 2009).

207 *Commission v Italy* (Case C-85/07, 18 December 2007); and *Greece* (Case C-264/07, 31 January 2008).

208 *Commission v Malta* (Case C-351/09, 22 December 2010).

209 *Commission v Greece* (Case C-297/11, 19 April 2012), *Belgium* (Case C-366/11, 24 May 2012), *Portugal* (Case C-233/11, 21 June 2012), *Spain* (Case C-403/11, 4 October 2012).

210 *European Commission v Kingdom of Spain* (Case C-556/18, 26 September 2019).

211 *Commission v Luxembourg* (Case C-32/05, 30 November 2006); *Commission v Germany* (Case C-67/05, 15 December 2005); *Commission v Poland* (Case C-648/13, 30 June 2016).

relating to the environmental objectives,[212] cost recovery for water services,[213] and the Directive's relationship with other EU laws.[214]

5.5 REVISED SADC PROTOCOL ON SHARED WATERCOURSES

5.5.1 Evolution and Normative Content

Established in 1960, the Southern African Development Community (SADC) seeks to foster regional integration in the areas of economic growth, poverty alleviation, peace and security, and the sustainable management of natural resources.[215] There are now 16 member states of SADC, which include 12 continental states and four island states.[216]

SADC member states initially adopted a protocol on shared watercourse systems in 1995 (SADC Protocol),[217] which was later revised in 2000 (Revised SADC Protocol).[218] The importance of shared watercourses for the SADC

---

[212] *Bund für Umwelt und Naturschutz Deutschland e.v. v Bunderrepublik Deutschland* (Case C-461/13, 1 July 2015); *European Commission v Republic of Austria* (Case C-346/14, 4 May 2016).

[213] *Commission v Germany* (C-525/12, 11 September 2014); *Vodaopskrba I advadnja d.o.o v. Željka Klufurič* (Case C-686/15, 7 December 2016).

[214] *Protect Natur-, Arten- und Landschaftsschutz Umweltorganisation v Bezirkshauptmannschaft Gmünd* (Case C-664/15, 20 December 2017); *Folk* (Case C-529/15, 15 July 2015); *European Commission v Kingdom of Spain* (Case C-559/19, 24 June 2021); *IL and Others v Land Nordrhein-Westfalen* (Case C-535/18, 28 May 2020).

[215] Treaty of the Southern African Development Community (adopted 17 August 1992) <https://www.sadc.int/document/declaration-treaty-sadc-1992-0> accessed 9 July 2024 (SADC Treaty).

[216] The continental states of SADC are Angola, Botswana, Democratic Republic of Congo, Eswatini, Lesotho, Malawi, Mozambique, Namibia, South Africa, Tanzania, Zambia and Zimbabwe; and the island states are Comoros, Madagascar, Mauritius and Seychelles.

[217] Protocol on Shared Watercourses in the Southern African Development Community (adopted 28 August 1995) <https://leap.unep.org/en/countries/ao/national-legislation/protocol-shared-watercourses-systems-southern-african-development/> accessed 9 July 2024.

[218] Revised Protocol on Shared Watercourses in the Southern African Development Community, Windhoek (adopted 7 August 2000, entered into force 22 September 2003), 40 ILM 321 (Revised SADC Protocol). SADC countries decided to revise the Protocol because they felt it did not adequately address environmental matters, and there was a desire to update it in line with the Watercourses

region is clear. All the continental states of the SADC region share transboundary waters, and the region is home to several major rivers shared by multiple countries, such as the Congo,[219] the Zambezi,[220] the Orange-Senqu,[221] the Okavango[222] and Limpopo Rivers.[223] Shared waters account for 70% of all renewable water resources within the region.[224]

In terms of normative commitments, although there are some notable differences, the 2000 Revised SADC Protocol closely follows the Watercourses Convention. Article 3 of the Revised SADC Protocol sets out key substantive requirements upon its parties, including the obligation to utilise shared watercourses in an equitable and reasonable manner, and to take all appropriate measures to prevent the causing of significant harm. These principles closely mirror the related provisions of the Watercourses Convention, i.e., Articles 5, 6, and 10. For instance, the Revised SADC Protocol includes the same list of factors and circumstances that should be taken into account when determining what is equitable and reasonable, and in line with the Watercourses Convention, stipulates that all factors should be considered together and a conclusion reached on the basis of the whole.[225] The Revised SADC Protocol

---

Convention. See Mapule Kgomongoe and Richard Meissner, 'The Revised Protocol on Shared Watercourses and the Management of Water Resources in SADC' in SAIIA (ed), *South African Yearbook of International Affairs 2003/04* (South African Institute of International Affairs 2004); Salman M.A. Salman, 'Legal regime for the use and protection of international watercourses in the Southern African region: evolution and context' (2001) 41(4) Natural Resources Journal 981; and Phera Ramoeli, 'The SADC protocol on shared watercourses: its origins and current status', in Anthony Turton and Roland Henwood (eds), *Hydropolitics in the developing world: A Southern African perspective* (African Water Issues Research Unit 2002), 105–112.

219 Shared by Angola, Burundi (non-SADC), Cameroon (non-SADC), Central African Republic (non-SADC), Democratic Republic of Congo, Republic of Congo (non-SADC), Rwanda (non-SADC), Tanzania and Zambia.

220 Shared by Angola, Botswana, Malawi, Mozambique, Namibia, Tanzania, Zambia and Zimbabwe.

221 Shared by Botswana, Lesotho, Namibia and South Africa.

222 Shared by Angola, Botswana, Namibia and Zimbabwe.

223 Shared by Botswana, Lesotho, Namibia and South Africa.

224 SADC, 'Regional Water Policy' (August 2005) <https://www.sadc.int/sites/default/files/2021-08/Regional_Water_Policy.pdf> accessed 9 July 2024, 6.

225 Article 3(8), Revised SADC Protocol (n 217). The only slight difference in the list of factors is that the Watercourses Convention includes as one of the factors, 'the social and economic needs of the Watercourses states concerned'; whereas the 2000 Revised Protocol refers to the 'social, economic and *environmental* needs of the Watercourse states concerned' [emphasis added]. It is questionable whether this

also contains the same requirement found in Article 7(1) of the Watercourses Convention to take all appropriate measures to prevent significant harm.[226] However, a notable departure in the 2000 Revised SADC Protocol is Article 3(10)(b), which stipulates that state parties should, where significant harm occurs, have due regard to Article 3(10)(a) of the Protocol. Article 3(10)(a) of the Protocol includes the same obligation as contained in Article 7(2), i.e., the duty to take all appropriate measures to prevent harm. Article 3(10)(b) therefore appears to do little more than elaborate on the obligation that can already be found in Article 3(10)(a). The equivalent provision to Article 3(10)(b) in the Watercourses Convention, i.e., Article 7(2), serves a different purpose, stipulating that if significant harm does nevertheless occur, the parties should determine whether or not that harm is consistent with the principle of equitable and reasonable utilisation. The overarching nature of the principle of equitable and reasonable utilisation, albeit with its limitations, is therefore clearly set out in the Watercourses Convention, whereas in the Revised SADC Protocol, it is unclear which principle takes priority.

Along similar lines to the Watercourses Convention, state parties to the Revised SADC Protocol are subject to a series of procedural requirements, including the duty to notify and consult over planned measures,[227] enter into consultations concerning the establishment of joint management mechanisms and the adoption of watercourse agreements,[228] cooperate on matters concerning the maintenance and protection of installations,[229] regulation of flow,[230] prevent and mitigation of harmful conditions,[231] and notify each other of emergency situations.[232] State parties are also obliged to settle their disputes in a peaceful manner and in accordance with the SADC Treaty.[233] Where the state

addition in the 2000 Revised Protocol is significant, given that both instruments also recognise the importance of taking into account the environmental impacts of any uses within other factors, and subsequent provisions of the Protocol (see, for example Article 4(2) of the Revised SADC Protocol (n 217)). See also Daniel Malzbender and Anton Earle, 'Southern Africa', in Flavia R. Loures and Alistair Rieu-Clarke (eds), *The UN Watercourses Convention in Force – Strengthening international law for transboundary water management* (Routledge 2013), 115.

226 Article 10(a), Revised SADC Protocol (n 217).

227 Article 4(1), ibid.

228 Article 4(3)(a) and Article 6, ibid.

229 Article 4(3)(c), ibid.

230 Article 4(3)(b), ibid.

231 Article 4(4), ibid.

232 Article 4(5), ibid.

233 Article 7, ibid.

parties are unable to resolve a dispute bilaterally, the Protocol requires them to submit the dispute to the SADC Tribunal.[234]

5.5.2 Reporting Under the Revised SADC Protocol

Pursuant to the Protocol, there is an obligation on 'shared watercourses institutions', which include river basin organisations (RBOs), commissions, authorities, boards, or similar, to regularly provide the Water Sector Co-ordinating Unit with information concerning progress in implementing the Protocol.[235] A broader reporting mandate is also provided for in SADC's regional water policy, which calls for a system by which to assess SADC Water Sector's 'achievement of its development goals, objectives, strategies, programmes and institutional performance'.[236] This is complemented by the regional water strategy, which sets out key definitions and principles to consider in monitoring and evaluation, whilst at the same time stressing that a detailed system of monitoring and evaluation should be developed through regional strategic action plans (RSAPs).[237]

Successive RSAPs have sought to establish reporting requirements, including the need for annual reports from Shared Watercourse Institutions and SADC member states, and the development of indicators aligned to the commitments under the Revised SADC Protocol, such as the establishment of RBOs and watercourse agreements, the harmonisation of water policy and legislation, and the development of strategies related to stakeholder participation and dispute resolution.[238]

---

[234] Article 7(2), ibid.

[235] Article 5(3)(c).

[236] SADC (n 224), 48–49.

[237] SADC, 'Regional Water Strategy' (June 2006) <https://www.sadc.int/sites/default/files/2021-08/Regional_Water_Strategy..pdf> accessed 9 July 2024, 111.

[238] See SADC, 'Regional Strategic Action Plan on Integrated Water Resources Development and Management 2005–2010' (April 2005) <https://www.sadc.int/sites/default/files/2021-08/Regional_Strategic_Action_Plan_RSAP-IWRM_2_.pdf> accessed 9 July 2024, 33; SADC, 'Regional Strategic Action Plan on Integrated Water Resources Development and Management (2011–2015)' (December 2011) <https://www.sadc.int/sites/default/files/2021-11/Regional_Strategic_Action_Plan_-IWRM_III.pdf> accessed 9 July 2024; and SADC, 'Regional Strategic Action Plan on Integrated Water Resources Development and Management (2016–2020)' (2016) <https://www.sadc.int/sites/default/files/2021-08/SADC_Water_4th_Regional_Strategic_Action_Plan_English_version.pdf> accessed 9 July 2024; SADC, 'Regional Strategic Action Plan on Integrated Water Resources Development and Management (2021–2025)' (2023) <https://www

However, there is a notable distinction between the reporting under the Water Convention and the SADC system. While the Water Convention reporting template is closely aligned with its provisions, the monitoring and evaluation framework under SADC is rather focused on monitoring progress in implementing the RSAPs themselves. While there is, therefore, some overlap with the provisions of the Revised SADC Protocol, the SADC approach cannot be categorised as a system that specifically and systematically monitors progress in the implementation of the Revised SADC Protocol itself. A more specific request to develop indicators that Shared Watercourse Institutions could use to report on progress in implementing the Revised SADC Protocol was called for in the fourth RSAP but has so far not been developed to the extent of reporting under the Water Convention.[239]

5.5.3 Implementation and Compliance Review

While the Revised SADC Protocol does not have a specific system for reporting on compliance and implementation, there is an institutional framework in place for supporting implementation. The so-called SADC Council of Water Ministers, with support from the Committee of Water Senior Officials, has overall responsibility for monitoring the implementation of the Revised SADC Protocol.[240] The aforementioned committee is in turn supported by the Water Resources Technical Committee, which is made up of national directors responsible for water from each SADC member state.[241] Additionally, the SADC Water Sector Co-ordinating Unit, which was later transformed into the Water Division, is responsible for monitoring the Protocol's implementation and submitting annual reports on progress to the Council via the Committee of Water Ministers.[242] However, as noted above, to date, these institutions have not reviewed specific incidences of weak implementation or non-compliance

.sadc.int/document/regional-strategic-action-plan-integrated-water-resources-development-and-management-phase> accessed 9 July 2024.

[239] Ibid, 13.

[240] Article 5 (2)(a)(i), Revised SADC Protocol (n 217).

[241] Article 5(2)(b) and (d), Revised SADC Protocol (n 217).

[242] Ibid, Article 5(2)(c)(i). The SADC Water Sector Co-ordination Unit was established in 1996 and later became the SADC Water Division (SADC, 'Regional Strategic Action Plan for Integrated Water Resources Development and Management 2005–2010' (n 238), 4).

but have rather reviewed the progress of the projects and programmes that fall under the umbrella of the RSAPs.

5.5.4 Addressing Incidences of Weak Implementation or Non-compliance

In line with the more general procedures that are in place for reporting and reviewing the implementation of the Revised SADC Protocol, there are no specific mechanisms for addressing weak implementation or non-compliance of the Protocol. As noted above, the SADC secretariat, through the Water Division, plays a general role in supporting the implementation of, and compliance with, the Protocol.[243] More general support for the implementation of the Revised SADC Protocol has also evolved through the adoption of several important regional policies by the SADC member states, including the SADC Regional Indicative Strategic Development Plan (RISDP).[244] The original RISDP was adopted by SADC in 2003 and later revised for the periods 2015–2020, and 2020–2030.[245] Several water-specific policy instruments also provide an enabling environment by which to implement the Revised SADC Protocol. In 2005, SADC member states adopted a Regional Water Policy, which covers nine thematic themes, including regional cooperation, development and poverty reduction, environmental sustainability, water-related disasters, water resources information and management, water resources development and management, regional water resources institutional framework, stakeholder participation and capacity building, and financing.[246] This policy is complemented by SADC's Regional Water Strategy.[247] While the Regional Water Policy and the Revised SADC Protocol set out the general policy landscape by which SADC member states agree to cooperate over water,

---

243 Key activities of the Water Division include reporting on progress in implementing the Protocol to the council of ministers, senior officials and technical committee; supporting the harmonisation of national water policy and legislation; co-ordinating with national water directorates within SADC member states; leveraging resources for implementation projects and programmes; supporting the establishment of joint institutions at the basin level; and assessing compliance with the protocol (see SADC Regional Water Policy (n 156), 44–45; and SADC Regional Water Strategy (n 237), 77–79).

244 SADC, 'Regional Indicative Strategic Development Plan (RISDP) 2020–2030' (2020) <https://www.sadc.int/pillars/regional-indicative-strategic-development-plan-2020-2030> accessed 9 July 2024.

245 Ibid, 12.

246 SADC Regional Water Policy (n 224), 16–56.

247 SADC Regional Water Strategy (n 237).

the Regional Water Strategy has been described as providing 'the "How," "Who," and "When" in the implementation of the Policy'.[248] RSAPs then set out more specific detail on how the strategy might be realised. While the aims and objectives of the RSAPs are broader than the Revised SADC Protocol, i.e., covering water resources management at all levels, they do provide an opportunity for SADC member states to identify and address general issues that may be preventing the effective implementation of the Protocol. In the past, RSAPs have been used to support the strengthening of legal and regulatory frameworks, the establishment of river basin organisations, river basin management planning, promoting public participation, capacity building, and infrastructure development.[249]

The only more specific mechanism by which non-compliance with the Revised SADC Protocol can be addressed is by recourse to traditional dispute settlement mechanisms. Article 7 of the Revised SADC Protocol obliges SADC member states to settle any disputes by peaceful means.[250] Where state parties are unable to settle their disputes, they are obliged to refer the dispute to the SADC Tribunal for a final and binding decision.[251] The SADC Tribunal has had a chequered history and since 2014 has ceased to function.[252] Later watercourse agreements adopted by SADC member states therefore tend to avoid reference to the SADC Tribunal and call upon parties to establish an independent tribunal to make a final and binding decision.[253]

---

248 SADC, Regional Strategic Action Plan on Integrated Water Resources Development and Management (2016–2020) (n 238), 4.

249 See RSAPs (n 238).

250 Article 7, Revised SADC Protocol (n 217). See also Article 4, Consolidated Treaty of the Southern African Development Community (adopted 21 October 2015), <https://www.sadc.int/sites/default/files/2021-08/Consolidated_Text_of_the_SADC_Treaty_-_scanned_21_October_2015.pdf> accessed 15 January 2025.

251 Ibid.

252 See Janelle Mangwanda, 'One Step Forward, Two Steps Back: The Rise and Fall of the SADC Tribunal' (2021) 22(2) Economic & Social Rights Review in Africa 17. See also, SADC, 'Communiqué Extraordinary Summit Heads of State and Government of the Southern African Development Community' (Windhoek, Namibia, 20 May 2011) <https://www.gov.za/news/media-statements/communiqu%C3%A9-extraordinary-summit-heads-state-and-government-southern-african> accessed 9 July 2024.

253 See for example, Article 13 of the Agreement between Angola and Namibia on the Establishment of the Cuvelai Watercourse Commission (adopted 16 September 2014) <https://faolex.fao.org/docs/pdf/bi-156656.pdf> accessed 9 July 2024.

5.6 CONCLUSION

This chapter set out to examine the extent to which regional and global agreements support the implementation of, and compliance with transboundary water agreements. What is clear from the analysis is that no one system operates at the global level in a comparable way to some of the CIMs considered in Chapter 3.

The Water Convention offers the most promising example of a multilateral agreement that aligns closely with the type of CIMs found in MEAs. However, while it now operating at a global level, the Water Convention is currently binding only on its 55 parties. Despite the Water Convention's significant potential to increase its membership, around two-thirds of states sharing transboundary waters are not currently obliged to report on their transboundary water agreements under the Convention, and do not have full recourse to the implementation committee and the support it might offer. Parts of the system are also more evolved than others. While the reporting mechanism is well established and benefits from all parties reporting every three years, the implementation committee is still in its infancy, having so far only considered one advisory procedure.

The SDG indicator 6.5.2 monitoring process shares a lot in common with the reporting mechanism under the Water Convention, including the use of the same reporting questionnaire. In addition, the secretariat of the Water Convention, in partnership with UNESCO for SDG indicator 6.5.2, oversees both exercises. However, while engagement in the exercises, i.e., 80% of the countries sharing transboundary waters, can be seen as a positive feature, SDG indicator 6.5.2 should not be confused with a mechanism that formally requires parties to report on treaty compliance and implementation. Rather, the exercise was set up to periodically assess the proportion of transboundary basin area with an operational arrangement for water cooperation for the purpose of measuring progress towards SDG target 6.5. While countries are invited to provide supplementary data on their bilateral, basin and sub-basin agreements, including challenges in their implementation – and most countries do so – the assessment of treaty compliance and implementation is not strictly part of the exercise. It is also uncertain whether so many countries would engage with the exercise if the primary objective was to monitor and assess at the global level the implementation of, and compliance with, transboundary water agreements. Additionally, while it is hoped that such a major exercise would continue in some shape or form, the future of the exercise is not certain given that the SDG framework is only in place until 2030.

At the regional level, both the EU Water Framework Directive and the Revised SADC Protocol, together with their associated institutions, contain key aspects of a CIM. Within both contexts, states commit to periodically report on their progress in implementing the regional agreements. However, such reporting is more general than what can be found in the reporting questionnaire under the Water Convention. States, as well as shared water institutions in the case of the Revised SADC Protocol, are not required to report in such detail on the implementation of, and compliance with, their bilateral, basin and sub-basin agreements. In the case of the Revised SADC Protocol, reporting is rather aligned to more general water resource management issues as set out in the RSAPs. In the case of the Water Framework Directive, both national and international measures for achieving the objectives of the Directive must be reported on. Along similar lines, while both the EU and SADC play a role in assessing progress, this does not tend to focus on specific bilateral, basin, or sub-basin agreements. Also, in terms of addressing incidences of weak implementation and non-compliance, neither the EU nor SADC have developed anything similar to the implementation committee that can be found within the Water Convention or many MEAs. These regional instruments and institutions therefore rely on more traditional means by which to address issues of non-compliance through dispute settlement procedures.

Ultimately, the analysis of global and regional approaches shows that there is no CIM that operates at the global level in relation to transboundary water agreements. However, elements of such a system are evident. The 1992 Water Convention offers the closest similarity to the types of CIMs found in MEAs, and with the prospect of more countries becoming party to it, it may play a stronger role in the future. While less evident, certain features of CIMs can also be found in the EU Water Framework Directive, the revised SADC Protocol, and SDG indicator 6.5.2. Whether these elements could be, or should be, developed into a universal CIM for the world's transboundary waters will be considered further in Chapter 9.

6. The Mekong River Basin

6.1 INTRODUCTION

The Mekong River, located in South East Asia, has a total length of 4,900 km, covers a basin area of 795,000 km^2, and is the tenth largest river in the world.[1] Its headwaters are located in the Tibetan Plateau, and from there, the river flows through China, Myanmar, Laos, Thailand, Vietnam and Cambodia before emptying into the South China Sea. 21% of the basin is located in China, 3% in Myanmar, 25% in Laos, 23% in Thailand, 20% in Cambodia, and 8% in Vietnam.[2]

About 65 million people live within the Lower Mekong River Basin (Cambodia, Laos, Thailand and Vietnam), and 7 million people live within the Upper Mekong River Basin (China and Myanmar).[3] Agriculture, predominantly for rice production, is the largest water user in the Mekong River Basin. In the Lower Mekong River Basin alone, the area under irrigation has expanded from approximately 3.1 million hectares in 1995 to over 4 million hectares in 2013.[4] Farmers in the Mekong River Basin produce enough rice to feed 300 million people per year, and irrigation accounts for 90.5% of the total water withdrawal in the Mekong River Basin.[5] The value of this rice production is estimated at US$ 7.7 billion.[6]

---

[1] FAO, 'Aquastat – Mekong River Basin' (2011) <http://www.fao.org/nr/water/aquastat/basins/mekong/index.stm> accessed 9 July 2024.

[2] Ibid.

[3] Mekong River Commission (MRC), 'State of the Basin Report 2018' (2018) <https://reliefweb.int/report/world/state-basin-report-2018> accessed 22 January 2025, 15 and 172.

[4] Ibid, 110.

[5] Cambodia's Development Policy Research Institute, 'Framework Research on Water Resources Management and Governance in Cambodia: A Literature Review' (May 2008) <https://cdri.org.kh/storage/pdf/wp37e_1617794531.pdf> accessed 9 July 2024; and FAO (n 1).

[6] MRC (n 3), 110.

As well as being an important driver for economic development and sustainable livelihoods, the Mekong River Basin represents one of the most biologically diverse areas in the world. The Lower Mekong River Basin contains 14 of the World Wildlife Fund's global 200 critical ecoregions, and new species continue to be discovered.[7]

Fish are central to regional food security.[8] An estimated 40 million people are involved in fishery-related activities within the basin.[9] 70% of rural households in Laos are dependent on fishing to sustain their livelihoods, and 40% of the total population of Cambodia relies on the Tonle Sap Lake and its floodplain for their livelihoods.[10] The Tonle Sap Lake in Cambodia also provides a critical regulatory service for the entire Mekong River system. This lake, the largest freshwater body in Southeast Asia, essentially acts as a bladder for the Mekong River Basin.[11] During the dry season, the lake, with an approximate area of 3,000 km^2, augments downstream water levels, while in the wet season, the lake stores floodwaters as the pattern reverses, and the lake expands to an area over 10,000 km^2.[12]

High rates of economic growth within the Mekong region have led to large increases in energy demand.[13] Hydropower is considered by all states of the Mekong as an important means by which to meet these growing energy needs. An estimated 2,401 megawatts of installed capacity was in place in the Lower

---

7 Ibid, 80.

8 Guy Ziv and others, 'Trading-off fish biodiversity, food security, and hydropower in the Mekong River Basin' 109(15) Proceedings of the National Academy of Sciences of the United States of America 5609.

9 A Belay and others, 'The Challenges of Integrated Water Resources Management in the Mekong River Basin in terms of People's Livelihood' (2010) 2(1) Journal of Water Resources Protection 61.

10 MRC (n 3), 118.

11 Karen Bakker, 'The Politics of Hydropower: Developing the Mekong' (1999) 18 Political Geography 209.

12 Ibid.

13 MRC (n 3), 34. Economic growth and energy demand have both increased on average by an annual rate of 8%. Other reasons behind the increased influence in hydropower within the region include the governments of Laos and Cambodia seeing the export of hydropower as a useful source of foreign exchange; the increased availability of quasi-public and private sector finance; the proliferation of hydropower developers in the region; and the expected increase in dry season flows from the development of dams on the Upper Mekong in China (see Xinlin Li, 'Hydropower in the Mekong River Basin: A balancing test' (2012) 24(1) Environmental Claims Journal 51).

Mekong River Basin alone in 2005, which rose to 12,285 megawatts in 2019.[14] In terms of projects, there are 89 projects on the Lower Mekong River, with 44 dams expected to become operational by 2040.[15] There are 11 projects planned for the mainstream of the Lower Mekong, two of which (Xayaburi and Don Sahong) are already operational.[16] On the upper mainstream, China has built 11 dams, two of which are large storage dams, and it has plans to develop a further 11 dams.[17]

These hydropower developments pose a significant threat to the equitable and sustainable management of the Mekong.[18] It is estimated that the developments could lead to a US$ 23 billion loss of fisheries by 2040 and a US$ 145 billion loss of forests, wetlands and mangroves.[19]

Climate change also poses a challenge for the Mekong River Basin.[20] Projected impacts of climate change in the Mekong River Basin include less rain during the dry season, more rain during the wet season, and a greater frequency of extreme weather events.[21] The Mekong Delta is particularly vulnerable due to the projected changes in freshwater flow, saltwater intrusion, sea level rise and population density.[22] However, some commentators have also cautioned against tackling climate change in isolation, as the hydropower developments are likely to induce change that is at least, if not more, radical

---

14 MRC (n 3), 112; MRC, 'Hydropower', <https://www.mrcmekong.org/hydropower> accessed 9 July 2024.

15 Ibid. See also Marko Koskinen and others, 'Mekong at the crossroads: Next steps for impact assessment of large dams' (2012) 41 Ambio 319.

16 MRC (n 14).

17 Ibid.

18 Stuart Orr and others, 'Dams on the Mekong River: Lost fish protein and the implications for land and water resources' (2012) 22 Global Environmental Change 925; Ziv (n 8), 5609.

19 MRC, 'The Study of the Sustainable Management and Development of the Mekong river Basin including impacts of Mainstream Hydropower Projects' (December 2017, revised November 2018) <https://ebook.tnmc-is.org/show/63/pdf> accessed 12 August 2024, 7–11.

20 Marko Keskinen and others, 'Climate change and water resources in the Lower Mekong River Basin: putting adaptation into the context' (2010) 1 Journal of Water and Climate Change 103.

21 Lancang-Mekong Water Resources Cooperation Center and Mekong River Commission, 'Technical Report – Phase 1 – Historical Changes of Featured Hydrological Conditions and their Causes' (September 2023) <https://www.mrcmekong.org/publications/technical-report-phase-1-of-the-joint-study-on-the-changing-patterns-of-hydrological-conditions-of-the-lancang-mekong-river-basin-and-adaptation-strategies/> accessed 28 August 2024.

22 Ibid.

than the impacts of climate change.[23] In 2019, the water levels of the Mekong River dropped to a 100-year low.[24] Abnormally low water levels were repeated in 2021.[25] While El Niño and climate change were identified as causal factors, upstream dams in China and Laos were also identified as contributors, and recent subsidence and coastal erosion within the Mekong Delta – the so-called 'food basket' of South East Asia – has also been attributed to several dams that have been constructed upstream.[26]

Additional challenges faced by the Mekong River Basin include overfishing, pollution, sand mining and deforestation.[27]

The multiple and complex challenges faced across the Mekong River Basin require the riparian states to work together in the search for joint solutions. The aim of this chapter will be to consider how the Mekong River Basin states have utilised transboundary water agreements to foster that cooperation and more specifically how they have addressed compliance and implementation. The analysis will focus on the Agreement on the Cooperation for the Sustainable Development of the Mekong River Basin, which was adopted by the parties of the lower Mekong (Cambodia, Laos, Thailand and Vietnam) on 5 April 1995 (1995 Mekong Agreement).[28] In order to understand why the 1995 Mekong Agreement was adopted and to identify the factors that shaped its design, the chapter will first offer an overview of the evolution of cooperation amongst the states of the Mekong River Basin. To ascertain the strength of commitments amongst the states party to the Mekong Agreement, the chapter will analyse the normative content of the Agreement itself. As well as ascertaining the key normative commitments, the chapter will consider: i) what mecha-

23 Keskinen (n 20).

24 Steve K.L. Chan, 'Transboundary Water Governance: The Impacts of Upstream Dams on the Mekong River in Cambodia' (2023) 18 GMSARN International Journal 9, 12.

25 Reuters, 'Mekong group urges better water management collaboration as record drought persists' (12 January 2022) <https://www.reuters.com/world/asia-pacific/mekong-group-urges-better-water-management-collaboration-record-drought-persists-2022-01-13/> accessed 10 July 2024.

26 Ian G. Baird and Michael A.S. Thorne, 'The downstream impacts of dams on the seasonally flooded riverine forests of the Mekong River in northeastern Cambodia' (2023) 31(4) South East Asia Research 377; Edward J. Anthony and others, 'Linking rapid erosion of the Mekong River delta to human activities' (2015) 5 Scientific Reports 14745.

27 Mekong River Commission (n 3). See also Karen Bakker, 'The Politics of Hydropower: Developing the Mekong' (1999) 18 Political Geography 209.

28 Agreement on the Cooperation for the Sustainable Development of the Mekong River Basin (adopted 5 April 1995), (1995) 34 ILM 864 (Mekong Agreement).

nisms are contained within the Mekong Agreement to monitor and report on its implementation; ii) what formal institutional arrangements exist to review the implementation of, and compliance with, the agreement; and iii) what mechanisms are in place to address any incidences of non-compliance or weak implementation. Having examined the formal architecture for addressing issues of compliance and implementation under the 1995 Mekong Agreement, the chapter will look at what has happened in practice. Such an analysis will first involve considering how programmes and policies adopted by the Mekong River Commission (MRC) have helped foster compliance and implementation. Second, the analysis will identify specific instances where compliance with or the implementation of the 1995 Agreement has been challenged.

6.2 THE EVOLUTION OF COOPERATION IN THE MEKONG BASIN

The origins of cooperation amongst the riparian states of the Mekong Basin can be found within the United Nations Economic Commission for Asia and the Far East (ECAFE).[29] In 1952, ECAFE's Bureau of Flood Control drew up a working paper that, as well as addressing flood control, also offered a wider vision for water resources development in the Mekong Basin.[30] A follow-up report laid out a preliminary development scheme for the Mekong that focused primarily on irrigation, flood control and hydropower development.[31] Five main dam projects on the Lower Mekong mainstream were proposed (Pa Mong, Khemerat, Khone Falls, Sambor and Tonle Sap), together with two additional mainstream possibilities (near Luang Pabang and Thakhek), and a tributary site (Nam Theun River).[32] The prospect of developing the resources of the Mekong then led Cambodia, Vietnam, Thailand and Laos to establish the Committee for Coordination and Investigations of the Lower Mekong Basin

---

[29] For an overview of the early efforts to foster cooperation within the Mekong Basin, see Jeffrey W. Jacobs, 'Mekong Committee History and Lessons for River Basin Development' (1995) 161 The Geographical Journal 135.

[30] UN ECAFE, *Preliminary Report on Technical Problems Relating to Flood Control and Water Resources Development of the Mekong, An International River* (ECAFE 1952).

[31] UN ECAFE, *Development of Water Resources in the Lower Mekong Basin* (ECAFE 1957).

[32] Ibid. See also United States Bureau of Reclamation, *Lower Mekong River Basin – a reconnaissance report prepared for International Cooperation, Administration* (USBR 1956), which was produced in collaboration with ECAFE.

(Mekong Committee) in 1957.[33] The Committee was heavily supported by the US, which saw collaboration between the Lower Mekong states and economic development through hydropower as a way to curb communist influences.[34]

Several studies were carried out by the Mekong Committee, which reaffirmed the potential of the Mekong Basin for hydropower, flood control and irrigation both along its mainstream and tributaries as means of addressing poverty.[35] An *Indicative Basin Plan* was produced in 1970, which identified 180 possible projects, including a cascade of seven dams on the mainstream of the Mekong.[36] The plan was supplemented in 1975 by the Joint Declaration of Principles for Utilisation of the Waters of the Mekong Basin, which sought to 'ensure that conservation, development and control of the water resources of the Basin are directed towards their optimum utilization for the benefit of all the peoples of the Basin states', and 'to promote the regional cooperation required for the proper management of the water resources of the Basin'.[37] Political turmoil in the 1970s slowed the progress of the collaboration amongst the basin states, which resulted in Cambodia leaving the Committee in 1976, and Laos and Vietnam being absent in 1976 and 1977. The Committee was then re-established in 1978 as the 'Interim Mekong Committee' (IMC) comprised of Thailand, Laos and Vietnam.[38] Given the absence of Cambodia from the IMC, the Committee focused its attention on additional studies and

---

[33] Statute of the Committee for Co-ordination of Investigations of Lower Mekong Basin (adopted 17 September 1957) <http://gis.nacse.org/tfdd/tfdddocs/216ENG.pdf> accessed 10 July 2024.

[34] 37% of the total budget of US$ 86 million in the first 10 years (K. Friesen, 'Damming the Mekong: Plans and Paradigms for Developing the River Basin from 1951 to 1995' (PhD thesis, American University, 1999). See also Greg Browder and Leonard Ortolano, 'The evolution of an international water resources management regime in the Mekong River Basin' (2000) 40 Natural Resources Journal 499.

[35] UN ECAFE, *Programme of Studies and Investigation for Comprehensive Development of the Lower Mekong Basin* (UN 1958); Gilbert F. White and others, *Economics and Social Aspects of Lower Mekong Development* (UN ECAFE 1962).

[36] Mekong Secretariat, *Indicative Basin Plan: Committee for Co-ordination and Investigation of the Lower Mekong Basin* (ECAFE 1972).

[37] Joint Declaration of Principles for Utilization of the Waters of the Lower Mekong Basin (adopted 31 January 1975) <http://gis.nacse.org/tfdd/tfdddocs/374ENG.pdf> accessed 10 July 2024.

[38] Declaration Concerning the Interim Committee for Coordination of Investigations of the Lower Mekong Basin (adopted 5 January 1978) <http://gis.nacse.org/tfdd/tfdddocs/396ENG.pdf> accessed 10 July 2024.

domestic projects on the tributaries of the Mekong.[39] However, the Interim Committee did take it upon itself to revisit the *Indicative Basin Plan* of 1970, which continued to focus on a cascade of eight mainstream dams, and compared to the 1970 Plan, presented an even stronger emphasis on hydropower potential above other benefits, such as flood control, fisheries and navigation.[40]

While progress was hampered by Cambodia's absence, in December 1992 representatives of Cambodia, Laos, Thailand and Vietnam attended a meeting facilitated by the United Nations Development Programme (UNDP) in Kuala Lumpur to discuss the future framework of cooperation in the Mekong.[41] UNDP facilitated five subsequent meetings and two technical drafting meetings, which culminated in the signing of the 1995 Mekong Agreement in Chiang Mai, Thailand.[42]

6.3 COMMITMENTS UNDER THE 1995 MEKONG AGREEMENT

6.3.1 Scope and Aim of the Agreement

The 1995 Mekong Agreement sets out the ambitious aim of cooperating in 'all fields of sustainable development, utilisation, management and conservation of the water and related resources of the Mekong River Basin'.[43] In terms of scope, the intention of the 1995 Mekong Agreement is far-reaching both in geographic and functional terms. Activities to be covered by the Agreement include irrigation, hydropower, navigation, flood control, fisheries, timber floating, and recreation and tourism, and the Agreement relates to the entire drainage basin. However, a fatal flaw in adopting such a basin-wide approach is the absence of the two upper riparian states of China and Myanmar, neither of which took part in the negotiation of the instrument nor has since become a party to the Agreement.

---

[39] Jacobs (n 29).

[40] Interim Mekong Committee, *Perspectives for Mekong Development: Revised Indicative Plan (1987) for the Development of Land, Water and Related Resources of the Lower Mekong Basin* (IMC 1988).

[41] George E. Radosevich and Douglas C. Olson, 'Existing and emerging basin arrangements in Asia: Mekong River Commission Case Study' (Third Workshop on River Basin Institution Development, Washington DC, 24 June 1999).

[42] Mekong Agreement (n 28).

[43] Article 1, ibid.

6.3.2 Substantive Commitments

The substantive commitments placed upon the parties of the Mekong Agreement are primarily set out in Articles 3, 5, 6 and 7 of its text. Article 5 reflects the well-established customary international law requirement that states 'utilise the waters of the Mekong River system *in a reasonable and equitable manner* in their respective territories, pursuant to all relevant factors and circumstances' [emphasis added].[44] In determining equity, a state must, as set out in the Mekong Agreement, take into account 'relevant factors and circumstances'.[45] The Mekong Agreement does not explicitly set out what factors and circumstances should be taken into account. However, guidance can be drawn from Article 6 of the Convention on the Law of the Non-navigational Uses of International Watercourses (Watercourses Convention).[46] According to the Watercourses Convention, the factors and circumstances to be taken into account include the physical characteristics of the watercourse, population dependency, existing and potential uses, the impacts of existing and potential uses, the efficiency of uses, and the availability of alternative uses.[47]

In terms of the weight that each factor should be afforded, general guidance is given in the Watercourses Convention, which suggests that the weight to be given to each factor should be determined by its relative importance to the other factors, and a conclusion reached on the basis of the whole.[48] The Convention goes on to suggest that no use enjoys inherent priority, although 'special regard' should also be afforded to 'the requirements of vital human needs'.[49] The 'no priority rule' is also tempered by the requirement under the Watercourses Convention that states should aim to achieve an outcome that is both optimal and sustainable, and is 'consistent with adequate protection of the watercourse'.[50] This approach is consistent with the commitment under the 1995 Mekong Agreement to 'the sustainable development, utilisation, management and conservation of the water and related resources of the Mekong River Basin', and the aim to cooperate, 'in a manner to optimize the multiple-use and

---

[44] Ibid.

[45] Article 5, ibid.

[46] Convention on the Law of the Non-navigational Uses of International Watercourses (adopted 21 May 1997, entered into force 17 August 2014), 36 ILM 700 (Watercourses Convention).

[47] Ibid.

[48] Article 6(3) Watercourses Convention, ibid.

[49] Article 10, Watercourses Convention, ibid.

[50] Article 5(1), Watercourses Convention, ibid.

mutual benefits of all riparians and to minimise the harmful effects that might result from natural occurrences and man-made activities'.[51]

The equitable and reasonable utilisation requirement under the 1995 Mekong Agreement is supplemented by additional substantive requirements. Article 3 of the Mekong Agreement commits the parties to 'protect the environment, natural resources, aquatic life and conditions, and ecological balance of the Mekong River Basin from pollution or other harmful effects resulting from any development plans and uses of water and related resources in the Basin'.[52] When commenting on the similar obligation to protect ecosystems of international watercourses, the International Law Commission (ILC) suggested that such an obligation 'requires that watercourse states shield the ecosystem of international watercourses from harm or damage'; and that states 'protect those ecosystems from a significant threat of harm'.[53] The ILC suggests that a precautionary approach would be inherent within the duty to protect, although some commentators raise concerns that the Mekong Agreement does not include an explicit reference to the precautionary principle, and as a result the MRC 'has been too often subdued about the risks associated with many development projects'.[54]

Environmental considerations are further reflected in Article 6 of the Mekong Agreement, which obliges its parties to 'cooperate in the maintenance of the flows on the mainstream from diversions, storage releases, or other actions of a permanent nature; except in the cases of historically severe droughts and/or floods'.[55] The basis for this provision can be found in the historic interests of the parties.[56] A key concern for Vietnam was to ensure sufficient dry season flows into the Mekong Delta in order to sustain rice harvests and to combat saline intrusion.[57] Laos was also keen to maintain existing dry season flows in order to preserve the navigability of the Mekong River all year

[51] Article 1, Mekong Agreement (n 28).

[52] Article 3, ibid.

[53] International Law Commission, 'Report of the International Law Commission on the Work of its 46th Session' (2 May – 22 July 1994) UN Doc A/CN.4/SER.A/1994/Add.1 (Part 2), 119.

[54] John Dore and Kate Lazarus, 'De-marginalising the Mekong River Commission', in François Molle, Tira Foran and Mira Käkönen (eds), *Contested Waterscapes in the Mekong Region – Hydropower, Livelihoods and Governance* (Earthscan 2009).

[55] Mekong Agreement (n 28).

[56] Browder and Ortolano (n 34).

[57] Ibid. See Article 6(A), Mekong Agreement (n 28), which requires the signatories to maintain flows 'of not less than the acceptable minimum monthly natural flow during each month of the dry season'.

round.[58] Article 6(A) of the Mekong Agreement therefore provided that the states maintain the flow of the mainstream of the river 'of not less than the acceptable minimum monthly flow during each month of the dry season'.[59] Cambodia was also keen to safeguard sufficient reverse wet season flow from the Mekong River into the Tonle Sap.[60] Article 6(B) of the Mekong Agreement therefore sets out a requirement to protect this wet season flow.[61] Preserving wet season flows into the Tonle Sap River, which feeds off the Mekong River and into the Tonle Sap lake, requires large wet season flows of the Mekong River to be maintained.[62] High wet season flows also support the ecological integrity of various wetlands both upstream and downstream of the junction of the Tonle Sap and Mekong River.[63]

No numerical values for wet and dry season flows were set out in the Mekong Agreement. Rather, the Agreement requires the states, through the MRC, to adopt 'guidelines for the locations and levels of the flows'.[64] In 1995, the entire storage capacity from infrastructure in the Mekong was only 2% of annual flow, so the actual dry season flow in the Mekong River when the states were negotiating the agreement was almost equal to the natural flow.[65] While maintaining that natural flow safeguards aquatic ecosystem functioning, the aforementioned developments in the basin, particularly in relation to hydropower, have considerably affected the flow dynamics of the river.[66]

Additional substantive obligations are provided for in Article 7 of the Mekong Agreement, which requires the parties to 'make every effort to avoid, minimize and mitigate harmful effects that might occur to the environment, especially the water quantity and quality, and aquatic (ecosystem) conditions, and ecological balance of the river system, from the development and use of the Mekong River Basin water resources or discharge of wastes and return flows'.[67] The terminology used in the Watercourses Convention, which could be argued is reflective of customary international law, differs from Article 7 of the Mekong Agreement. Under the Watercourses Convention, the requirement is to adopt 'all appropriate measures' to prevent the causing of significant

---

58 Browder and Ortolano (n 34).
59 Mekong Agreement (n 28).
60 Browder and Ortolano (n 34).
61 Mekong Agreement (n 28).
62 Browder and Ortolano (n 34).
63 Mekong Agreement (n 28).
64 Article 6, Mekong Agreement (n 28).
65 Browder and Ortolano (n 34).
66 Lancang-Mekong Water Resources Cooperation Center and MRC (n 21).
67 Mekong Agreement (n 28).

harm.[68] Assessing whether a state has complied with this 'due diligence' standard requires an assessment of both the nature of the harm itself *and* the conduct of a state in seeking to prevent that harm.[69] Such a requirement brings in a strong procedural element whereby an alleged breach must be assessed not just for the harm itself, but also on whether a state adopted the necessary legal, administrative or technical measures to prevent such harm.[70] Differentiated responsibilities may also apply to the application of this due diligence stand-

---

[68] Article 7, Watercourses Convention (n 46); See also Stephen C. McCaffrey, *The Law of International Watercourses* (OUP 2007), 406–445.

[69] Alistair Rieu-Clarke, *International Law and Sustainable Development – Lessons from the Law of International Watercourses* (IWA Publishing 2005), 118. The ILC has commented that, 'due diligence is manifested in reasonable efforts by a state to inform itself of factual and legal components that relate foreseeably to a contemplated procedure and to take appropriate measures, in timely fashion, to address them' (ILC, 'Report of the International Law Commission on the Work of its 53rd Session (23 April – 1 June and 2 July – 10 August 2001), UN Doc A/CN.4/SER.A/2001/Add.1 (Part 2), 154). The ILC goes on to suggest that 'states are under an obligation to take unilateral measures to prevent significant transboundary harm or at any event to minimize the risk thereof arising out of activities within the scope of article 1. Such measures include, first, formulating policies designed to prevent significant transboundary harm or to minimize the risk thereof and, secondly, implementing those policies. Such policies are expressed in legislation and administrative regulations and implemented through various enforcement mechanisms', ibid.

[70] Article 3 of the Convention on the Protection and Use of Transboundary Watercourses and International Lakes (adopted 17 March 1992, entered into force 6 October 1996), 1936 UNTS 269, lists a number of measures that may be deemed appropriate depending on the context, including: point source prevention, control and reduction of pollution through application of low- and non-waste technology; prior licencing of wastewater discharges by competent national authorities, and the monitoring and control of authorised discharges; limits on wastewater discharges stated in permits and based on best available technology for discharges of hazardous substances; stricter requirements, leading to prohibition where appropriate, for sensitive water bodies or their ecosystems; use of at least biological treatment or equivalent process for municipal wastewater; appropriate measures taken, such as the use of best available technology, in order to reduce nutrient inputs from industrial and municipal sources; appropriate measures and best environmental practices developed and implemented for the reduction of inputs of nutrients and hazardous substances from diffuse sources; the application of environmental impact assessment and other means of assessment; the promotion of sustainable water resources management, including the application of the ecosystem approach; contingency planning; additional measures to prevent the pollution of groundwater; and the risk of accidental pollution is minimised.

ard, whereby states with a greater capacity to adopt legal, administrative and/or technical measures to prevent harm may be subject to a higher standard than other states.[71]

A question can be raised over whether the 'make every effort' requirement under the Mekong Agreement constitutes a higher standard than the 'take appropriate measures' requirement under the Watercourses Convention. It could be argued that a standard by which a state must make *every* effort does not concern itself with whether or not that effort is appropriate based on the capacity of the states concerned, or the risk and magnitude of harm involved. However, Article 7 of the Mekong Agreement goes on to require its signatories to 'make every effort to *avoid, minimise and mitigate* harmful effects that might occur to the environment' [emphasis added].[72] The option to 'minimise and mitigate' harm would imply that some harm may be tolerated based on whether or not the effort made to minimise and mitigate such harm is appropriate. Such a due diligence approach would be consistent not only with the Watercourses Convention but also customary international law.[73]

A further point to observe is that the Watercourses Convention explicitly stipulates that states should have due regard to the principle of equitable and reasonable utilisation, when determining whether harm should be eliminated or mitigated, and whether compensation might be claimed.[74] The Mekong Agreement does not make any explicit reference to the relationship between the duty to prevent, minimise and mitigate harm (Article 7), and the equitable

---

[71] The ILC states that 'the standard of due diligence against which the conduct of the state of origin should be examined is that which is generally considered to be appropriate and proportional to the degree of risk of transboundary harm in the particular instance. For example, activities which may be considered ultrahazardous require a much higher standard of care in designing policies and a much higher degree of vigour on the part of the state to enforce them. Issues such as the size of the operation, its location, special climate conditions, materials used in the activity, and whether the conclusions drawn from the application of these factors in a specific case are reasonable, are among the factors to be considered in determining the due diligence requirement in each instance. What would be considered a reasonable standard of care or due diligence may change with time; what might be considered an appropriate and reasonable procedure, standard or rule at one point in time may not be considered as such at some point in the future. Hence, due diligence in ensuring safety requires a state to keep abreast of technological changes and scientific developments' (ILC n 69, 154).

[72] Article 7, Mekong Agreement (n 28).

[73] See Attila Tanzi and Alexandros Kolliopoulos, 'The No-Harm Rule', in Attila Tanzi and others (eds), *The UNECE Convention on the Protection of Transboundary Watercourses and International Lakes* (Brill 2015), 133.

[74] Article 7, Watercourses Convention (n 46).

and reasonable utilisation principle (Article 5). However, a systemic approach to the interpretation of the Agreement would suggest that both provisions, Articles 5 and 7, are a package along similar lines to the 'package of norms' approach adopted under the Watercourses Convention, and reflective of customary international law.[75]

An analysis of the substantive commitments under the Mekong Agreement demonstrates that there is considerable discretion in how these provisions may be interpreted and implemented. The Mekong Agreement can even be described as an 'agreement to agree', with the expectation that more detailed commitments will be developed as the cooperation between the parties evolves. Such an approach is provided for in Article 26 of the Mekong Agreement, for instance, whereby the parties are required to develop 'rules for water utilisation and inter-basin diversions, that in addition to setting out certain procedural requirements, request the states to determine and maintain flow requirements; and set out criteria for determining surplus quantities of water during the dry season on the mainstream'.[76] However, so far, the parties have made little progress in the development of any concrete substantive rules, which, as will be illustrated below, places considerable strain on the more general substantive principles found in Articles 3, 5, 6 and 7 of the Mekong Agreement.

6.3.3 Procedural and Institutional Commitments

The 1995 Mekong Agreement sets out a suite of procedural and institutional requirements. The primary institutional body established under the Mekong Agreement is the MRC.[77] The MRC is made up of a Council, a Joint Committee and a secretariat. The Council, which is obliged to meet at least once per year, represents the main decision-making body of the MRC and is made up of one member from each participating state at the Ministerial and Cabinet level.[78] The Joint Committee, which is obliged to meet at least twice a year, is made up of one member from each participating riparian state at no less than the Head of Department level.[79] The Joint Committee plays a supporting role in the implementation of the decisions of the Council. The secretariat then provides technical and administrative services to both the Council and the Joint Committee.[80]

---

75 McCaffrey (n 68).
76 Article 26, Mekong Agreement (n 28).
77 Articles 11–33, ibid.
78 Article 15, ibid.
79 Article 21 and 23, ibid.
80 Article 38, ibid.

Several provisions of the Mekong Agreement provide procedural elements, but Article 5 is central. Article 5 introduces a multi-tiered approach to planned measures. For activities taking place on the tributaries, including the Tonle Sap, the Joint Committee must be notified of any intra-basin uses and inter-basin diversions.[81] Intra-basin use during the wet season is also subject to notification to the Joint Committee.[82] 'Notification' is elaborated upon within Chapter II of the Mekong Agreement, which describes it as 'timely providing information by a riparian to the Joint Committee on its proposed use of water'.[83]

A stricter requirement, of 'prior consultation' through the Joint Committee, is required for inter-basin diversions within the wet season, and intra-basin use within the dry season.[84] Chapter II of the Mekong Agreement describes 'prior consultation' as being the provision of 'timely notification plus additional data and information … that would allow the other member riparians to discuss and evaluate the impact of the proposed use upon their uses of water and any other affects, which is the basis for arriving at an agreement'.[85] In seeking to strike a balance between the interests of the planning state and any potentially affected states, the Agreement goes on to point out that 'prior consultation is neither a right to veto the use nor a unilateral right to use water by any riparian without taking into account other riparians right'.[86] Such a requirement should be seen within a more general legal obligation upon states to consult in *good faith*.[87]

The strictest commitment is afforded to planned inter-basin diversions during the dry season, which are subject to *agreement* by the parties through the Joint Committee.[88]

The Mekong Agreement also imposes procedural commitments in relation to harm and damages. Article 7 provides that, 'where one or more states is notified with proper and valid evidence that it is causing substantial damage to one or more riparians from the use and/or discharge to water of the Mekong River, that state or states shall cease immediately the alleged cause of harm until such harm is determined in accordance with Article 8'.[89] Article 8 then stipulates that, where harmful effects cause substantial damage to one or more

81 Article 5(A), ibid.

82 Article 5(B)(1)(a), ibid.

83 Ibid.

84 Article 5(B), ibid.

85 Chapter II, ibid.

86 Chapter III, ibid.

87 *Gabčíkovo-Nagymaros Project (Hungary/Slovakia)* (Judgment) [1997] ICJ Rep 7, para 142.

88 Article 5(B)(2)(a), Mekong Agreement (n 28).

89 Ibid.

riparians from the use of and/or discharge to waters of the Mekong River by any riparian state, the party or parties concerned shall determine all relevant factors, the cause, extent of damage and responsibility for damage caused by the state. They should then, in conformity with the principles of international law relating to state responsibility, address and resolve all issues, differences and disputes in an amicable and timely manner by peaceful means.

These procedural rules concerning damages are supplemented by procedural requirements related to dispute settlement. The Mekong Agreement simply offers a flexible option whereby the parties must address any difference or dispute via the Joint Committee or Council.[90] If that proves unsuccessful in resolving the dispute, then they are required to seek a resolution by 'negotiation through diplomatic channels within a timely manner'.[91] Considerable discretion is therefore placed upon the parties in terms of the specific means they use, and the extent to which they might involve third parties.

A further set of procedural commitments is contained within the Mekong Agreement through the obligations imposed on the MRC. The Joint Committee is obliged to prepare and propose for approval of the Council Rules for Water Utilisation and Inter-Basin Diversions, as stipulated in Articles 5 and 6 of the Agreement.[92] Functions of the Joint Committee also include: formulating a basin development plan, which should be periodically reviewed and approved by the Council;[93] regularly obtaining, updating and exchanging information and data necessary to implement the Agreement;[94] and conducting appropriate studies and assessment for the protection of the environment and maintenance of the ecological balance of the Mekong.[95]

The procedural commitments set out in the Mekong Agreement follow a similar approach to the substantive commitments, with considerable discretion left to the parties to either develop further details through subsequent measures or agree on their application on a case-by-case basis. To date, the parties to the Mekong Agreement have not managed to agree on legally binding rules for water utilisation and inter-basin diversions, as stipulated in Articles 5 and 6 of the Agreement. Rather, the signatories to the Mekong Agreement have chosen to develop softer procedures.[96] The value of these procedures and accompanying guidelines will be explored in the following section.

---

[90] Article 34, ibid.

[91] Article 35, ibid.

[92] Article 26, ibid.

[93] Article 24(B), ibid.

[94] Article 24(C), ibid.

[95] Article 24(D), ibid.

[96] See for example, Procedures for Notification, Prior Consultation and Agreement (30 November 2003) <https://www.mrcmekong.org/mrc-procedures/>

6.4 EXPERIENCE IN IMPLEMENTATION AND COMPLIANCE

In assessing the record of compliance and implementation vis-à-vis the Mekong Agreement, this section will follow the structure of Chapter 4 and pay particular attention to key areas of monitoring and reporting, mechanisms to review implementation, and strategies employed to address weak implementation and non-compliance. Any measures adopted by the parties to the Mekong Agreement in support of compliance and implementation will be examined, together with the factors that have or are likely to influence the effectiveness of the measures.

6.4.1 Monitoring and Reporting

Exchange of data and information

No formal requirement to report on compliance and implementation is contained in the Mekong Agreement or any subsidiary procedures of the MRC. However, various measures have been put in place by the parties to the Mekong Agreement with the aim of indirectly monitoring the implementation of the agreement and reporting on progress. These measures include efforts to exchange data and information, monitor the conditions of transboundary waters, and develop joint strategies, plans and programmes. While not explicitly covered in the Mekong Agreement, non-state actors are also playing an increasingly stronger role in monitoring and reporting the efforts of the lower Mekong states to implement the agreement. The latter activities will therefore also be considered in this section.

As noted in the previous section, responsibility for the exchange of data and information rests with the Joint Committee.[97] In support of this commitment, the parties to the Mekong Agreement adopted Procedures for Data

---

accessed 28 August 2024 (PNPCA); Procedures for Water Use Monitoring (30 November 2003) <https://www.mrcmekong.org/mrc-procedures/> accessed 28 August 2024; Procedures for Data and Information Exchange and Sharing (PDIES) (1 November 2001) <https://www.mrcmekong.org/mrc-procedures/> accessed 28 August 2024; Procedures for Water Quality (26 January 2011) <https://www.mrcmekong.org/mrc-procedures/> accessed 28 August 2024; Procedures for the Maintenance of Flows on the Mainstream (22 June 2006) <https://www.mrcmekong.org/mrc-procedures/> accessed 28 August 2024. See also Philip Hirsch and others, *National Interests and Transboundary Water Governance in the Mekong*, <http://www.cawater-info.net/bk/water_law/pdf/hirsch-et-al.pdf> accessed 15 January 2025, 30.

[97] Article 24(C), Mekong Agreement (n 28).

and Information Exchange and Sharing (PDIES) on 1 November 2001.[98] The objectives of the PDIES are stated as being to: 'operationalize the data and information exchange among the four MRC member countries'; 'make available, upon request, basic data and information for public access as determined by the NMCs concerned'; and 'promote understanding and cooperation among the MRC member countries in a constructive and mutually beneficial manner to ensure the sustainable development of the Mekong Basin'.[99] The PDIES also list the types of data and information required for the implementation of the Mekong Agreement,[100] and assigns the MRC secretariat with responsibility for managing an MRC Information System (MRC – IS).[101] The MRC secretariat has the responsibility to report annually to the Joint Committee on the overall effectiveness of the PDIES.[102] In support of the PDIES, the parties to the Mekong Agreement adopted Guidelines on Custodianship and Management of the MRC Information System in 2002 and supplementary technical documents in 2005.[103]

The establishment of data and information sharing procedures within the MRC builds on a tradition that dates back to the establishment of the Mekong Committee in 1957.[104] The Mekong Committee spent its first 15 years gathering hydrologic data in order to support decision-making on the potential construction of dams on the mainstream and tributaries of the Mekong.[105] However, despite a long tradition and the introduction of the PDIES and MRC-IS, there have been significant challenges related to the exchange of data

---

98 PDIES (n 96).

99 PDIES (n 96), 2.

100 The groups of data and information listed under the Procedures are: water resources, topography, natural resources, agriculture, navigation and transport, flood management and mitigation, infrastructure, urbanisation and industrialisation, environment and ecology, administrative boundaries, socio-economy and tourism (Article 5(b), PDIES (n 96), 3).

101 Article 5(1), PDIES n 96, 3. An MRC Data and Information Services Portal was subsequently established (see MRC, 'Data and Information Systems and Services', <https://www.mrcmekong.org/data-and-information-systems-and-services/> accessed 28 August 2024).

102 Article 5(2), PDIES (n 96), 4.

103 MRC (n 101).

104 Andrea Gerlak, Jonathan Lautze and Mark Giordano, 'Water resources data and information exchange in transboundary water treaties' (2011) 11 International Environmental Agreements: Politics, Law and Economics 179.

105 Chris Sneddon and Coleen Fox, 'Rethinking transboundary waters: A critical hydropolitics of the Mekong Basin' (2006) 25(2) Political Geography 181.

and information within the basin, which has led to repeated calls to improve the implementation of PDIES.[106]

One challenge concerns ambiguity in what is being asked for. Bach and others observe that, 'what is needed can … be interpreted in many ways, which translates into gaps in time series and geographic coverage of databases, including even basic hydro-meteorological data'.[107] While a lack of a shared understanding might therefore be seen as a key challenge, others have argued that the high rate of MRC staff turnover, and the shortage of technically competent staff, has meant that 'too few efforts have been made by the MRC to collect and analyse data and then publish the results'.[108] Plengsaeng and others highlight the significance of capacity and the institutional environment at the national level in ensuring that transboundary platforms for data and information sharing are effective.[109] According to the MRC's Guidelines on Custodianship and Management of the MRC-IS, National Mekong Committees or Line Agencies in each country 'are the ones that initially collect, process, and store the data and information to be exchanged and shared under the Exchange and Sharing procedures'.[110] In taking on such a responsibility, National Mekong Committees must identify 'primary custodians' among various national agencies that commit to providing the 12 types of data and information requested pursuant to the PDIES.[111] In analysing the Thai context, Plengsaeng and others suggest

---

[106] Chuan Aligha, 'Environmental Clearinghouse as an Institutional Incentive for Data and Information Sharing and Conflict Reduction in the Mekong River Basin' (UCOWR Conference, 20 July 2004); See, for example, MRC, Hua Hin Declaration (5 April 2010) <https://www.preventionweb.net/files/13499_MRC HuaHinDeclaration05Apr101.pdf> accessed 28 August 2024; MRC, 'Strategic Plan 2011–2015', <https://www.mrcmekong.org/wp-content/uploads/2024/08/Stratigic-Plan-2011-2015.pdf> accessed 28 August 2024; Bastien Affeltranger, 'Sustainability of environment regimes: The Mekong River Commission', in Han G. Bruach and others (eds), *Facing Global Environmental Change: Environmental, Human, Energy, Food, Health and Water Security Concepts* (Springer 2009), 593.

[107] Hanne Bach and others, *Transboundary River Basin Management: Addressing Water, Energy and Food Security* (MRC 2014).

[108] Ian Campbell, 'Perceptions, data, and river management: Lessons from the Mekong River' (2007) 43 Water Resources Research 2.

[109] Bunthida Plengsaeng, Uta Wehn and Pieter van der Zaag, 'Data-sharing bottlenecks in transboundary integrated water resources management: a case study of the Mekong River Commission's procedures for data sharing in the Thai context' (2014) 39(7) Water International 933.

[110] MRC, Guidelines for Custodianship and Management of the Mekong River Commission Information System (11 July 2002) <https://www.mrcmekong.org/publications_cat/policies-procedures-and-guidelines/> accessed 28 August 2024.

[111] PDIES (n 96).

that domestic law and regulations inhibit data sharing due to national security concerns.[112] Along similar lines, ambiguity and uncertainty in national organisational data policies have allegedly led to overcautious approaches to data and information sharing, or the lack thereof.[113] Additional national factors affecting data and information sharing include insufficient technological skills, e.g., IT skills, spatial data-related skills, and English language skills.[114]

A critical area where the exchange of data and information between Lower Mekong states has been particularly challenging is in relation to planned transboundary hydropower projects. As noted previously, the Lower Mekong states adopted the Procedures for Notification, Prior Consultation and Agreement (PNPCA) in 2003.[115] These procedures were then supplemented by guidelines in August 2005.[116] The procedures and guidelines set out the form, content and institutional procedures that should be followed when states are planning projects that may have a transboundary impact.

Five hydropower projects situated on the mainstream of the Mekong in Laos have gone through the MRC's prior consultation process – the Xayaburi, Don Sahong, Pak Beng, Pak Lay and Luang Prabang. This stands in stark contrast to the significant number of existing and planned dams within the Basin. Arguably, the greatest impact from hydropower developments has resulted from developments in the tributaries of the Mekong, where 87 are at some stage of development, and a further 36 projects are expected to be operational by 2040.[117] However, the PNPCA requirements under the Mekong Agreement have been interpretated by its parties to apply primarily to mainstream projects and not those taking place on the tributaries of the Mekong.[118] This is because the Mekong Agreement makes a distinction between tributaries and

---

112 Plengsaeng (n 109), 945.

113 Ibid.

114 Ibid.

115 PNPCA (n 96).

116 Mekong River Commission, Guidelines on Implementation of the Procedures for Notification, Prior Consultation and Agreement (31 August 2005) <https://archive.iwlearn.net/mrcmekong.org/download/agreement95/Procedures_Guidlines/Tech-Guidelines-PNPCA-Final-26Jul05.pdf> accessed 28 August 2024.

117 Mekong River Commission (n 3), at 112. See also Keskinen and others (n 15).

118 Alistair Rieu-Clarke and Geoffrey Gooch, 'Governing the tributaries of the Mekong: the contribution of international law and institutions to enhancing equitable cooperation over the Sesan' (2010) 22 Pacific McGeorge Global Business and Development Law Journal 193; Bennett Bearden, 'The Legal Regime of the Mekong River: a look back and some proposals for the way ahead' (2010) 12(6) Water Policy 798.

the mainstream when stipulating in Article 5(A) that 'on the tributaries of the Mekong River, including Tonle Sap, intra-basin uses and inter-basin diversions shall be subject to notification to the Joint Committee'.[119] In other words, they are not subject to the more collaborative requirement of prior consultation. A further distinction between tributaries and the mainstream of the Mekong is made when the Mekong Agreement stipulates that notification involves 'timely providing information by a riparian to the Joint Committee on its proposed use of water'.[120] The definition of proposed use sets a threshold requirement that any impact must first be 'significant' and secondly have an impact on the mainstream flows. Any inter-tributary impact would therefore be excluded from the definition of a proposed use.[121]

Several projects on the tributaries of the Lower Mekong have called into question the value of adopting such a narrow reading of the Mekong Agreement. The Yali Falls dam, built on the Sesan River in Vietnam, resulted in significant impacts downstream in Cambodia. These impacts included unusual flooding events, fluctuations in river flow, water quality issues and riverbank erosion, which led to loss of livelihoods among downstream communities.[122] The project did not undergo any prior consultation process.[123] Such a restrictive interpretation of the Mekong Agreement also ignores the cumulative impacts that arise from the multiple hydropower projects on the tributaries of the Mekong River.[124] Moreover, an argument could be made that the need for notification

---

119 Mekong Agreement (n 28).

120 Chapter II, ibid.

121 Ibid.

122 SWECO Grøner and others, 'Final Report – Environmental Impact Assessment on the Cambodian Part of the Se San River due to Hydropower Developments in Vietnam' (2006) <https://www.riverresourcehub.org/resources/environmental-impact-assessment-on-the-cambodian-side-of-the-srepok-river-due-to/> accessed 10 July 2024; NGO Forum on Cambodia, 'Down River – The Consequences of Vietnam's Se San River Dams on Life in Cambodia and their Meaning in International Law' (2005) <https://hrp.law.harvard.edu/wp-content/uploads/2013/02/Down-River-2005.pdf> accessed 10 July 2024; Fisheries Office Ratanakiri Province, 'A Study of the Downstream Impacts of the Yali Falls Dam in the Se San River Basin in Ratanakiri Province' (2000) <https://www.academia.edu/6222865/A_Study_of_the_Downstream_Impacts_of_the_Yali_Falls_Dam_in_the_Se_San_River_Basin_in_Ratanakiri_Province_Northeast_Cambodia> accessed 10 July 2024.

123 Rieu-Clarke and Gooch (n 118).

124 Matti Kummu and Marko Keskinen, 'Impact Assessment in the Mekong: Review of Strategic Environmental Assessment (SEA) & Cumulative Impact Assessment (CIA)' (Working Paper), <https://www.academia.edu/2758065/Impact_Assessment_in_the_Mekong_Review_of_Strategic_Environmental

and consultation, including the production of a transboundary Environmental Impact Assessment (EIA), is now part and parcel of customary international law and should therefore be followed regardless of whether there is an explicit provision to cover transboundary impacts within the Mekong Agreement.[125]

A further issue relates to the way in which the PNPCA prior consultation processes have been applied in the cases of the Xayaburi, Don Sahong, Pak Beng, Pak Lay, Luang Prabang and Sanakham Hydropower projects, which are all situated on the mainstream of the Mekong in Laos. In terms of the timing of notification, the Mekong Agreement requires that any notification should be 'timely'.[126] The PNPCA guidelines require that 'submission to the MRC Joint Committee must be at least 6 months prior to commencement of project implementation, preferably greater'.[127] The guidelines go on to suggest that 'in actual practice it is likely that projects … would be submitted far in advance of the intended start-up date because they are long-term large scale projects requiring considerable technical, economic, social and impact analyses'.[128]

The Lao government signed a Memorandum of Understanding (MoU) with a Thai energy company, Ch. Karnchang Public Company Limited, to conduct a survey and study the development of the Xayaburi project on 4 May 2007.[129] An EIA and social impact assessment (SIA) were then conducted between September 2007 and April 2008.[130] However, it was not until 20 September

---

_Assessment_SEA_and_Cumulative_Impact_Assessment_CIA_> accessed 10 July 2024; International Centre for Environmental Management, 'Strategic Environmental Assessment of Hydropower on the Mekong Mainstream' (October 2010) <https://icem.com.au/portfolio-items/strategic-environmental-assessment-of-hydropower-on-the-mekong-mainstream/> accessed 15 January 2025.

[125] *Case Concerning Pulp Mills on the River Uruguay (Argentina v Uruguay)* [2010] ICJ Rep 14 (Pulp Mills Case). The Court in the Pulp Mills Case declared that 'it may now be considered a requirement under general international law to undertake an environmental impact assessment where there is a risk that the proposed activity may have a significant adverse impact in a transboundary context, in particular, on a shared resource' (para 205, ibid). *Certain Activities Carried out by Nicaragua in the Border Area (Costa Rica v Nicaragua)* (Compensation) [2018] ICJ Rep 15, para 104.

[126] Chapter II, Mekong Agreement (n 28).

[127] PNPCA Guidelines (n 116), 5.

[128] PNPCA Guidelines (n 116), 5.

[129] Team Consulting Engineering and Management Co. Ltd and Power Engineering Ltd, 'Feasibility Study Xayaburi Hydroelectric Power Project Lao, PDR—Final Report' (Ch. Karnchang Public Company Limited, March 2010), 1.

[130] Team Consulting Engineering and Management Co. Ltd, 'Social Impact Assessment—Xayaburi Hydroelectric Power Project' (Ch. Karnchang

2010 that the Lao National Mekong Committee submitted prior consultation documents to the MRC secretariat.[131] In the case of Don Sahong, the Lao government and a Malaysian private company, Mega First Corporation Berhad (MFCB), signed a MoU to instigate the feasibility of the project on 23 March 2006,[132] but it was not until 20 September 2013 that the Lao government notified the MRC of the project.[133] In the case of the Pak Beng project, a project MoU was adopted in August 2007, but the project was not submitted to the PNPCA process until 4 November 2016.[134] Similarly, a feasibility study for the Pak Lay project commenced in November 2007, while it was not until 13 June 2018 that the project was submitted to the PNPCA process.[135] For the Luang Prabang project, a project MoU was adopted in October 2007,[136] while the PNPCA process was not initiated until 31 July 2019.[137] Finally, in the case

---

Public Company Limited, August 2010); and Team Consulting Engineering and Management Co. Ltd, 'Environmental Impact Assessment—Xayaburi Hydroelectric Power Project' (Ch. Karnchang Public Company Limited, August 2010).

131 MRC, 'Xayaburi's Prior Consultation Road Map', <https://www.banktrack.org/download/prior_consultation_project_review_report_volume_2_stakeholder_consultations_related_to_the_proposed_xayaburi_dam_project/110707_reportonstakeholderconsonxayaburi.pdf> accessed 28 August 2024.

132 National Consulting Company, 'Don Sahong Hydropower Project, Lao PDR, Environmental Impact Assessment – Final' (January 2013) <https://data.laos.opendevelopmentmekong.net/library_record/2013ko>, viii.

133 MRC, 'Don Sahong Project's Prior Consultation Road Map', <https://www.mrcmekong.org/news_and_events/don-sahong-hydropower-project/> accessed 8 June 2023.

134 MRC, 'Roadmap – The Pak Beng PNPCA Prior Consultation Process', <https://www.mrcmekong.org/news_and_events/pak-beng-hydropower-project/> accessed 8 June 2023.

135 MRC, 'Draft Pak Lay PNPCA Prior Consultation Roadmap', <https://www.mrcmekong.org/news_and_events/pak-lay-hydropower-project/> accessed 8 June 2023.

136 Luang Prabang Power Company Limited, 'Feasibility Study Report', <https://www.mrcmekong.org/news_and_events/luang-prabang-hydropower-project/> accessed 8 June 2023, iv.

137 MRC, Luang Prabang 'PNPCA Prior Consultation Process Roadmap', <https://www.mrcmekong.org/news_and_events/luang-prabang-hydropower-project/> accessed 8 June 2023.

of the Sanakham project, a MoU was signed in December of 2007,[138] but the PNPCA process did not start until 9 September 2019.[139]

While the term 'timely' is open to interpretation, it could be argued that the PNPCA process should have been triggered earlier in the aforementioned cases. In the *Pulp Mills* case, for instance, the International Court of Justice, albeit within the confines of a bilateral treaty, suggested that an initial requirement to inform should be satisfied, 'at the stage when the relevant [national] authority has had the project refereed to it with the aim of obtaining initial environment authorisation and before the granting of that authorisation'.[140] The Convention on Environmental Impact Assessment in a Transboundary Context (ESPOO Convention) ties notification strongly to the process of EIAs, stipulating that: 'the formal stage for the identification of issues to be examined in the EIA, often called scoping, provides a suitable moment for an early notification'.[141] Along similar lines, McCaffrey has suggested that 'timely' should be defined as, 'sufficiently early in the preliminary planning stages to permit meaningful consultation and negotiation, if these are necessary'.[142]

What data and information should be shared has also posed a challenge in the implementation of the MRC's PNPCA prior consultation processes. A considerable amount of data and information was made available during all the PNPCA processes. Laos shared the feasibility studies, together with EIAs and SIAs, and completed PNPCA prior consultation forms.[143] The states also

---

[138] Datang (Lao) Sanakham Hydropower Co. Ltd, 'Sanakham Hydropower Project, Transboundary Environmental and Social Impact Assessment & Cumulative Impact Assessment' (October 2018) <https://www.mrcmekong.org/news_and_events/sanakham-hydropower-project/> accessed 8 June 2023, 13.

[139] MRC, 'Revised Proposed Roadmap of SNHPP PC Process' (September 2021) <https://www.mrcmekong.org/news_and_events/sanakham-hydropower-project/> accessed 8 June 2023.

[140] Pulp Mills Case (n 125), para 105.

[141] See UNECE, 'Guidance on Notification According to the Espoo Convention', UN Doc ECE/MP.EIA/12 (2009), 8. Convention on Environmental Impact Assessment in a Transboundary Context (adopted 25 February 1991, entered into force 10 September 1997), (1991) 30 ILM 802.

[142] Second Report on the Law of the Non-navigational Uses of International Watercourses, by Stephen C. McCaffrey, Special Rapporteur, in ILC, 'Report of the International Law Commission on the Work of its 42nd Session' (23 February and 7 June 1990), UN Doc A/CN.4/SER.A/1990/Add.1 (Part 1), 42.

[143] The PNPCA prior consultation form should include the following information: the notifying state; date of submission; notifying Ministry or Agency; contact person and address; name, location and description of the project, including scope, scale, site, type, quantity, capacity and characteristics; nature of the proposed use, e.g., on tributary or mainstream; purpose of the proposed project; expected date

had access to various studies that had been conducted by the MRC, including the *Basin Development Strategy*, the Strategic Environmental Assessment of Hydropower on the Mekong Mainstream, the Study on the Sustainable Management and Development of the Mekong River, including impacts of mainstream hydropower projects, and the Preliminary Design Guidance for Proposed Mainstream Dams in the Lower Mekong Basin.[144] However, during all the PNPCA prior consultations, questions were raised by downstream countries over the sufficiency of the available data and information.[145] In the case of the Sanakham Dam, the lack of data on the cumulative and transboundary impacts of the project constituted a major hurdle in finalising the PNPCA process.[146]

---

for implementation, including the start and end dates for construction, and date for operation; and the duration and timing for water use, see PNPCA (n 96).

144 MRC, 'Integrated Water Resources Management-based Basin Development Strategy 2011–2015' (January 2011) <https://data.opendevelopmentmekong.net/dataset/ddcdb9ad-3885-4c97-8f9e-a5ba3d66a786/resource/7609e625-91a5-40b1-88ed-3df371f7c968/download/iwrm-basin-development-strategy-fourth-draft-2010.pdf> accessed 10 July 2024; International Centre for Environmental Management, 'Strategic Environmental Assessment of Hydropower on the Mekong Mainstream – Final Report' (October 2010) <http://www.icem.com.au/documents/envassessment/mrc_sea_hp/5.%20final%20report/pdf/SEA_FP_summary_07Oct_updated12oct.pdf> accessed 15 January 2025. MRC, 'Preliminary Design Guidance for Proposed Mainstream Dams in the Lower Mekong Basin' (August 2009) <https://www.preventionweb.net/files/15958_mrcpreliminarydesignguidanceforprop.pdf> accessed 10 July 2024.

145 Cambodia National Mekong Committee, 'Reply to Prior Consultation', <https://www.banktrack.org/download/mekong_river_commission_procedures_for_notification_prior_consultation_and_agreement_form_format_for_reply_to_prior_consultation/110707_cambodiareplyform.pdf> accessed 28 August 2024; Thailand National Mekong Committee, 'Reply to Prior Consultation', <https://www.mrcmekong.org/news_and_events/xayaburi-hydropower-project/> accessed 8 June 2023; Vietnam National Mekong Committee, 'Reply to Prior Consultation', <https://www.banktrack.org/download/1_mekong_river_commission_procedures_for_notification_prior_consultation_and_agreement_vietnam/110707_vietnamreplyform.pdf> 28 August 2024. See also, Bangkok Tribune, 'Thailand insists on "sufficient" data on transboundary impacts of Lao PDR's Sanakham Dam before consultation wrap-up' (22 April 2022) <https://bkktribune.com/thailand-insists-on-sufficient-data-on-transboundary-impacts-of-lao-pdrs-sanakham-dam-before-consultation-wrap-up/> accessed 10 July 2024.

146 'New Indicative Ending Date Set for Sanakham Dam Consultation' (*The Laotian Times*, 22 September 2021) <https://laotiantimes.com/2021/09/22/new-indicative-ending-date-set-for-sanakham-dam-consultation/> accessed 28 August 2024.

Monitoring

While PNPCA relates to individual projects, joint monitoring potentially offers an important means by which to more generally assess the implementation and effectiveness of the Mekong Agreement. Unlike other basin agreements, there is no explicit joint monitoring requirement in the Mekong Agreement itself. The Joint Committee is simply tasked to carry out, 'appropriate studies and assessment for the protection of the environment and maintenance of the ecological balance of the Mekong River Basin'.[147] Through this general mandate, the MRC established the Water Utilisation Programme (WUP) in 2008, with the support of the Global Environment Facility. The objective of WUP was to develop both a real-time hydrological monitoring system and a longer-term strategic assessment of water availability for energy and agricultural development.[148] In terms of the real-time system, the MRC provides river level monitoring all year round through 22 water level monitoring stations, which provide daily updates during the flood season (June to December) and weekly updates during the dry season (January to May).[149] There is also a tradition of monitoring water quality in the Mekong, which dates back to the establishment of a water quality monitoring network in 1985.[150] The network has since grown to monitor water quality through 48 stations.[151] Through this programme, 12 water quality parameters are monitored on a monthly basis, and an additional six are monitored monthly during the dry season.[152] At the national level, each of the member states has committed to providing a water quality laboratory to support the monitoring, sampling and analysis of water quality.[153] While the implementation of a joint water quality monitoring system throughout the Mekong is generally perceived as positive, some challenges remain. These

147 Article 24(D), Mekong Agreement (n 28).

148 Global Environment Facility, 'Mekong River Basin Water Utilisation Project', <https://www.thegef.org/projects-operations/projects/615> accessed 10 July 2024.

149 MRC, 'Monitoring the Health of the Mekong River', <https://www.mrcmekong.org/basin-monitoring/> accessed 28 August 2024.

150 Kongmeng Ly, Henrik Larsen and Nguyen Van Duyen, 'Lower Mekong Regional Water Quality Monitoring Report' (MRC Technical Paper No. 51, February 2015), 2.

151 MRC, 'Water Quality Monitoring', <https://www.mrcmekong.org/water-quality-monitoring/> accessed 28 August 2024.

152 Kongmeng, Larsen and Van Duyen (n 150), 9. The water quality parameters monitored are temperature, pH, conductivity (salinity), alkalinity/acidity, dissolved oxygen, chemical oxygen demand, total phosphorous, total nitrogen, ammonium, total nitrite and nitrate, faecal coliform, total suspended solids, calcium, magnesium, sodium, potassium, sulphate and chloride.

153 Ibid, 3.

challenges include insufficient capacity to monitor and analyse emerging toxic contaminants and the need to continuously update Quality Assurance/Quality Control in all aspects of water quality monitoring and reporting.[154]

Through the MRC, member states have also established a fisheries monitoring programme to monitor the impacts of fisheries management and basin development activities, such as dam construction.[155] This programme has sought to develop time series indices of fish diversity, fish (and their larvae) abundance, biomass and size for the multispecies assemblage and for important species. Data are collected from over 100 fisheries monitoring sites in the Lower Mekong Basin.[156]

Additional monitoring systems have been implemented through the MRC's Data and Information Services.[157] These include monitoring systems related to groundwater, discharge and sediment, and water use. The effectiveness of these systems has been strengthened through technical assistance, financial support, human resources training, and legal, institutional, regulatory and procedural enhancements at the national level through the National Mekong Committees and line agencies.[158]

However, while there have been these positive developments in relation to joint monitoring within the Mekong, the monitoring has tended to focus more on bio-physical aspects of the resources than on the more politically sensitive socio-economic dynamics of transboundary cooperation, or the development and implementation of domestic political, institutional and legal arrangements.[159]

Joint strategies, plans and programmes

A further area where the lower Mekong states have sought to strengthen cooperation relates to basin-wide planning. Pursuant to the Mekong Agreement, the parties are encouraged to formulate a basin development plan 'that would be used to identify, categories and priorities the projects and programs to seek assistance for and to implement at the basin level'.[160] The origins of joint basin

---

154 Ibid, 49.

155 See generally, MRC, 'Integrated Analysis of Data from MRC Fisheries Monitoring Programmes in the Lower Mekong Basin' (MRC Technical Paper 33, August 2013).

156 Ibid, 25–30.

157 See MRC (n 101).

158 Qi Gao, *A Procedural Framework for Transboundary Water Management in the Mekong – Shared Mekong for a Common Future* (Brill Nijhoff 2014), 88.

159 Ibid, 90.

160 Article 2, Mekong Agreement (n 28).

planning can be traced back to the 'Indicative Basin Plan' produced by the secretariat of the Mekong Committee in 1970, and later revised in 1987.[161]

This earlier plan has been described as providing 'shopping lists of mainstream and tributary dams that represented the culmination of hydro-engineering-driven feasibility studies'.[162] The MRC therefore sought to adopt a more holistic approach by employing the concept of integrated water resources management (IWRM). In 2011, the MRC produced an IWRM-based Basin Development Strategy.[163] A key outcome of this strategy has been described as being that:

> For the first time since the signing of the 1995 Mekong Agreement, the MRC member countries have developed shared understandings of the opportunities and risks of the national plans for water resources development in the LMB and agreed on a number of Strategic Priorities to optimise the development opportunities and minimise uncertainty and risks associated with them.[164]

Through a roadmap, the strategy sets out priority actions that are needed to implement the strategy, together with suggested timeframes, expected outcomes, and a monitoring and reporting programme.[165] In 2013, the strategy was complemented by a regional action plan and national action plans for each of the Lower Mekong Basin states.[166] These action plans set out how the strategy should be implemented. Although these early Basin Development Plans provided an important means by which to identify and co-ordinate national plans with regional-level planning, they were criticised for taking an overly hydrological approach, which neglects more complex ecosystemic considerations.[167] The more recent Basin Development Strategies for the periods 2016–2020, and 2021–2030 have therefore sought to move beyond just water resources

161 MRC (n 36).

162 Ben Boer, *The Mekong: A Socio-legal Approach to River Basin Development* (Earthscan 2015). Öjendal suggests that this makes the Mekong unusual for a river of its size in that a basin plan for development of the water resources was completed prior to the initiation of any major projects; see Joakim Öjendal, 'Mainland Southeast Asia: co-operation or conflict over water?', in Leif Ohlsson (ed), *Hydropolitics: Conflicts over Water as a Development Constraint* (Zed Books 1995), 149–177.

163 MRC (n 144).

164 Ibid, i.

165 Ibid, 37.

166 MRC, 'Basin Action Plan', <https://www.mrcmekong.org/strategic-plans/> accessed 8 June 2023.

167 Boer (n 162).

planning.[168] The 2021–2030 strategy, for instance, encompasses issues related to the co-ordinated operation of dams and other water infrastructure, progress towards the Sustainable Development Goals, and gender.[169]

Reporting requirements

Both within the 2021–2030 Basin Development Strategy and the 2021–2015 MRC Strategy Plan, there is little mention of monitoring the implementation of the 1995 Mekong Agreement itself. While the Basin Development Strategy adopts a monitoring, evaluation and reporting system, the focus is on broader strategic issues based on an agreed Mekong Basin Indicator framework.[170] The indicator framework is structured in a way that captures five key dimensions: environment, social, economic, climate change and cooperation, and examines issues such as the conditions of water flow and water quality, the preservation and protection of environmental assets, social benefits from water resource developments, the economic value of water uses in the Mekong, water, food and energy security, navigation, and the protection against floods and droughts.[171] In terms of the Mekong Agreement itself, countries are simply obliged to report on the added value of the Agreement, and more broadly the extent to which the Mekong River Basin is moving towards optimal and sustainable development.[172]

The monitoring, evaluation and reporting system under the Basin Development Strategy and Plan is supplemented by a requirement for the MRC secretariat to produce a state of the Basin report every five years.[173] The state of the Basin report adopts a similar approach to the Basin Development Strategy in covering a range of 'dimensions', including social, economic, environmental, climate change and cooperation.[174] Some consideration of the commitments under the 1995 Mekong Agreement is included within the analysis. For example, in relation to the environmental dimension, the report notes that 'the requirements of the PMFM [Procedures for Maintenance of Flows on the

---

168 MRC, 'Basin Development Strategy 2021–2030 and MRC Strategic Plan 2021-2025' (April 2021) <https://www.mrcmekong.org/strategic-plans/> accessed 28 August 2024.

169 Ibid.

170 MRC, 'Mekong River Basin Indicator Framework' (2019) <https://www.mrcmekong.org/wp-content/uploads/2024/08/Mekong-River-Basin-Indicator-Framework.pdf> accessed 28 August 2024.

171 Ibid, 113–115.

172 Ibid.

173 MRC, 'State of the Basin Report 2018', <https://www.mrcmekong.org/publications/summary-state-of-the-basin-report-2018-5/> accessed 28 August 2024.

174 Ibid.

Mainstream] are generally being met'.[175] Along similar lines, the state of the Basin report observes that 'a substantial level of cooperation is evident among member Countries towards the objectives of the 1995 Mekong Agreement'.[176] The report goes on to note that 'the PNPCA process is being used by countries to notify the other countries of projects with potential trans-boundary impacts, notwithstanding some misunderstanding of the rights afforded to member Countries during the process, and the not always satisfactory reconciliation of issues identified even when substantial re-design occurs'.[177] While therefore picking up on implementation issues, the Basin report falls far short of a systematic and detailed assessment of the implementation of the Mekong Agreement.

The mandate of the Joint Committee also requires it to review progress in the implementation of the various plans, programmes and policies of the Mekong Agreement.[178] However, such a review also falls short of having a structured mechanism by which to explicitly review compliance and implementation of the Agreement itself.

Public information

As noted in the previous chapter, non-state actors can play an important role in monitoring and reporting issues related to compliance and implementation. Under the Mekong Agreement, there is no explicit reference to non-state actors. Despite this, the MRC has engaged with non-state actors through the implementation of specific projects and programmes. In 1999, the MRC adopted a set of principles for stakeholder participation, which were followed by a public participation strategy in 2003, and an associated action plan in 2004.[179]

A central activity for engaging stakeholders in the implementation of the Mekong has been through the basin planning described above. Several regional stakeholder forums have sought to bring together member countries, dialogue partners, universities, research institutions, NGOs, civil society groups, community representatives, river basin organisations, and development partners in order to discuss the MRC's basin development plan at key stages. To date,

---

[175] Ibid, v.

[176] Ibid, xv.

[177] Ibid.

[178] Article 24, Mekong Agreement (n 28).

[179] MRC, Mekong River Commission Stakeholder Engagement Handbook (1st edn, MRC 2021). Pursuant to these principles, stakeholders were defined as 'any person, group of institutions that has an interest in activity, project or programme'. This includes both intended beneficiaries and intermediaries, those positively affected, and those involved and/or those who are generally excluded from the decision-making process.

there have been 13 regional stakeholder forums – the first one took place in 2008 in Vientiane.

However, some scholars have criticised the level of stakeholder engagement in the Mekong. Cooper, for instance, points to the need for the MRC to use the ten sub-basin areas of the Basin Development Plan in order to conduct more localised stakeholder engagement.[180] Failing to reach the local level has raised concerns that the Mekong Agreement and the work of the MRC do not 'necessarily conform to the needs and aspirations of the majority of inhabitants of the basin nor do they take into account the multiple effects on the environment in a wide range of cultural, social, economic and ecological settings'.[181] In relation to stakeholder engagement within the context of the PNPCA processes, Suhardiman and Geheb observe that,

> The way in which both national and regional consultation meetings have been conducted suggests that participation has been dealt with as a procedural issue, a formal bureaucratic step that both the MRC and LNMC needed to fulfil, and not necessarily as a platform upon which to capture stakeholders' views, or a way to specifically influence resettlement and/or dam design.[182]

A further challenge when considering the role of non-state actors at the transboundary level is the national context. In all lower Mekong countries, civil society is afforded certain rights to participate in national decision-making processes through specific national legislation and constitutional guarantees.[183] However, in practice, the degree of freedom to participate varies, and in all four countries, civil society participation in decision-making remains constrained.[184]

---

180 Rachel Cooper, 'The Potential of MRC to Pursue IWRM in the Mekong: Trade-offs and Public Participation', in Joakim Öjendal, Stina Hansson and Sofie Hellberg, *Politics and Development in a Transboundary Watershed – The Case of the Lower Mekong Basin* (Springer 2012), 78.

181 Mahfuzuddin Ahmed and Philip Hirsch (eds), *Common Property in the Mekong – Issues of Sustainability and Subsistence* (ICLARM 2000). See also Nigel Hawkesworth and others, 'Independent Organisational, Financial and Institutional Review of the MRC Secretariat and the National Mekong Committees' (January 2007) <https://archive.iwlearn.net/mrcmekong.org/download/free_download/Financial_and_Institutional_Review.pdf> accessed 10 July 2024, 16.

182 Diana Suhardiman and Kim Geheb, 'Participation and politics in transboundary hydropower development: The case of the Pak Beng dam in Laos' (2021) 32(4) Environmental Policy and Governance 320.

183 See Boer (n 162).

184 Ibid. See also Yumiko Yasuda, *Rules, Norms and NGO Advocacy Strategies: Hydropower Development on the Mekong River* (Routledge 2015).

6.4.2 Reviewing Treaty Compliance and Implementation

The previous section has shown that while the Lower Mekong states have undertaken efforts to foster cooperation in the basin, any monitoring and reporting activities have not explicitly assessed the extent to which the Mekong Agreement itself has been implemented or complied with. Unsurprisingly, there is therefore no explicit institutional mandate by which the Lower Mekong states review specific incidences of weak implementation or non-compliance. More generally, the MRC Council is required to 'make decisions necessary to successfully implement' the Mekong Agreement.[185] In addition, the Joint Committee is required to, 'regularly obtain, update and exchange information and data necessary to implement this Agreement'; and the MRC secretariat is tasked with assisting the Joint Committee, 'in the implementation and management of projects and programs as requested'.[186] As noted above, the only other option by which to address compliance and implementation matters is through the dispute settlement provisions of the Mekong Agreement.[187]

In practice, most of the activities conducted by the MRC Council, which meets annually, and the Joint Committee, which meets twice a year, involve the review of the various plans, programmes and projects that have been developed under the auspices of the MRC. Some writers have suggested that the heavy influence of donors who can 'pick and choose' plans, programmes and projects, also influences what the MRC can achieve in terms of implementation.[188] While such plans, programmes and projects are strongly based on the Mekong Agreement, reviewing them falls short of systematically assessing whether the main rules and principles of the Mekong Agreement are being implemented and complied with.

One challenge that the MRC faces in reviewing implementation and compliance relates to its political mandate. King and others, for instance, suggest that the role of the MRC has been 'reduced to mostly research and discussion about mainstream cooperation, with speculative emphasis on the impact of Chinese mainstream developments, but with tributary developments mysteriously

[185] Article 18(B), Mekong Agreement (n 28).

[186] Article 24(C) and Article 30(D), ibid, respectively.

[187] Articles 34 and 35, ibid.

[188] MRC prioritises projects in a 'shopping list', 'from which donors can pick and choose … donors determine the work programme that will be implemented' (M. Miller, 'Transformation of a River Basin Authority: the case of the Mekong Committee', in Asit K. Biswas, Tsuyoshi Hashimoto (eds), *Asian Waters: From Ganges Brahmaputra to Mekong* (OUP 1996), 235).

scoped out of formal Council and JC discussions'.[189] Along similar lines, Boer and others argue that:

> The decision-support framework of the MRC, based on the principle of technical studies informing strategic and operational decisions, is backed up by a significant investment in the science of the basin through various program initiatives. These initiatives employ science as a generator of normative standards, rather than as an inflexible judgment tool, in support of better decision-making over hydropower and other forms of development. Much of the donor support for the MRC over the years has gone into programs, studies, modelling exercises and assessments on which more rational and sustainable decisions are to be predicated. However, these programs have not stipulated how their outputs are to be used and have laid down few clear pathways for the science to be utilized in project-specific assessments or governmental decisions based on such assessments.

Others have more explicitly pointed to the MRC being marginalised from political decision-making processes.[190]

It is not surprising that given the institutional challenges of the MRC to review implementation and compliance issues, the role of non-state actors in any formal decision-making process is also extremely limited. The aforementioned stakeholder consultations offer the main means by which non-state actors can raise implementation and compliance issues. However, decision-makers at the national level and within the MRC are not explicitly required to explain how any non-state actor's views have been taken into account. The only influence that non-state actors have is that from 2001 'partner regional organisations' can participate in MRC Council and Joint Committee meetings, but only upon invitation and only as observers.[191]

6.4.3 Addressing Incidences of Weak Implementation and Non-compliance

Under the Mekong Agreement, there is no specific provision setting out how issues of weak implementation and non-compliance should be addressed. As

---

189 Peter King, Jeremy Bird and Laurence Haas, 'Environmental Criteria For Hydropower Development in the Mekong Region' (Technical Report, March 2007) <https://wwfint.awsassets.panda.org/downloads/hydropowerdevelopment_mekongregion.pdf> accessed 10 July 2024.

190 Diana Suhardiman, Mark Giordano and François Molle, 'Scalar Disconnect: The Logic of Transboundary Water Governance in the Mekong' (2012) 25(6) Society and Natural Resources 572.

191 Mekong River Commission, 'Partner Organisations', <https://www.mrcmekong.org/development-partners-and-partner-organisations/> accessed 28 August 2024.

noted previously, the MRC Council and Joint Committee have the general responsibility to address compliance and implementation issues, whereby the Council has a broad mandate to 'entertain, address and resolve issues, differences and disputes referred to it by any Council member, the Joint Committee, or any member state on matters arising under' the Mekong Agreement;[192] and the Joint Committee is expected to 'address and make every effort to resolve issues and differences that may arise between regular sessions of the Council, referred to it by any Joint Committee member or member state on matters arising under this Agreement, and when necessary to refer the matter to the Council'.[193] Additionally, the Joint Committee is tasked with the obligation to 'review and approve studies and training for the personnel of the riparian member countries involved in Mekong River Basin activities as appropriate and necessary to strengthen the capability to implement the Agreement'.[194]

In practice, any efforts by the Lower Mekong Basin states to address weak implementation or non-compliance of the Mekong Agreement must be reconciled with the overarching 'Mekong spirit' based on non-confrontational politics and consensus-based decision-making.[195] It is in relation to the aforementioned hydropower developments on the mainstream of the Mekong that both the limitations of this approach, and the strategies that the countries have employed to indirectly address compliance and implementation issues, are most evident.

One such example relates to prior consultation under the PNPCA. While the Mekong Agreement is silent on the period required for prior consultation, the PNPCA stipulates that 'the timeframe for Prior Consultation shall be six months from the date of receiving documents on Prior Consultation'; and can be extended 'if necessary' through a decision of the MRC Joint Committee.[196] The PNPCA guidelines go on to suggest that, 'in effect, a prior consultation submission should be at a minimum be [sic] at least 6 months before intended commencement of project implementation', and that 'in actual practice, it is likely that projects for proposed water uses falling within the "prior consultation" category would be submitted far in advance of the intended start-up date because they are long-term large scale projects requiring considerable technical, economic, social and impact analyses'.[197] In terms of terminating the PNPCA process, again no detail is provided in the Mekong Agreement itself,

192 Article 18(C), Mekong Agreement (n 28).

193 Article 18(F), ibid.

194 Article 18(G), ibid.

195 Michael Buxton, Jennifer Martin and Max Kelly, 'Conflict Resolution and Policy Making Mediation in the Mekong River Basin' (2006) 41 Just Policy 26.

196 PNPCA (n 96), 2.

197 PNPCA Guidelines (n 116), 5.

but section 5.4.2 of the PNPCA document states that the Joint Committee should aim to reach '*an agreement* on the proposed use and issue a decision that contains the agreed upon conditions' [emphasis added].[198]

Both in the case of the Xayaburi and the Don Sahong PNPCA processes, the Lower Basin states failed to reach a consensus on whether the projects should proceed.[199] In both instances, Laos took the unilateral decision to end the consultation process after the initial six-month period, while the other states called for additional time to assess the impacts of the projects and voiced concerns over data gaps and the potential cumulative and transboundary impacts of the projects.[200] While this unsatisfactory outcome might be seen as a failure of the PNPCA process, and evidence that the countries had reached an impasse on a key issue of treaty compliance, some positive actions resulted. Laos took the unilateral decision to redesign the Xayaburi project with the aim of appeasing some of the concerns that Cambodia, Thailand and Vietnam had raised during the PNPCA process. Amendments to the original proposal included providing additional measures for fish passage, navigation and sediment risk, as well as investigations of seismic risk.[201] A review of these changes by the MRC secretariat observed that 'the developer has made significant efforts and investments towards addressing the concerns raised in the Xayaburi TRR', but also cautioned that 'insufficient information has been provided to fully assess the likely efficacy of these measures'.[202]

Another result of the failure to reach consensus during the Xayaburi PNPCA process was a decision by the MRC Council at its 18th Meeting on 8 December 2011 to conduct a Study on Sustainable Management and Development of the Mekong River, including impacts of Mainstream Hydropower Projects.[203] While not specifically assessing the cases of Xayaburi and Don Sahong, the study, which was completed in December 2017, explored both the benefits and likely impacts of national water resource development plans.[204] A key finding of the study was that 'combined investments in water resources for 2020 and 2040 were likely to negatively affect community resilience and vulnerability

198 PNPCA (n 96), 7.

199 An Pich Hatda, 'From Transparent to Transparency: The Evolution of the Mekong River Commission's Prior Consultation Process' (Asia Pacific Bulletin, 8 October 2020) <https://www.eastwestcenter.org/sites/default/files/private/apb527_0.pdf> accessed 10 July 2024.

200 See for example See MRC (n 134), MRC (n 135).

201 MRC, 'Review of the Design Changes Made for Xayaburi Hydropower Project' (Technical Reference Paper No. 65, January 2019), 5.

202 Ibid, 4.

203 MRC (n 19).

204 Ibid.

as well as sustainability and that the main trade-off was benefits accrued by power companies at the expense of fishing households'.[205] The study went on to conclude that 'such an outcome is not consistent with the goals of the Mekong Agreement of 1995'.[206]

Another result of the less than satisfactory outcome of the Xayaburi and Don Sahong PNPCA processes was for the MRC to convene a 'dialogue workshop' on the lessons learned from the implementation of the PNPCA in February 2016.[207] This dialogue workshop, which brought together MRC member state representatives and international experts, developed a series of recommendations on how the PNPCA process might be improved. Several of these recommendations were taken onboard by the countries, including the development of Guidelines for Transboundary EIA in the Lower Mekong River Basin,[208] and a Commentary to the PNPCA.[209] In addition, the workshop called for greater clarity regarding the commencement and conclusion of the Prior Consultation process. This recommendation led to a change in the PNPCA process whereby the Lower Mekong states agree to issue a 'statement' at the end of the prior consultation process.[210] The statement marked a shift away from a 'yes/no' decision on whether or not the project should go ahead, to a focus on putting in place joint recommendations on how the design of the project might avoid, minimise and mitigate any transboundary harmful effects.[211] As well as the statement itself, the lower Mekong states agreed to adopt a joint action plan aimed at monitoring progress in implementing any actions set out in the statement.[212] While the addition of the statement and joint action plan has generally been seen to have improved the PNPCA process, some tensions are also evident in Vietnam's reply to Prior Consultation for the Luang Prabang PNPCA, where they call on Lao to 'continue working closely with other member states in *fully*

205 Ibid.

206 Ibid.

207 MRC, 'Dialogue Workshop Report' (Bangkok, Thailand, 2016).

208 MRC, 'Guidelines for Transboundary Environmental Impact Assessment in the Lower Mekong River Basin (TbEIA)' (MRC, 20 February 2023).

209 MRC, 'Working Document – PNPCA Commentary' (MRC, April 2019).

210 MRC (n 207).

211 Hatda (n 199).

212 See for example, MRC, 'Statement on the Prior Consultation Process for the Luang Prabang Hydropower Project in Lao PDR' (MRC, 30 June 2020), and MRC, 'Joint Action Plan for the Implementation of the Statement on the Prior Consultation Process of the Luang Prabang Hydropower Project' (MRC, 30 June 2020).

implementing the Joint Statements for Pak Beng and Pak Lay Hydropower Projects [emphasis added]'.[213]

These enhancements also sidestep any fundamental decision on whether or not a project should go ahead. This is evident in the case of the Sanakham PNPCA process, where Thailand has voiced serious concerns over the transboundary and cumulative impacts of the project.[214] The PNPCA process and its enhancements, as well as the Council Study, have also not appeared to dampen Laos' appetite for the development of hydropower projects on the mainstream despite the concerns raised by its downstream riparians.[215]

Another aspect to consider in addressing compliance and implementation vis-à-vis the Mekong Agreement relates to financial and technical assistance. Since its establishment in 1995, a significant amount of financial and technical assistance has been provided by donor agencies.[216] As the activities of the MRC increased, the Lower Mekong states recognised that such an approach to financing the MRC was unsustainable.[217] At the Mekong Summit in April 2010, the Lower Mekong states therefore committed to ensuring that 'core river basin functions' are fully financed by member countries by 2030.[218] These core river basin functions include data acquisition, exchange and monitoring; analysis, modelling and assessment; planning support; forecasting, warning and emergency response; implementing MRC procedures; administration and management; facilitating dialogue and co-ordination; and reporting and dissemination.[219] In the 2021–2025 Basin Strategic Plan, the total budget for MRC activities is estimated at US$ 60.5 million, of which US$ 48 million is recognised as core river basin function costs. US$ 25 million of the MRC budget is to be covered by member countries.[220] This shift away from reliance on external funding for the MRC is likely to strengthen the Lower Mekong

---

213 Viet Nam National Mekong Committee, 'Reply to Prior Consultation' (22 June 2020).

214 Bangkok Tribune (n 145).

215 Radio Free Asia, 'Laos to proceed with seventh Mekong Dam despite impact concerns' (7 June 2023) <https://www.benarnews.org/english/news/thai/dam-project-06082023153318.html> accessed 10 July 2024.

216 Between 2010 and 2015 the level of donor funding to the MRC was US$ 115 million (the Phnom Penh Post, 'Donors slash funding for MRC' (14 January 2016) <http://www.phnompenhpost.com/national/donors-slash-funding-mrc> accessed 10 July 2024.

217 MRC, 'Review of the Decentralisation of Core River Basin Management Function Activities' (MRC, 22 February 2019).

218 MRC Hua Hin Declaration (n 106).

219 MRC (n 168), 125.

220 Ibid, 183.

states' sense of ownership of the MRC and river basin management. However, there is also a risk that such a shift might influence the priorities of the MRC. The Development Partners of the MRC have traditionally been keen to support activities that enhance dialogue and science-based decision-making amongst the basin states, such as efforts to enhance stakeholder participation, improve the PNPCA process, and develop guidelines on Transboundary EIAs.[221]

Another important proposed mechanism by which to provide financial and technical assistance to implement the Mekong Agreement is the Mekong Fund. Potentially financed from a range of sources, including the private sector, development partners, and climate funds, the Mekong Fund is envisaged *inter alia* to provide direct and indirect assistance to communities that may suffer from any adverse impacts, as a result of both natural factors, e.g., flood and droughts, and human-induced changes, e.g., infrastructure development, changes to the river system.[222] Such a fund could therefore be used by communities to tackle some of the negative impacts they face from the development of hydropower projects upstream, and thus help address the commitment in the Mekong Agreement, 'to make every effort to avoid, minimise and mitigate harmful effects that might occur to the environment … from the development and use of the Mekong River Basin'.[223] In September 2023, the Joint Committee approved such a funding model in principle and agreed to trial an 'ecosystem window' of the fund designed to support community engagement in wetland and watershed biodiversity conservation and the enhancement of sustainable livelihoods.[224]

6.5 CONCLUSION

The analysis of the Mekong River Basin has shown the tensions countries face in reconciling their national interests with their treaty commitments. The basin plays a vital role in supporting the development goals of its six riparian countries, while at the same time, the need to preserve a unique biologically diverse ecosystem is clear. The challenge of reconciling competing interests is perhaps most evident in relation to hydropower. Hydropower developments have exposed the need for a co-ordinated response among countries to ensure

---

221 Ibid.

222 Ibid, 112.

223 Article 7, Mekong Agreement (n 28).

224 Phontham Visapra, 'MRC moves closer to making "Mekong Fund" a reality' (*The Laotian Times,* 29 September 2023) <https://laotiantimes.com/2023/09/29/mrc-moves-closer-to-making-mekong-fund-reality/#:~:text=The%20governing%20body%20of%20the,drought%20and%20flooding%2C%20combined%20with> accessed 28 August 2024.

that they do not jeopardise the needs and interests of the communities reliant upon the waters of the Mekong to sustain their livelihoods through fisheries, tourism, agriculture and other water uses. An added complication is climate change. On the one hand, the shift away from fossil fuels has provided a justification for the transition towards so-called 'clean energy', including hydropower. On the other hand, climate change combined with these developments has undoubtedly placed greater strain on the availability of water for other uses and heightened the likelihood and magnitude of droughts, such as those experienced by the lower riparian states of the Mekong in 2019 and 2021. Of course, co-ordinated regulation of hydropower infrastructure also holds the potential to mitigate the negative impacts of extreme hydrological events.

The Mekong states have demonstrated a commitment to addressing their challenges cooperatively. While cooperation with the upper basin states has been limited primarily to data exchange and dialogue, the Lower Mekong states have a long history of cooperation. The 1995 Mekong Agreement both signifies an important milestone in that cooperation and illustrates some of the difficulties faced by the countries in seeking to reconcile their competing interests over the uses of the Mekong River. Ultimately, this has led to an agreement that has strong aspirations, i.e., the sustainable development of the Mekong Basin, but leaves many questions unanswered. In terms of substantive norms, the agreement does not go further than setting out key principles of customary international law, i.e., the principle of equitable and reasonable utilisation, the duty to take all appropriate measures to prevent significant transboundary harm, and the obligation to protect and preserve ecosystems. The Lower Mekong states have used the flexibility, or ambiguity, inherent in these principles to accommodate their own national interests. This is most evident in Laos's plans to develop hydropower on the mainstream of the Mekong River. It also means that as interpretations of how these principles should be applied in practice differ, identifying clear examples of non-compliance has been difficult for the states to evidence. The procedural commitments of the Mekong Agreement have followed a similar pattern. Again, this is most evident in relation to the mainstream hydropower developments and the implementation of the PNPCA process. Laos, as the state planning the projects, has consistently claimed to be in compliance with its procedural commitments to notify and consult on planned measures, whereas Cambodia, Thailand and Vietnam have consistently pointed to the need to extend the consultation period and take more time to assess the cumulative and transboundary impacts of these planned projects.

In the absence of any specific compliance and implementation mechanism (CIM), the Lower Mekong states have employed different strategies to address compliance and implementation. For example, while no formal reporting requirement exists under the Mekong Agreement, the Lower Mekong states have made significant efforts to exchange data and information, both with respect to the basin itself and specifically via the PNPCA processes. The Lower Mekong states have also invested significantly in joint and co-ordinated monitoring within the basin, with a view to better understanding the likely impacts of water use developments. These efforts have contributed to a better scientific understanding of the basin, which in turn has helped the states more effectively cooperate in joint basin planning. Particularly through the Basin Development Plans and Strategies, the states have been able to identify where cooperation is needed at the basin level and have sought to adopt joint and co-ordinated plans and programmes to make that a reality. The increasing, although arguably still inadequate, role of stakeholder communities in the development of these plans and strategies is an important means of both ensuring that key priorities of the population of the Mekong are addressed and progress is transparently monitored.

While the aforementioned activities might be seen as indirectly and positively supporting the implementation of the Mekong Agreement, they fall short of specifying and systematically assessing compliance and implementation. Where compliance and implementation issues arise, the Lower Mekong states have demonstrated a reluctance to invoke the dispute settlement mechanisms contained in the Agreement and have rather employed softer means to encourage better compliance and implementation. These efforts are most evident in relation to the PNPCA process, where a combination of additional studies, joint statements, guidance and financial incentives have been employed. These efforts have no doubt helped to enhance the implementation of, and compliance with, the Mekong Agreement, although it is hard to assess at this stage whether they have been fully successful. Laos has mitigated its plans but also continues to develop hydropower projects on the mainstream despite the concerns expressed by Cambodia, Thailand and Vietnam on the downstream cumulative impacts of these projects. A question to be considered further in Chapter 9 of this book is therefore whether the Lower Mekong Basin states would profit from the adoption of a CIM under the Mekong Agreement.

7. The Orange-Senqu River Basin

7.1 INTRODUCTION

The Orange-Senqu River is the third largest river basin in Southern Africa, after the Congo and the Zambezi, with a catchment area of 1,000,000 km^2 and an approximate natural run-off of 11,300 km^3 per annum.[1] The river originates in the Maluti Mountains of the Lesotho Highlands, where it is known as the Senqu River.[2] Four states share the Orange-Senqu River: Botswana, Lesotho, Namibia and South Africa. Of the total catchment area, 12.9% is situated in Botswana, 3% in Lesotho, 24.8% in Namibia and 59.3% in South Africa. In terms of annual run-off, South Africa contributes 55% and Lesotho 41% of the total waters of the Orange-Senqu River, whereas Namibia only contributes 4% and Botswana provides no annual run-off contribution.[3] After leaving Lesotho, the river flows in a westerly direction through South Africa until it forms a 450 km border between Namibia and South Africa before finally

---

[1] UNDP-GEF Orange-Senqu Strategic Action Programme, *Orange-Senqu River Basin: Transboundary Diagnostic Analysis* (ORASECOM 2014).

[2] Richard Meissner, *Interest Groups, Water Politics and Governance – The Case of the Lesotho Highlands Project* (Springer 2015), 21.

[3] R.S. McKenzie and C. Roth, *The evaluation of river losses from the Orange River downstream of the PK le Roux dam* (Water Research Commission: Pretoria 1994). Botswana is recognised as a basin state because of the basin's geomorphological links to the ephemeral Nossob and Molopo Rivers, which are historically suspected to have contributed surface runoff before they were blocked by the Kalahari Desert dunes (see Pieter Heyns, 'Water resources management in Southern Africa', in Mikiyasu Nakayama (ed), *International Waters in Southern Africa* (United Nations University Press 2003), 5–37). It is also speculated that groundwater originating in Botswana may contribute to the river, but no precise contribution has been ascertained (Inga M. Jacobs, 'A community in the Orange: the development of a multi-level water governance framework in the Orange-Senqu River basin in Southern Africa' (2012) 12 International Environmental Agreements 187).

reaching the Atlantic Ocean.[4] Less than half of the total run-off is estimated to reach Alexander Bay and the Atlantic Ocean due to the impacts of evapotranspiration, large dams, and inter-basin transfers.[5]

The Orange-Senqu Basin is highly susceptible to seasonal and spatial variation in precipitation, with a low conversion of rainfall to runoff and high variability between seasons and from year to year.[6] Climate change is bringing added challenges to the basin, including greater variability and unpredictability.[7]

Out of all the transboundary river basins within the Southern Africa region, the Orange-Senqu is considered to be the most developed.[8] There are 29 dams and reservoirs in the basin that control the river flow and an extensive infrastructure of inter-basin transfers.[9] The dams serve both the purpose of hydropower generation and regulation of flows for irrigation. Agriculture accounts for 61% of the water demand throughout the basin and employs 50% of the population.[10] Industrial and domestic uses of the Orange River are limited, except within the Vaal River, a major tributary of the Orange within South

---

4 Wanjiku Kaniaru, 'From scarcity to security: Water as a potential factor for conflict and cooperation in Southern Africa' (2015) 22(3) South African Journal of International Affairs 386; Heyns (n 3).

5 Department of Water Affairs and Forestry, 'Internal Strategic Perspective – Orange River System Overarching' (February 2004) <https://www.dws.gov.za/Documents/Other/WMA/13/OrangeOverarchingISPFeb04intro.pdf> accessed 6 August 2024.

6 A.H. Conley and P.H. van Niekerk, 'Sustainable management of international waters: the Orange River case' (2000) 2 Water Policy 132; Pieter Heyns, 'Achievements of the Orange-Senqu River Commission in integrated transboundary water resources management' (General Assembly of the International Network of Basin Organisations, Martinique, 24–28 October 2004).

7 S.K. Mgquba and S. Majozi, 'Climate Change and its Impacts on Hydropolitics in Transboundary Basins: A Case Study of the Orange-Senqu River Basin' (2020) 11(1) Journal of Water and Climate 150.

8 Jacobs (n 3), 192.

9 Glenn-Marie Lange, Eric Mungatana and Rashid Hassan, 'Water accounting for the Orange River Basin: An economic perspective on managing a transboundary resource' (2007) 61 Ecological Economics 660.

10 Mahasa Pululu, Palamuleni Lobina and Ruhiiga Tabukeli, 'The Upper Orange River Water Resources Affected by Human Interventions and Climate Change' (2015) 6(3) Hydrology Current Research <https://www.hilarispublisher.com/open-access/the-upper-orange-river-water-resources-affected-by-human-interventions-and-climate-change-2157-7587-1000212.pdf> accessed 5 August 2024.

Africa, where water is supplied to most of South Africa's industries and major population centres, including Johannesburg and Pretoria.[11]

South Africa, a water-scarce country, is heavily dependent on the Orange-Senqu River.[12] An estimated 24% of South Africa's population is located within the basin, and the country accounts for between 82%–97% of all the basin's water use.[13] Namibia, the most downstream state, is also highly reliant on the Orange-Senqu for its agricultural needs.[14] The strategic interest of the Orange-Senqu for Namibia is heightened due to the country being extremely arid and also primarily dependent upon transboundary rivers to satisfy its internal water demand.[15] Namibia uses 2% of the waters of the Orange-Senqu River.[16] Lesotho is mainly dependent on the Orange-Senqu for hydropower generation and the royalties it receives from South Africa for the inter-basin water transfers that result from the Lesotho Highlands Water Project.[17] As noted above, Botswana's use of the Orange-Senqu is negligible and limited to groundwater sources and ephemeral rivers.[18] However, they do hold plans to divert water from the Lesotho Highlands.[19]

The Orange-Senqu River has been described as a 'closed basin', meaning that the actual uses of the water exceed long-term water availability.[20] Despite this predicament, population growth and demographic changes in the basin, as

---

[11] Ibid, 662.

[12] Meissner (n 2), 12.

[13] Anthony Turton, 'An overview of the hydropolitical dynamics of the Orange River Basin', in Mikiyasu Nakyama (ed), *International waters in Southern Africa* (United Nations University 2003).

[14] Nicole Kranz, Eduard Interwies and Rodrigo Vidaurre, 'Transboundary Regimes in the Orange Senqu Basin', <https://www.ecologic.eu/sites/default/files/publication/2015/1951_del131_orangesenqu.pdf> accessed 5 August 2024, 13–14.

[15] Ibid.

[16] Pululu and others (n 10).

[17] Jacobs (n 3).

[18] Pieter Heyns, Marion Patrick and Anthony R. Turton, 'Transboundary Water Resources Management in Southern Africa: Meeting the Challenge of Joint Planning and Management in the Orange River Basin' (2008) 24(3) International Journal of Water Resources Development 371, 376.

[19] Sabine Blumstein and Jacob D. Petersen-Perlman, 'When the Water Runs Dry: Supporting Adaptive Governance in Transboundary River Basins' (2021) 46(3) Water International 306.

[20] Peter Ashton and Anthony Turton, 'Water and Security in Sub-Saharan Africa: Emerging Concepts and Their Implications for Effective Water Resource Management in the Southern Africa Region', in H.G. Brauch and others (eds), *Globalisation and Environmental Challenges: Reconceptualising Security in the 21st Century* (Springer 2008).

well as economic growth and development aspirations, are set to place additional pressures on the basin.[21] These pressures will, in turn, require the states of the Orange-Senqu River to develop cooperative arrangements that are capable of ensuring that the waters of the river are utilised in an equitable and reasonable manner.

In light of the challenges faced by the states of the Orange-Senqu River Basin, this chapter will explore the cooperative arrangements that the states have already entered into concerning the river. The chapter will focus primarily on the basin-wide cooperative arrangement that is in place, namely the Agreement on the Establishment of the Orange-Senqu River Commission (ORASECOM Agreement), which was adopted by all riparian states on 3 November 2000.[22] However, several other bilateral cooperative arrangements will also be considered. Prior to examining the content of these cooperative arrangements, the chapter will explore the evolution of cooperation between the Orange-Senqu River states with a view to identifying the factors that have influenced the states in adopting such arrangements. Then, following an analysis of the substantive and normative commitments contained within the cooperative arrangements, and the ORASECOM Agreement in particular, the chapter will explore the extent to which the parties to the agreement have put in place measures to support its compliance and implementation.

7.2 THE EVOLUTION OF COOPERATION IN THE ORANGE-SENQU RIVER BASIN

Competition over water and grazing in the Orange River valley amongst indigenous peoples was believed to be fierce.[23] The river also proved to be of great interest to European explorers of the 18th and 19th centuries, who were keen to assess both its navigability and its natural resources.[24] The discovery of diamonds in the Hopetown District and Kimberley in the late 19th century is believed to have led to significant migration of people into the basin.[25]

[21] Elizabeth Kistin and Peter J. Ashton, 'Adapting to Change in Transboundary Rivers: An Analysis of Treaty Flexibility on the Orange-Senqu River Basin' (2008) 24(3) International Journal of Water Resources Development 385.

[22] Agreement on the Establishment of the Orange-Senqu River Commission (adopted 3 November 2000) <https://orasecom.org/wp-content/uploads/2020/09/ORASECOM_Agreement_Reprint-August-2012.pdf> accessed 5 August 2024.

[23] A.R. Wilcox, *Great River: The Story of the Orange River* (Drakensberg Publications 1986).

[24] Anthony R. Turton and others, *A Hydropolitical History of South Africa's International River Basins* (Water Research Commission 2004), 102–104.

[25] Meissner (n 2), 27.

Together with this migration, the potential of the basin for irrigation became increasingly recognised and subsequently developed through the so-called 'hydraulic mission'.[26]

In the first half of the 20th century, it was recognised that the growing demands for water within the Orange River could not be satisfied by projects within South Africa alone.[27] Attention therefore turned to the Lesotho Highlands – the water tower of the basin. In 1950, the High Commissioner to Lesotho, Sir Evelyn Baring, requested a survey of the country's water potential.[28] This led to the *Oxbow Scheme* which laid out plans to construct a high-altitude dam, hydropower station and tunnel in the upper reaches of the Senqu River to harness and transport water to South Africa's gold mines.[29] Lesotho, by itself, did not have the means to construct the scheme. However, broader political issues, and worsening relations between Lesotho and South Africa, delayed any progress on the project.[30] It was not until October 1986, and closely following a *coup d'état* in Lesotho, that the countries signed the Lesotho Highlands Water Project Treaty.[31]

The design of the Lesotho Highlands Water Project comprises five dams, over 200 km of tunnels, and a 72 megawatt hydropower plant.[32] Phase one of the project resulted in the construction of the 195m Katse Dam, the 72MW Muela Hydropower Station in Lesotho, and a network of transfer and delivery tunnels to South Africa.[33] Subsequently, the Mohale Dam, Motosoku Weir and additional tunnels to transfer water to the Katse Dam were constructed.

---

[26] Anthony R. Turton, 'Precipitation, people, pipelines and power in Southern Africa', in Philip Stott and Sian Sullivan (eds), *Political Ecology: Science, Myth and Power* (Arnold 2000).

[27] Meissner (n 2), 29.

[28] Ibid.

[29] Ibid.

[30] Van Robbroeck, *The Lesotho Highlands Water Project: An authoritative overview* (Department of Water Affairs 1986).

[31] Treaty on the Lesotho Highlands Water Project Between the Government of the Republic of South Africa and the Government of the Kingdom of Lesotho (adopted 26 October 1986) <https://www.lhda.org.ls/uploads/documents/governance/lhwp_treaty.pdf> accessed 5 August 2024.

Some commentators have speculated that South Africa was the main instigator of the coup (see Simon Baynham and Greg Mills, 'Lesotho: Between dependence and destabilisation' (1987) 43 The World Today 52–54).

[32] WRP (Pty) Ltd and others, 'Orange River Integrated Water Resources Management Plan – Institutional Structures in the four Orange Basin states' (August 2007) <https://orasecom.org/wp-content/uploads/2020/05/1941INSTITUTIONAL.pdf> accessed 5 August 2024.

[33] Ibid.

The financial cost of this phase of the project, which was fully borne by South Africa, is estimated at 18.08 billion South African rand.[34] The project provides 20 million South African rand per month in royalties to Lesotho, and the production of power from the Muela Hydropower Station makes Lesotho virtually self-sufficient in electricity.[35] The income generated by the project accounts for 25% of Lesotho's total annual revenue, while the transfer of 30.2 m^3 per second of water benefits the Gauteng Province of South Africa by providing a relatively cheap and secure water supply to major cities in the economic heartland of the country.[36]

Whilst the Lesotho Water Highlands Project provides significant benefits to both countries and has been heralded as a positive example of benefit-sharing between two states, it is not without its critics.[37] Concerns have been voiced over the resettlement and compensation of people living in and near the dam sites in Lesotho, and whether the benefits generated from the project have fairly trickled down to local communities.[38] The project has also been plagued with problems concerning corruption.[39] Additionally, environmental concerns have been raised over the project, with the adequacy of the initial Environmental Impact Assessment (EIA) being questioned.[40]

The Lesotho Highlands Water Project is overseen by the Lesotho Highlands Water Commission, which is a bi-national institution established under the

---

[34] Article 10(1), Lesotho Highlands Treaty (n 31). According to Article 10(2) of the Lesotho Highlands Treaty, Lesotho are responsible for the implementation, operation and maintenance of the Muela Hydropower Plant.

[35] Prior to the project, Lesotho was reliant on South Africa's state-owned power supply company (Electricity Supply Commission) to meet its energy needs.

[36] Shani Wallis, *Lesotho Highlands Water Project – Volume 5* (Laserline 1992).

[37] See Claudia W. Sadoff, Dale Whittington and David Grey, *Africa's International Rivers: An Economic Perspective* (World Bank 2002), 50.

[38] Korinna Horta, 'The Mountain Kingdom's White Oil: The Lesotho Highlands Water Project' (1995) 22(6) Ecologist 227; and Ryan Hoover, *Pipe Dreams: The World Bank's Failed Efforts to Restore Lives and Livelihoods of Dam-Affected People in Lesotho* (International Rivers Network 2001).

[39] 'Putting corruption on trial in Lesotho', *BBC News* (7 August 2001) <http://news.bbc.co.uk/1/hi/business/1477523.stm> accessed 5 August 2024.

[40] Khabele Matlosa, 'The Lesotho Highlands Water Project: Socio-Economic Impacts', in David Tevera and Sam Moyo (eds), *Environmental Security in Southern Africa* (SAPES Books 2000); and Jo-Ansie Van Wyk, 'The International Politics of Dams with Special Reference to Lesotho' (2000) 22(1) Strategic Review of Southern Africa 56.

terms of the Lesotho Highlands Water Treaty.[41] Three representatives from each country form the Lesotho Highlands Water Commission. Two national institutions support the activities of the Commission. In South Africa, the Trans-Caledon Tunnel Authority (TCTA) manages and maintains the delivery tunnel, which transfers water from Lesotho to South Africa.[42] In Lesotho, the Lesotho Highlands Development Authority (LHDA) takes responsibility for the management of the project, including resettlement and compensation of displaced communities, water supply to resettled communities, irrigation and tourism.[43] Some commentators have observed that while the roles and responsibilities of the LHDA are well set out in the Lesotho Highlands Water Treaty, those of the TCTA are less detailed, with little focus on downstream responsibilities.[44] This, in turn, has been highlighted as evidence of the failure of Lesotho and South Africa to fully account for the interests of Namibia and Botswana in the implementation of the project.[45] However, as Kaniaru warns, 'any increase in offtake from the Orange River Basin upstream of the Namibia–South Africa border must have an impact on water availability for Namibia and the estuary'.[46] He goes on to maintain that 'any subsequent phases of the Lesotho Highlands Water Project will be required to factor in the water quantity, quality and environmental needs of Namibia'.[47]

While Namibia did not participate in the Lesotho Highlands Water Project, there is evidence of cooperation between South Africa and Namibia pertaining to the Orange-Senqu river. In 1987, an agreement was entered into between South Africa and South West Africa (which subsequently became Namibia) concerning the control, development and utilisation of the water of the Orange River.[48] This agreement established the Joint Technical Commission, which was made up of three representatives from each party, and served as an advi-

---

[41] Protocol VI, Supplementary Arrangements Regarding the System of Governance for the Project, Lesotho Highlands Treaty (n 31). Activities of the Lesotho Highlands Water Commission include the appointment of auditors and consultants, operating and maintenance plans, tendering procedures, the allocation of costs between parties and the assessment of quantities of water to be delivered.

[42] Ibid.

[43] Ibid.

[44] Jennifer Mohamed-Katerere, *Review of the legal and policy framework for transboundary natural resources management in southern Africa* (IUCN Regional Office in South Africa 2001).

[45] WRP and others (n 32), 9.

[46] Kaniaru (n 4), 386.

[47] Ibid.

[48] Elizabeth Kistin and others, 'An overview of the content and historical context of the international freshwater agreement that South Africa has entered into

sory body to the parties.[49] The Joint Technical Commission was replaced in 1992 by agreements to establish the Permanent Water Commission (PWC), and the Vioolsdrift and Noordoewer Joint Irrigation Scheme (VNJIS) between Namibia and South Africa.[50] The PWC, made up of three representatives from each party, monitors the activities of the Joint Irrigation Authority (JIA) established under the VNJIS agreement.[51] The JIA is comprised of four delegates from each party, at least three of whom must be landowners within the district, and the fourth usually being a representative of the government, e.g., Department of Water.[52] The JIA is responsible for the operation and maintenance of the VNJIS and the control of water abstractions from the Orange River.

Despite these examples of cooperation between Namibia and South Africa, the lower reaches of the Orange River have also been a source of tension.[53] Both countries question the precise position of the international boundary.[54] Namibia claims that the border lies in the middle of the river, while South Africa alleges it is on the northern high-water mark.[55] The precise determination of the border between the countries has implications in terms of the control of mineral deposits present in the river bed and the alluvial terraces

---

with neighbouring countries' (2009) 9 International Environmental Agreements: Politics, Law and Economics 1.

49 Ibid.

50 The agreements between Namibia and South Africa essentially formalised an arrangement that predates the sovereignty of Namibia. In 1933, when South West Africa was under South African control, the government established a scheme to irrigate both sides of the Orange River with a view to encouraging agricultural development and employment (Sue Matthews, 'South Africa and Namibia ensuring enough irrigation water together', *The Water Wheel* (November/December 2014) <https://journals.co.za/doi/pdf/10.10520/EJC162538#:~:text=A%20reconciliation%20strategy%20for%20the,users%20to%20the%20year%202040> accessed 5 August 2024, 27.

51 Kistin and others (n 48).

52 Ibid.

53 Peter Ashton, 'Southern African Water Wars: Are they inevitable or preventable?' in Hussein Solomon and Anthony Turton (eds), *Water Wars: Enduring Myth or Impending Reality?* (Accord 2000), 87.

54 Maria Konokhova, 'Namibia Urges South Africa to Advance Talks Over Disputed Orange River Border', *Sputnik Africa* (15 October 2023) <https://en.sputniknews.africa/20231015/namibia-urges-south-africa-to-advance-talks-over-disputed-orange-river-border-1062818754.html> accessed 5 August 2024.

55 Wanda Ruitshauser, 'The Orange River Boundary and the Ongoing Border Dispute Between Namibia and South Africa' in Luregn Lenggenhager and others (eds), *The Lower !Garib-Orange River* (Bielefeld 2023).

that mark the early positions of the river bed.[56] Demarcation of the border also has important implications for the local residents who rely on the islands in the river as grazing ground for their livestock.[57]

Returning to the agreements relating to the VNJIS, there was a close correlation between the adoption of those agreements and the launch in 1994 of the *Orange River Replanning Study*.[58] According to Earle and others, the study was initially intended to ascertain South Africa's own water priorities.[59] However, formal invitations were later extended to Namibia and Lesotho to participate.[60] This initiative by South Africa caused some unease among Namibia and Lesotho as they felt that the study should have been conducted within an international forum.[61] Both countries then proceeded to conduct their own studies, with the results being subsequently shared among the three riparian states. These events triggered appetite among all of the states – motivated in particular by Namibia, who had originally proposed the establishment of a Permanent Orange River Basin Commission in 1994 – to negotiate a basin-wide regime for the Orange Senqu River.[62] The negotiations culminated in the adoption of the ORASECOM Agreement on 7 August 2000.[63] The ORASECOM Agreement was the fourth basin-wide regime to be established in Southern Africa and the first to follow the Revised SADC Protocol on Shared Watercourse (Revised SADC Protocol).[64] The relationship between the latter two instruments will be explored in the following section.

In 2009, the Orange-Senqu River Commission (ORASECOM) undertook a review of the 2000 ORASECOM Agreement and concluded that it would be preferable to revise the agreement in light of the aspirations of the parties as set out in their basin-wide plan.[65] A revised Agreement was subsequently adopted by the parties in 2018 but has not as yet been ratified by all parties.

---

56 Kaniaru (n 4), 392.

57 Ibid.

58 Earle and others, 'A Preliminary Basin Profile of the Orange/Senqu River' (University of Pretoria, February 2005) <https://www.anthonyturton.com/assets/my_documents/my_files/Orange_Profile_4_Apl_2.pdf> accessed 5 February 2025, 27.

59 Ibid.

60 Ibid.

61 Ibid.

62 Ibid. See also Heyns (n 3), 20–21.

63 ORASECOM Agreement (n 22)

64 Revised Protocol on Shared Watercourses in the Southern African Development Community (adopted 7 August 2000), 40 ILM 321.

65 ORASECOM, 'Legal Opportunities and Constraints for ORASECO' (April 2009) <https://orasecom.org/wp-content/uploads/2020/05/661ORASECOM-Legal-Analysis.pdf> accessed 5 August 2024.

The analysis below therefore focuses on the 2000 ORASECOM Agreement while also highlighting notable changes that would be introduced if the revised Agreement enters into force.

7.3 COMMITMENTS UNDER THE ORANGE-SENQU AGREEMENT

7.3.1 Scope and Aim of the Agreement

The preamble of the ORASECOM Agreement recognises the common interest between Botswana, Lesotho, Namibia and South Africa in the development of the Orange-Senqu River System as a means to contribute towards 'mutual benefit, peace, security, welfare and prosperity of their people'.[66] The involvement of Botswana, as a state 'with a common interest' in the Orange-Senqu River System, is worthy of note given that, as mentioned previously, their reliance on the system is limited to ephemeral rivers and groundwater. However, according to Turton, the recognition of Botswana as a riparian state within the agreement provides them with a wider range of diplomatic options when negotiating water-sharing arrangements across the other basins they share with their neighbours, including the Limpopo and Okavango basins.[67]

The ORASECOM Agreement adopts a broad approach to its aims. The preamble commits the parties to 'the realisation of the principle of equitable and reasonable utilisation, as well as the principle of sustainable development with regard to the River System'.[68] In addition, the preamble recognises the desire of its parties to promote, 'close and co-ordinated cooperation in the development of all the resources of the River System'.[69]

Another point to note on scope is the relationship between the ORASECOM Agreements and other legal arrangements. As mentioned previously, part of the impetus in establishing the ORASECOM agreement was the adoption of the region-wide SADC Protocol on Shared Watercourse Systems in 1995 (SADC Protocol).[70] Due to concerns that Angola and Mozambique had during the

---

[66] Revised Agreement on the Establishment of the Orange-Senqu Watercourse Commission (adopted 14 December 2018), (Revised ORASECOM Agreement).

[67] Turton (n 13).

[68] ORASECOM Agreement (n 22).

[69] Ibid.

[70] Protocol on Shared Watercourse Systems in the Southern African Development Community (SADC) Region (adopted 28 August 1995, entered into force 29 September 1998) <https://www.internationalwaterlaw.org/documents/regionaldocs/sadc1.html> accessed 5 August 2024. See also Gavin Quibell and Guy Pegram, 'Strengthening Transboundary Water Management Institutions: The

time of its signing, and following a series of workshops with SADC member states to reflect on the text of the agreement, the SADC Protocol was subsequently amended.[71] The fifth and final workshop took place in Johannesburg, South Africa, in March 2000, and the text of a Revised Protocol on Shared Watercourses in SADC was adopted on 7 August 2000.[72] The latter instrument drew heavily on the provisions of the Convention on the Law of the Non-navigational Uses of International Watercourses, which had been adopted by the UN General Assembly three years earlier.[73]

It is curious that the Revised Protocol on Shared Watercourses in the SADC is not explicitly referred to in the preamble of the ORASECOM Agreement.[74] The former instrument was signed by Botswana, Namibia, Lesotho and South Africa on 7 August 2000; whereas the latter instrument was signed by the four countries on 3 November 2000. Instead, the Preamble to the ORASECOM Agreement refers to the 1995 SADC Protocol on Shared Watercourse Systems. However, any confusion is addressed by Article 16 of the Revised SADC Protocol, which stipulates that 'upon entry into force of this Protocol, the Protocol on Shared Watercourse Systems in the Southern African Development (SADC) Region ... shall be repealed and replaced by this Protocol'.[75] The Revised SADC Protocol entered into force on 22 September 2003.[76]

While not explicit within the preamble of the ORASECOM Agreement, the reach of the Revised SADC Protocol on the former instrument can be found in

---

case of the Orange-Senqu River Commission in Southern Africa', <https://www.inweb.gr/twm4/abs/QUIBELL%20Gavin.pdf> accessed 5 August 2024. See also Jacobs (n 3), 193–194.

71 E.M. Mokuoane, 'Revised Protocol on Shared Watercourses in the Southern African Development Community', in Charles L. Abernethy (ed), *Intersectoral Management of River Basins*, <https://publications.iwmi.org/pdf/H029128.pdf> accessed 5 August 2024, 348.

72 Ibid.

73 Salman M.A. Salman, 'Legal Regime for Use and Protection of International Watercourses in the Southern African Region: Evolution and Context' (2001) 41 Natural Resources Journal 981, 1004; Daniel Malzbender and Anthony Earle, 'The Impact and Implications of the Adoption of the 1997 UN Watercourses Convention in Southern African Countries', <http://www.unwatercoursesconvention.org/global-relevance/southern-africa> accessed 5 August 2024. South Africa was one of the first countries to ratify the Watercourses Convention on 26 October 1998, and Namibia subsequently ratified it on 29 August 2001. Botswana and Lesotho are not parties to the Watercourses Convention.

74 The Revised ORASECOM Agreement (n 66) makes explicit reference to the 2000 Revised SADC Protocol in its preamble.

75 Revised SADC Protocol (n 70).

76 Ibid.

its approach to the establishment of river basin management institutions. The Revised SADC Protocol requires SADC member states to 'establish appropriate institutions' for the 'effective implementation' of the Protocol, including 'River Basin Commissions between Basin states and in respect of each drainage basin'.[77] An extensive list of objectives and functions of the river basin management institutions is then provided for in Articles 4 and 5 of the Revised SADC Protocol.[78] The compatibility of these requirements with the ORASECOM Agreement will be studied below.

In relation to agreements entered into by SADC member states, the Revised SADC Protocol requests that such agreements are, in conformity with the main provisions of the Protocol.[79] Several provisions of the ORASECOM agreement do make reference to the Revised SADC Protocol, despite there being no reference to the latter instrument in the preamble.[80] There is therefore clearly a need to adopt a combined reading of the 2000 Revised SADC Protocol and the 2000 ORASECOM Agreement when determining the commitments entered into by the four riparians of the Orange-Senqu River.

A further issue concerning the relationship between legal arrangements relates to the agreements that have been entered into at the bilateral level, namely the 1992 Agreements establishing the Permanent Water Commission and Vioolsdrift and Noordoewer Joint Irrigation Scheme between Namibia and South Africa, and the 1986 Lesotho Highlands Treaty. This proved to be a contentious issue during the negotiation of the ORASECOM Agreement.[81] Namibia was keen to bring the 1986 Lesotho Highlands Treaty under the jurisdiction of the ORASECOM Agreement, but such a move was resisted by South Africa and Lesotho.[82] A compromise was to exclude the existing treaties from the ORASECOM agreement but ensure that there would be regular reporting of the bilateral arrangements to ORASECOM.[83]

No specific mention is made of the 1992 Agreements and the 1986 Agreement within the text of the ORASECOM Agreement. However, Article 1(3) of the Agreement stipulates that 'in the absence of an agreement to the contrary, nothing in this Agreement shall affect the rights and obligations of a party arising from other agreements in force prior to the date this Agreement

77 Article 3, ibid.

78 Articles 4 and 5, ibid.

79 Article 6, Revised SADC Protocol (n 70).

80 See for instance Article 7(2) and 7(3), ORASECOM Agreement (n 22).

81 ORASECOM, *Orange-Senqu River Commission 15 Years (2000–2015)*, (ORASECOM 2015), 14.

82 Ibid.

83 Ibid.

comes into force for such a party'.[84] Article 1(3) puts precedence on the commitments that the parties have already entered into in the 1992 Agreement and the 1986 Agreement.

The need to strike a balance between the bilateral agreements and the basin-wide ORASECOM Agreement is a key challenge for the cooperative governance of the basin.[85] Namibia sees ORASECOM as a means by which it might influence upstream developments, having largely been excluded from the Lesotho Highlands Water Project.[86] Additionally, inter-basin upstream water transfers within South Africa may also raise concerns for downstream interests. Heyns, for instance, estimates that of the various water-transfer schemes within its territory, 'South Africa has the capacity to export 2,120 MCM/year from the basin and can import only 925 MCM/year, leaving a deficit of 1,195 MCM/year'.[87] However, the wording of Article 1(3) does not call for a strong alignment of the existing agreements with the ORASECOM Agreement. As Jacobs observes, ORASECOM 'does not ... have any direct links (through formal mechanisms), or any formal oversight of co-ordinating powers with respect to the pre-existing bilateral commissions'.[88]

In terms of future arrangements, stronger wording is included in the ORASECOM Agreement. Article 1(4), whilst recognising 'the prerogative of any number of the parties to establish themselves river commissions with regard to any party of the River System', stipulates that such commissions 'will be subordinate to this Commission and existing Commissions will liaise with this Commission in terms of this Agreement'.[89] However, as will be discussed below, the appetite of the upstream states to table basin-wide planning discussions within ORASECOM has proven to be low.

A final point to note in terms of scope is the question of whether groundwater is included within the ORASECOM Agreement. The preamble to the agreement refers to the 'Orange-Senqu River System', which is then referred to as the 'River System' throughout the agreement.[90] There is no definition

---

84 ORASECOM Agreement (n 22).

85 Naho Mirumachi, *Transboundary Water Politics in the Developing World* (Routledge 2015), 102.

86 Ibid. Namibia was requested to raise no objections to the Lesotho Highland Water Project prior to Phase I of the project, see Heyns (n 3), 20–21.

87 Heyns (n 3), 23.

88 Inga M. Jacobs, *The Politics of Water in Africa: Norms, Environmental Regions, and Transboundary Cooperation in the Orange-Senqu and Nile Rivers* (Continuum 2012).

89 ORASECOM Agreement (n 22).

90 Ibid.

section of the Agreement.[91] The Revised SADC Protocol closely follows the Watercourses Convention by making reference to the 'Watercourse' rather than 'River'.[92] 'Watercourse' is defined in the Revised SADC Protocol as meaning, 'a system of surface and ground waters consisting by virtue of their physical relationship a unitary whole normally flowing into a common terminus such as the sea, lake or aquifer'.[93] While, at first glance, the ORASECOM Agreement may appear more restrictive than the Revised SADC Protocol, it could be argued that any groundwater connected to the Orange-Senqu River System is, at least implicitly, included within the scope of the Agreement. Such an interpretation could be inferred from some of the key substantive and procedural commitments that the states have entered into.[94] These commitments, as will be demonstrated below, require the riparian states of the Orange-Senqu River to take a basin-wide approach to its management. The importance of accounting for groundwater needs and interests when implementing the substantive and procedural commitments of the ORASECOM Agreement is heightened by the fact that groundwater is used extensively throughout the Orange-Senqu basin for irrigation, industry, mining, domestic and rural water supply schemes.[95] An additional factor to take into account is that there is a significant number of transboundary aquifers that fall within the catchment area of the Orange-Senqu River Basin.[96] Efforts are ongoing to better understand the physical characteristics of these aquifers and in turn explore the appropriate governance arrangements that may apply to them.[97]

---

91 In contrast, the Revised ORASECOM Agreement (n 66) includes a definitions section, but it is of limited value.

92 Article 1, Revised SADC Protocol (n 70).

93 Ibid.

94 In Article 8(1) of the Revised ORASECOM Agreement (n 66), 'groundwater management and use' is included as a specific objective of the Commission'. Additionally, throughout the text of the 2018 Revised ORASECOM Agreement, the term 'watercourse' is used rather than 'river system', which aligns the agreement more clearly with the 2000 Revised SADC protocol.

95 A. Viles, Review of Groundwater Resources in the Orange River Catchment (August 2007) <https://iwlearn.net/resolveuid/bc3600286b491676b3f75d64770cd089> accessed 5 August 2024.

96 Ibid.

97 See for instance, UNESCO-IHP, 'GGRETA Project' (*UN-IGRAC.org*) <https://www.un-igrac.org/special-project/ggreta> accessed 5 August 2024; The World Bank, *Sustainable Groundwater Management in SADC member states*, <https://projects.worldbank.org/en/projects-operations/project-detail/P127086> accessed 5 August 2024.

7.3.2 Substantive Commitments

Inspired by the 2000 Revised SADC Protocol and the Watercourses Convention, the ORASECOM Agreement sets out a series of substantive commitments in Article 7. Article 7(2) of the ORASECOM Agreement stipulates that:

> The parties shall, in their respective territories, utilise the resources of the River System in an equitable and reasonable manner with a view to attaining optimal and sustainable utilisation thereof, and benefits therefrom, consistent with adequate protection of the River System.

Article 7(2) corresponds to a truncated version of Article 7(a) of the Revised SADC Protocol and Article 5 of the Watercourses Convention. Whilst the essence is the same, it might be argued that the Revised SADC Protocol and the Watercourses Convention place more emphasis on the protection of the watercourse.[98]

The ORASECOM Agreement continues by stipulating that 'the term "equitable and reasonable" shall be interpreted in line with the Revised Protocol on Shared Watercourses in the Southern Africa Development Community (SADC) Region'.[99] While the Revised SADC Protocol could by no means be considered to provide an exhaustive interpretation of equitable and reasonable utilisation, it does go further than the ORASECOM Agreement by providing a list of relevant factors and circumstances that should be taken into account in determining what might constitute an equitable and reasonable use.[100] Further interpretative guidance is provided by the second part of Article 8 of the Revised SADC Protocol, which provides that:

> The weight to be given to each factor is to be determined by its importance in comparison with that of other relevant factors. In determining what is an equitable and reasonable use, all relevant factors are to be considered together and a conclusion reached on the basis of the whole.[101]

---

[98] Both instruments include a separate sub-Article relating to equitable *participation.* Article 7(b) of the Revised SADC Protocol, copied almost verbatim from the Watercourses Convention, Article 5(b), reads: 'Watercourse states shall participate in the use, development and protection of a shared watercourse in an equitable and reasonable manner. Such participation, includes both the right to utilise the watercourse and the duty to cooperate in the protection and development thereof, as provided in this Protocol'.

[99] ORASECOM Agreement (n 22).

[100] Article 4 of the 2018 Revised ORASECOM Agreement (n 22), in line with the 2000 Revised SADC Protocol, includes a non-exhaustive list of factors and circumstances to take into account when determining what is equitable.

[101] Article 8(b), ibid.

This requirement to weigh factors together should also be considered in light of the additional substantive commitments that are contained in the ORASECOM Agreement. The second major substantive norm that is set out in the ORASECOM agreement is the requirement that, 'the parties shall, in utilising the resources of the River System in their territories, take all appropriate measures to prevent the causing of significant harm to any other party'.[102] The ORASECOM agreement continues by stipulating that 'the term "significant harm" shall be interpreted in line with the Revised Protocol on Shared Watercourses in the Southern Africa Development Community (SADC) Region'.[103] The latter stipulation is clearly intended to link to Article 1 of the Revised SADC Protocol, which defines 'significant harm' as being 'non-trivial harm capable of being established by objective evidence without necessarily rising to the level of being substantial'.[104]

A point of departure between both instruments is that the ORASECOM Agreement simply provides that states must 'take all appropriate measures to prevent the causing of significant harm to any other party'.[105] The Revised SADC Protocol is, however, more nuanced in that it provides a requirement that:

> ... where significant harm is nevertheless caused to another Watercourse state, the state whose use causes such harm shall, in the absence of agreement to such use, take all appropriate measures, having due regard for the provisions of paragraph (a) above in consultation with the affected states, to eliminate or mitigate such harm and, where appropriate, to discuss the question of compensation'.[106]

The Revised SADC Protocol, pursuant to Article 10, and unlike the strict wording of the ORASECOM Agreement, therefore suggests that some harm may have to be tolerated by other states. What is not clear is whether such harm might only be tolerated where compensation is provided, or while measures are being taken to eliminate or mitigate such harm. The Watercourses Convention is much more definitive in this regard. It stipulates that due regard should be had to the principle of equitable and reasonable utilisation when determining whether or not significant harm might be tolerated.[107] This gives the effect, as suggested by the International Law Commission (ILC), that:

---

[102] Article 7(3), ORASECOM Agreement (n 22).

[103] Article 7(3), ibid.

[104] Article 1, Revised SADC Protocol (n 70).

[105] Article 7(3), ORASECOM Agreement (n 22).

[106] Article 10(b), Revised SADC Protocol (n 70).

[107] Article 7(2), Convention on the Law of the Non-navigational Uses of International Watercourses (adopted 21 May 1997, entered into force 17 August 2014), 36 ILM 700 reads:

> An activity [that] involves significant harm would not of itself necessarily constitute a basis for barring it. In certain circumstances "equitable and reasonable utilisation" of an international watercourse may still involve significant harm. Generally, in such circumstances, the principle of equitable and reasonable utilisation remains the guiding criterion in balancing the interests at stake.[108]

Additionally, the ILC has commented that, 'it is a generally accepted principle that when several norms bear on a single issue, they should, to the extent possible, be interpreted so as to give rise to a single set of compatible obligations'.[109] A strong argument could therefore be made that the provisions of the Watercourses Convention, the Revised SADC Protocol, and the ORASECOM Agreement should be interpreted holistically. While the latter two instruments do not explicitly set out the relationship between the principles of equitable and reasonable utilisation, and no significant harm, this is addressed by Article 7 of the Watercourses Convention.

A third and final area of substantive commitments contained within the ORASECOM Agreement relates to the protection of the river. Article 7(12) requires the parties to 'individually and joint take all measures that are necessary to protect and preserve the River System from its source and headwaters to its common terminus'.[110] This requirement is supplemented by obligations upon the parties to 'prevent, reduce and control pollution; protect the river system's estuary, including the marine environment; and prevent the introduction of alien and new species into the River system that may have a detrimental effect to its ecosystem'.[111] In relation to ecosystem protection, the ORASECOM Agreement is therefore more general than the text found in the Revised SADC Protocol, as the Agreement does not specifically refer to the protection and

---

> Where significant harm nevertheless is caused to another watercourse state, the state whose use causes such harm shall, in the absence of agreement to such use, take all appropriate measures, having due regard for the provisions of articles 5 and 6, in consultation with the affected state, to eliminate or mitigate such harm and, where appropriate, to discuss the question of compensation.

[108] 'Draft Articles on the Law of the Non-navigational Uses of International Watercourses' in Report of the International Law Commission on the Work of its 46th Session (2 May – 22 July 1994) UN Doc A/49/10, 103.

[109] 'Conclusions of the work of the Study Group on the Fragmentation of International Law: Difficulties arising from the Diversification and Expansion of International Law' in Report of the International Law Commission on the Work of its 58th Session (1 May – 9 June and 3 July – 11 August 2006) UN Doc A/61/10, 175. See also Article 31, Vienna Convention on the Law of Treaties (adopted 22 May 1969, entered into force 27 January 1980), 1155 UNTS 331.

[110] ORASECOM Agreement (n 22).

[111] Article 7(13)–(15), ibid.

preservation of 'ecosystems' of a shared watercourse.[112] However, the essence of the commitments is the same, and as noted above, the provisions of both instruments should be interpreted as a whole.

7.3.3 Procedural and Institutional Commitments

A key feature of the ORASECOM Agreement is its establishment of the Orange-Senqu River Commission or ORASECOM.[113] The Commission is comprised of a council that serves 'as technical advisor to the parties on matters relating to the development, utilisation and conservation of the water resources in the River System and shall perform such other functions pertaining to the development and utilisation of water resources as the parties may agree to assign to the Commission'.[114] Pursuant to the Agreement, the Council is comprised of not more than three permanent members and not more than three advisers unless otherwise agreed by the Council.[115] Meetings of the Council are to take place at least once a year, and any decisions taken therein must be made by consensus.[116]

According to the ORASECOM Agreement, the Council, 'shall take all measures required to make recommendations, or to advise the parties' on the implementation of the Agreement.[117] Specific matters to be addressed by the Council include measures to determine the long-term safe yield of the River System; the equitable and reasonable utilisation of the River System; joint and separate investigations and studies by the parties regarding the development of the River System; an assessment of the extent to which inhabitants in the territory of each party concerned must participate in respect of the planning, development, utilisation, protection and conservation of the River System; the standardisation of data and information collection, processing and dissemination; the prevention of pollution of water resources and the control of aquatic weeds within the River System; the establishment of contingency plans and measures for responding to emergency situations or harmful conditions resulting from natural causes (floods and droughts) or human conduct (industrial

---

112 Article 4(2)(a), Revised SADC Protocol (n 70). See also Article 20 of the Watercourses Convention (n 107).

113 Articles 1–6, ORASECOM Agreement (n 22).

114 Article 4, ibid.

115 Article 2(3), ibid.

116 Article 3(6)–(9), ibid. The 2018 Revised ORASECOM Agreement (n 22), in a reflection of how ORASECOM has evolved, sets out the institutional structure of the Commission as comprising a forum of the parties, a Council of Commissioners, task teams and a secretariat.

117 Article 5(1) & (2), ibid.

accidents); the regular exchange of information and consultation on the possible effects of planned measures; and measures to address disputes between two or more of the parties.[118]

In pursuit of its obligations, the Council is supported by several task teams, which cover communication, finance, legal, and technical matters.[119]

No secretariat was foreseen within the ORASECOM Agreement itself.[120] However, a decision was taken by the Council in July 2004 to establish a secretariat to *inter alia* co-ordinate ORASECOM activities and implement ORASECOM decisions; serve as a repository for information related to the Orange-Senqu River; act as a focal point for ORASECOM for external parties; perform ORASECOM administrative functions; conduct communication and promotion activities of ORASECOM; and mobilise additional resources.[121] The secretariat's offices were opened in Centurion, South Africa, on 24 February 2011.[122]

The procedural obligations under the ORASECOM Agreement are limited to the exchange of data and information, notification and consultation on planned measures, and dispute settlement. In terms of data and information exchange, the parties are obliged to 'exchange available information and data regarding the hydrological, hydrogeological, water quality, meteorological and environmental condition of the River System'.[123] In addition, they must 'employ their best efforts to, collect and, where appropriate, process data and information with regard to the River System in a manner which facilitates its utilisation by the other parties, technical experts or consultants who may be appointed by the Council'; and 'make every effort to employ the standardised form for collection, processing and disseminating data and information, where appropriate'.[124]

Where a party is planning a project, programme or activity which may have a significant adverse effect upon one or more other states within the

---

118 Article 5(2)–(10), ibid.

119 Article 6(1), ibid.

120 See Article 15, ibid. A secretariat is provided for in the 2018 Revised ORASECOM Agreement (n 22).

121 See ORASECOM, 'Structure of ORASECOM', <https://orasecom.org/structure-of-orasecom/#:~:text=ORASECOM%20is%20structured%20into%20the%20Council%2C%20Secretariat%20and%20Task%20Teams> accessed 5 August 2024.

122 ORASECOM, 'Newsletter' (July 2010 – February 2011) <https://orasecom.org/wp-content/uploads/2020/05/761Newsletter-No.-3-Jul-2010-to-Feb-2011.pdf> accessed 5 August 2024.

123 Article 7(4), ORASECOM Agreement (n 22).

124 Article 7(11), ibid.

Orange-Senqu River system, they shall notify the Council and provide available data and information on the plans.[125] Such an obligation to notify strongly aligns with the commitments contained in both the Revised SADC Protocol and the Watercourses Convention.[126] However, the ORASECOM Agreement arguably goes further by stipulating that a planning state must also notify the Council where their plans 'may adversely affect' the Orange-Senqu River System itself. This requirement, contained in Article 7(5), would suggest that any likely impacts may not necessarily need to transcend sovereign borders. Moreover, the threshold for notification would appear lower than the aforementioned requirement as there is no requirement that any potential adverse effects be significant.

Pursuant to the ORASECOM Agreement, notified parties have six months by which to reply to the notifying party, unless the parties agree otherwise.[127] Unlike the Revised SADC Protocol and the Watercourses Convention, there is no stipulation that the period be extended upon request of the notified state.[128] The ORASECOM Agreement also provides that, 'in the event that the implementation or execution of any planned measures is of the utmost urgency in order to save life, or to protect public health and safety, or other equally important interests as a result of an emergency situation, the party planning the measure may immediately proceed with implementation or execution'.[129] However, the party in question must lodge 'a formal declaration of the urgency of the measures' with the Council.

The ORASECOM Agreement also addresses the scenario where a party fails to notify of a particular plan, programme or activity. In such a scenario, the ORASECOM Agreement stipulates that not only other parties, but 'technical experts or consultants appointed by the Council' may request data and information 'which are available or obtainable on any planned project, programme or activity which may have a significant adverse effect upon the other parties'.[130] The Agreement goes on to clarify that such data and information must include the findings of an environmental impact assessment (EIA) that addresses the effects on the ecosystems of the watercourse as well as the social, cultural, economic and natural environment.[131] The ORASECOM Agreement is therefore more stringent in this regard than the Revised SADC Protocol, which only refers to Watercourse states, not technical experts or consultants;

---

125 Article 7(5), ibid.
126 Article 4(1), Revised SADC Protocol (n 70).
127 Article 7(6), ORASECOM Agreement (n 22).
128 See Article 4(1)(iii), ibid.
129 Article 7(7), ibid.
130 Article 7(8), ibid.
131 Article 7(9), ibid.

and only requires the sharing of an EIA if one is available.[132] Both the Revised SADC Protocol and the Watercourses Convention do, however, provide more detail on several aspects of the notification procedure, including stipulating that the implementation of the planned measures must not go ahead during the notification period without the consent of the notified state;[133] and setting out procedures for consultation and negotiations over planned measures, where necessary.[134] As noted previously, these more detailed provisions within the Revised SADC Protocol should be seen as providing supplementary requirements to the parties of the ORASECOM Agreement.

The final procedural element contained within the ORASECOM Agreement relates to the settlement of disputes. Pursuant to the Agreement, there is a general obligation on the parties to settle their disputes through consultation and/or negotiation.[135] However, where the parties are unable to reach an agreement through consultation or negotiation, and unless they agree otherwise, they have the option to bring the dispute before the SADC Tribunal.[136] If the dispute is submitted to the SADC Tribunal, the decision of the Tribunal is final and binding on the parties. While it would therefore appear that the states have some level of discretion when deciding whether or not to involve third parties in the resolution of disputes, the commitments under the Revised SADC Protocol in this regard are stricter. Article 7(2) of the latter instrument stipulates that 'disputes between state parties regarding the interpretation or application of the provisions of this Protocol which are not settled amicably, *shall* be referred to the [SADC] Tribunal'.[137] Given the strong overlap between the scope of the ORASECOM Agreement and the Revised SADC Protocol, riparian states of the Orange-Senqu are therefore under an obligation to submit their dispute to the SADC Tribunal pursuant to the latter instrument. However, as noted previously, the uncertain status of the SADC Tribunal would mean that practically, states would not be able to rely on this option.[138]

7.4 EXPERIENCE IN IMPLEMENTATION AND COMPLIANCE

In assessing the record of compliance and implementation with the ORASECOM Agreement, this section will closely follow the structure of

---

[132] Article 4(1)(b), Revised SADC Protocol (n 70).
[133] Article 4(1)(d)(ii), ibid.
[134] Article 4(1)(g), ibid.
[135] Article 8(1), ORASECOM Agreement (n 22).
[136] Article 8(2), ibid.
[137] Revised SADC Protocol (n 70).
[138] See section 5.5.4 above.

Chapter 4 and pay particular attention to key areas of monitoring and reporting, mechanisms to review implementation, and strategies to address weak implementation and non-compliance. Measures adopted by the parties to the ORASECOM Agreement in support of compliance and implementation will be examined, together with the factors likely to influence the effectiveness of those measures.

7.4.1 Monitoring and Reporting

Exchange of data and information

The exchange of data and information on a basin as complex as the Orange-Senqu is critical to its effective management.[139] Policymakers have repeatedly emphasised the need to improve knowledge and understanding of the Orange-Senqu Basin before any water allocations among the parties can take place.[140] Significant improvements in the exchange of data and information have occurred in recent decades due to political transformations in the region, technological advances and regional approaches.[141] It is suggested that these developments have in turn led to increased levels of trust between the parties and improved interpersonal relationships among basin managers operating in different countries.[142]

South Africa plays a critical role in the exchange of data and information concerning the Orange-Senqu River Basin. As noted previously, the largest proportion of the basin is in South Africa, and the river is of strategic importance to the economic development of the country. South Africa has therefore dedicated a significant amount of effort to the study of the basin since the mid-1980s.[143] More recently, data has been made available through various web-based tools that have been provided by the Department of Water Affairs in South Africa, such as the Water Management System, Hydstra, and the National Groundwater Information System (NGIS).[144] Improvements in inter-

---

139 Kranz and others (n 14).

140 Kistin and others (n 48).

141 Ibid.

142 Ibid, 19–20.

143 ORASECOM, UNDP and GEF, 'Orange-Senqu Strategic Action Programme – Hydro-meteorological Monitoring in the Orange-Senqu River Basin' (Technical Report 49, 6 December 2013) <https://wis.orasecom.org/content/study/UNDP-GEF/NAP-SAP/Documents/Strategic%20Action%20Programme%20for%20the%20Orange-Senqu%20River%20Basin.pdf> accessed 5 August 2024, 18.

144 Ibid.

net services within the last ten years or so have gone some way to ensure that the exchange of such data and information is more widely available.[145]

At the basin level, ORASECOM has sought to play a co-ordinating role in the exchange of data and information through the development of its web-based Water Information System (WIS).[146] WIS serves as a central repository for all data and information developed under the auspices of ORASECOM.

The Orange-Senqu basin hosts around 300 built structures, including 30 large dams and several large inter- and intra-basin transfers, and all the riparian countries have plans to develop further large-scale projects such as mines, gas-fired power stations, irrigation schemes, and additional phases of the Lesotho Highlands Water Project.[147] As noted in the previous section, ORASECOM has the responsibility to co-ordinate the exchange of data and information concerning these plans.[148] In furtherance of this requirement, ORASECOM has developed recommendations on Transboundary Environmental Assessment in the Orange-Senqu River Basin.[149] These recommendations cover requirements relating to both notification and the EIA process. In relation to notification, the recommendations suggest that there should be a preliminary notification of a policy, plan, programme or project when it is being developed conceptually.[150] Such notification would involve the communication of the broad outline of the proposed policy, plan, programme or project and might allow ORASECOM to participate in any EIA scoping phase.[151] According to the recommendations, 'full technical notification' would then occur,

> … when the (preliminary) findings of the full SEA [Strategic Environmental Assessment] or EIA are transmitted to the potentially affected state(s) and/or the joint technical institution [ORASECOM], including, *inter alia*, a full technical description of the policy, plan, programme or project, a full evaluation of the likely environmental, social, cultural and economic impacts, proposals for avoiding or mitigating such impacts, all available technical data and information, and a non-technical summary of these findings.[152]

---

145 ORASECOM and others (n 143).

146 See 'WIS Orange-Senqu Water Information System', <https://orasecom.org/water-information-system-wis/> accessed 5 August 2024.

147 ORASECOM (n 81), 42

148 Article 5, ORASECOM Agreement (n 22).

149 ORASECOM, UNDP and GEF, 'Orange-Senqu Action Programme – Transboundary Environmental Assessment in the Orange-Senqu River Basin – Recommendations of the ORASECOM Council' (Technical Report 14, 13 June 2013).

150 Ibid, 18.

151 Ibid.

152 Ibid.

Chapter four of the recommendations then provides a detailed outline of the requirements for notification, including the format for notification, the functions of the ORASECOM secretariat and Council, and consultation and negotiation procedures.[153]

Chapter three of the recommendations sets out the requirements when conducting an EIA or SEA.[154] The recommendations stipulate that an SEA should be carried out for 'policies, plans and programmes that have the potential to significantly influence the environment'.[155] According to the recommendations, SEAs should be carried out 'much earlier in the decision-making process, than ... project level EIAs', and are 'a more proactive tool that assesses impacts at a time when it may still be possible to consider alternatives'.[156] As part of the EIA or SEA process, the recommendations require the creation of a Public Participation and Disclosure Plan, which is designed to 'constructively engage the stakeholders in the project throughout the project planning, implementation, and evaluation'.[157] In addition, the recommendations set out principles for environmental assessment and management, including the precautionary principle, the ecosystems approach, inter-state equity, social equity, consideration of alternatives, mitigation strategies, and the polluter pays principle.[158]

While the recommendations signify a concerted effort by ORASECOM to strengthen notification and consultation procedures within the basin, challenges remain. There is a need to build trust amongst the parties to the ORASECOM Agreement due to perceived failures to notify in the past, or where notified countries have failed to respond within agreed timeframes.[159] Commentators have questioned whether meaningful discussions on large-scale infrastructure projects have been able to take place within ORASECOM.[160] Kistin, for instance, notes that when a consultant asked about plans for a feasibility study related to Phase 2 of the Lesotho Highlands Water Project in a 2007 ORASECOM meeting, 'a member of the South African delegation quickly replied, "We don't discuss those matters here. This is ORASECOM"'.[161]

Kistin goes on to suggest that:

---

153 Ibid, 28–32.

154 Ibid, 21–27.

155 Ibid, 21.

156 Ibid, 21.

157 Ibid, 22.

158 Ibid, 23–26.

159 ORASECOM (n 81), 23.

160 Elisabeth Kistin, 'Critiquing Cooperation: Transboundary Water Governance and Adaptive Capacity in the Orange-Senqu Basin' (2012) 149 Journal of Contemporary Water Research & Education 41.

161 Ibid, 43.

> What this exchange illustrated is that, despite the ample flexibility afforded in the formal water governance structures, the South African delegations' broader efforts to restrict the boundaries of what can and cannot be discussed limits the ability of ORASECOM to engage in serious basin-level planning or recognize and respond to changing circumstances.[162]

Broader constraints have also impeded the exchange of data and information. For instance, private consultants have played a significant role in the collection, exchange and utilisation of information relating to the basin.[163] This in turn has led to a 'quasi-internal network of consultants' that work within the basin and have at times proven to be reluctant to share information openly with competitors.[164] Additional constraints that have been suggested include a lack of human, financial, and technical resources, a high level of staff turnover, a lack of political will and national data protocols.[165] However, one positive in the sharing of data and information has been the development of the Integrated Water Resources Plan for the Orange-Senqu River Basin, which will be discussed below.

Additionally, at the regional level, data and information exchange has been bolstered by the SADC Hydrological Cycle Observing System (SADC-HYCOS), which serves as a central depository for water data.[166] As a key component of the SADC Regional Strategic Action Plan on Integrated Water Resources Management (RSAP-IWRM), SADC-HYCOS has enhanced hydro-meteorological monitoring, developed and operated an integrated regional water resources database and website, strengthened capacity within the region, and developed hydrological products.[167] SADC-HYCOS has been implemented through three phases: 1998–2001, 2005–2009, and 2014–2017.[168] However, as with other data-gathering efforts within the region, large staff turnover and non-continuous funding have affected the ability of SADC-HYCOS

---

162 Ibid. See also André Mueller and others, 'Stalemate of the Hydrological Master Variable? The Challenge of Implementing Environmental Flows in the Orange-Senqu Basin' (2022) 47(3) Water International 458.

163 Kistin (n 160), 53.

164 Ibid.

165 Ibid, 46.

166 See A.J. Andrews, S. Pieyns and E. Servat, 'The Design of an International Real Time Data Collection System: SADC-HYCOS' (1999) 13 Water Resources Management 253.

167 WMO, 'SADC-HYCOS (Southern Africa)', <https://wmo.int/site/wmo-hydrohub> accessed 5 August 2024.

168 WMO, 'Status of HYCOS components', <https://library.wmo.int/viewer/56215/download?file=wmo_z_whycos_sadc-hycos-phase3_draft_en.pdf&type=pdf&navigator=1> accessed 5 August 2024.

to fully reach its objectives. There has therefore been an overall decrease in hydro-meteorological observations within the basin.[169] Efforts are ongoing to address these gaps through the development of a fourth phase of SADC-HYCOS focused on climate resilience.[170]

Monitoring

There are no formal requirements for ORASECOM to monitor compliance and implementation vis-à-vis the ORASECOM agreement. As will be discussed below, ORASECOM does, however, have a role to play in the monitoring and evaluation of certain projects and programmes.

In terms of monitoring water quality and quantity issues, ORASECOM has played a key role. The first joint monitoring of the Orange-Senqu River Basin, supported by all four member states, was carried out in 2010.[171] A survey aimed to assess the quality of the water resources, and to serve as a baseline upon which future activities might be measured, was conducted.[172] There were four key elements to the survey, namely aquatic ecosystem health surveys, water and sediment chemistry, biological water quality, and public participation and outreach.[173] The survey included 50 to 60 sample sites throughout the Orange-Senqu River System, and the core team was made up of two experts from each member state with the support of specialists from international collaborating partners.[174] A second joint basin survey was conducted in 2015, and a subsequent survey in 2021.[175] A challenge in such monitoring activities, as noted by a representative from Namibia, is too strong a reliance on external consultants at the cost of enhancing the capacity of locals to conduct such monitoring.[176] The 2014 Transboundary Diagnostic Analysis for the Basin also

---

169 ORASECOM (n 143), 17.

170 Green Climate Fund, 'Approved Project Preparation Facility Application, Climate Resilient Systems for SADC Water Sector: SADC Hydrological Cycle Observation System (SADC-HYCOS IV Project)' (13 May 2023) <https://www.greenclimate.fund/sites/default/files/document/ppf067-dbsa-multi-country.pdf> accessed 5 August 2024.

171 ORASECOM, 'A report on ORASECOM's First Joint Basin Survey' (October and November 2010) <http://the-eis.com/elibrary/sites/default/files/downloads/literature/RASECOM%20Joint%20Basin%20Survey%201%20Booklet.pdf> accessed 5 August 2024.

172 Ibid, 6.

173 Ibid.

174 ORASECOM (n 81), 25.

175 GEF, ORASECOM and UNDP, 'Mid-term Review of "Support to the Orange-Senqu River Strategic Action Programme Implementation" Project' (May–June 2022) <https://erc.undp.org/evaluation/documents/download/21427> accessed 5 August 2024.

176 ORASECOM (n 81), 25.

highlighted the need to 'increase the basin-wide monitoring network of relevant variables at strategic monitoring stations', and a mid-term review noted the inadequate levels of national ownership of such initiatives.[177]

Joint strategies, plans and programmes

A significant challenge for basin-wide management of the Orange-Senqu Basin is that many infrastructure developments reflect national interests.[178] As Mirumachi notes, 'while there is rhetoric of regional benefits to be gained from developing the river, the way the river flow is engineered and modified emphasises *national* water planning – and ultimately the sovereignty over its share of water'.[179] This tussle between national interests and working together at the basin level is clearly evident within the aspirations to develop a basin-wide Integrated Water Resources Management (IWRM) plan for the Orange-Senqu.

The origins of basin planning can be traced back to the 1920s, when the government of South Africa developed plans to utilise the Orange-Senqu River for various irrigation projects.[180] However, it was not until the 1960s, under considerable political influence by the South African government, that a plan was formulated. The objectives of the first plan were to provide irrigation for agriculture, municipal water supply, hydro-electric power generation, flood prevention, recreational facilitation, population settlement (mainly white farmers), employment opportunities, and regional economic stimulation through water and agriculture-based industry.[181] The plan led to the construction of the Gariep and Vanderkloof Dams in the 1960s. Public participation in the development of these projects was extremely limited, and only the white population in the area was notified and compensated for the negative impacts of the project.[182]

Given political transformations in South Africa and the growing recognition of environmental issues in the 1990s, the need to reconsider the Orange River Development Plan was recognised. This led to the development of the Orange River Replanning Study (ORRS) between 1992 and 1998, which resulted in a greater degree of participation, a deeper analysis

---

177 ORASECOM, *Orange-Senqu River Basin Transboundary Diagnostic Analysis* (ORASECOM 2014), 18; GEF, ORASECOM and UNDP (n 175), xi.

178 See also ORASECOM, *The Orange-Senqu River Basin Infrastructure Catalogue* (ORASECOM 2013).

179 Naho Miumachi, *Transboundary Water Politics in the Developing World* (Routledge 2015).

180 WRP (Pty) Ltd (n 32), 10.

181 Ibid.

182 Ibid.

of environmental considerations, and a study of the basin-wide implications for improved co-ordination with the Lesotho Highlands Water Project.[183] The ORRS has to a large extent been subsumed by the more recent development of the Orange-Senqu Basin-Wide IWRM Plan (IWRMP).[184] Under the auspices of ORASECOM, the IWRMP has been developed through three phases. Phases one and two focused on laying the foundations upon which the states could develop a basin-wide IWRM plan. Phase one, which was implemented between 2004 and 2007, sought to collate existing information relating to the basin, including hydrology and water resource availability; economics and current use of economic tools in water management and allocation; demographics, water demand and water resources development in the basin; water infrastructure in the basin; policy, legal and institutional frameworks related to water resource management in the basin; water quality and pollution; groundwater availability and use; and environmental considerations.[185]

Phase two of IWRMP was implemented between 2009 and 2011 and aimed to address the gaps identified in Phase one. A number of key focus areas were identified, including an assessment and upgrading of an Integrated Orange-Senqu River Basin Model; updating and extension of the hydrology; assessment of requirements for, and the development of, an Integrated Water Resources Quality Management Plan; an assessment of the impact of global climate change on the hydro-climatology, water resources, vulnerability and adaptation requirements; an assessment of environmental flow requirements; and an assessment of the potential for water demand management in the irrigation sector.[186]

While not strictly part of the IWRMP, a notable contribution was made through the development of a Transboundary Diagnostic Analysis (TDA) and Strategic Action Plan (SAP) for the Orange-Senqu Basin. The Orange-Senqu TDA is described as:

> … an objective, non-negotiated analysis using best available verified scientific information and an objective, participatory process that examined the state of the environment and the root causes for its degradation. It provides the factual basis for the formulation of a Orange-Senqu Strategic Action Programme, which will embody specific actions (policy, legal, institutional reforms or investments) that

[183] Ibid.

[184] ORASECOM, 'Orange-Senqu Basin-Wide Integrated Water Resources Management Plan Development', <https://orasecom.org/orange-senqu-basin-wide-integrated-water-resources-management-plan-development/#:~:text=The%20development%20of%20the%20Orange,water%20resources%20of%20the%20basin> accessed 5 August 2024.

[185] Ibid.

[186] Ibid.

> can be adopted nationally, usually within a harmonized multinational context, to address the major priority transboundary problems identified in the TDA, and over the longer term enable the sustainable development and environmental protection of the Orange-Senqu river basin.[187]

Completed in 2008, the Orange-Senqu TDA was later updated in 2014. By engaging with a range of stakeholders, the TDA identified several transboundary problems, including increasing water demands, changes in flow, the spread of alien invasive species, declining water quality, and land degradation.[188] The TDA formed the basis upon which to develop the SAP, which, as discussed below, provided the environmental component of phase three of the IWRMP.[189]

Development of a basin-wide plan for the Orange-Senqu has proven challenging. As one commentator remarks:

> ... parties have performed well in collecting and exchanging information when commitment requirements are perceived to be low (e.g., the execution of joint studies or the compilation of existing information). However, when commitment requirements are perceived as more substantial (e.g., establishing a basin-wide data protocol, opening Phase 2 [of LHWP] discussions, or engaging in planning at the basin level) progress has been blocked, stalled, or slower to materialize.[190]

The parties, through the ORASECOM Council, did however manage to adopt phase three of the IWRM Plan for the Orange-Senqu River Basin in December 2014.[191] The IWRM Plan for the Orange-Senqu Basin covers the period 2015–2024. The overarching objective of the plan is:

> ... to provide a framework for sustainable development and management of the water resources, taking into account the need for improved distribution and equitable allocation of benefits, in order to contribute towards socio-economic upliftment of communities within the basin, and ensure future water security for the basin.[192]

---

[187] ORASECOM, 'Preliminary Transboundary Diagnostic Analysis Adopted by ORASECOM in April 2008', <https://iwlearn.net/documents/5089> accessed 5 August 2024, 1.

[188] ORASECOM (n 81).

[189] Ibid, 24.

[190] Kistin (n 160).

[191] ORASECOM, 'IWRM Plan for the Orange Senqu River Basin', <https://renoka.org/wp-content/uploads/2021/08/019_2014_IWRM-Plan-Main-Report.pdf> accessed 5 August 2024.

[192] Ibid, 7.

This overarching objective is complemented by a vision for the Orange-Senqu River Basin, of 'a well-managed water secure basin with prosperous inhabitants living in harmony in a healthy environment'.[193]

The Plan therefore aligns well with the purpose of the ORASECOM Agreement, namely to 'realize the principle of equitable and reasonable utilization, as well the principle of sustainable development with regard to the River System'.[194] Whilst the IWRM plan is not structured around the key provisions of the ORASECOM Agreement, it can be seen as a tool by which the parties to the Agreement implement their commitments thereunder.[195] In so doing, the plan sets out 11 key objectives, some of which are considered central and enabling, and others cross-cutting.[196] A series of strategic actions and more specific actions are then assigned to the strategic objectives.[197] The specific actions are broken down into a description of the particular activity, whether they are transboundary and/or national, a timeline, the institution(s) responsible for their implementation, estimated costs, and potential funding sources.[198]

At the outset, the scope of the plan is set out as being:

> … focused on defining and prioritizing only ORASECOM's actions and activities over the next ten years. However, in order to do this it has been necessary to develop a holistic plan within the spirit of IWRM, even though the majority of actions and activities in the Plan will be planned, prioritized and carried out (or are already being carried out) at the national level by national institutions without any interference from ORASECOM.[199]

This statement clearly shows the tension between national and transboundary priorities. However, the inclusion of both national and transboundary aspects within the plan should go some way to ensuring that activities being carried out at different levels are co-ordinated. Several other features within the plan help to foster such co-ordination. For instance, in the breakdown of specific actions within the plan, the involvement of ORASECOM bodies is classified into high, significant, facilitator or support, and review or no involvement.[200]

---

193 Ibid.

194 Preamble, ORASECOM Agreement (n 22).

195 Ibid.

196 Ibid, 45.

197 Ibid, 52–58, 71–86.

198 Ibid, 81.

199 Ibid, 1.

200 The IWRM plan describes four classifications of ORASECOM involvement, namely: (i) High level of ORASECOM involvement. For the majority of activities under the specific action, ORASECOM bodies (Technical Task Team

A further means by which to foster co-ordination, and a significant step towards a basin-wide approach within the Orange-Senqu Basin, was the adoption of a 'core development and management scenario' as an integral part of the IWRM plan.[201] This scenario takes the existing baseline and identifies key management and infrastructure development choices that would support the attainment of the IWRM plan. In so doing, the Plan seeks to enhance the transparency and co-ordination of infrastructure and management strategies, which are ongoing or planned across the basin.

While making reference to the ORASECOM Agreement, the IWRM plan does not specifically call for monitoring its compliance and implementation. The closest areas relate to ensuring 'effective policy, legal and institutional arrangements', and the cross-cutting theme of 'capacity building and institutional strengthening'.[202] However, little detail is provided on how these areas will be realised.

Reporting requirements

As noted above, ORASECOM is made up of a council, technical task teams, and secretariat, with the former being responsible for making recommendations and advising the parties on the implementation of the ORASCOM Agreement.[203] In March 2011, the Ministers of the four Orange-Senqu River Basin states committed to holding annual meetings to review ORASECOM programme delivery.[204] In this regard, six priority areas have been identified for review, namely i) institutional and organisational strengthening; ii) specific capacity building on shared watercourses management; iii) development of shared information system; iv) enhancing ORASCOM communication and

(TTT), Communications Task Team (CTT) etc., and secretariat) will be involved in execution or management during project/programme planning; (ii) Significant level of ORASECOM involvement. For some of the activities under the specific action, ORASECOM bodies (Technical Task Team (TTT), Communications Task Team (CTT) etc., and secretariat) will be involved in management, for most in the facilitation role during project/programme implementation; (iii) For the majority of activities under the specific action, ORASECOM bodies (Technical Task Team (TTT), Communications Task Team (CTT), etc., and secretariat) will be involved only in facilitation or support of project/programme implementation; (iv) ORASECOM involvement limited to review or none in most of the activities under the specific action (see ORASECOM (n 191), at 72).

201 ORASECOM (n 191), 59.

202 Ibid, 78.

203 Ibid, 44.

204 See ORASECOM, 'Programmes' (*Orasecom.org*) <https://orasecom.org/#> accessed 5 August 2024.

awareness building; v) specific transboundary projects and studies; and vi) promotion of conservation and environmental strategies and policies.[205]

Whilst there is therefore a general remit within the ORASECOM institutional structure to review implementation, this falls short of an explicit mechanism that requires the states to report on their progress in the implementation of the ORASECOM agreement itself, or to identify incidences of non-compliance. Rather, issues related to compliance and implementation vis-à-vis the ORASECOM agreement take place indirectly through the reporting of plans, programmes and projects that have been approved by the ORASECOM Council, with the monitoring of the implementation of the IWRM plan constituting a central component of this effort.

Public information

The ORASECOM Agreement does not explicitly provide any role for the public to provide ORASECOM with information concerning the agreement's compliance and implementation. However, as discussed below, a role for the 'inhabitants in the territory of each party' is envisaged in the 'planning, development, utilisation, protection and conservation of the River System'.[206]

The important role that the public can play in the management of the Orange-Senqu Basin was recognised in the adoption of the Roadmap Towards Stakeholder Participation by the ORASECOM Council in 2007.[207] A key objective of the Roadmap was:

> … to develop and maintain open and effective horizontal and vertical communication between and among the structures of ORASECOM and basin stakeholders via the development of accessible, timely and good quality information and dissemination mechanisms to build trust, and improve participation and decision making in the basin.[208]

The adoption of the roadmap led to several activities aimed at enhancing communication. Much of the effort to engage with stakeholders focused on improving the way in which ORASECOM disseminated information. For instance, a communication strategy adopted by ORASECOM in 2010 had key objectives of better informing stakeholders about ORASECOM, its institutional setup, mandate and functioning; and ORASECOM communicating to

205 Ibid.

206 Article 5(2)(4), ORASECOM Agreement (n 22).

207 ORASECOM, 'Integrated Water Resources Management Plan for the Orange Senqu Basin - Main Report' (December 2014), <https://renoka.org/wp-content/uploads/2021/08/019_2014_IWRM-Plan-Main-Report.pdf> accessed 22 March 2025.

208 Ibid, 9.

stakeholders and target audiences how the organisation's actions contribute to improved management of the water resources of the Orange-Senqu Basin.[209] A number of communication tools were created to enhance the dissemination of knowledge. For instance, as noted above, the ORASECOM WIS was created to improve access to credible and quality-assured data and information on the Orange-Senqu River System.[210] As an online platform, WIS is open to anyone with an interest in the basin, and it even has a provision whereby anyone can submit information to the system. ORASECOM WIS is complemented by the Orange-Senqu River Awareness Kit, which was launched on 19 October 2009, with a second version coming online in 2011.[211] The river awareness kit is described as 'an information and knowledge management tool for the Orange-Senqu River Basin' which is targeted at 'the broad spectrum of stakeholders in the Orange-Senqu River Basin, including government agencies, river basin managers, Non-Governmental Organisations (NGOs), education establishments and the general public, as well as the international community'.[212] This online resource covers a wide range of aspects of the Orange-Senqu River Basin, including the physical characteristics of the system; social, cultural and economic characteristics; governance aspects; and water resource management issues.[213] Additionally, in a bid to reach younger stakeholders, ORASECOM has developed the Orange-Senqu 'learning box', which can be used by schools to inform children about the characteristics and management challenges faced within the Orange-Senqu River System.[214]

The Orange-Senqu IWRM planning process was also an opportunity for stakeholders within the basin to provide inputs concerning the challenges faced within the basin. The development of the basin-wide and national Strategic Action Plans for the Orange-Senqu Basin involved a significant level of stakeholder consultation.[215] The Strategic Action Plan's development at the national level was guided by inter-sectoral working groups that represented different ministries, as well as civil society. These working groups combined to guide the development of the Strategic Action Plan at the basin level. Wider

---

209 ORASECOM, 'The ORASECOM Communications Strategy 2010 – 2012', <https://orasecom.org/wp-content/uploads/2020/05/661The-ORASECOM-Communications-Strategy.pdf> accessed 5 August 2024.

210 See ORASECOM (n 146).

211 See ORASECOM, 'Orange-Senqu River Awareness Kit', <https://orasecom.org/orange-senqu-river-awareness-kit/> accessed 5 August 2024.

212 Ibid.

213 Ibid.

214 See ORASECOM, 'Learning Box', <https://orasecom.org/learning-box/> accessed 5 August 2024.

215 ORASECOM (n 1), 7.

stakeholder interaction was fostered through the establishment of national stakeholder platforms. These platforms were open to key stakeholders and provided input into the development of the Strategic Action Plans at key phases, as well as more general input into the development of the Orange-Senqu IWRM plan.

Moving forward, the IWRM plan envisages a strong role for stakeholders in the implementation of the plan, through the realisation of the aforementioned stakeholder roadmap, and through a revision of the ORASECOM community strategy. An additional feature of the IWRM plan was to recognise the importance of gender mainstreaming, and the under-representation of women in water management structures at the grass-roots level.[216] A key strategic action for the IWRM Plan is therefore to ensure appropriate and effective mainstreaming of gender considerations into planned and ongoing actions.[217]

7.4.2 Reviewing Treaty Compliance and Implementation

The ORASECOM Agreement sets out a series of 'powers' of the Council, which are to a large extent coupled with the obligations of the parties. For instance, the Council is required to advise or make recommendations to the parties on measures and arrangements to determine the long-term safe yield of the water sources of the River System; the equitable and reasonable utilisation of the water sources of the River System to support sustainable development in the territory of each party; and the prevention of pollution of water resources and the control over aquatic weeds in the River System.[218]

As noted above, from a procedural standpoint, the ORASECOM Agreement places the parties under an obligation to notify the Council and provide all available data and information on planned projects, programmes and activities that may have an adverse effect upon one or more other parties, or the river system itself.[219] The Council must then take all measures required to make recommendations or advise the parties on investigations and studies related to the development of the river system, including any project or the construction, operation and maintenance of any water works, and the regular exchange of information and consultation on the possible effects of planned measures.[220] In addition, the parties are under a general obligation to collect, process, harmonise and disseminate data and information relating to the Orange-Senqu River System; and the Council is required to advise on the standardised form

216 ORASECOM (n 191), 37.
217 Ibid, 53
218 Article 5(2)(1), (2) and (6), ibid.
219 Article 7(5)–(10), ibid.
220 Article 5(2)(3) & (8), ibid.

of collecting, processing and disseminating data or information with regard to all aspects of the river system.[221]

While the Council is therefore given a broad remit to support, and at least implicitly oversee, the implementation of key obligations of the ORASECOM Agreement, no explicit role is given to the Council to review compliance or implementation. An assessment of the extent to which the agreement is being complied with and implemented only takes place implicitly through the review of the various projects and programmes that are initiated by the parties, with the support of the secretariat. In this regard, the monitoring and evaluation of the IWRM plan provides a particularly important means by which to, at least indirectly, progress the implementation of the ORASECOM Agreement.

The Council is obligated to 'take the decisions necessary to implement this agreement', and to make recommendations or advise the parties on 'such other matters as may be determined by the parties'.[222] These provisions could therefore provide the parties with the basis upon which they might develop a specific compliance and implementation mechanism (CIM). However, it is important to note that the Council, which itself is constituted by representatives of the parties, is limited in that it can only advise and make recommendations. Ultimately, the decision on whether to strengthen mechanisms relating to compliance and implementation must therefore be collectively agreed upon by all the parties. In this regard, several constraints might be envisaged, including a power asymmetry between the parties, 'covert efforts to shape decision-making processes', lack of trust, national interests, and the need to reach consensus.[223]

In terms of public involvement in reviewing compliance and implementation, the possibilities are limited. There is a general role for the ORASECOM Council to make recommendations on:

> ... the extent to which the inhabitants in the territory of each party concerned shall participate in respect of the planning, development, utilisation, protection and conservation of the River System, as well as the harmonisation of policies in that regard and the possible impact on the social, cultural, economic and natural environment.[224]

However, this falls well short of the public being provided with the active right to participate in any decision-making process.

[221] Articles 5(2)(5) & 7(11), ibid.
[222] Article 5(1) & 5(2)(1), ibid.
[223] Kistin and Ashton (n 21), 51; Jacobs (n 3).
[224] Article 5(2)(4); ORASECOM Agreement (n 22).

7.4.3 Addressing Incidences of Weak Implementation and Non-compliance

The ORASECOM Agreement provides limited options for addressing incidences of weak implementation and non-compliance. As noted previously, Article 8 provides that any disputes must 'be settled amicably through consultation and/or negotiation'; and if that fails then adjudication through the SADC Tribunal is envisaged.[225]

Supporting incidences of weak implementation and non-compliance through other means, such as financial and technical assistance, is not envisaged in either the Agreement itself or any of the projects or programmes adopted by ORASECOM. However, indirectly it could be maintained that financial and technical assistance, supported to a large extent by external donors, has promoted the implementation of the agreement.[226] Here, the adoption, implementation and review of the IWRM plan, as described above, is the central means by which implementation of the Agreement can, at least in part, be supported – although its reliance on external funding may run the risk of skewing priorities in the basin. As Kistin notes, 'donor initiatives in the basin tend to focus on technocratic approaches to enhancing cooperation and overlook the political barriers constraining adaptive capacity in the basin'.[227]

7.5 CONCLUSION

The Orange-Senqu River Basin is of great importance to its riparians, especially in light of population pressures, growing demands, and threats associated with climate change. There is already significant development within the basin, as exemplified by the Lesotho Highlands Water Project. This project demonstrates the benefits of countries cooperating over their shared waters. The project also shows the importance that South Africa places on the waters of the Orange-Senqu River, and how it has used its relative power in the basin to enhance its own water security.

The Orange-Senqu River Basin sits within the wider context of SADC, and it is clear that regional efforts to foster transboundary water cooperation have influenced the development of a basin-wide framework. The 2000 ORASECOM Agreement, as well as its 2018 revision, follows closely the 2000 Revised SADC Protocol, and both instruments should be read in combination. Such combined agreements show that, like the 1995 Mekong Agreement,

---

[225] Article 8, ibid.

[226] Kistin and Ashton (n 21), 51.

[227] Kistin (n 160).

the 2000 ORASECOM Agreement sets out general principles upon which the states of the Orange-Senqu cooperate rather than precise and prescriptive substantive and procedural requirements. States are therefore obliged to follow the key substantive principles of customary law, namely the equitable and reasonable use principle, and the duty to take all appropriate measures to prevent significant harm. Also, in relation to procedural commitments, the agreement simply sets out general provisions relating to data and information exchange, notification and consultation, and dispute settlement. Much of the focus of the agreement is on the establishment of ORASECOM, the institutional structure by which the countries progress their cooperation. ORASECOM's role, which is further elaborated in the 2018 revision of the agreement, is limited to an advisory role. Ultimately, the extent to which that advice is taken on board will be determined by the riparians on an *ad hoc* basis and by consensus. This setup, like with most river basin organisations, has important implications for the ability of ORASECOM to address implementation issues, but especially its ability to tackle incidences of non-compliance.

While the substantive and procedural commitments within the 2000 ORASECOM Agreement, and the assigned role of ORASECOM itself, might be seen as a limitation, considerable progress has been made to 'ensure long-term conservation and sustainable use of the water resources of the Orange-Senqu Watercourse'.[228] In relation to data and information exchange, the countries have deepened their knowledge and understanding of the basin, both in terms of its hydrological features and its social, environmental and economic characteristics. Through recommendations on notification and impact assessments, the riparian states have also made efforts to put in place measures to jointly assess plans that may have an impact in the basin. However, it should be noted that these are only recommendations, which in turn speaks to the sensitivities faced by the countries in making such provisions legally binding, particularly in relation to large infrastructure projects within the basin.[229] It can also be argued that much of what is contained in the recommendations is already reflective of customary international law, and issues of trust remain.

As well as data and information exchange, the experience within the Orange-Senqu River Basin shows that the riparian states have made concerted efforts to monitor the basin, particularly through the periodic basin surveys that have taken place. While these surveys have no doubt deepened knowledge and understanding of the basin, they have tended to focus on water quantity

---

[228] Article 2, Revised ORASECOM Agreement (n 66).

[229] André Mueller and others, 'Stalemate of the Hydrological Master Variable? The Challenge of Implementing Environmental Flows in the Orange-Senqu Basin' (2022) 47(3) Water International 458.

and quality issues, rather than directly monitoring progress in implementing the agreement itself.

Another significant area of cooperation between the riparian states concerns basin-wide planning. While the origins of such plans go back over 100 years, the three most recent phases of developing the Orange-Senqu Basin-wide IWRM Plan are of particular significance. These plans, coupled with the data and information exchange and monitoring described above, have gone a long way in deepening knowledge and understanding of the basin, together with its pressures, and the likely costs and benefits of future national and basin-level development scenarios. While some attention placed on the legal and institutional framework within the current basin-wide plan (2014–2024), there is little focus on issues related to the implementation of, and compliance with, the agreement itself. This is therefore an area that might be strengthened in the future, possibly once the 2018 revised ORASECOM agreement enters into force. As it stands, any reporting requirements are at a programme level. ORASECOM could potentially take on a more explicit role in monitoring the implementation of, and compliance with its Agreement through the annual ministerial meetings of ORASECOM. The role of the public could also be enhanced in this regard. Significant efforts have been placed on garnering information from the public, and local communities in particular, through the development of the basin plans. However, no explicit platform exists for the public to raise any implementation and compliance issues. Enhancing transparency among the parties, and between the parties and non-state actors, offers a promising means of not only systematically and effectively improving the implementation of the Agreement but also to help build trust among the key stakeholders of within the basin.

In relation to addressing incidences of weak implementation and non-compliance, it would appear that there are opportunities for strengthening the existing practice. As it stands, the provisions of the ORASECOM agreement simply refer to traditional dispute settlement provisions. Given the current status of the SADC tribunal, it is questionable how workable these provisions are in practice. South Africa and Namibia have yet to resolve their border dispute, which points to the ineffectiveness of dispute settlement mechanisms in the region.[230] States might therefore explore alternative ways to address compliance and implementation issues with the support of third parties.

---

230 M.K. Mahlakeng, 'The Orange-Senqu River Basin – An Analysis of Regime Capacity and Nascent Environmental Conflict' (2020) 24(1) World Affairs 142. A border dispute between Botswana and Namibia concerning the Chobe River ultimately went to the International Court of Justice, see *Case Concerning Kasikili/Sedudu Island (Botswana/Namibia)* [1999] ICJ Rep 1045.

More generally, it might be noted that development partners have played a significant role in supporting cooperation between the riparian states. The development of the basin-wide TDA and the SAP are both reflective of significant support from development partners and provide an important basis upon which the basin-wide IWRM plan has been developed. These might, therefore, be seen as indirect ways in which development partners have supported compliance and implementation of the agreement. However, there is a question over whether the priorities of actors from outside the basin might detract from the riparian states' ability to comprehensively implement the commitments set out in the agreement.

In conclusion, this chapter, just like the Mekong basin analysis, raises a question over whether the incorporation of a CIM, or parts thereof, would enhance cooperation over the Orange-Senqu River basin. This question will be revisited in Chapter 9.

8. The Danube River Basin

8.1 INTRODUCTION

The Danube River is one of Europe's major waterways.[1] The river is 2,857 km in length, has a drainage basin area of 817,000 km^2, and a mean annual discharge of 6,486 m^3 per second.[2] The basin area – which covers approximately 10% of continental Europe – reaches across 19 countries, 14 of which have more than 2,000 km^2 of their territory within the basin.[3] This makes the Danube the most international river in the world. The basin can be divided into three sub-basins: the upper basin extends from the source in the Black Forest of Germany to Bratislava in Slovakia; the middle basin, the largest of the sub-basins, extends from Bratislava to the Iron Gates Gorge between Serbia and Romania; the lower Danube reaches from Romania and Serbia to Ukraine, encompassing the Danube Delta and flowing into the Black Sea.[4] Twenty-seven large and 300 small tributaries are encompassed within the basin, as well as several major lakes.[5] Significant transboundary tributaries of the Danube include the Tisza (966 km in length and shared between Hungary, Romania, Serbia, Slovakia and Ukraine); the Prut (950 km in length and shared between Moldova, Romania and Ukraine); the Sava (861 km in length and shared between Slovenia, Croatia, Bosnia and Herzegovina, and

[1] Nike Sommerwerk, 'Managing the World's Most International River: The Danube River Basin' (2010) 61(7) Marine & Freshwater Research 736.

[2] Nike Sommerwerk and others, 'The Danube River Basin', in K. Tockner, C. T. Roberts and U. Uehliner (eds), *Rivers of Europe* (Academic Press 2009), 59–112; Jacqueline McGlade, 'Governance of Transboundary Pollution in the Danube River' (2002) 5 Aquatic Ecosystem Health & Management 95.

[3] Austria, Bosnia and Herzegovina, Bulgaria, Croatia, Czech Republic, Germany, Hungary, Moldova, Montenegro, Romania, Serbia, Slovakia, Slovenia and Ukraine.

[4] ICPDR, 'The Danube River Basin', <https://www.icpdr.org/sites/default/files/nodes/documents/icpdr_facts_figures.pdf> accessed 6 August 2024.

[5] Ibid.

Serbia); the Inn (517 km in length and shared between Austria, Germany and Switzerland); and the Drava (749 km in length and shared between Austria, Croatia, Hungary and Slovenia).[6]

The Danube River Basin is home to more than 80 million people.[7] The basin population represents considerable diversity in terms of languages, traditions, histories, religions and cultures. As a result of the break-up of the Soviet Union and the collapse of Yugoslavia, the basin has also witnessed significant political change. These political changes have led to the creation of newly independent states, namely Bosnia and Herzegovina, Croatia, the Czech Republic, Montenegro, North Macedonia, Slovakia and Slovenia. More recently, there has been a notable transition due to additional Danube riparian states joining the European Union, i.e., Bulgaria, Croatia, the Czech Republic, Hungary, Romania, Slovenia and Slovakia, and a drive from others to join, such as Albania, Bosnia and Herzegovina, Moldova, Montenegro, North Macedonia, Serbia and Ukraine.

In economic terms, there is considerable disparity between the riparian countries of the basin, with the Upper Danube countries being amongst the most economically prosperous in Europe, while the countries in the lower part of the basin are amongst the poorest.[8] Despite these disparities, all the riparian countries of the Danube River Basin have a common reliance upon the river's ecosystem for their socio-economic needs, including agriculture, industries, water and sanitation services, navigation, hydropower generation, tourism and recreation.[9]

In addition, the importance of the Danube River as a navigable transport route has long been recognised. For instance, in 1845, the Ludwig-Main-Danube Canal was constructed in order to link the sub-basins of the Danube.[10] Currently the Danube is navigable for 2,414 km from Sulina in Romania to Kelheim in Germany, and there is a strong economic interest to increase

---

[6] Ibid.

[7] Sommerwerk (n 1).

[8] Ibid.

[9] For an overview of the needs and interests of Danube Basin states, see Appendix 5.2 in Susanne Schmeier, *Governing International Watercourses – River Basin Organisations and the Sustainable Governance of Internationally Shared Rivers and Lakes* (Routledge 2013).

[10] Helmut Haversack and others, 'Challenges of River Basin Management: Current Status of, and Prospects for, the River Danube from a River Engineering Perspective' (2016) 543 Science of the Total Environment 828.

navigation on the river and its tributaries as part of the EU's Trans-European Network for Transportation.[11]

Agriculture also has a long tradition in the Danube, with fertile areas along the middle and lower parts of the Danube ranking among the most important agricultural regions in Europe.[12] Agricultural land cover constitutes 42% of the basin area.[13] Significant expansion in agriculture took place in central and eastern European countries during the Soviet era with the drive to develop intensive and large-scale farming practices.[14]

Industry, including mining, is also a major user of the waters of the Danube and an important economic driver in all countries of the Danube River Basin. It is estimated that industry accounts for between 31–42% of gross domestic product within Danube countries and 29–50% of total employment.[15] In addition, the Danube has, mainly since the second half of the 20th century, been extensively exploited as a source of hydropower.[16] There are estimated to be 8,557 hydropower stations in operation within the basin, with Austria having the largest percentage, i.e., over 60%, of generated electricity.[17] In the majority of Danube countries, hydropower currently represents the most important source of 'renewable' energy production, and the potential to develop hydropower, particularly in the Western Balkan region of the Danube, is well recognised.[18]

While the Danube River Basin is therefore critical to the economic development of its riparian countries, it is also unique in terms of its biodiversity and is

---

[11] Ibid. See also Eva Feldbacher and others, 'Twenty Years of Research on Water Management Issues in the Danube Macro-region – past developments and future directions' (2016) 572 Science of the Total Environment 1297.

[12] UNDP-GEF, 'Danube Regional Project', <http://www.undp-drp.org/drp/danube_agriculture.html> accessed 6 February 2025.

[13] Armagan Karabulut and others, 'Mapping water provisioning services to support the ecosystem-water-food-energy nexus in the Danube river basin' (2016) 17 Ecosystem Services 278.

[14] UNDP-GEF (n 12).

[15] ICPDR, 'Industry', <https://archive.iwlearn.org/icpdr.org/icpdr-pages/industry.htm> accessed 6 February 2025.

[16] Libor Jansky and others, 'The Danube: A Case Study of Sharing International Waters' (2004) 14 Global Environmental Change 39.

[17] A. Pistocchi and others, *Water Scenarios for the Danube River Basin* (EU Publications Office 2015).

[18] Ibid. F. McGrath, P. Gallop and A.C. Lesoska, 'Can the International Financial Institutions do more to support new renewables and energy efficiency in Southeast Europe?' (2010) 3(2) Analytical Journal 8.

considered one of the world's most important ecoregions.[19] The Danube Delta in particular acts as a key biodiverse region but also a very sensitive part of the basin's ecosystem.[20] The delta is considered to be one of Europe's most significant wetlands and has been designated a UNESCO World Heritage Site and a Man and Biosphere Reserve.[21] Unfortunately, due to the competing demands placed on the basin, the Danube is also listed among the world's 'top 10 rivers at risk'.[22] Through the years, the delta has been embanked and drained, and the total channel network in the delta doubled to improve navigation. One example is the Bystroe navigation canal, which has been under construction since 2004 in the Ukrainian part of the Danube Delta biosphere reserve and poses a threat to biodiversity in the region.[23]

The development of the Danube to meet economic needs has already taken its toll on the physical integrity of the river, its wetlands and floodplains; as well as affecting both its water quality and quantity.[24] The Danube and its tributaries have been progressively constrained for the purposes of flood protection, navigation and hydropower generation.[25] Hydropower projects, such as Iron Gate I and II (built in the 1970s), and the Gabčíkovo Dam in Slovakia (built in the 1980s), are believed to disrupt fish migration in the Lower and Middle Danube, and have altered the sediment flow and groundwater regime.[26] The negative effects of the aforementioned developments have included a reduction in river length, unstable river banks, riverbed erosion and degradation, loss of floodplains and wetlands, a disconnection of tributaries for fish migration, a loss of species, aquatic plants and natural spawning habitats, the need for increased dredging, and a reduction in reservoir efficiency due to sediment surplus.[27] It is estimated that over 80% of the Danube's natural floodplain has been lost due to land use changes, including agricultural expansion and

---

19 David M. Olson and Eric Dinerstein, 'The Global 200: A Representation Approach to Conserving Earth's Most Biologically Valuable Ecoregions' (1998) 12(3) Conservation Biology 502.

20 Feldbacher and others (n 11).

21 Dora Banaduc and others, 'The Lower Danube River – Danube Delta – North West Black Sea: A Pivotal Area of Major Interest for Past, Present and Future of its Fish Fauna – A Short Review' (2016) 545 Science of the Total Environment 137.

22 CM Wong and others, *World's top 10 rivers at risk* (WWF 2007).

23 Tache Bocaniala, 'The Legal Implications for the Navigation Development of Bystroye Channel' (2009) 1 Acta Universitatis Danubius Administratio 13.

24 See generally ICPDR, *Joint Basin Survey 3* (ICPDR 2015).

25 Haversack (n 10).

26 G. Klaver, B. van Os, P. Negrell and E. Petelet-Giraud, 'Influence of Hydropower Dams on the Composition of the Suspended and River Bank Sediments in the Danube' (2007) 148(3) Environmental Pollution 718.

27 For a full account, see Haversack (n 10).

forestry development; and less than 15% of the Upper Danube remains free-flowing.[28] Only in small areas, such as the Danube national park in Austria, has the original Danube ecosystem and adjacent wetlands remained intact.[29]

At the basin level, water availability is not an issue *per se*. Bulgaria is estimated to have the highest rate of water withdrawal per capita at just 28%, while Bosnia and Herzegovina, Croatia and Slovakia are thought to only use 1% of their renewable water resources.[30] There is, however, a strong co-dependency amongst states within the basin, with Hungary, Moldova and Serbia being highly dependent on renewable water resources originating from outside their respective territories.[31] A further challenge has been the impact of major floods on the Danube, the most notable recent events occurring in 2002, 2005, 2006, 2009, 2010, 2013 and 2014.[32] While flooding provides multiple benefits to the Danube's ecosystem, the magnitude and frequency of recent flood events, coupled with pressures to develop flood plains and natural storage, have led to increased economic damages.[33]

Haversack characterises the upper part of the Danube basin as having good water quality but a highly regulated flow, and the downstream areas as being less modified but with poor water quality.[34] Many parts of the Danube River suffer from pollution, which derives from numerous large urban centres, as well as agriculture, forestry, mining and navigation activities.[35] While there has been an overall improvement in water quality over the past few decades, the Danube and its tributaries remain susceptible to multiple point and non-point pollution sources.[36] In response to such pressures, there has been significant investment in wastewater treatment plants, which has had a positive impact on reducing biodegradable organic matter, although major centres still

---

[28] Sommerwerk (n 1).

[29] Roy Brouwer and others, 'Valuation and Transferability of the Non-market Benefits of River Restoration in the Danube River Basin' (2016) 17 Ecosystem Services 278.

[30] Pistocchi and others (n 17).

[31] Ibid.

[32] Günter Blöschl and others, 'Thematic Issue on Floods in the Danube basin – processes, patterns, predictions' (2016) 64(4) Journal of Hydrology and Hydromechanics 301.

[33] The economic damage from the 2012 floods was estimated at €15 billion; see Risk Management Solutions, 'Central Europe Flooding, August 2002 – Event Report', <http://forms2.rms.com/rs/729-DJX-565/images/fl_2002_central_europe_flooding.pdf> accessed 6 August 2024.

[34] Haversack (n 10).

[35] Carmen Gasparotti, 'The Main Factors of Water Pollution in the Danube River Basin' (2014) 1(33) EuroEconomica 91.

[36] Sommerwerk (n 1).

lack sufficient treatment plants.[37] Reductions in nitrate and phosphate loads are also evident, although pollution loads still pose a threat to the Danube ecosystem, as well as that of the Black Sea.[38] Hazardous substances, including heavy metals, persistent organic pollutants, and micro-pollutants, constitute a major threat to water quality in the Danube basin. Major industrial disasters, such as the Baia Mare tailings spill from a mine site in Romania, have also had a significant transboundary impact on the water quality in the Danube River Basin.[39]

Within this context, the chapter will explore the cooperative arrangements that have been entered into by the states pertaining to the Danube Basin. In particular, the chapter will focus on the main basin-wide arrangement, which is the 1994 Convention on the Protection and Use of the Danube River (Danube Convention).[40] Following an analysis of the evolution of cooperation in the basin, the chapter will examine the normative commitments set out in the 1994 Danube Convention. This will be followed by an assessment of the efforts the parties have made to support its compliance and implementation. Consistent with the previous two case study chapters, the analysis of compliance and implementation will concentrate on measures that are in place to report on progress, to analyse any progress, and to address any incidences of weak implementation or non-compliance.

8.2 THE EVOLUTION OF COOPERATION IN THE DANUBE BASIN

For many centuries, the driver of cooperation in the Danube Basin was trade and commerce.[41] Cooperation has been traced back to Roman times, where a

---

37 European Court of Auditors, *EU-funding of urban wastewater treatment plants in the Danube river basin: further efforts needed in helping Member States achieve EU wastewater policy objectives* (EU Publications Office 2015).

38 Sommerwerk (n 1).

39 Aaron Schwabach, 'From Schweizerhale to Baia Mare: The Continuing Failure of International Law to Protect Europe's Rivers' (2000) 19(4) Virginia Environmental Law Journal 431; Chris Hudson, 'The Role of International Environmental Law in the Protection of the Danube River Basin: the Baia Mare Cyanide Spill' (2001) 12(2) Colorado Journal of International Environmental Law and Policy 367.

40 Convention on the Protection and Sustainable Use of the Danube River (adopted 29 June 1994, entered into force 22 October 1998) <https://www.icpdr.org/sites/default/files/DRPC%20English%20ver.pdf> 5 July 2024 (1994 Danube Convention).

41 Kenneth Irvine, 'Educating for action: Aligning skills with policies for sustainable development in the Danube River Basin' (2016) 543 Science of the

major road connected four provincial capitals, trade centres, and around 200 military forts along the river.[42] At the end of the Crimean War, the Treaty of Paris in 1856 was signed between Great Britain, France, the Ottoman Empire, Russia and Sardinia. This treaty marked a key milestone in the evolution of cooperation in the Danube Basin, whereby the Black Sea was demilitarised, and the freedom of navigation for merchant ships of all countries along the Danube was realised.[43] The Treaty also established two Commissions that were responsible for the regulation of navigation along the Danube and the improvement of the river's navigability. In commenting on one of the Commissions, Campbell observed that '[by] its physical presence at the mouth of the Danube it was a symbol and sentinel of the political interest of the west in preserving south-eastern Europe and Turkey from Russian domination'.[44] The tussle between east and west would remain a major influence shaping cooperation over the Danube during much of the 20th century. This tussle was evident in the 1921 Convention Instituting the Definitive Statute of the Danube.[45] At face value, the convention could be heralded as a symbol of cooperation.[46] Navigation of the Danube was to be 'unrestricted and open to all flags on a footing of complete equality', and the Danube was described as an 'internationalised river system'.[47] However, Russia and Germany were conspicuously absent as parties to the Convention, which was seen as an attempt by western powers 'to block the resurgence of German or Russian power in the Danube basin'.[48] By the 1940s, the political balance had shifted and a new Convention was adopted

---

Total Environment 765. Rhoda Margesson, 'Reducing Conflict Over the Danube Waters: Equitable Utilisation and Sustainable Development' (1997) 21(1) Natural Resources Forum 23.

[42] M. Grant, *Atlas of Classical History* (OUP 1994).

[43] Treaty of Paris between Great Britain, France, the Ottoman Empire, Sardinia and Russia (adopted 30 March 1865) <https://content.ecf.org.il/files/M00934_TreatyOfParis1856English.pdf> accessed 6 August 2024. The Paris Treaty built upon a general provision on the freedom of navigation on international rivers contained in the Vienna Congress Acts of 1815.

[44] John C. Campbell, 'Diplomacy on the Danube' (1949) 27(2) Foreign Affairs 315.

[45] Convention Instituting the Definitive Statute of the Danube (adopted 23 July 1921, entered into force 1 October 1922) (1923) 17(1) American Journal of International Law 13.

[46] Josef L. Kunz, 'The Danube Régime and the Belgrade Conference' (1949) 43(1) American Journal of International Law 104; Joanne Linnerooth and Susan Murcott, 'The Danube River Basin: International Cooperation or Sustainable Development' (1996) 36 Natural Resources Journal 521.

[47] Article 1, 1921 Danube Convention (n 45).

[48] Campbell (n 44).

in 1948. Drafted in Moscow, the 1948 Convention Regarding the Regime of Navigation on the Danube was a cooperative effort amongst the communist governments of the Danube to the exclusion of western powers.[49] However, the Commission that was established pursuant to the 1948 Convention gradually became less politicised, and east–west technical cooperation developed in relation to navigation, hydropower generation, and the building of a trans-European waterway system. Membership of the Commission eventually expanded to include Austria, Bulgaria, Croatia, Germany, Hungary, Moldova, Romania, Russia, Serbia, Slovakia and Ukraine.[50] Several countries also have observer status in the Commission.[51]

Although navigation may have fostered cooperation amongst Danube states, Irvine observes that the influence of that cooperation has been an increased modification of the river's hydromorphology, and since the 1950s, 'the separation of back waters from main channels and artificial connection of water bodies'.[52] Additionally, Irvine notes that by the 1980s, growing environmental concerns were being voiced over other uses of the Danube, including large parts of the floodplains of the lower Danube that were being drained for agriculture; severe pollution from a mix of heavy industry, intensive agriculture and urban settlement; and heavy nutrient loads resulting in anoxia and ecological regime shifts in the Black Sea.[53]

These environmental concerns led Austria, Bulgaria, Czechoslovakia, Germany, Hungary, Romania, the Soviet Union and Yugoslavia to adopt the Bucharest Declaration in 1985,[54] which, as noted by Nachtnebel, was a result of the 'political and economic changes of the former socialist countries which started toward the end of the eighties'.[55] The Bucharest Declaration stressed

---

49 Convention Regarding the Regime of Navigation on the Danube (adopted 18 August 1948) <http://www.danubecommission.org/dc/en/danube-commission/convention-regarding-the-regime-of-navigation-on-the-danube> accessed 6 August 2024. The convention was signed by the USSR, Bulgaria, Hungary, Romania, Ukraine, Czechoslovakia and Yugoslavia.

50 Danube Commission <http://www.danubecommission.org/dc/en/danube-commission> accessed 6 August 2024.

51 Ibid. The observer states are Belgium, Greece, Georgia, Cyprus, Macedonia, the Netherlands, Turkey, France, Montenegro and the Czech Republic.

52 Feldbacher and others (n 11).

53 Irvine (n 41).

54 See generally Aurel Varduca, 'The 1985 Bucharest Declaration – An important step toward Danube water quality protection', in Irene Lyons Murphy (ed), *Protecting Danube River Basin Resources – Ensuring Access to Water Quality Data and Information* (Kluwer 1997).

55 H.P. Nachtnebel, 'The Danube River Basin Environmental Programme: Plans and Actions for a Basin Wide Approach' (EU-SADC Conference on

the importance of ecosystem protection as a prerequisite to the sustainable management of the Danube River Basin and also established a network for standardised water quality measurements.[56] This initial step to foster cooperation over environmental matters relating to the Danube was quickly followed by the Environmental Programme for the Danube River Basin, which was initiated by the Danube states and international institutions in Sofia in September 1991. The Programme aimed to conduct priority actions and studies in preparation for the basin states eventually being able to adopt a basin-wide legal framework for the protection and sustainable use of the Danube.[57] The Danube Convention was subsequently signed on 29 June 1994 in Sofia, Bulgaria, by eleven Basin states (Austria, Bulgaria, Croatia, Czech Republic, Germany, Hungary, Moldova, Romania, Slovakia, Slovenia and Ukraine) and entered into force in 1998.[58] Fifteen contracting parties have now ratified the Danube Convention, namely Austria (1998), Bosnia and Herzegovina (2005), Bulgaria (1999), Croatia (1998), Czech Republic (1998), Germany (1998), Hungary (1998), Moldova (1999), Montenegro (2008), Romania (1998), Serbia (2003), Slovakia (1998), Slovenia (1998), Ukraine (2003) and the European Community (1998).[59]

8.3 COMMITMENTS UNDER THE 1994 DANUBE CONVENTION

8.3.1 Scope and Aim of the Agreement

The overarching goal of the Danube Convention is to achieve equitable and sustainable water management across the basin.[60] Central to achieving this aim is the recognition of the need to *inter alia* conserve, improve and rationally use surface water and groundwater within the basin; 'control the hazards

---

Shared River Basins, Maseru, Lesotho, May 1997) <https://iwhw.boku.ac.at/LVA816338/Background%20material/Specific_Course_material/Environmental%20Programme%20Danube.pdf> accessed 6 August 2024.

56 Varduca (n 54).

57 Nachtnebel (n 55). See also Ruby Moynihan, 'The Contribution of the UNECE Water Regime to Transboundary Cooperation in the Danube River Basin', in Attila Tanzi and others (eds), *The UNECE Convention on the Protection and Use of Transboundary Watercourses and International Lakes – Its Contribution to International Water Cooperation* (Brill 2015).

58 1994 Danube Convention (n 40).

59 ICPDR, 'Contracting parties', <https://www.icpdr.org/main/icpdr/contracting-parties> accessed 6 August 2024.

60 Article 2(1), 1994 Danube Convention (n 40).

originating from accidents involving substances hazardous to water, floods and ice hazards of the Danube river'; and 'to contribute to reducing the pollution loads of the Black Sea from sources in the catchment area'.[61]

In order to achieve its overarching aim of equitable and sustainable water management, the Danube Convention sets out a number of specific objectives. These objectives include taking 'all appropriate legal, administrative and technical measures to maintain and improve water quality within the Danube basin, and prevent and reduce adverse impacts and changes occurring or likely to be caused'; and setting priorities for the sustainable development and environmental protection of the Danube, while also strengthening, harmonising and co-ordinating measures taken and planned at both domestic and international levels in that regard.[62] Compared to both the 1995 Mekong Agreement and the 2000 ORASECOM Agreement, the 1994 Danube Convention is more precise in terms of what it seeks to achieve, which in turn opens up the possibility to measure performance towards these objectives more precisely.

Article 1 of the Danube Convention defines its geographic scope as being the 'catchment area', which encompasses, 'the hydrological river basin as far as it is shared by the contracting parties'.[63] The scope of the Convention is, however, slightly qualified in that Article 1 defines 'Danubian states' as being 'sovereign states sharing a considerable part of the hydrological catchment area of the Danube River'.[64] A state that has 2,000 km^2 or less of the Danube catchment within its territory is not considered a Danubian state for the purposes of the Convention.[65] Albania, Italy, North Macedonia, Poland and Switzerland are therefore not party to the Danube Convention even though a small part of their territories lies within the basin area.[66]

In terms of functional scope, the Danube Convention is focused on planned and ongoing activities that cause or may cause transboundary impact.[67] In accordance with the Convention on the Protection and Use of Transboundary Watercourses and International Lakes (Water Convention), 'transboundary impact' is defined as, 'any significant adverse effect on the riverine environment resulting from a change in the conditions of waters caused by human

---

61 Ibid.

62 Article 2(3), ibid.

63 Article 1(b), ibid.

64 Article 1(a), ibid.

65 Ibid.

66 In accordance with the Danube Basin Analysis 2005, 126 km^2 of the Danube basin is within Albania, 565 km^2 is within Italy, 109 km^2 is within Macedonia, 430 km^2 is within Poland and 1,809 km^2 is within Switzerland.

67 Article 2, 1994 Danube Convention (n 40).

activity and stretching out beyond an area under the jurisdiction of a contracting party'.[68]

More specifically, the Danube Convention sets out key activities that should be carried out pursuant to the agreement, which include addressing wastewater discharges from point and non-point sources, water infrastructure (planned and existing), flood control, runoff and storage control, the abatement of ice hazards, the handling of substances in water, and controlling other water uses, including fishery and inland navigation as far as water protection against pollution is concerned.[69] Again, in comparison with the 1995 Mekong Agreement and the 2000 ORASECOM Agreement, the Danube Convention sets out more specific activities that the parties are responsible for implementing.

8.3.2 Substantive Commitments

As noted above, the Danube Convention aligns closely with the Water Convention – an alignment that is clearly reflected in its substantive commitments. At a general level, three guiding principles inform the interpretation and application of the substantive requirements of the Danube Convention, namely the polluter pays principle, the precautionary principle, and the principle of non-deterioration.[70] These principles are also found in the Water Convention.[71]

In terms of substantive requirements, the Danube Convention then includes two key Articles entitled 'prevention, control and reduction of transboundary impact' (Article 5) and 'specific water resources protection measures' (Article

68 Article 1(c), 1994 Danube Convention (n 40). The Article further stipulates that, 'such changes may affect life and property, safety of facilities and the aquatic ecosystems concerned'. See also Convention on the Protection and Use of Transboundary Watercourses and International Lakes (adopted 17 March 1992, entered into force 6 October 1996), 1936 UNTS 269 (Water Convention), which defines 'transboundary impact' as 'any significant adverse effect on the environment resulting from a change in the conditions of transboundary waters caused by human activity, the physical origin of which is situated wholly or in part within an area under the jurisdiction of a party, within an area under the jurisdiction of another party' (Article 1(2)). While the difference in the use of the phrase 'effect on the riverine environment' (Danube Convention), and simply, 'effect on the environment' (Water Convention), may suggest that the Danube Convention has a narrower focus – however, in practice, the Danube's focus on the catchment area is likely to make any difference negligible at best.

69 Article 3(2), 1994 Danube Convention (n 40).

70 Articles 2(4) and (6), 1994 Danube Convention (n 40). Article 2(4) stipulates that, 'the application of this Convention by no means shall cause any significant direct or indirect increase of impacts to the riverine environment'.

71 Article 2(5) and (7) of the Water Convention (n 68).

6). Article 5, whilst named transboundary impact, has a two-fold commitment: firstly, 'to ensure efficient water quality protection and sustainable water use', and secondly, 'to prevent, control and reduce transboundary impact'.[72]

The importance of sustainability and ecosystem protection is further reflected in other parts of the Danube Convention. Article 3(5), for instance, stipulates that 'water management cooperation', as prescribed within the Convention, must be oriented on 'sustainable water management', which in turn demands 'stable, environmentally sound development'.[73] Article 3(5) of the Convention goes further by setting out key requirements of 'sustainable water management', including to 'maintain the overall quality of life; maintain continuing access to natural resources; avoid lasting environmental damage and protect ecosystems; and exercise preventive approach'.[74] Article 6 also places considerable emphasis on the need for sustainable water management, while focussing on the long-term protection of groundwater resources, the prevention of pollution to groundwater resources, and minimising the risks of accidental pollution.[75]

8.3.3 Procedural and Institutional Commitments

In line with the Water Convention, the majority of the provisions of the Danube Convention focus on procedural and institutional arrangements. Central to the implementation of the Danube Convention is the establishment of the International Commission for the Protection of the Danube River (ICPDR).[76] Both the structure and procedures of the ICPDR are set out in an Annex to the Convention.[77] Pursuant to this structure, the ICPDR is formed by the delegations of each of the contracting parties, who meet 'at least once a year', in a so-called 'ordinary meeting', wherein political decisions on the implementation of the Convention are taken.[78]

The implementation of the Convention is also supported through various expert and task groups, including those on flood protection, accident prevention and control, public participation, information management, monitoring and assessment and river basin management.[79] These groups are made up of

---

72 1994 Danube Convention (n 40).

73 Ibid.

74 Ibid.

75 Ibid.

76 Article 18, ibid.

77 Annex IV, ibid.

78 Article 3, Annex IV, ibid.

79 See ICPDR, 'Expert Groups', <http://www.icpdr.org/main/icpdr/expert-groups> accessed 6 August 2024.

delegates and experts that are nominated by the delegations to the ICPDR.[80] The activities of these bodies are supported by a permanent secretariat, which, pursuant to the Convention, has a broad mandate to 'perform the functions that are necessary for the administration of this Convention and for the work of the International Commission as well as other tasks entrusted to the Executive Secretary by the Commission'.[81]

The Convention also sets out a suite of procedural requirements to support the implementation of its substantive norms. In line with the Water Convention, there is a requirement to 'develop, adopt and implement relevant legal, administrative and technical measures' to prevent, control and reduce transboundary impact, and ensure 'efficient water quality protection and sustainable water use'.[82] The Convention goes on to specify a series of measures that should be adopted to address transboundary impact, including adopting at the national level and where appropriate harmonising legal standards and permitting systems related to waste water discharge limits, the handling of hazardous substances, the reduction of nutrients or hazardous substances from non-point pollution sources,[83] and defining water quality objectives and criteria.[84] To support these measures, the parties are obliged to periodically undertake inventories of the relevant point and non-point sources of pollution.[85] These inventories should form the basis of joint action programmes that address pollution loads and concentrations.[86]

The Danube Convention also includes several provisions related to planned activities within the Danube River Basin. For instance, pursuant to Article 11 of the Convention, there is a requirement for any party involved in planned activities likely to cause transboundary impact to exchange information and enter into consultations on those activities within the framework of the ICPDR.[87] Such an approach is supported by the requirement that parties adopt measures related to 'environmental impact assessment in line with supranational and international regulations or other procedures for evaluation and assessment

[80] Article 6, Annex IV, 1994 Danube Convention (n 40).

[81] Article 7, ibid.

[82] Article 5, ibid. Along similar lines, Article 3 of the Water Convention (n 68) calls upon its parties to 'develop, adopt, implement and, as far as possible, render compatible relevant legal, administrative, economic and financial measures'.

[83] Article 5, 1994 Danube Convention (n 40).

[84] Article 7, ibid; see also Annex III of the Danube Convention, which sets out general guidance on the establishment of water quality objectives and criteria.

[85] Article 8, ibid.

[86] Article 8, ibid.

[87] Article 11, ibid.

of environmental effects'.[88] These requirements are supplemented by the more detailed provisions contained in the 1991 Convention on Environmental Impact Assessment in a Transboundary Context, and EU legislation related to notification and consultation, as well as environmental impact assessment (EIA).[89]

Parties to the Danube Convention are also obliged to cooperate in relation to critical situations concerning both natural conditions and accidental pollution. A key requirement in this regard is the obligation upon the parties to establish 'coordinated or joint communication, warning and alarm systems in the basin-wide context'.[90] There is also the requirement to inform other parties of any emergency event, which may include 'accidental pollution, other critical water conditions, floods and ice-hazards'.[91] Where a critical situation arises, the parties are further obliged to 'provide mutual assistance upon the request of other contracting parties'.[92] Pursuant to these requirements, the parties have established an accident emergency warning system, which is activated whenever there is a risk of transboundary water pollution or threshold danger levels of certain hazardous substances are exceeded.[93] Additionally, the parties have developed an early flood warning system, which was put into practice in 2008 following a series of disastrous floods in the Danube River Basin.[94]

---

88 Article 7, ibid.

89 The Convention on Environmental Impact Assessment in a Transboundary Context (adopted 25 February 1991, entered into force 10 September 1997) (1991) 30 ILM 802 (all riparian countries of the Danube River Basin are parties to the Espoo Convention); Directive 2011/92/EU of 13 December 2011 on the assessment of the effects of certain public and private projects on the environment [2011] OJ L 26/1 (as amended by Directive 2014/52/EU of 16 April 2014 [2014] OJ L 124/1); and Directive 2001/42/EC of 27 June 2001 on the assessment of the effects of certain plans and programmes on the environment [2001] OJ L 197/30.

90 Article 16, 1994 Danube Convention (n 40).

91 Article 16(2), ibid.

92 Article 17, ibid.

93 See ICPDR, 'International Operations Manual for PIACs of the Danube AEWS', <https://www.icpdr.org/sites/default/files/2023-09/aews_manual_2019_public.pdf> accessed 6 August 2024.

94 See ICPDR, 'New Early Flood Warning System Launched (5 July 2012) <https://www.icpdr.org/tasks-topics/tasks/flood-risk-management/new-early-flood-warning-system-launched> accessed 6 August 2024.

8.4 EXPERIENCE IN IMPLEMENTATION AND COMPLIANCE

In assessing the record of implementation and compliance with the Danube Convention, this section will follow the structure of Chapter 4 and pay particular attention to key areas of monitoring and reporting, mechanisms to review implementation, and strategies to address non-compliance.

8.4.1 Monitoring and Reporting

Exchange of data and information

The Danube Convention obliges its parties to exchange data on a range of topics, including:

(a) the general condition of the riverine environment within the catchment area of the Danube River;
(b) experience gained in the application and operation of best available techniques and the results of research and development;
(c) emission and monitoring data;
(d) measures taken and planned to be taken to prevent, control and reduce transboundary impact;
(e) regulations for wastewater discharges; and
(f) accidents involving substances hazardous to water.[95]

Additionally, in the pursuit of harmonised emission limits, the Convention provides that the parties must share 'information on their regulations'.[96] The ICPDR has been central to fostering data exchange between the parties to the Convention. In this regard, an expert group on Information Management and GIS deals with data collection, including the creation and maintenance of DanubeGIS, a shared data platform that is accessible to both the parties and the general public. DanubeGIS brings together a range of data that has been provided by the parties. This data covers matters including the general condition of the riverine environment, emission and monitoring data, and planned infrastructure projects.[97] Much of the data contained in the DanubeGIS database

[95] Article 12, 1994 Danube Convention (n 40).

[96] Article 12, ibid.

[97] The following maps are included in DanubeGIS: Danube River Basin District Overview; Ecoregions; Surface Water Bodies; Transboundary Groundwater Bodies; Urban Wastewater Treatment; Main Industrial Facilities; Nitrogen Pollution; Phosphorus Pollution; River Continuity Alterations; Morphological Alterations; Wetlands/Floodplains Reconnection; Hydrological Alterations; Future

has been provided by the parties pursuant to their commitments to develop River Basin Management Plans under the EU Water Framework Directive.[98] The parties have also adopted a series of inventories. For example, following the cyanide spills affecting the Tisa River in 2000, a tributary of the Danube, the parties to the Danube Convention developed a basin-wide inventory of potential accidental risk spots.[99] The parties to the Danube Convention have also developed an inventory of municipal and industrial discharges.

Monitoring

The parties to the Danube Convention are obliged to harmonise monitoring and assessment methods related to river quality, emission control, flood forecast and water balance; and to develop joint programmes related to monitoring the riverine conditions of the Danube.[100] The parties must also agree on monitoring points, river quality characteristics and pollution parameters to be regularly evaluated.[101] The TransNational Monitoring Network (TNMN) was formally launched in 1996, relatively soon after the adoption of the Convention, to support monitoring requirements under the Convention.[102] It was then updated in 2006 to reflect the requirements of the EU Water Framework Directive.[103] Currently there are 101 monitoring stations within the TNMN, and sampling is carried out at a minimum frequency of 12 times per year for chemical

---

Infrastructure Projects; Invasive Alien Species; Protected Areas; Transnational Monitoring Network; Heavily Modified and Artificial Bodies; Ecological Status/Potential; Chemical Status; Urban Wastewater Treatment; Nitrates Vulnerable Zones; Fish Migration; Flood Hazard and Flooding Scenarios. See generally Danube GIS (*danube.org*) <https://www.danubegis.org> accessed 6 August 2024.

[98] Directive 2000/60/EC of 23 October 2000 establishing a framework for Community action in the field of water policy [2000] OJ L 327/1 (EU Water Framework Directive).

[99] ICPDR, 'Inventory of Potential Accidental Risk Spots in the Danube River Basin' (November 2001) <https://www.icpdr.org/sites/default/files/ARS%20Inventory.pdf> accessed 6 August 2024.

[100] Article 9, 1994 Danube Convention (n 40).

[101] Article 9(1), ibid.

[102] Early beginnings of the TNMN date back to 1985, when the riparian countries of the Danube adopted the Bucharest Declaration, which had as one of its objectives to develop a monitoring programme (see ICPDR, 'The Flow of Danube Cooperation: A history of shared responsibility' (*Danube Watch* 2014) <https://www.icpdr.org/publications/flow-danube-cooperation-history-shared-responsibility> accessed 6 August 2024.

[103] Ibid.

determinants and twice a year for biological parameters.[104] The key objective of the TNMN is to monitor the overall status and long-term changes of surface water and, where applicable, groundwater, with a particular focus on transboundary pollution load. In line with EU Water Framework Directive commitments, the ecological status and potential, as well as the chemical status of surface waters, is monitored, together with groundwater quality (chemical) and quantitative status.[105] As a result of the adoption of the ICPDR Strategy on Adaptation to Climate Change, the TNMN was enhanced to include the monitoring of the impacts of climate change.[106] Additionally, to meet the requirements of the EU Water Framework Directive, different types of monitoring have been incorporated into the TNMN, including surveillance, operational and investigative monitoring.[107]

Joint strategies, plans and programmes

A key driver of joint strategies, plans and programmes within the Danube Basin has been EU legislation, and the EU Water Framework Directive in particular.[108] Pursuant to the Directive, the first River Basin Management Plan was adopted by the parties to the Danube Convention in 2009, and then updated in 2015 and 2021.[109] In addition to this basin-level plan and national plans, sub-basin management plans were adopted for the Danube Delta, the Tisza, the Sava and the Prut rivers.[110] In addition, the parties to the Danube Convention have adopted joint strategies, plans and programmes concerning

---

104 Pollution loads are also calculated for Biochemical Oxygen Demand (BOD); inorganic nitrogen; ortho-phosphate-phosphorus; dissolved phosphorus; total phosphorus; suspended solids; and chlorides.

105 ICPDR, 'Danube River Basin Management Plan – Update 2021', <https://www.icpdr.org/tasks-topics/tasks/river-basin-management/danube-river-basin-management-plan-2021> accessed 6 August 2024, 148.

106 Ibid, 136.

107 ICPDR (n 102).

108 EU Water Framework Directive (n 98).

109 ICPDR, 'Danube River Basin District Management Plan' (14 December 2009) <https://www.icpdr.org/sites/default/files/DRBM_Plan_2009.pdf> accessed 6 August 2024; ICPDR, 'Danube River Basin District Plan – Update 2015' <https://www.icpdr.org/sites/default/files/nodes/documents/drbmp-update2015.pdf> accessed 6 August 2024; ICPDR (n 105).

110 Ibid.

flood management,[111] climate change,[112] inland navigation and environmental protection,[113] private sector cooperation,[114] early warning and alarm systems for accidents,[115] sustainable hydropower development,[116] cooperation with the EU,[117] and joint basin survey and monitoring.[118]

As a precursor to the first River Basin Management Plan, the Danube countries undertook a Danube Basin Analysis, which sought to assess the pressures and impacts on the basin, with the aim of classifying water bodies that were at risk, possibly at risk, or not at risk of failing to meet the environmental objectives of the Water Framework Directive.[119] Through this analysis, four

---

[111] ICPDR, 'Action Programme for Sustainable Flood Protection in the Danube River Basin' (14 December 2004) <https://www.icpdr.org/sites/default/files/ICPDR_Flood%20_Action_Programme.pdf> accessed 6 August 2024; ICPDR, 'Flood Risk Management Plan for the Danube River Basin District' <https://www.icpdr.org/sites/default/files/nodes/documents/1stdfrmp-final.pdf> accessed 6 August 2024.

[112] ICPDR, 'Strategy on Adaptation to Climate Change' (2019) <https://www.icpdr.org/sites/default/files/nodes/documents/icpdr_climate_change_adaptation_strategy_web.pdf> accessed 6 August 2024.

[113] ICPDR, International Sava Basin Commission and Danube Commission, 'Joint Statement on Guiding Principles – Development of Inland Navigation and Environmental Protection in the Danube River Basin' (October 2007) <https://www.icpdr.org/tasks-topics/water-users/navigation/joint-statement-navigation-environment> accessed 6 August 2024.

[114] ICPDR, Principles for Cooperation and Relations with Business and Industry (1 June 2005) <https://www.icpdr.org/about-icpdr/partners/business-cooperation> accessed 6 August 2024.

[115] ICPDR, 'Transboundary Accident Prevention and Control in the Danube River Basin' (2021) <https://www.icpdr.org/sites/default/files/nodes/documents/icpdr_apc_public_report_a4_v12c_web.pdf> accessed 6 August 2024.

[116] ICPDR, 'Guiding Principles on Sustainable Hydropower Development in the Basin', <https://www.icpdr.org/tasks-topics/water-users/hydropower> accessed 6 August 2024.

[117] ICPDR 'Joint Paper on Cooperation and Synergy for the EU Strategy for the Danube Region' (September 2014) <https://www.icpdr.org/about-icpdr/partners/eu-danube-strategy/icpdr-eu-strategy-danube-region> accessed 6 August 2024.

[118] ICPDR, 'Joint Danube Survey 3 – A Comprehensive Analysis of Danube Water Quality' (2015) <https://www.danubesurvey.org/jds3/results> accessed 6 August 2024; ICPDR, 'Joint Basin Survey 4 – A Scientific Selfie of the Danube River', <https://www.danubesurvey.org/jds4/publications/public-report.html> accessed 6 August 2024.

[119] See ICPDR (n 109), 5.

'significant water management issues' were identified in the basin, namely pollution by organic substances, nutrients and hazardous substances, as well as hydromorphological alterations associated mainly with hydropower generation, flood protection and navigation.[120] A fifth significant water management issue was added during the 2021 update of the basin plan to cover 'effects of climate change (drought, water scarcity, extreme hydrological phenomena and other impacts)', as well as a recognition of the need to place particular focus on groundwaters of basin-wide importance.[121]

In addition to assessing the main uses, pressures and impacts within the Basin, the first River Basin Management Plan also sets out a *joint programme of measures* designed to address those pressures and impacts, which was subsequently updated in the 2015 and 2021.[122] This programme of measures represents a collection of co-ordinated measures adopted at multiple levels (sub-national, national, sub-basin and basin levels) in order to achieve the objectives of the Water Framework Directive. Such measures are targeted at reducing pollution from organic substances, nutrients, and hazardous substances, improving the hydromorphological conditions of the basin, improving the management of groundwater quality and quantity, and promoting green infrastructure as a way to enhance climate change resilience.[123]

An important milestone in the evolution of the Danube's River Basin Management Plan took place in 2016 when it was agreed by all the parties to the Danube Convention, both EU and non-EU member states, to implement the EU Water Framework Directive and Floods Directive throughout the entire Danube River Basin.[124] A comparison between the requirements of the EU Water Framework Directive and the 1994 Danube Convention shows that there is considerable overlap. The overarching objective of the EU Water Framework Directive is to achieve 'good' water status in all EU waters.[125] 'Good' water status correlates to the notion of the sustainable use of waters.[126] This objective is in line with the overarching goal contained in the 1994 Danube Convention of 'sustainable and equitable water management, including the conservation, improvement and the rational use of surface waters and groundwater in the catchment area as far as possible'.[127] Sustainability is therefore at the core

[120] Ibid.

[121] ICPDR (n 105), 48.

[122] See ICPDR (n 109), 51.

[123] ICPDR (n 105), 197–272.

[124] Ibid.

[125] Article 4, EU Water Framework Directive (n 98).

[126] Ibid.

[127] Article 2, 1994 Danube Convention (n 40). Article 2 of the Danube Convention also calls upon its parties, 'to ensure the sustainable use of water

of both instruments. The only slight difference is the emphasis on both sustainability and equity within the Danube Convention, although it could be maintained that equity – both intra- and inter-generational – is an inherent characteristic of the sustainability principle.[128]

Additionally, the programme of measures and the significant water management issues identified by the Danube countries in accordance with the requirements of the EU Water Framework Directive align closely with some of the provisions of the 1994 Danube Convention. For instance, a key area within the scope of the 1994 Danube Convention is 'the discharge of wastewaters, the input of nutrients and hazardous substances both from point and non-point sources as well as heat discharge'.[129] Similarly, the joint programme of measures adopted by Danube countries under the EU Water Framework Directive has focused considerable attention on organic, nutrient and hazardous substances pollution from both point and non-point source pollution.[130] A suite of measures designed to combat pollution has been adopted by the Danube countries as part of their efforts to implement the EU Water Framework Directive and related EU legislation. While more progress is needed,[131] these efforts have seen a significant reduction in levels of organic pollution, nutri-

---

resources for municipal, industrial and agricultural purposes as well as the conservation and restoration of ecosystems and to cover also other requirements occurring as to public health' (Article 2(3)); and notes that, 'water management shall be orientated on sustainable water management, that means on the criteria of stable, environmentally sound development, which are at the same time directive to: maintain the overall quality of life; maintain continuing access to natural resources; avoid lasting environmental damage and protect ecosystems; exercise a preventive approach' (Article 2(5)). Additionally, pursuant to Article 5 of the Danube Convention, the contracting parties must, 'develop, adopt and implement relevant legal, administrative and technical measures as well as provide for the domestic preconditions and basis required in order to ensure efficient water quality protection and sustainable water use'.

[128] Alistair Rieu-Clarke, 'The Sustainability Principle', in Attila Tanzi and others (eds), *The UNECE Convention on the Protection and Use of Transboundary Watercourses and International Lakes – Its Contribution to International Water Cooperation* (Brill Nijhoff 2015).

[129] Article 3(2)(a), 1994 Danube Convention (n 40).

[130] ICPDR (n 105), 12–13.

[131] The Danube River Basin Management Plan sets out a basin-wide vision that would see no emission of untreated wastewater into the waters of the Danube River basin, the balanced management of nutrient emissions via point and diffuse sources, and no risk or threat to human health and the aquatic ecosystem of the waters in the Danube River Basin and the Black Sea from hazardous substances; see ICPDR (n 105), 198, 205 and 218.

ent emissions, and hazardous substances.[132] They have also aligned with key requirements contained in the 1994 Danube Convention, such as the Article 4 obligations to set emission limits for industrial sectors and municipal wastewater, the requirements in Articles 5 to 7 related to waste water discharge based on best available technologies, the handling of hazardous substances, the reduction of nutrients and hazardous substances from non-point sources based on best environmental practices, and Article 8 requirements to develop emission inventories for point and non-point sources of pollution and establish a list of further prevention and abatement measures to be taken.

As well as pollution, the implementation of the EU Water Framework Directive within the Danube River Basin has highlighted the need to address hydromorphological issues that mainly concern hydropower generation, flood protection and navigation.[133] While receiving less attention within the text of the 1994 Danube Convention, the need to account for hydromorphological issues is within the scope of the Convention. For instance, the Convention's scope of application explicitly includes 'planned activities and measures in the field of water construction works, in particular regulation as well as run-off and storage level control of water courses, flood control and ice-hazards abatement, as well as the effect of facilities situated in or aside the watercourse on its hydraulic regime'; 'other planned activities and measures for the purposes of water use, such as water power utilisation, water transfer and withdrawal'; and 'the operation of the existing hydrotechnical constructions e.g. reservoirs, water power plants: measures to prevent environmental impact including: deterioration in the hydrological conditions, erosion, abrasion, inundation and sediment flow'.[134] The programme of measures contained in the Danube River Basin Management Plan sets out more detailed measures to tackle hydromorphological issues, including highlighting planned restoration measures in 222 water bodies of the Danube River basin.[135]

Groundwater issues are also dealt with in much more detail in the Danube's River Basin Management Plan compared to the Convention. The only two explicit references found in the Convention concerning groundwater relate to the need for parties to 'enumerate groundwater resources subject to a long-term protection as well as protection zones valuable for existing or future drinking water supply purposes', and 'prevent the pollution of groundwater resources, especially those in a long-term perspective reserved for drinking water supply'.[136] Conversely, pursuant to the requirements of the EU

---

[132] Ibid, 12–13.

[133] Ibid, 88–115.

[134] Article 3(2)(a), 1994 Danube Convention (n 40).

[135] ICPDR (n 105), 23.

[136] Article 6, 1994 Danube Convention (n 40).

Water Framework Directive and associated legislation, the Danube's River Basin Management Plan places emphasis both on groundwater quantitative and qualitative issues, with a focus on 12 groundwater bodies of basin-wide importance.[137]

Along similar lines, there is no explicit mention of climate change within the 1994 Danube Convention, which is reflective of the time when the text was negotiated and adopted. However, many climate change adaptation measures would align with the more explicit requirements within the Convention related to sustainable water management, and as noted above, in 2012 the ICPDR adopted a Strategy on Adaptation to Climate Change.[138] The Danube's River Basin Management Plan, which reflects the 2012 strategy, includes a series of measures designed to mitigate impacts of climate change, adapt to it, and minimise the related damages.[139]

Reporting requirements

The Danube Convention places specific reporting requirements on the contracting parties. However, these reporting requirements do not strictly relate to compliance and implementation of the provisions of the Convention. In rather general terms, the parties are required to report to the ICPDR on the 'existence, conclusion, amendment or withdrawal' of any arrangements that they have entered into related to the Danube River Basin; national legislation that relates to the management of the Danube; and the competent national institutions designated to implement the Convention.[140] While the adoption of arrangements, particularly at the sub-basin and bilateral levels, might support the implementation of the Convention, reporting on them will not go far in assessing the extent to which the normative commitments of the Convention have been implemented or complied with. Similarly, the adoption of national legislation is undoubtedly critical to the implementation of the Convention, such as the requirement to adopt legal provisions related to wastewater discharges or hazardous substances.[141] However, this level of reporting will not provide a full picture of the extent to which those national laws are effective, let alone the extent to which they are contributing to the implementation of the substantive commitments of the Convention.

---

[137] ICPDR (n 105), 258–264.

[138] See ICPDR (n 112).

[139] ICPDR (n 105), 264–266.

[140] See Article 10(b) and (c), 1994 Danube Convention (n 40).

[141] See, for example, Article 5 of the Danube Convention, requiring the adoption of 'legal provisions' related to 'time limits for waste water discharges', 'the handling of substances hazardous to water', and 'reducing inputs of nutrients or hazardous substances from non-point sources'.

An additional area of national reporting that is required by the Danube Convention relates to 'action-oriented decisions at the domestic level'.[142] When these decisions are taken by the ICPDR, the contracting parties are obliged to report on the 'timeframe and the financial experiences' required for their implementation.[143] Contracting parties are also obliged to report on 'planned activities, which for reasons of their character are likely to cause transboundary impacts'.[144] This complements the requirement that the contracting parties have to exchange information on 'planned activities and measures in the field of water construction works, in particular regulation as well as run-off and storage level control of water courses, flood control and ice-hazards abatement, as well as the effects of facilities situated in or aside the watercourse on its hydraulic regime';[145] and 'other planned activities and measures for the purpose of water use, such as water power utilisation, water transfer and withdrawal',[146] that cause or are likely to cause transboundary impact. Lastly, the Danube Convention provides a very general reporting requirement related to 'reports and documents being foreseen in this Convention or requested by the Commission'.[147]

In practice, the most significant area of reporting relates to the implementation of the River Basin Management Plan and the EU Water Framework Directive, which requires countries to report periodically on the status of the waters, and their progress in implementing the programme of measures.[148]

Public information

The Danube Convention provides that the contracting parties:

> ... ensure that their competent authorities are required to make available information concerning the state or the quality of riverine environment in the Danube Basin to any natural or legal person, with payment of reasonable charges, in respect to any reasonable request, without that person having to prove an interest, as soon as possible.[149]

All the contracting parties to the Danube Convention are also party to the Convention Access to Information, Public Participation in Decision-making and Access to Justice in Environmental Matters (Aarhus Convention), which

---

142 See Article 10(d), 1994 Danube Convention (n 40).
143 Ibid.
144 See Article 10(f), ibid.
145 See Article 3(b), ibid.
146 Article 3(c), ibid.
147 Article 10(a), ibid.
148 See section 5.4 above.
149 Article 14(1), ibid.

sets out more detailed requirements on government authorities to provide information to the public on matters related to the environment.[150]

The ICPDR plays a significant role in the provision of public information through the ICPDR website (www.icpdr.org), which includes annual reports of the ICPDR, databases and inventories, legal documents, technical papers, terms of reference and work plans of the expert groups, and general information about the ICPDR's past and current programmes. Additionally, the public is able to access the Danube Geographic Information System (https://www.danubegis.org), which provides a significant amount of data that has been generated and made publicly available through the course of reporting on the implementation of the EU Water Framework Directive and the EU Floods Directive.[151] The Danube Basin Analysis, for example, provides detailed information to the public on the general characteristics of the basin, its water bodies, significant pressures, impacts and risks, protected areas, and water and wastewater services provision.[152] As part of their obligations to implement the EU Water Framework Directive, countries are also obliged to publish draft versions of the river basin management plan for comment.[153]

Other means by which to provide the public with information on the Danube include the publication of the 'Danube Watch', a periodic magazine produced by the ICPDR; the 'Danube Box', social media postings, an educational tool related to the basin; and public events related to 'International Danube Day'.[154]

8.4.2 Reviewing Treaty Compliance and Implementation

The ICPDR is a critical institution in terms of the implementation of the Danube Convention.[155] Through several provisions of the Convention, the ICPDR is mandated to carry out certain specific tasks related to implementation, including elaborating additional procedures on matters such as the exchange of

150 Convention on Access to Information, Public Participation in Decision-Making and Access to Justice in Environmental Matters (adopted 25 June 1998, entered into force 30 October 2001), 2161 UNTS 447.

151 Article 14 of the EU Water Directive obliges EU member states to encourage the active involvement of all interested parties in the implementation of the Directive, and in particular in the production, review and updating of the river basin management plans.

152 ICPDR, 'The 2013 Update of the Danube Basin Analysis Report' (16 October 2014) <https://www.icpdr.org/sites/default/files/nodes/documents/dba_2013_-_report_0.pdf> accessed 6 August 2024.

153 Article 14, EU Water Framework Directive (n 98).

154 ICPDR (n 105), 275.

155 Article 18(1), 1994 Danube Convention (n 40).

information,[156] joint scientific and technical research programmes,[157] accidental and natural disasters,[158] and mutual assistance.[159] As well as developing procedures, the ICPDR is tasked with certain facilitatory roles, such as being a platform for consultations on planned activities,[160] assisting in the resolution of disputes,[161] and registering competent authorities in case of emergency events.[162] An additional task related to implementation is the requirement for the Commission to submit to the contracting parties an annual report on its activities.[163]

Central to fulfilling its mandate is the Convention's conference of the parties (CoP). CoPs take place on an annual basis,[164] and have a mandate to 'review policy issues concerning the implementation of this Convention upon the report of the International Commission and shall adopt appropriate recommendations or decisions'.[165] Decisions are adopted by consensus with each delegation receiving one vote. Between CoPs, the work of the Commission is co-ordinated by the Standing Working Group, which has the task of preparing 'the main strategic issues to be resolved by the International Commission'.[166] The heads of delegations and/or their nominated representatives make up the Standing Working Group.[167] As noted above, the work of the Commission is further supported by expert groups, which are complemented by four task groups.

Another key organ of the ICPDR is its secretariat based in Vienna, Austria, which is headed by an Executive Secretary. The secretariat has the responsibility 'to perform the functions necessary to maintain and support the ICPDR in the implementation of the Danube River Protection Convention'.[168] Pursuant

---

156 Article 12, ibid.
157 Article 15, ibid.
158 Article 16, ibid.
159 Article 17, ibid.
160 Article 11, ibid.
161 Article 24, ibid.
162 Article 16, ibid.
163 Article 10, ibid.
164 ICPDR, 'Rules of Procedure' (13 April 2006) <https://www.icpdr.org/sites/default/files/Final%20IC%20002-Rev3%20-%20RoP.pdf> accessed 6 August 2024, 1. Pursuant to Annex IV, article 3(2) of the Danube Convention (n 40), extraordinary meetings of the Commission may take place at the request of at least three delegations.
165 Article 22, 1994 Danube Convention (n 40).
166 ICPDR (n 164), 1.
167 Ibid.
168 ICPDR, 'Main Functions and Job Descriptions of the Permanent Secretariat of the ICPDR', <https://www.icpdr.org/about-icpdr/organisation/secretariat#:~

to the ICPDR's rules of procedure, the Executive Secretary has the responsibility 'for the administration of the secretariat, and for drawing up the budget and calculating contributions for the income and expenditure of the International Commission in a year', as well as supporting 'the International Commission and its Expert Groups in developing their annual work programmes'.[169] The Executive Secretary is also responsible for producing an annual report that accounts for the activities carried out by the Commission in the previous year.[170]

The ICPDR therefore represents a complex institutional structure that brings together both political decision-makers and technical expertise in order to advance the Danube Convention. However, strictly speaking, none of the bodies of the ICPDR have a clear and structured mandate to methodically review implementation of, and compliance with, the Convention. At the decision-making level, the CoP has an important general role in reviewing progress. While this exercise aligns closely with the commitments in the Convention, it does not provide a systematic review of the extent to which all commitments contained therein have been fulfilled. Along similar lines, the tasks of the expert groups and task groups go a long way toward supporting the implementation of the Convention. However, both in their objectives and in their tasks, there is not a strict alignment with the provisions of the Convention. The same might be said about the annual reports produced by the Commission. These reports, which are available to the public, showcase activities that have been implemented by the Commission over the course of a year, as well as the associated budget and expenditure. The reports do not, however, provide a detailed account of the extent to which the commitments contained within the Convention have been implemented and complied with.

As noted above, decision-making powers within the ICPDR rest with the contracting parties. However, there are some opportunities for non-state actors to be involved in the decision-making process. Non-state actors can, for example, apply for observer status in the Commission.[171] If approved by the parties, observers have the right to 'participate in meetings organised in the framework of the Convention, in which they are entitled to participate, with the possibility to express their position and views, and to have them reflected in the relevant

:text=The%20Secretariat%20of%20the%20ICPDR,ICPDR's%20'DANUBIS'%20information%20system.> accessed 6 August 2024.

169 ICPDR (n 151), at 4–5.

170 Ibid.

171 ICPDR, 'Guidelines for Observers to the ICPDR' (6 November 2024) <https://www.icpdr.org/sites/default/files/nodes/documents/ic_185_-_guidelines-for-observers.pdf> accessed 6 August 2024.

documents'.[172] There are currently 24 observer organisations that represent both non-governmental organisations and inter-governmental organisations.[173]

Founded upon the legal requirements of the EU and the Aarhus Convention, public participation also takes place in the development of plans and programmes of the ICPDR.[174] This is supported through an expert group dedicated to public participation and a staff member of the ICPDR secretariat dedicated to working on public consultation, communication and outreach.[175] A major focus of stakeholder involvement relates to the development and review of River Basin Management Plans. For example, during the 2021 update of the Danube River Basin Development Plan, the public were asked to comment on the draft timetable of work, the work programme and the significant water management issues during 2018 and 2020. Activities for gaining public opinion included a dedicated email address, an online questionnaire, an online public consultation workshop and via social media.[176]

8.4.3 Addressing Incidences of Weak Implementation and Non-compliance

The ICPDR, with its broad aim to 'implement the objectives and provisions of this Convention',[177] has a role to play in addressing issues of weak implementation and non-compliance. Of course, most of the activities undertaken by the ICPDR support the implementation of the Convention, and therefore in turn hopefully pre-empt non-compliance issues. However, at the basin level there is no specific mechanism, such as an implementation or compliance committee, that the parties can turn to when they experience or identify incidences of

---

172 Ibid.

173 Organisations with observer status in the ICPDR include the Black Sea Commission, Carpathian Convention, Central Dredging Association, Danube Civil Society Forum, Danube Competence Centre, Danube Commission, Danube Environmental Forum, Danubeparks, Danube Sturgeon Task Force, Danube Tourist Commission, European Anglers Alliance, European Barge Union, European Water Association, Friends of Nature International, Global Water Partnership, International Association for Danube Research, International Association of Water Services Companies in the Danube River Catchment Area, International Hydrological Programme of the UNESCO, International Sava River Basin Commission, Ramsar Convention on Wetlands, Regional Environmental Centre for Central and Eastern Europe, VGB PowerTech e.v., Vidonau, World Wide Fund for Nature – Danube Carpathian Programme.

174 See (n 89).

175 Ibid.

176 ICPDR (n 105), 273–278.

177 Article 18, 1994 Danube Convention (n 40).

weak implementation or non-compliance. The closest option that the parties have is to raise an issue at the CoP, or within one of the subsidiary bodies, e.g., expert groups. However, as the CoP and expert groups are made up of all parties, a party may be reluctant to use that route.

The only other mechanism would be via the dispute settlement mechanism included within the Convention. Where a dispute arises over the interpretation or application of the Convention, the contracting parties are obliged to notify the Commission and 'seek a solution by negotiation or by any other means of dispute settlement acceptable to the parties to the dispute'.[178] In such a situation, the parties may, 'if appropriate', seek the assistance of the ICPDR.[179] The use of the words 'if appropriate' would suggest that the ICPDR has a subsidiary role at best in addressing any dispute between the parties and can only do so at the discretion of the parties concerned.

If parties are unable to resolve their dispute, 'by negotiation or by any other means of dispute settlement', within a 'reasonable time', and not more than twelve months after notifying the ICPDR, then they are obliged to submit the dispute to the International Court of Justice (ICJ) or Arbitration.[180]

The options for contracting parties of the Danube Convention to address issues of compliance and implementation through collaborative procedures therefore appear to be limited. Raising issues of weak implementation or non-compliance within the CoP may prove counterproductive given the expectation that decisions and recommendations be adopted by consensus.[181] In theory, where consensus is not attainable, the parties have the option to adopt a decision or recommendation by a four-fifths majority vote.[182] However, the decision or recommendation would not become binding on any party that did not vote for it and is not willing to implement it.[183] The possibility of using the CoP as a forum to address incidences of non-compliance therefore appears to be very limited. Similarly, the dispute settlement mechanism envisaged under the Convention would face the same challenges as other dispute settlement mechanisms due to their adversarial nature.

The difficulties in addressing disputes between contracting parties of the Danube Convention are evident in two cases: the Bystroe Canal Project

[178] Article 24(1), ibid.

[179] Ibid.

[180] Article 24(2), ibid. The procedures for Arbitration are set out in an Annex to the Danube Convention.

[181] Annex IV, Article 5(1), ibid.

[182] Annex IV, Article 5(1), ibid.

[183] Annex IV, Article 5(2), ibid.

involving Romania and Ukraine;[184] and the Gačíkovo-Nagymaros Project between Hungary and Slovakia.[185]

The Bystroe Canal Project on the Danube Delta illustrates the compliance challenges faced in the implementation of basin arrangements. Navigation in the Danube Delta, shared between Moldova, Romania and Ukraine, has a long history. Following the Crimean War, the 1856 Treaty of Paris created the European Commission of the Danube River, which had as its main task to ensure that seagoing vessels could navigate the Danube Delta wetland and reach upstream ports.[186] During the late 19th and 20th centuries, a navigable canal through the delta was developed using the Sulina branch of the river in Romania.[187] For strategic reasons, the Soviet Union then decided to develop the northern part of the Danube Delta, the Kilia branch, in order to reach Soviet (Ukrainian) ports without using the Romanian-controlled Sulina canal.[188] However, in the 1990s, investment in the canal waned and the channel became harder to navigate.[189] The Sulina channel, cutting across Romanian territory, therefore became the primary navigable route for large ships traversing the Danube River to and from the Black Sea.[190]

In 2001, a feasibility study, which included an EIA, was submitted by a Ukrainian company (Delta-Lotsman Company, now called Delta Prospect) to the Ukrainian government concerning the dredging of a Danube-Black Sea Deep Water Navigation Route.[191] This study was subsequently revised

---

184 See generally Mari Koyano, 'Effective Implementation of International Environmental Agreements: learning lessons from the Danube Delta conflict', in Teruo Komori and Karel Wellens (eds), *Public Interest Rules of International Law – Towards effective implementation* (Ashgate 2009), 261.

185 See Gábor Baranyai and Gábor Bartus, 'Anatomy of a deadlock: a systemic analysis of why the Gabčíkovo-Nagymaros dam dispute is still unresolved' (2016) 18 Water Policy 39, 40.

186 Treaty of Paris (n 43).

187 Felix Zaharia, 'Public Participation and Water Resources Management in the Danube Delta: the Bystroe Canal project and the Espoo Convention', in Mara Tignino and Komlan Sangbana (eds), *Public Participation and Water Resources Management: Where Do We Stand in International Law?* (UNESCO 2015), 122.

188 Ibid.

189 Ibid.

190 Koyano (n 184), 261.

191 Espoo Inquiry Commission, 'Report on the Likely Significant Adverse Transboundary Impacts of the Danube-Black Sea Navigation Route at the Border of Romania and the Ukraine' (July 2006) <https://unece.org/fileadmin/DAM/env/eia/documents/inquiry/Final%20Report%2010%20July%202006.pdf> accessed 6 August 2024, 8.

in 2002 and approved by the Ukrainian Cabinet in 2003.[192] Also in 2003, a UNESCO/Ramsar Joint Mission visited Ukraine with a view to assessing the impact of the proposed project.[193] The mission concluded that the project was likely to produce adverse effects on the transboundary biosphere reserve.[194] Additionally, the mission observed that they had not seen any evidence of consultation or co-ordination between Romania and Ukraine related to the project and called upon Ukraine to cooperate with Romania to develop a Strategic Environmental Assessment (SEA) of navigation through the different parts of the Danube Delta.[195] Despite this finding, a more detailed project approval was granted by the Ukrainian government in May 2004 for the first phase of the project, which involved deepening the sandbar section of the Bystroe branch of the Danube in Ukraine and dredging a river section between two Ukrainian cities that border Romania (Ismail and Vilkove).[196] This work was completed by August 2004, and the waterway was subsequently opened for navigation that month.[197]

Ukraine's actions invoked a response from the ICPDR. Initial concern over the project was expressed at the ICPDR's ordinary meeting in December 2003, and the ICPDR issued a resolution on the matter in 2004.[198] In line with the resolution, the Ukrainian government was asked, 'to halt the future stages of construction until a proper internal evaluation of environmental consequences of the project can be undertaken'. The resolution further stated that, 'to continue to proceed further with the project without completing a proper assessment and discussion of potential transboundary impacts is contrary to the spirit and requirements of the Danube River Protection Convention'.[199]

The project could be seen as falling within the scope of the Danube Convention, which *inter alia* includes 'planned activities and ongoing measures as far as they cause or are likely to cause transboundary impacts' within

---

192 Ibid.

193 Jan Kvet and Tobias Salathé, 'UNESCO (Man and Biosphere Programme) and Ramsar Convention Mission Report – Danube Biosphere Reserve / Kyliiske Mouth Ramsar Site Ukraine, 27–31 October 2003' (31 October 2003) <https://whc.unesco.org/en/documents/140886/> accessed 6 August 2024.

194 Ibid.

195 Kvet and Salathé (n 193), 8.

196 Ibid.

197 Ibid.

198 Koyano (n 184), 266.

199 ICPDR Statement on the Opening of the Danube Black Sea – Deep Navigation Canal (Bystroe Area) in Ukraine, <http://archive.iwlearn.net/icpdr.org/icpdr/static/dw2004_2/dw0204p21.htm> accessed 6 February 2025.

the catchment area of the Danube River.[200] As suggested by the ICPDR, the actions of Ukraine also appeared to break certain procedural requirements in the Convention, including the requirements to exchange information,[201] to conduct an EIA, 'in line with supranational and international regulations',[202] and to enter into consultations on planned activities.[203]

However, the ICPDR was not the only multilateral institution to raise concerns about the planned project and its compliance with Ukraine's treaty commitments. Actions were also taken by the UNESCO Man and Biosphere Reserve Council,[204] the Secretary-General of the Ramsar Convention,[205] the World Heritage Convention,[206] the Standing Committee of the Convention on the Conservation of European Wildlife and Natural Habitats (Bern Convention)[207] and the European Commission.[208] The co-ordinated response from these institutions reflects an interesting feature of addressing non-compliance concerns. This was cemented by a meeting held in September 2004 in Geneva, which brought together representatives from several international programmes and agreements to discuss a combined approach to the Bystroe project, which was followed by a joint mission organised by the European Commission.[209]

Cases were also submitted by Romania to the Aarhus Convention,[210] and the Convention on Environmental Impact Assessment in a Transboundary Context (Espoo Convention).[211] In relation to the Aarhus Convention, the meeting of

---

200 Article 3, 1994 Danube Convention (n 40).

201 Article 12, ibid.

202 Article 7(5)(f), ibid.

203 Article 11, ibid.

204 Ramsar, 'Bystroe Canal Project under International Scrutiny' (16 May 2008) <https://www.ramsar.org/news/bystroe-canal-project-under-international-scrutiny> accessed 6 August 2024, paras 15–16.

205 Ibid, para 14.

206 Decision 29 COM 7B.18, Danube Delta (Romania) (2005) <https://whc.unesco.org/en/decisions/373> accessed 6 August 2024.

207 'Recommendation no. 11 of the Standing Committee under the Convention criticised Ukraine for not conducting enough consultation with neighbouring states, and noted that the planned activities may have significant adverse environmental impacts' in the Council of Europe, Convention on the Conservation of European Wildlife and Natural Habitats, Standing Committee, Report (14 December 2004) <https://rm.coe.int/09000016807468b0> accessed 6 August 2024.

208 See generally Koyano (n 184), 264.

209 Ibid, 264.

210 Decision II/5b – Compliance by Ukraine with its obligations under the Aarhus Convention, in 'Report of the Second Meeting of the parties', UN Doc ECE/MP.PP/2005/2/Add.8 (13 June 2005).

211 See (n 191).

the parties endorsed the findings of its compliance committee that Ukraine was not in compliance with the Convention in relation to the provision of information to the public, and the requirements of EIA and environmental decision-making procedures concerning the project.[212] The Espoo Convention's Inquiry Commission also concluded that Ukraine had failed to fulfil its requirements under the Convention given that the project was likely to cause a significant adverse transboundary impact.[213] This implied that Ukraine should have fulfilled its obligations under the Convention to notify Romania about the project, and to invoke the consultation procedure therein, which includes the participation of the public from both countries in that consultation.[214]

The international pressure on Ukraine appeared to have some effect, with Ukraine stating that it would revise the EIA of Phase 2 of the project. Around the same time, an International Conference for the Sustainable Development of the Danube Delta was hosted by Ukraine in February 2006.[215] A key conclusion of the Conference was a shared 'vision for the conservation and sustainable development of the Danube Delta', whereby, 'individual project decisions could be taken'.[216] In addition, Ukraine accelerated progress on ratification of a trilateral agreement between itself, Romania and Moldova, which then entered into force in October 2006.[217] A follow-up to the conference was the development of a River Basin Management Plan for the Delta initiated by the ICPDR.[218]

However, Ukraine appeared to change tack in late 2006 when it recommenced work on the Bystroe Canal project, with the canal subsequently being put into operation in 2007, and an official opening of the deep-water shipping canal in 2009.[219] At the same time, international organisations and institutions sought to increase pressure on Ukraine. At a co-ordination meeting in Geneva

---

212 Ibid.

213 Ibid.

214 Ibid, 7.

215 ICPDR and UNESCO, 'Conference Conclusions – International Conference on the Conservation and Sustainable Development of the Danube Delta' (27–28 February 2006, Odessa, Ukraine) <https://www.icpdr.org/danube-basin/sub-basins/danube-delta/danube-delta-conference-february-06> accessed 6 August 2024.

216 Ibid.

217 Agreement between the Minister of Environment and Territorial Planning of the Republic of Moldova, the Minister of Waters, Forests and Environmental Protection of Romania, and the Minister of the Environment and Natural Resources of Ukraine for the creation and management of a cross-border protected area of Danube Delta and the lower River Prut (adopted 5 June 2000).

218 Koyano (n 184), 266.

219 Ibid.

in May 2008, these organisations and institutions reaffirmed their efforts and concluded that, 'commitments and obligations of Ukraine under international conventions have not been adhered to'.[220]

Generally, the ICPDR took a back seat in addressing Ukraine's non-compliance with its treaty commitments. Much of the focus during this stage of the dispute was on the implementation committee of the Espoo Convention, and to a lesser extent the Aarhus Convention. Several submissions were considered by the implementation committee of the Espoo Convention, and decisions were adopted by successive meetings of the parties. In July 2008, for example, the fourth session of the meeting of the parties to the Espoo Convention issued a declaration of non-compliance on the Government of Ukraine, and urged it to 'repeal without delay the final decision of 28 December 2007 concerning the implementation of the project for the Danube-Black Sea Deep Water Navigation Canal in the Ukrainian sector of the Danube Delta, and not to implement Phase II of the project before applying fully the provisions of the Convention'.[221] The fifth session of the meeting of the parties to the Espoo Convention in 2011 noted some progress by Ukraine, including its participation in an EU-funded project to support its implementation of the Convention, and to bring the Bystroe project in line with the Convention.[222] The meeting of the parties also noted the steps taken by Ukraine to repeal the decision of 28 December 2007 on Phase II of the project, to notify Romania of the project and to submit EIA assessment documentation, to hold public consultations in Romania on 9 June 2009, and to hold a bilateral meeting with Romania in Kyiv on 15 July and 16 July 2009.[223] However, the meeting of the parties also noted with concern:

> … the insufficient progress with the realization of the strategy of the Government of Ukraine to implement the Convention, in particular the recent changes in the legislative framework for development control that appear to be not corresponding

[220] Ramsar (n 204). The meeting brought together representatives from the Permanent secretariat of the ICPDR, the secretariat of the Bern Convention, the secretariat of the Ramsar Convention, the secretariat of the Convention on Biological Diversity, UN Environment, UNESCO Man and Biosphere Programme and the World Heritage Convention, and the secretariats of the Espoo Convention, the Water Convention, and the Aarhus Convention.

[221] UNECE, 'Report of the Meeting of the parties to the Convention on Environmental Impact Assessment in a Transboundary Context on its Fourth Meeting', UN Doc ECE/MP.EIA/10 (28 July 2008), 81.

[222] UNECE, 'Report of the Meeting of the parties to the Convention on Environmental Impact Assessment in a Transboundary Context on its Fifth Meeting' UN Doc ECE/MP.EIA/15 (28 July 2008), 20.

[223] Ibid.

> to the strategy, but in fact diminishing rather than strengthening the capacity of the legislative framework to ensure compliance with the Convention.[224]

Not much had changed by the sixth session of the meeting of the parties in 2014. While a new draft law on the implementation of the Convention had been developed, no concrete legislative measures had been adopted by Ukraine, and 'no steps' had been taken to bring the Bystroe Project into 'full compliance with the Convention'.[225] However, by the seventh session of the meeting of the parties in 2017, some progress had been made with the adoption of a national legal framework to implement the Convention.[226] While this went some way to bringing Ukraine into compliance with the Convention, the requisite secondary legislation was lacking. A lot of focus therefore turned to developing the national legal framework to ensure Ukraine was in compliance with the Espoo Convention. The Bystroe Project itself still remained a major challenge to Ukraine's compliance. In 2020, Ukraine had started a new project called 'Bystroe Route', which was intended to cover the two phases of the Bystroe Canal Project. Ukraine had notified Romania in accordance with the Convention, and Romania had confirmed its intent to participate in the related transboundary procedure.[227] The implementation committee highlighted a number of areas that remained outstanding with regard to the project and bringing it in line with Ukraine's obligations under the Convention, including assessing the damage to the environment, particularly of a transboundary nature, finalising and approving a plan for compensatory or mitigation measures in cooperation with Romania, and carrying out all the necessary steps of a transboundary EIA for the new 'Bystroe Route' project.[228] More recently, concerns were sparked by Romania when Ukraine initiated further dredging of the canal in February 2023.[229] In the context of Russia's invasion,

---

[224] Ibid.

[225] UNECE, 'Report of the Meetings of the parties to the Convention on its Sixth Session and of the Meeting of the Parties to the Convention serving as the Meeting of the parties to the Protocol on its second', UN Doc ECE/MP.EIA/20/Add.1 (15 July 2014), 10.

[226] UNECE, 'Report of the Meeting of the parties to the Convention on its Seventh Session and of the Meeting of the Parties to the Convention serving as the Meeting of the parties to the Protocol on its Third Session', UN Doc ECE/MP.EIA/21 (19 September 2017), 8.

[227] UNECE, 'Report of the Implementation Committee on its 48th Session', UN Doc ECE/MP.EIA/IC/2020/4 (20 October 2020), 3.

[228] Ibid.

[229] Luiza Ilie, 'Romania asks to check Ukrainian canal dredging in sensitive Danube Delta' (*Reuters,* 20 February 2020) <https://www.reuters.com/article/idUSL8N3502B4/> accessed 6 August 2024.

the Bystroe canal is seen by Ukraine as an important alternative for transporting grain.[230] Despite some progress, including Romania and Ukraine entering into a bilateral agreement on 18 November 2022 on the implementation of the Espoo Convention, concerns were expressed over Ukraine's dredging activities at the ninth meeting of the parties to the Espoo Convention in December 2023.[231] Romania and Ukraine were, however, able to come to an agreement on the project whereby Ukraine provided assurances that any environmental authorisations would be conditioned on initiating a monitoring programme for species of special interest, such as sturgeons, and protected ecosystems.[232] A sign of significant progress was evident at the meeting of the implementation committee in February 2024 where the initial caution issued to Ukraine in 2008 was lifted, and the Committee noted that, 'Ukraine had taken all the necessary measures to fully comply with the Convention'.[233]

In parallel to the activities of the Espoo Convention, the ICPDR embarked on a couple of initiatives related to the Danube Delta that demonstrate how they indirectly sought to address issues related to the Bystroe canal. Within the framework of activities concerning the adoption of river basin management plans, the ICPDR facilitated work on the preparation and implementation of a sub-basin management plan for the Danube Delta.[234] This resulted in the adoption of a trilateral memorandum of understanding between Moldova, Romania and Ukraine at the end of 2007.[235] Additionally, the ICPDR sought to improve the co-ordination of inland navigation and environmental protection more generally through the development of a joint statement with the Danube Commission and the Sava River Basin Commission on Guiding Principles on the Development of Inland Navigation and Environmental Protection in the Danube River Basin, December 2007.[236]

---

230 Ibid.

231 Decision IX/4k on compliance by Ukraine with its obligations under the Convention in respect of the Danube-Black Sea Deep Water Navigation Canal in the Ukrainian sector of the Danube Delta, UN Doc ECE/MP.EIA/32/Add.2, <https://unece.org/sites/default/files/2024-05/IX.4_k_Convention_Compl_UA_Bystroe.pdf> accessed 29 August 2024.

232 Ilie (n 229).

233 UNECE, 'Report of the Implementation Committee on its fifty-eighth Session' UN Doc ECE/MP.EIA/IC/2024/2 (31 May 2024), para 32.

234 Koyano (n 184), at 267.

235 Ibid.

236 ICPDR, 'Joint Statement on Guiding Principles for the Development of Inland Navigation and Environmental Protection in the Danube River Basin' (December 2007/January 2008) <https://www.icpdr.org/sites/default/files/Joint_Statement_FINAL.pdf> accessed 16 August 2024.

Contrasting the activities under the Espoo Convention and the Danube Convention, it appears that, while the former focused on addressing incidences of non-compliance directly via its inquiry commission, the implementation committee and the meeting of the parties, under the Danube Convention a different role was played, which did not focus specifically on compliance but rather provided a platform by which the states could strengthen the foundations upon which to achieve more effective and concrete cooperation.

The co-ordination between different international conventions and intergovernmental organisations may have had a lot to do with this separation as there was a clear recognition of complementarity in approaches. However, the lack of a compliance mechanism under the Danube Convention might also have been a reason to favour the route of the Espoo Convention and, to a lesser extent, the Aarhus Convention. The states may have been more reticent to trigger the formal dispute settlement provisions contained under the Danube Convention, which would also require their consent. In contrast, unilateral submissions by Romania could be filed with the Espoo and Aarhus Conventions. Other commentators have pointed to the need for the ICPDR to walk a fine line, whereby they felt more comfortable playing a facilitatory or mediatory role.[237] However, ICPDR may be on less firm ground in seeking to directly resolve disputes between parties, especially when there might be ambiguity over whether the issue is of basin-wide relevance or bilateral.

The line between bilateral and basin-wide issue competence was also evident in the dispute between Hungary and Slovakia concerning the Gabčíkovo-Nagymaros Project. In many respects, this dispute can be seen as taking place in a pre-Danube Convention and pre-ICDPR era. The project was originally conceived in the 1960s as a joint development programme between two then-communist states, namely the Czechoslovak Socialist Republic and the Hungarian People's Republic.[238] The original scheme, as set out in an agreement entered into by the parties in 1977, envisaged the construction of a series of dams or locks that would divert the waters of the Danube mainstream near Dunakiliti in Hungary, through a canal and a series of locks near Gabčíkovo in Czechoslovakia.[239] The scheme would produce energy through the holding and release of water twice per day during peak power demand, and would

[237] Schmeier (n 9), 107.

[238] Gábor Baranyai and Gábor Bartus, 'Anatomy of a deadlock: a systemic analysis of why the Gabčíkovo-Nagymaros dam dispute is still unresolved' (2016) 18 Water Policy 39, 40.

[239] Czechoslovakia and Hungary Agreement concerning mutual assistance in the construction of the Gabčíkovo-Nagymaros system of locks, 16 September 1977.

also help improve navigation and protect against floods.[240] To compensate for the twice-daily release of water from Gabčíkovo, an additional re-regulation dam was planned downstream at Nagymaros in Hungary.[241] Both the benefits deriving from the project and the costs of the project were to be borne by the countries in equal measure.[242]

While work on the project commenced in 1978, Hungary, following intense criticism from a domestic audience, decided to suspend the works on the project on 13 May 1989.[243] At that stage, while no construction works had been undertaken at the Nagymaros site in Hungary, part of the project near Dunakiliti in Czechoslovakia had been completed.[244] Czechoslovakia, frustrated with the lack of progress, decided in July 1991 to implement the so-called 'Variant C' of the project, which would divert water further upstream, fully within Czechoslovakian territory.[245] Work commenced on this unilateral damming of the Danube on 15 October 1992.[246]

At the time, Hungary requested the dispute be heard by the ICJ, although without Czechoslovakia's consent to the proceedings, the Court had no jurisdiction. However, third-party intervention took place in the form of the European Commission. Through a meeting of the European Commission on 28 October 1992, it was agreed that a case would be submitted jointly by the parties to the ICJ.[247] At the same time, it was agreed that the European Commission would arrange a tripartite fact-finding mission by three independent experts to visit the site and report on 'Variant C', and any emergency measures that might need to be undertaken.[248] However, these recommendations only proposed temporary measures prior to the decision of the ICJ, and ultimately were not taken up by the countries. Through bilateral negotiations, they finally adopted an Agreement concerning Certain Temporary Technical

---

240 Baranyai and Bartus (n 238), 40.

241 Ibid.

242 1977 Agreement (n 239).

243 *Case Concerning the Gabčíkovo-Nagymaros Project (Hungary/ Slovakia)* [1997] ICJ Rep 7 [Gabčíkovo-Nagymaros Case], 22.

244 Ibid.

245 Ibid.

246 Ibid.

247 Sands suggests that it was the pressure placed upon the countries by the Commission of the European Communities that ultimately led to them agreeing to refer the case to the ICJ (see Philippe Sands, 'International Environmental Litigation and its Future' (1999) 32(5) University of Richmond Law Review 1619, 1630).

248 Ibid.

Measures and Discharges in the Danube and Mosoni branches of the Danube in April 1995.[249]

The case before the ICJ took place between 2 July 1993, when a special agreement between Hungary and the Slovak Republic to submit the case to the ICJ was notified to the Court, and 24 September 1997, when a decision of the ICJ was made.[250] This period also encompassed the negotiation and adoption of the Danube Convention. However, no mention was made of the Danube Convention in the decision of the Court, which was made just over a year before the Convention entered into force in 1998 and prior to the ICPDR being established.

While it is therefore unrealistic to consider that the Danube Convention and the ICPDR might play a role in addressing the dispute, the decision of the ICJ in 1997 was by no means the end of the issue. In its final judgment, the ICJ concluded that Hungary was not entitled to suspend and subsequently abandon its commitments under the 1977 Treaty and that the Slovak Republic was not entitled to put into operation 'Variant C'.[251] Having found fault with both countries, the ICJ stipulated that, 'Hungary and Slovakia must negotiate in good faith in light of the prevailing situation, and must take all necessary measures to ensure the achievement of the objectives of the Treaty of 16 September 1977, in accordance with such modalities as they may agree upon'.[252] Additionally, the ICJ requested the countries reach an agreement on compensation.[253] This request was based on the Court's determination that Slovakia was entitled to compensation for costs associated with Hungary's abandonment of the original scheme, and Slovakia should provide compensation for any damages sustained through the putting of Variant C into operation.[254]

The decision of the ICJ has been criticised for creating 'an ambiguous legal situation that actually helped the parties to reinforce their pre-litigation positions'.[255] However, immediately after the judgment, Hungary and Slovakia did

---

[249] Ibid. The agreement was to be in place until 14 days after the judgment of the Court.

[250] See ICJ, Special Agreement between the Republic of Hungary and the Slovak Republic for Submission to the International Court of Justice of the Differences between them Concerning the Gabčíkovo-Nagymaros Project, <https://www.icj-cij.org/public/files/case-related/92/10835.pdf> accessed 6 August 2024.

[251] Ibid.

[252] Gabčíkovo-Nagymaros Case (n 243), 80.

[253] Ibid.

[254] Ibid.

[255] Baranyai and Bartus (n 238), 39. See also Boldizsár Nagy, 'The ICJ Judgment in the Gabčíkovo-Nagymaros Project Case and Its Aftermath: Success

enter into bilateral negotiations with a view to implementing the ICJ's decision. Several major milestones can be observed during the period between 1997 and 2020. An intense phase of bilateral negotiations took place following the judgment of the ICJ in September 1997 and on 27 February 1998, when a 'framework agreement' was concluded by the two countries.[256] However, in largely aligning, at least with the spirit of the 1977 Treaty and the original project, the framework agreement faced serious opposition from the Hungarian population.[257] Elections in May 1998 led to a change in government, which may, in part, have been a result of the stance taken by the former government on the Gabčíkovo-Nagymaros Project and the terms of the framework agreement.[258] This change of government meant that the framework agreement was not signed by Hungary.

Frustrated at Hungary's about-face, Slovakia requested the ICJ make an additional judgment on the basis that Hungary bore responsibility for failing to conclude an agreement on the matter. Hungary did not agree to the submission of this additional judgment. Both countries then sent a joint letter to the ICJ dated 28 January 2010, informing the court that bilateral negotiations had resumed.[259]

The parties exchanged draft proposals on potential solutions to the dispute through the course of 1999 and 2001. This led to a decision in the summer of 2001 to set up working groups that would study the various proposals in more detail with a view to finding common ground. However, as noted by Nagy, 'the task was not promising as the two positions were based on different expectations, philosophy and methodology'.[260] Nagy also observes that the countries, contrary to expert advice, chose not to involve a third party at this stage, which

or Failure?', in Serena Forlati, Makane Moïse Mbengue and Brian McGarry (eds), *The Gabčíkovo-Nagymaros Judgment and its Contribution to the Development of International Law* (Brill 2020); Sands (n 247), 1631; John Fitzmaurice, 'The Ruling of the International Court of Justice in the Gabcikovo-Nagymaros Case: A critical analysis' (2000) 9 European Environmental Law Review 80; Stephen Deets, 'Constituting Interests and Identities in a Two-Level Game: Understanding the Gabčíkovo-Nagymaros Dam Conflict' (2009) 5(1) Foreign Policy Analysis 37.

256 Nagy (n 255), 41.

257 Ibid.

258 Ibid, 41.

259 Joint Statement of the Agent of the Republic of Hungary and the Agent of the Slovak Republic on the state of affairs in the Case Concerning the Gabčíkovo-Nagymaros Project (28 January 2010) <https://www.gabcikovo.gov.sk/old.gabcikovo.gov.sk/arch/Z100128-VD-SK_HU-priloha2.pdf> accessed 6 August 2024.

260 Nagy (n 255), 46.

led to 'less than inspiring' exchanges between legal and technical working groups.[261]

While little progress was made from 2001 to 2009, this period also witnessed both countries joining the EU.[262] Hungary seized on this opportunity to suggest that the parties might find a solution to the dispute through the implementation of EU law related to water management, environmental protection, energy and transport.[263] However, this was dismissed by Slovakia, which argued that EU law could not be applied retroactively, and the directives were implemented at a national level.[264]

A notable development took place on 7 March 2007 when the countries agreed to carry out a joint SEA.[265] The SEA not only envisaged the two countries working together to find a technical solution, it also involved the establishment of a six-expert steering committee comprised of two national experts from each country and two international experts.[266] Unfortunately, in a letter dated 10 February 2009, Slovakia informed Hungary that it did not have the financial resources to produce the SEA.[267] Little progress was made in the following years until a flurry of negotiations took place in 2015, which culminated in the production of the 'Joint Conclusions on the Strategic Environmental Assessment'.[268] These joint conclusions were submitted to both governments in September 2015.[269] The Joint Conclusions observe in a section entitled 'legal obligations', that it is necessary to consider, 'all the rules relating in particular to the protection of the natural environment and navigation, as well as the documents and policies governing the use of renewable and waste-free energy'.[270] However, except for the ICJ decision and the 1977 Treaty, there is no specific reference to what those rules are or even where they might be found. Instead, the document even suggests that there is a need for the parties to clarify 'the basic international legal framework for negotiations'.[271]

---

261 Ibid, 46–47.

262 Both Hungary and Slovakia became members of the EU on 1 May 2004.

263 Nagy (n 255), 48.

264 Ibid.

265 Joint Conclusion of Strategic Environmental Assessment of the Gačíkovo-Nagymaros Project', <https://mta.hu/data/dokumentumok/hatteranyagok/konferenciak/szigetkozi_konferencia/JOINT_CONCLUSIONS_SEA_25092015-fin_GYOR.doc> accessed 6 August 2024.

266 Ibid, 49.

267 Ibid, 50.

268 Ibid.

269 Ibid, 3.

270 Ibid, 9.

271 Ibid, 9.

While the conclusion of the Gabčíkovo-Nagymaros dispute is yet to be realised, for the purposes of the chapter it might be questioned whether the Danube Convention and the ICPDR could have played a stronger role in assisting the two countries in finding a solution. As noted earlier, it would be unrealistic to think that the Convention and the ICPDR could play much of a role while the case was being heard by the ICJ. However, what of the situation since the entry into force of the Danube Convention and the establishment of the ICPDR in 1998?

An interesting dynamic in the development of the Danube Convention is that the Gabčíkovo-Nagymaros dispute might be expected to have influenced how the parties engaged in the negotiation of the Danube Convention; however, there is little evidence of any such influence.[272]

In terms of scope, the dispute would appear to fit squarely within the Convention's mandate, which is to regulate 'planned activities and *ongoing measures* as far as they cause or are likely to cause transboundary impacts' [emphasis added].[273] From a procedural standpoint, the Convention might also apply. For example, the parties are obliged to cooperate in the field of monitoring and assessment, exchange information on planned activities likely to cause transboundary impacts, and enter into consultations within the framework of

[272] For example, it might be argued that France's initial reluctance to become party to the 1992 Water Convention and the Watercourses Convention was in part due to the dispute between the Netherlands and the upstream Rhine riparian states concerning the discharge of chlorine into the Rhine river and its resultant impacts downstream in the Netherlands. The dispute lasted from the 1930s to 2004 (see Carel Dieperink, 'International Water Negotiations under Asymmetry: Lessons from the Rhine Chlorides Dispute Settlement (1931 – 2003)' (2011) 11 International Environmental Agreements: Politics, Law and Economics 139). Even upon its approval of the 1992 Water Convention on 30 June 1998, France submitted a declaration that read, 'The Government of the French Republic, in approving the Convention on the Protection and Use of Transboundary Watercourses and International Lakes, declares that reference to the concept of reasonable and equitable uses of transboundary waters does not constitute recognition of a principle of customary law, but illustrates a principle of cooperation between the parties to the Convention; the scope of such cooperation is specified in agreements, to which the Convention between the states bordering the same transboundary waters – such agreements being concluded on the basis of equality and reciprocity', UN Treaty Collection, 'Status of Treaties', <https://treaties.un.org/Pages/ViewDetails.aspx?src=TREATY&mtdsg_no=XXVII-5&chapter=27&clang=_en#3> accessed 6 August 2024.

[273] Article 3(2), 1994 Danube Convention (n 40).

the ICPDR.[274] In terms of the substantive provisions of the Convention, the Gabčikovo-Nagymaros project is at variance with the environmental objectives of the Convention. The operation of the Gabčíkovo hydropower dam continues, despite the ICJ declaring that Slovakia was not entitled to put in place 'variant C'. This project has led to the diversion of the Danube into the 19 km-long bypass canal, and only 20% of its discharge (which is reduced to about 10% in the winter period) remains in the riverbed.[275] At the time of the judgment, the ICJ noted that such a unilateral measure was clearly at variance with Hungary's 'right to an equitable and reasonable share of the natural resources of the Danube'.[276] Environmental problems in Hungary associated with the diversion of the Danube and the operation of the Gabćíkovo dam in Slovakia include low water levels and unnatural flow patterns in the Danube's old riverbed, sediment loss and riverbed erosion, and a reduction in groundwater levels.[277] These effects have in turn threatened the quality of the recharged water used for drinking water supply, as well as the region's biota.[278] The environmental impacts of the Gabčíkovo Dam might therefore be seen as potentially at variance with the Danube Convention's substantive requirements, including 'sustainable water management', 'stable, environmentally sound development'; and the requirement for parties to 'take appropriate measures aiming at the prevention or reduction of transboundary impacts and at a sustainable and equitable use of water resources as well as at the conservation of ecological resources'.[279]

In light of the transboundary environmental impacts of the project, there may therefore have been scope for the ICPDR to play a more direct role in the dispute, but it would have been difficult for the institution to play such a role when the two countries in question have demonstrated a commitment to finding a solution to the dispute through the ICJ and subsequent bilateral negotiations.

---

[274] Article 9 and 11, ibid. Article 11 states that consultations may, however, be excluded from the scope of the Convention if they are 'covered by bilateral or other international cooperation'. Such cooperation might include the special agreement to submit the Gabčíkovo-Nagymaros case to the ICJ, and the subsequent consultations.

[275] Gábor Guti and Ladislav Pekarik, 'A brief overview of the long-term changes of fish fauna in the Slovak-Hungarian section of the Danube River' (2016) 47(2) Opuscula Zoologica (Budapest) 203, 203.

[276] Gabčíkovo-Nagymaros Case (n 243), 56.

[277] Joint Conclusion of Strategic Environmental Assessment of the Gačíkovo-Nagymaros Project (n 265), 8.

[278] Ibid.

[279] Article 2(5) and Article 6, 1994 Danube Convention (n 40).

However, while the ICPDR did not play a direct role in the dispute, some indirect influence might be evident from ICPDR activities.[280] As noted above, a key activity for the ICPDR has been joint monitoring. Initially, Hungary and Slovakia agreed to establish joint monitoring concerning the effects of the Gabčíkovo Dam at the bilateral level.[281] This monitoring was originally agreed upon by the two countries in 1995 and was to be in place until an agreement on the implementation of the ICJ decision was reached. Given the nature of the decision, the agreement to jointly monitor was extended on 17 December 1997 by mutual consent.[282] The Agreement obliged the parties to exchange and evaluate data obtained by environmental monitoring in Slovakia and Hungary that is necessary to assess the impacts of the increased flow rate in the Danube and the water supply on the Hungarian side.[283] A complementary statute set out the technical requirements of environmental monitoring.[284] Joint annual reports have been produced by the countries based on the data collected. This has coincided with the work of the ICPDR on joint monitoring. For instance, the first Joint Danube Survey took place in 2002, with the aim to 'make a thorough analysis of water, sediments, suspended solids and river flora and fauna in the Danube and its major tributaries'.[285] In its basin-wide approach, the survey covers the length of the Danube River, including major tributaries. To date, four Joint Danube Surveys have been conducted in 2001, 2007, 2013 and 2019. This survey also complements the TNMN, as mentioned above, which seeks to monitor water quality and pollution loads in the waters of the Danube River Basin.

Another complementary activity that indirectly encourages cooperation between Hungary and Slovakia is the work related to the development,

---

280 See Schmeier (n 9), 209.

281 Agreement between the Government of the Slovak Republic and the Government of Hungary about Certain Temporary Measures and Discharges to the Danube and Mosini Danube (19 April 1995) <https://www.gabcikovo.gov.sk/old.gabcikovo.gov.sk/doc/jr2006en/> accessed 6 August 2024. As well as agreeing to joint environmental monitoring, the Agreement sets out measures for increased discharges into the Danube and Mosoni branches of the Danube, and the construction of an underwater weir in the main Danube at Dunakiliti to supply Hungarian river branches with water.

282 Gabriel Jenčík and Janák Emil, 'Joint Annual Report on the Environment Monitoring in 2006' (September 2007) <http://www.gabcikovo.gov.sk/old.gabcikovo.gov.sk/doc/jr2006en> accessed 6 August 2024.

283 Ibid.

284 Ibid.

285 ICPDR, 'Summary of the Final Report Joint Danube Survey' (May 2002) <https://www.icpdr.org/sites/default/files/jds_summary_english.pdf> accessed 6 August 2024, 7.

adoption and implementation of the 2013 *Guiding Principles on Sustainable Hydropower.*[286] These guidelines aim to integrate 'environmental aspects in the use of hydropower in order to ensure a balanced and integrated development', both in relation to existing and planned projects.[287] An assessment report on hydropower within the Danube Basin, which informed the development of the Guiding Principles, mentions Gabčíkovo-Nagymaros dam but only talks generally about the impacts of such projects within the basin.

8.5 CONCLUSION

The Danube River Basin countries have enjoyed a long history of cooperation. While early cooperation focused on navigation, it is evident, particularly in the adoption of the 1994 Danube Convention, that the riparian countries are committed to taking a basin-wide approach to the sustainable and equitable management of the Danube River. The 1994 Danube Convention sets out the basic parameters for that cooperation, with a particular focus on the prevention of transboundary pollution from both point and non-point sources. Quantitative aspects of transboundary water management are not covered in as much detail within the text of the Convention, but they are no less relevant in the Convention's overarching aim of equity and sustainability. Influenced by the Water Convention, the Danube Convention sets out a suite of procedural measures that states must adopt in order to prevent, control and reduce transboundary impacts, including joint monitoring and assessment, exchange of information, and public information. However, it is the establishment of the ICPDR that is most significant in progressing transboundary water cooperation in the Danube Basin. Through the meetings of the parties, expert and task groups, and the secretariat, the ICPDR has embarked on a range of programmes and activities within the basin, and adopted a series of policies, strategies, plans and guidelines designed to support that cooperation.

Similar to the experiences of the Orange-Senqu and Mekong River Basins, there has not been any direct focus on managing compliance and implementation within the Danube Basin. Much of the attention of the ICPDR and its contracting parties has been on addressing implementation through various programmes, activities, policies, strategies, plans and guidelines. However, indirectly, compliance and implementation issues have been tackled. In terms of data and information, the ICPDR, with support of the contracting parties, has developed a significant body of data and information on the basin and has embarked on major joint monitoring and assessment programmes. While the

286 ICPDR (n 116), 5.

287 Ibid.

requirement for joint monitoring and assessment is clearly set out in the text of the 1994 Danube Convention, the implementation of the EU Water Framework Directive has heavily influenced the type of data gathered, including data related to the characteristics of the basin, impacts of human activity, the ecological status of waters and an economic analysis of water use. Public access to information is also something that is jointly supported by commitments contained in both the EU Water Framework Directive and the 1994 Danube Convention. Concerted efforts have been made to make data and information available through measures such as the Danube Geographic Information System.

Indirectly, data gathered by ICPDR and the Danube Basin states offers insight into the degree to which the Danube Convention has been implemented. However, this falls short of a systematic assessment of the extent to which the key provisions of the Danube Convention have been implemented or are being complied with – although where there is overlap between the provisions of the Danube Convention and the EU Water Framework Directive, a review of implementation does take place through the process of adopting, reviewing and updating the river basin management plan and the programme of measures contained therein. As noted above, there is significant overlap here in relation to the prevention, control and reduction of point and non-point source pollution from a range of sectors, including agriculture and industry. Quantitative water management issues are also captured in both instruments. Through their periodic review, basin management plans have the capacity to capture emerging issues in a way that is not always possible within a text of an international treaty. Issues such as groundwater management and climate change, which have emerged as significant water management issues for the Danube Basin, are therefore addressed much more in the basin management plans than in the text of the 1994 Danube Convention. The process of developing, reviewing and updating the basin management plan also offers an important opportunity to engage the public of the Danube River Basin in water management issues.

There is no formal direct mechanism akin to the compliance and implementation mechanisms found in multilateral environmental agreements by which the parties to the Danube Convention tackle issues of weak implementation or non-compliance. The only formal option for addressing alleged breaches of the Convention would be via its traditional dispute settlement procedures. However, as in other river basin organisations, the desire to take decisions by consensus constrains what a river basin organisation can do.

The river basin management plan has therefore become an important means by which to support the implementation of the provisions of the 1994 Danube Convention. Issues of weak implementation are identified through the basin planning process, and support is subsequently provided. A benefit of this process being aligned to EU commitments is that countries can leverage EU funding to help implement their commitments. For instance, in the last 15 years, Danube countries have invested around €28 billion in wastewater infrastructure to meet requirements under the EU Urban Waste Water Treatment Directive and the EU Water Framework Directive.[288]

In terms of non-compliance, the examples of the Bystroe Canal and the Gabčíkovo-Nagymaros Project illustrate both the challenges and opportunities that are present in the basin for tackling non-compliance. The Bystroe Canal example illustrates how compliance mechanisms may still have a role to play within the basin, given the prominent role that the Espoo Convention and its implementation committee played in addressing the issue between Romania and Ukraine. The fact that Romania and Ukraine entered into a bilateral agreement, and the Espoo implementation committee has removed the caution on Ukraine, is a testament to the value of such a process – although the dispute did endure for almost 20 years. The differences between Hungary and Slovakia concerning the Gabčíkovo-Nagymaros Project remain on the table, and despite, or perhaps because of, the involvement of the ICJ, the two countries have proven reluctant to involve third parties in the resolution of the ongoing dispute. The ICPDR has evidently sought to help address the challenges surrounding the Gabčíkovo-Nagymaros Project through indirect activities, such as the implementation of the Water Framework Directive across the basin and the development of guidelines on sustainable hydropower. These efforts suggest that there might be limitations on the extent to which multilateral river basin organisations are both able and willing to get involved in bilateral disagreements between countries. These potential limitations will be explored further in the next chapter.

---

[288] ICPDR (n 105), 198.

9. Towards stronger implementation of treaty commitments

9.1 INTRODUCTION

The previous chapters have extensively explored both the potential value and opportunities that currently exist to incorporate compliance and implementation mechanisms (CIMs), or at least elements thereof, within a transboundary water context. Chapter 2 examined how the context of transboundary waters might affect the willingness of countries to introduce CIMs within their transboundary water arrangements. Chapter 3 then explored how CIMs have become part and parcel of multilateral environmental agreements (MEAs), and identified three key components, namely reporting, reviewing and addressing compliance or implementation issues. A review of transboundary water agreements in Chapter 4 demonstrated that while the text of agreements includes some elements of these three key components, the adoption of CIMs is not widespread within a transboundary water context. Similarly, the case studies of the Danube, Orange-Senqu and Mekong River Basins demonstrated that in practice, compliance and implementation with transboundary water agreements is not tackled in the same way as it is in MEAs. The focus of this chapter is to pull all this analysis together and ultimately ask whether there is merit in incorporating CIMs within transboundary water agreements, or at least learning from some of the existing practices.

The chapter is structured into four key sections. The next section asks what can be learned from MEA practice related to CIMs, and more specifically whether the arguments for incorporating CIMs within MEAs are relevant within a transboundary water context. Then, the chapter explores the role that multi-level governance plays within a transboundary water context, and in relation to compliance and implementation. As a CIM already exists under the Water Convention, the prospect and merit of enhancing the role of that Convention at the global level is a particular focus of this section. Following the analysis of the global and regional context, the chapter explores the basin level and pays particular attention to lessons learned from the analysis of practice within the Danube, Orange-Senqu and Mekong River Basins, as well as the comparative analysis of the text of transboundary water agreements. Finally, the chapter considers whether a focus on CIMs might help encourage states to adopt transboundary water agreements where they are currently lacking, or help states address potential bottlenecks in their negotiations.

9.2 WHAT CAN TRANSBOUNDARY WATER AGREEMENTS LEARN FROM MULTILATERAL ENVIRONMENTAL AGREEMENTS?

Scholars have identified several reasons for the introduction of CIMs within MEAs.[1] As observed in Chapter 3, the central argument for the incorporation of CIMs within MEAs is that they address some of the limitations of the rules of state responsibility and traditional dispute settlement procedures.[2] Rather than an unwillingness to meet treaty obligations, one of the root causes of non-compliance, it is argued, often centres on capacity issues.[3] In such a scenario, traditional dispute settlement mechanisms, it is maintained, would not be able to address non-compliance.[4]

Capacity issues clearly influence the implementation of transboundary water agreements. In general terms, UN-Water highlights capacity development as one of five factors where greater attention is needed to deliver Sustainable Development Goal (SDG) 6 – water and sanitation for all.[5] Within a transboundary context, a lack of resources has been identified as a key difficulty in the operation of joint bodies, such as river basin organisations or bilateral commissions, within 40% of transboundary river basins, including those covering

---

[1] See generally Malgosia Fitzmaurice and Catherine Redgwell, 'Environmental Non-compliance Procedures and International Law' (2000) 31 Netherlands Yearbook of International Law 39–43, 42.

[2] Haroldo Machado Filho, 'Looking for Adequate Tools for the Enforcement of Multilateral Environmental Agreements: Compliance Procedures and Mechanisms' (ESIL Research Forum, Geneva May 2005).

[3] Abraham Chayes and Antonia Handler Chayes, *The New Sovereignty – Compliance with International Regulatory Agreements* (Harvard University Press 1995), 13–15.

[4] Justine Bendel, *Litigating the Environment – Process and Procedure Before International Courts and Tribunals* (Edward Elgar 2023), 213–248.

[5] UN-Water, 'The Sustainable Development Goal 6 – Global Acceleration Framework' (2020) <https://www.unwater.org/sites/default/files/app/uploads/2020/07/Global-Acceleration-Framework.pdf> accessed 20 May 2024, 10–11. See also Carla Sabbatini and Damian Indij, 'Capacity development for SDG 6.5 on IWRM and transboundary cooperation: opportunities and barriers' (2022) 24(5) Water Policy 814.

major transboundary rivers and lakes such as the Amazon, Aral Sea, Colorado, Columbia, Congo, Danube, Gambia, Lake Chad, Limpopo, La Plata, Niger, Nile, Okavango, Rhine, Senegal, Volta and Zambezi.[6] Moreover, capacity issues played at least some part in the Bystroe Canal dispute between Ukraine and Romania, where EU funding was provided to Ukraine as a means by which it could strengthen its compliance with the Convention on Environmental Impact Assessment in a Transboundary Context (Espoo Convention).[7] Similarly, the implementation committee of the Convention on the Protection and Use of Transboundary Watercourses and International Lakes (Water Convention),[8] provided direct technical assistance and leveraged financial assistance to aid Albania and Montenegro in the implementation of their commitments under the Water Convention within the context of the Cijevna/Cem River.[9]

A further argument made in favour of CIMs over traditional dispute settlement procedures concerns causality and the nature of environmental disputes.[10] It is argued that traditional dispute settlement mechanisms are only useful when it is possible to ascertain causality, and it is difficult to ascertain causality within the context of environmental problems.[11] However, it could be argued that even where causality can be determined, CIMs may play a role. Within a transboundary water context, both the basin context, i.e., bilateral or multilateral, and the nature of the issue, i.e., collective action or unidirectional, are likely to affect the determination of causality.[12] Within the context of 'unilateral problems', where changes in water quality or quantity in one state, usually upstream, affect another, usually downstream, it may be possible

---

[6] UNECE, UNESCO and UN-Water, 'Progress on Transboundary Water Cooperation: Mid-term status of SDG indicator 6.5.2 – with a special focus on Climate Change', UN Doc ECE/MP.WAT/76 (2004). See also, UN, 'Concept Paper prepared by the Secretariat – Interactive dialogue 4: Water for cooperation' UN 2023 Water Conference (New York, 22–24 March 2023) UN Doc A/CONF.240.2023/7, para 31.

[7] Convention on Environmental Impact Assessment in a Transboundary Context (adopted 25 February 1991, entered into force 10 September 1997), 1989 UNTS 309.

[8] Convention on the Protection and Use of Transboundary Watercourses and International Lakes (adopted 17 March 1992, entered into force 6 October 1996), 31 ILM 1312 (Water Convention).

[9] UN Water Convention Implementation Committee, 'Report of the Implementation Committee on its sixteenth meeting', UN Doc ECE/MAP.WAT/IC/2023/2 (28 March 2024).

[10] Fitzmaurice and Redgwell (n 1), 41.

[11] Ibid.

[12] Frank Marty, *Managing International Rivers – Problems, Politics and Institutions* (European Union Studies 2001), 36.

to ascertain causality.[13] Indeed, the majority of cases before traditional dispute settlement mechanisms concerning transboundary waters, such as the *Indus Waters Kishenganga Arbitration*,[14] the *Case Concerning the Gabčíkovo-Nagymaros Project*,[15] the *San Juan River Cases*,[16] the *Pulp Mills Case*,[17] and the *Silala Case*[18] – address these types of upstream-downstream problems.[19] However, from a procedural standpoint, most CIMs also have the option for one state party to trigger a procedure based on the actions or omissions of another state party.[20] While this so-called 'state-to-state trigger' might be considered at variance with the consultative and non-confrontational nature of CIMs, it has been used within a transboundary context.[21] All the procedures before the Espoo Convention's implementation committee, for example, have involved neighbouring states, including the 2019 procedure which Montenegro initiated due to concerns it had with Albania's plans to build several small hydropower plants on the transboundary Cijevna/Cem River.[22] As noted above, Montenegro also requested the assistance of the implementation com-

---

[13] Ines Dombrowsky, *Conflict, Cooperation and Institutions in International Water Management – An Economic Analysis* (Edward Elgar 2007), 52. Some commentators note that harm can also flow upstream (see for example Salman Salman, 'Downstream riparians can also harm upstream riparians: the concept of foreclosure of future uses' (2010) 35(4) Water International 350).

[14] *Indus Waters Kishenganga Arbitration (Pakistan v India)* (Final Award) (20 December 2013) <https://pca-cpa.org/en/cases/20> accessed 21 May 2024 (Kishenganga Arbitration).

[15] *Case Concerning the Gabčíkovo-Nagymaros Project (Hungary/Slovakia)* [1997] ICJ Rep 7 (Gabčíkovo-Nagymaros Case).

[16] *Certain Activities Carried out by Nicaragua in the Border Area (Costa Rica v Nicaragua) and Construction of a Road in Costa Rica along the San Juan River (Nicaragua v Costa Rica)* [2015] ICJ Rep 665 (San Juan River Cases).

[17] *Case Concerning Pulp Mills on the River Uruguay (Argentina v Uruguay)* [2010] ICJ Rep 14 (Pulp Mills Case).

[18] *Dispute over the Status and Use of the Waters of the Silala (Chile v Bolivia)* [2022] ICJ Rep 614 (Silala Case).

[19] Rüdiger Wolfrum, 'Enforcing Community Interests through International Dispute Settlement' in Ulrich Fasternrath and others (eds), *From Bilateralism to Community Interest – Essays in Honour of Judge Bruno Simma* (OUP 2011), 1137.

[20] Justine Bendel and Yusra Suedi, 'State-to-State Procedures before Environmental Compliance Committees: Still Alive?' in Christina Voigt and Caroline Foster (eds), *International Courts versus Non-Compliance Mechanisms – Comparative Advantages in Strengthening Treaty Implementation* (CUP 2024), 121.

[21] Ibid.

[22] Espoo Convention Implementation Committee, 'Findings and recommendations on compliance by Albania with its obligations under the Convention and

mittee of the Water Convention in the same matter, although the Committee decided to interpret the letter from Montenegro as a request for advice under its advisory procedure rather than a party-to-party submission.[23] As noted in the previous chapter, the construction of the Bystroe Canal by Ukraine in the Danube Delta has also triggered CIM procedures by Romania under the Espoo Convention and the Convention on Access to Information, Public Participation in Decision-making and Access to Justice in Environmental Matters (Aarhus Convention).[24]

When faced with similar disputes, traditional dispute settlement mechanisms have proven to have their limitations. In the *Construction of a Road in Costa Rica along the San Juan River* case, for example, Nicaragua sought to argue that Costa Rica's construction of a road had altered the sediment flows within the river, which had in turn changed the morphology of the river and had affected its navigability.[25] Ultimately, Nicaragua was unsuccessful in its claim, with the International Court of Justice (ICJ) stating that, 'Nicaragua has produced no direct evidence of changes in the morphology of the Lower San Juan or of a deterioration of its navigability since the construction of the road began'.[26] The ICJ dismissed the expert modelling and estimates that Nicaragua put forward, and concluded that their claims had not been substantiated by empirical data.[27] Such empirical data would, however, be difficult for Nicaragua to obtain without a long-term joint monitoring and assessment system being in place. This might be contrasted with the experience of Albania and Montenegro before the implementation committee of the Water Convention, where the states received support to collaboratively establish a joint technical working group on monitoring and assessment.[28]

---

the Protocol in respect of the planned construction of several small hydropower plants on the Cijevna River', UN Doc ECE/MP.EIA/IC/2023/9 (6 June 2023).

[23] UN Water Convention Implementation Committee, 'Report of the Implementation Committee on its tenth meeting', UN Doc ECE/MP.WAT/IC/2019/2 (27 May 2020), para 7. The advisory procedure might be considered as a softer submission than a 'state-to-state' trigger given that it, 'shall not be regarded as alleging non-compliance' (see Decision VI/I – Support to implementation and compliance', UN Doc ECE/MP.WAT/37/Add.2).

[24] See Espoo Convention, 'EIA/IC/S/1 Ukraine', <https://unece.org/environmental-policy/environmental-assessment/eiaicsl-ukraine> accessed 21 May 2024; Aarhus Convention Compliance Committee, 'Report on the Seventh Meeting', UN Doc ECE/MP.PP/C.1/2005/2/Add.3 (14 March 2005).

[25] San Juan River Cases (n 16), para 203.

[26] Ibid.

[27] Ibid.

[28] UN Water Convention Implementation Committee, 'Report of the Implementation Committee on its fifteenth meeting', UN Doc ECE/MP.WAT/

Similarly, in the *Silala* case before the ICJ, the adversarial nature of the proceedings may have done more to exacerbate than solve the dispute. The dispute has its origins in the early 1900s when the Silala waters were diverted for the use of potable water for the coastal city of Antofagasta, the towns of Sierra Gorda and Baquedano in Chile by the Bolivia Railway Company (FCAB) and several mining companies.[29] Since 1942, the Chile-Bolivia Mixed Boundary Commission had a mandate to address transboundary water issues between the two countries.[30] However, relations were strained when, in 1997, Bolivia 'reversed and annulled' the concessions granted in relation to the Silala waters, claiming that the waters were Bolivian and had been artificially diverted for the provision of water to suit Chilean interests.[31] Following several diplomatic exchanges, the countries agreed to establish a bilateral working group in the early 2000s to deepen knowledge and understanding of the characteristics of the Silala waters.[32] During the following ten years, Chile and Bolivia made some progress through technical studies and regular meetings to develop a common understanding of the physical characteristics of the Silala waters.[33] However, relations broke down from 2010 onwards following Bolivia's stance of claiming full ownership of the Silala waters and its insistence that Chile pay compensation for its historic use of the Silala.[34] In 2016, Chile then decided to institute proceedings before the ICJ.[35] During the proceedings, both countries expended considerable time, effort and expense on scientific studies designed to shore up their respective legal positions.[36] However, during this

---

IC/2022/4 (2 May 2023), para 7.

29 ICJ, 'Application Instituting Proceedings filed in the Registry of the Court on 6 June 2016 – Dispute over the Status and Use of the Waters of the Silala' (Chile v Bolivia) (30 May 2016) <https://www.icj-cij.org/sites/default/files/case-related/162/162-20160606-APP-01-00-EN.pdf> accessed 19 August 2024, para 12.

30 The Commission was established through the Protocol on the Conservation of Boundary Markers (adopted 10 August 1942) <https://nuevo.leychile.cl/servicios/Consulta/Exportar?radioExportar=Normas&exportar_formato=pdf&nombrearchivo=DTO-300_17-MAY-1949&exportar_con_notas_bcn=False&exportar_con_notas_originales=False&exportar_con_notas_al_pie=False&hddResultadoExportar=400273.1949-05-17.0.0%23> accessed 19 August 2024.

31 ICJ (n 29), para 23.

32 Ibid, para 27.

33 Ibid, paras 27–33.

34 Ibid, para 32.

35 Ibid.

36 Howard S. Wheater and others, 'Understanding the Silala River – Scientific insights from the dispute over the status and use of the waters of the Silala (Chile v. Bolivia)' (2023) 11(1) WIREs Water <https://wires.onlinelibrary.wiley.com/doi/epdf/10.1002/wat2.1663> accessed 19 August 2024.

effort Bolivia's scientific experts conceded that the Silala waters were indeed 'a coupled groundwater-surface water system originating in Bolivian territory (upstream) and extending into Chile (downstream)'.[37] This concession led the ICJ to find *inter alia* in its judgment of the first of December 2022, that Chile's claim 'no longer has any object'.[38] In the opinion of the court, no dispute existed as both countries appeared to agree that the Silala is international in nature.[39] Ultimately, the ICJ therefore left it to the parties, on the basis of this finding, to reach an agreement on the use and protection of the Silala waters.

In this instance, resorting to the ICJ was an inefficient means by which Bolivia and Chile could reach consensus on their shared use of the Silala waters.[40] While the fact that both countries now recognise the Silala waters as being international in nature might be seen as progress, the process can be contrasted with a hypothetical scenario whereby the countries used a similar setup to the implementation committee under the Water Convention. In such a scenario, independent legal and technical experts could have assisted the parties to reach consensus on the physical characteristics of the Silala waters through a collaborative process. Working together collaboratively on deepening the knowledge base related to the Silala waters might have also helped the countries build trust bilaterally at both a technical and political level. This building of trust, with the support of independent technical and legal experts, could also provide a more solid foundation upon which the countries could reach an agreement on how the Silala waters might be shared in the future. As it stands, and after eight years of adversarial proceedings before the ICJ, it is unclear how the countries will reach such a determination. Already, both countries have expended considerable time and resources on the ICJ proceedings. In contrast, the use of a process such as the implementation committee under the Water Convention, as can be seen in the example of the Cijevna/Cem River and Albania and Montenegro's cooperative efforts, may have saved the countries considerable time and expense, while ultimately leading to a more satisfactory outcome.

As well as fostering collaboration between states, CIMs may also have an advantage over international courts and tribunals in bringing together a wider range of interested parties. For instance, in the case of the Bystroe Canal, CIMs were triggered in the case of the Espoo Convention and the Aarhus

37 ICJ, 'Written statement of the experts of Bolivia' (10 January 2022) <https://www.icj-cij.org/index.php/node/106148> accessed 19 August 2024.

38 Silala case (n 18), 53–54.

39 Ibid.

40 For a general discussion on the ability of international courts and tribunals to handle the level of scientific knowledge and understanding that environmental issues often demand, see Bendel (n 4), 10.

Convention, as well as a broader co-ordination effort amongst the relevant MEAs.[41] In the example of Albania and Montenegro concerning the Cijevna/Cem River, both the implementation committee under the Espoo Convention and the implementation committee under the Water Convention sought to co-ordinate their activities.[42] Such co-ordination might help identify a wider range of technical and financial support that can be brought to bear efficiently upon a particular issue. In contrast, proceedings before international courts or tribunals will limit the opportunities for scientific and technical knowledge to be shared, and for third parties, such as convention bodies and international organisations, to engage in the proceedings and offer technical or financial assistance in a co-ordinated manner.

Within the context of bilateral transboundary water disputes, the ICJ appears to have had more traction in determining breaches of procedural obligations. In the *Pulp Mills* case, for instance, the Court found that Uruguay had breached its procedural obligations under the 1975 Statute of the River Uruguay to notify Argentina via its bilateral commission of certain planned activities, but the Court was of the opinion that Argentina had not proven that Uruguay had breached its substantive obligations to protect and preserve the Uruguay River.[43] Even when commenting on these substantive obligations in the *Pulp Mills* case, the ICJ felt more comfortable stressing the importance of procedure, namely the 'requirement under general international law to undertake an environmental impact assessment where there is a risk that the proposed industrial activity may have a significant adverse impact in a transboundary context'.[44] These procedural considerations were revisited by the ICJ in the *San Juan River* cases, where the Court held that, pursuant to international environmental law, a state planning an activity is under an obligation to notify and consult potentially affected states, where there is a risk of significant transboundary harm.[45] In addition, the Court stressed the need for the state planning the activity to carry out an environmental impact assessment (EIA) where there is a risk of significant transboundary harm.[46] The Court determined that Nicaragua's plans did not risk causing significant

---

[41] Laura Pineschi, 'International Courts versus Compliance Mechanisms through the Lens of the *Gabčíkovo-Nagymaros* and *Bystroe Canal* Cases' in Christina Voigt and Caroline Foster (eds), *International Courts versus Non-Compliance Mechanisms – Comparative Advantages in Strengthening Treaty Implementation* (CUP 2024), 81–82.

[42] UN Water Convention Implementation Committee (n 23), para 10.

[43] Pulp Mills Case (n 17), para 282.

[44] Ibid, para 204.

[45] San Juan River Cases (n 16), para 105.

[46] Ibid.

transboundary harm, so there was no need to notify and consult, or conduct an EIA. Conversely, the Court held that Costa Rica's plans to build a road were of a scale that would risk causing significant transboundary harm and would therefore require an EIA.[47]

While traditional dispute settlement mechanisms might therefore play a role, particularly in the case of the breach of procedural obligations between two states, not all transboundary water issues are bilateral. In many cases, transboundary river basins are shared by more than two states.[48] For instance, the Danube River basin is shared by 19 states, the Nile by 14 states, the Niger by 11 states, the Congo by ten states, the Rhine by nine states, Lake Chad, Ganges-Brahmaputra-Meghna, and Zambezi by eight states, the Amazon and Indus by seven states, and the Aral Sea, Jordan, Tarim, Tigris-Euphrates, Volta and Mekong by six states.[49] In these basins, all, or at least the majority of basin states, may have a 'community interest' in achieving certain actions, such as flood and drought protection, increased biodiversity and ecosystem protection, or improved water quality.[50] Similarly, parties to a transboundary water agreement may have a common interest in enhancing the treaty regime, through, for example, joint monitoring and assessment or basin-wide planning. It is in relation to these types of community interests that commentators argue CIMs are best suited. As Brunnée puts it, 'addressing the community concern animating an agreement requires the greatest possible degree of compliance by the widest possible range of parties, rather than finding that an individual party has breached its obligations'.[51]

---

[47] Ibid, para 157–162.

[48] 75 out of a total of 310 transboundary river basins are shared by more than two states (see Oregon State University, 'International River Basin Register' (*Oregonstate.edu*) <https://transboundarywaters.ceoas.oregonstate.edu/international-river-basin-register> accessed 7 February 2025).

[49] Ibid. The International River Basin Register notes that a further 13 basins are shared by four states, and 42 are shared by three states.

[50] Anders Jägerskog and others, 'Transboundary Water Management as a Regional Public Good' (SIWI Report No. 20, 2007) <https://www.researchgate.net/publication/42765906_Transboundary_Water_Management_as_a_Regional_Public_Good_Financing_Development_An_Example_from_the_Nile_Basin/link/545caf500cf295b5615cc281/download?_tp=eyJjb250ZXh0Ijp7ImZpcnN0UGFnZSI6InB1YmxpY2F0aW9uIiwicGFnZSI6InB1YmxpY2F0aW9uIn19> accessed 21 May 2024.

[51] Jutta Brunnée, International Environmental Law and Community Interests: Procedural Aspects' in Eyal Benvenisti and Georg Nolte (eds), *Community Interests Across International Law* (OUP 2018), 171. See also Malgosia Fitzmaurice, 'The New Generation of Environmental Non-Compliance Procedures and the Question of Legitimacy' in Christina Voigt and Caroline Foster (eds), *International Courts*

As illustrated in Chapter 3, MEA reporting mechanisms play an important role in managing compliance within a multilateral setting as they focus on managing compliance through mutual knowledge and understanding, transparency and persuasion.[52] Regular reporting offers the opportunity to keep the implementation of a treaty arrangement under continuous review, which in turn can help the parties identify areas where greater attention is required. Reporting can also help build trust amongst the parties, through the assurance that all the parties are making efforts to progress towards a common interest. Additionally, where reporting is conducted in a transparent manner, non-state actors can enhance the quality of that reporting process and act as a 'quality of control' of the data and information submitted by parties.

Regular reporting has been considered to be particularly helpful in relation to environmental problems for several inter-related reasons.[53] Firstly, there may be a need for the parties to work together to deepen their scientific knowledge and understanding of an issue; secondly, scientific uncertainty may have resulted in the parties adopting vague environmental rules in the original agreement; and thirdly, there may be a need for the parties to develop a common understanding of what action is required.[54] Transboundary water cooperation certainly faces similar challenges. A lack of scientific knowledge and understanding is often seen as a key barrier to effective decision-making concerning the protection and use of transboundary rivers, lakes and aquifers.[55] As the experiences of the Danube, Mekong and Orange-Senqu River Basins demonstrate, the riparian states have put significant effort into deepening their knowledge and understanding of their basin, and they have used their respective basin commissions in order to co-ordinate those efforts. However, regular reporting on the implementation of the respective transboundary water agreements may still be a useful means by which states take stock of their progress in deepening scientific knowledge and understanding of the basin, while at the same time identifying any gaps, and building trust and transparency amongst the parties, as well as between the parties and non-state actors.

States might also use regular reporting as a means to deepen knowledge and understanding of how key rules and principles contained within a

---

versus Non-Compliance Mechanisms – Comparative Advantages in Strengthening Treaty Implementation (CUP 2024), 58.

[52] Birgit Hollaus, *Multilateral Compliance Mechanisms in EU Environmental Law – Internationalising EU Environmental Action and Beyond* (Edward Elgar 2023), 45.

[53] Chayes and Chayes (n 3), 10–17.

[54] Ibid.

[55] Derek Armitage and others, 'Science-policy processes for transboundary water governance' (2015) 44(5) Ambio 353.

transboundary water agreement should be implemented. Transboundary water agreements may experience similar issues to MEAs in terms of the vagueness of certain norms. The substantive norms of equitable and reasonable utilisation, the duty to take all appropriate measures to prevent significant harm, and the obligation to protect ecosystems, which enjoy widespread inclusion within transboundary water agreements, including those relating to the Danube, the Orange-Senqu and the Mekong, may be interpreted differently by riparian states. As demonstrated by the Mekong Agreement, procedural obligations – such as the duty to cooperate, notify, and consult on planned measures, and to conduct EIAs – may also be open to differing interpretations between riparian states. Reporting potentially offers a transparent means by which countries can develop a shared understanding of how these commitments are implemented and complied with in practice. Again, experience in river basins, such as the Danube, Orange-Senqu and Mekong, demonstrates that countries are already doing this to some extent through the work of their respective commissions. Regular reporting, however, offers a more systematic means by which to gather and share experience in the implementation of and compliance with the key rules and principles of an agreement. Moreover, having a dedicated body with the responsibility for reviewing implementation and compliance could help to further enhance a shared understanding of how those key rules and principles should be implemented and complied with.

9.3 SUPPORTING IMPLEMENTATION AND COMPLIANCE OF TRANSBOUNDARY WATER AGREEMENTS THROUGH MULTI-LEVEL GOVERNANCE?

Transboundary water agreements are influenced by multiple governance levels.[56] At the global level, the UN General Assembly, based on a proposal by Bolivia in 1959, took up the study of 'the legal problems relating to the utilisation and use of international rivers', which ultimately led to the adoption of the Watercourses Convention in 1997.[57] This effort reflected an attempt by the UN to extrapolate universal rules and principles for the protection and use of

---

56 See Laurence Boisson de Chazournes, 'Freshwater and International Law: The Interplay between Universal, Regional and Basin Perspectives' (*UN World Water Assessment Programme Side Publications Series* 2009) <https://unesdoc.unesco.org/ark:/48223/pf0000185080> accessed 23 May 2024.

57 Preliminary Studies on the Legal Problems Relating to the Utilisation and Use of International Rivers, UNGA Res 1401(XIV) (21 November 1959). An earlier attempt to develop international law in this area was made through the adoption of the Convention relative to the development of Hydraulic Power affecting

transboundary waters from state practice. The International Law Commission (ILC) did this by an extensive review of the bilateral and multilateral treaties that states had adopted pertaining to their transboundary waters, as well as other relevant material on the topic including decisions of international tribunals, declarations of international organisations, and the work of non-governmental organisations.[58] The draft rules and principles that the ILC came up with were then used as a basis by which states negotiated the text of the Watercourses Convention in the Sixth Committee of the General Assembly in 1996 and 1997.[59]

On the one hand, this effort demonstrates the 'bottom-up' influence state practice related to transboundary waters has had on global efforts to codify and progressively develop universal rules and principles relating to the protection and use of transboundary waters. On the other hand, these global norms have influenced the negotiation, adoption, interpretation and implementation of numerous agreements at the regional and basin levels.[60] It could therefore be argued that globally a common language of rules and principles exists, which states have utilised in their negotiation, adoption, interpretation and implementation of transboundary water agreements. If this common language exists, is there scope for reporting, reviewing and addressing compliance and implementation of transboundary water agreements at the global level?

As noted in Chapter 5, while the Watercourses Convention lacks any institutional framework, there is scope under the Water Convention, which is now also operating at a global level, and has a track record in supporting countries.[61]

---

more than one state (adopted 9 December 1923) 26 LNTS 774, although a lack of widespread support meant that the convention never entered into force.

[58] Alistair Rieu-Clarke, 'Determining Sovereign Rights and Duties over International Watercourses: The Contribution of the International Law Commission and the UN General Assembly' in Terje Tvedt, Owen McIntyre and Tadesse Kasse Woldetsadik (eds), *A History of Water – Sovereignty and International Water Law* (IB Tauris 2005).

[59] Ibid.

[60] See Stephen McCaffrey, 'The 1997 U.N. Watercourses Convention: Retrospect and Prospect' (2008) 21 Global Business & Development Law Journal 165; Inga Jacobs, *The Politics of Water in Africa – Norms, Environmental Regions, and Transboundary Cooperation in the Orange-Senqu and Nile Rivers* (Continuum Books 2012).

[61] UNECE, 'The Water Convention: 30 Years of Impact and Achievement on the Ground' UN Doc ECE/MP.WAT/69 (2022); Bo Libert, 'The UNECE Water Convention and the Development of Transboundary Cooperation in the Chu-Talas, Kura, Drin and Dniester River Basins' (2014) 40(1) Water International 168.

The Water Convention is a typical framework convention.[62] General rules and principles are set out in the text, and there is sufficient scope to develop the terms of cooperation amongst the parties through the Convention's work programme, meetings of the parties, and other subsidiary bodies. In this respect, the Water Convention shares a lot in common with global MEAs.[63]

While the Espoo Convention does not enjoy global membership, some of the most direct parallels with the Water Convention might be drawn with its implementation committee, where parties appear to be willing for the committee to assist in addressing issues that are both transboundary and bilateral in nature.[64] As the implementation committee under the Water Convention evolves, it is therefore not much of a stretch to imagine how it might support compliance and implementation in a similar way. As seen in the cases of the Danube, Mekong and Orange-Senqu, for certain situations, the respective river basin organisation may be constrained in what they can do, and it may be that countries are more willing to rely on technical and legal expertise from outside the basin to address certain compliance or implementation issues. For instance, in both the case of the Cijevna/Cem River and that of the Bystroe Canal, the value of involving institutions and expertise from outside the basin is evident.

Given that the Water Convention already has a CIM in place, which includes a reporting mechanism and an implementation committee, is it feasible for it to play a stronger role globally? One possibility would be for more countries to become party to the Water Convention. The Convention certainly appears to be growing in stature at the global level. As well as the 55 parties to the Convention, at least 20 countries are actively in the process of becoming a party to the Convention.[65] In the foreseeable future, a scenario might therefore

62 Nele Matz-Lück, 'Framework Convention as a Regulatory Tool' (2009) 1 Goettingen Journal of International Law 439; Francesca Bernardini, 'The Normative and Institutional Evolution of the Convention' in Attila Tanzi and others (eds) *The UNECE Convention on the Protection and Use of Transboundary Watercourses and International Lakes – Its Contribution to International Water Cooperation* (Brill 2015).

63 Ibid.

64 Bendel and Suedi (n 20). To date, there are 45 parties to the Espoo Convention (see UNTS, '4. Convention on Environmental Impact Assessment in a Transboundary Context' (21 August 2024) <https://treaties.un.org/Pages/ViewDetails.aspx?src=TREATY&mtdsg_no=XXVII-4&chapter=27&clang=_en> accessed 21 August 2024.

65 UNECE, 'South Sudan eyes Water Convention accession for stronger water governance and development opportunities' (26 July 2024) <https://unece.org/media/environment/Water-Convention/news/393078> accessed 30 August 2024.

be envisaged where over half of the countries sharing transboundary waters become parties to the Water Convention and therefore formally fall under the reporting requirements of the Convention. Increased membership of the Convention might also result in a bigger workload for the implementation committee. New parties, representing a more diverse membership, might look to the Convention and the committee's expertise to address the challenges they face in the implementation of their transboundary water agreements.

In theory, the implementation committee could also increase its workload through greater use of its 'committee initiative' function, whereby it uses reporting under the Water Convention to identify individual incidences of non-compliance and invites the relevant party or parties to explain the reasons for such non-compliance. However, this is an unlikely option given that the parties' original rationale for including the implementation committee was to *support* countries having difficulties with the implementation of, and compliance with, the Convention rather than confronting non-complying parties. Moreover, the practice of the Convention has been to use reporting as a softer tool to inform its Programme of Work and to address implementation and compliance gaps and challenges through the activities included therein.

While the CIM under the Water Convention may grow in significance with the increase in the number of Parties to the Convention, there is still the question of what options are available to countries that are not party to the Convention. The Water Convention is having more of an influence on, and is influenced by, non-parties. Around 130 countries are estimated to have engaged in the activities of the Water Convention in recent years.[66] For example, the last meeting of the parties brought together official representation from over 100 countries that share transboundary waters.[67] Perhaps more significant is the role that states not party to the Convention play in some of the work of the Convention, such as the development of material designed to support the interpretation and implementation of international water law. Recent publications, such as the Handbook of Water Allocation in a Transboundary Context,[68] the Practical Guide for the Development of Agreements or Other Arrangements

---

66 UNECE, 'Water for peace on World Water Day: momentum builds for cross-border cooperation through UN Water Convention' (22 March 2024) <https://unece.org/climate-change/press/water-peace-world-water-day-momentum-builds-cross-border-cooperation-through> accessed 19 April 2024.

67 UNECE, 'Ninth Session of the Meeting of the Parties to the Water Convention', <https://unece.org/info/Environmental-Policy/Water-Convention/events/356707> accessed 19 August 2024.

68 UNECE, 'Handbook on Water Allocation in a Transboundary Context', UN Doc ECE/MP.WAT/62 (2021).

for Transboundary Water Cooperation,[69] and the Guide to Reporting under the Water Convention,[70] have all benefited from the input from both parties and non-state parties. Similarly, the Water Convention's Work Programme areas have brought together expertise from a wide range of basins, such as the global network of basins working on climate change, which includes 14 basins from across Africa, Central and South America, Central and South-East Asia, and Europe.[71] However, while non-parties are increasingly engaging with the work of the Water Convention, they are not formally required to report under the Water Convention. Similarly, the implementation committee under the Water Convention is essentially only available to parties. The only way in which non-parties could become involved in the Committee's work is if the issue relates to difficulties a party is having in the implementation of the Convention. Unless all countries sharing transboundary waters commit to becoming party to the Water Convention, a scenario would therefore always remain whereby only a proportion of states sharing transboundary waters could rely upon the CIM under the Water Convention.

An alternative would be to establish or strengthen CIMs at the regional level. However, as noted in Chapter 5, currently the only legal frameworks that address transboundary waters operate within the regions encompassing the European Union (EU) and Southern African Development Community (SADC). Both the EU and SADC already have systems in place that support compliance and implementation. While adopting more specific arrangements for transboundary waters, such as those found in CIMs, might support the implementation of the EU Water Framework Directive and the Revised SADC Protocol on Shared Watercourses, their value added could be questioned. With the exception of the Republic of Ireland, all EU countries sharing transboundary waters are already party to the Water Convention and are therefore likely to use that framework if required. The situation in the SADC region is different, given that of the 12 SADC countries sharing transboundary waters, only Namibia, Zambia and Zimbabwe are currently parties to the Water Convention. While there might therefore be added value in introducing a CIM to support the Revised SADC Protocol on Shared Watercourses, it would become less

---

[69] UNECE, 'Practical Guide for the Development of Agreements or Arrangements for Transboundary Water Cooperation', UN Doc ECE/MP.WAT/68 (2021).

[70] UNECE, 'Guide to Reporting under the Water Convention and as a Contribution to SDG indicator 6.5.2', UN Doc ECE/MP.WAT/60 (2020).

[71] See UNECE, 'Progress report of the Global network of basins working on climate change adaptation as of April 2023', <https://unece.org/sites/default/files/2023-07/Global_network_overview_pilot%20projects_progress_May2023_ENGL_Final_0.pdf> accessed 19 August 2024.

pertinent to do so if more countries from the SADC region became party to the Water Convention. Botswana and Tanzania have already expressed interest in becoming party to the Water Convention, which, unless countries see the merits of having a system that is more reflective of the SADC context, means that the case for introducing a CIM under the Revised SADC Protocol on Shared Watercourses may not receive much support.[72] In other regions, where no regional legal frameworks for transboundary waters currently exist, the prospect of establishing a CIM at the regional level would seem far-fetched.

Another hypothetical might be to rely on the framework that exists under SDG indicator 6.5.2. As noted in Chapter 5, the reporting template for SDG indicator 6.5.2 and for reporting under the Water Convention is the same. However, a key distinction is that countries are not formally obliged to report under SDG indicator 6.5.2. Any information provided is given on a voluntary basis by the countries involved in the SDG indicator 6.5.2 exercise. Along similar lines, the review of SDG indicator 6.5.2 national reports by the custodian agencies for 6.5.2, UNECE and UNESCO, also has a different function compared to reviewing progress in the implementation of, or compliance with, transboundary water agreements, and no implementation or compliance committee is in place to address any issues that countries might raise in their SDG indicator 6.5.2 reports. Adopting a CIM within the context of the SDG indicator 6.5.2 reporting process would therefore require countries to negotiate and agree on a revised process. As noted above, given that a CIM already exists within the Water Convention, and is to some extent already aligned to SDG indicator 6.5.2, it is unlikely that countries sharing transboundary waters would commit to such an exercise. What is perhaps more likely is that a non-Party to the Water Convention may become more 'acclimatised' to the reporting mechanism under the Water Convention, and the commitments under the Convention more generally, through participation in the SDG indicator 6.5.2

---

[72] UNECE, 'Botswana accelerates progress on Water Convention accession and shared river agreements' (31 October 2023) <https://unece.org/environment/news/botswana-accelerates-progress-water-convention-accession-and-shared-river> accessed 19 August 2024; Ndawana Norest, 'Zimbabwe holds historic national workshop for the accession to UN water conventions' (*The Water Diplomat*, 26 June 2024) <https://www.waterdiplomat.org/story/2024/06/zimbabwe-holds-historic-national-workshop-accession-un-water-conventions> accessed 19 August 2024; UNECE, 'National Workshop related to the Convention on the Protection and Use of Transboundary Watercourses and International Lakes: Tanzania's accession process' (1–2 December 2022) <https://unece.org/sites/default/files/2022-11/Tanzania_National%20Workshop_Concept%20Note_DRAFT.pdf> accessed 19 August 2024.

exercise, which in turn may raise their interest in becoming a party to the Convention.

In sum, the greatest prospects for a CIM to operate at the global level would therefore appear to be for more states to become party to the Water Convention.

9.4 STRATEGIES AND RECOMMENDATIONS FOR STRENGTHENING THE IMPLEMENTATION OF, AND COMPLIANCE WITH, TRANSBOUNDARY WATER AGREEMENTS

While the previous section considered compliance and implementation within a multi-level governance context, this section will focus on compliance and implementation within the context of specific transboundary water agreements. In so doing, this chapter will assess the extent to which some of the rationale for adopting CIMs within MEAs might be incorporated into transboundary water agreements and their regimes.

In relation to regular reporting, the analysis of transboundary water agreements in Chapter 4, and experience from the Danube, Mekong and Orange-Senqu basins, demonstrates that states have put in place mechanisms by which to regularly report on their activities. However, it is rare that these measures report specifically on the implementation of the provisions of a transboundary water agreement *per se*, or provide an opportunity to highlight specific incidences of non-compliance. A common approach has been for parties to include more general provisions within their transboundary water agreements to regularly exchange data and information or, in some instances, to jointly monitor and assess the conditions of transboundary waters. This therefore begs the question of whether a more systematic approach to reviewing the implementation of and/or compliance with the actual transboundary water agreement itself would add value.

Context would be important to take into account when considering this question. In some instances, agreements may have evolved to an extent that any meaningful review of the original provisions may not be of merit. For example, reviewing the provisions of the 1909 Boundary Water Treaty between Canada and the United States would give a very misleading representation of transboundary water cooperation between the two countries given that their cooperation has evolved significantly since the adoption of the Treaty.[73] Similarly, within the Danube, Orange-Senqu and Mekong contexts, reviewing the implementation of the provisions of each basin agreement may

[73] Daniel Macfarlane, '75 years of Canada-US transborder water quantity hydropolitics' (2023) 48(4) Canadian Water Resources Journal 350.

have little value. Cooperation has clearly evolved since the adoption of these basin-wide agreements, with much of the focus in each of the basins on the management plans instead. In the case of the Danube, for instance, the text of the 1994 Danube Convention has to a large extent been effectively superseded by the requirements of the EU Water Framework Directive and subsequent legislation. Periodic review of the Basin Management Plan might therefore be a more appropriate means by which to review progress and address compliance and implementation challenges. Here, parallels might be drawn with the way in which the Water Convention is implemented, whereby the parties have demonstrated a willingness to address compliance and implementation issues through more general means, such as through the use of the Programme of Work under the Convention, rather than calling out individual incidences of weak implementation or non-compliance.

However, regular reporting on progress in implementing basin management plans could still include an opportunity for countries to highlight difficulties they face in implementing or complying with the agreement itself, which in turn might enhance transparency and trust between the parties to the agreement. For example, reporting could provide an opportunity to highlight any inconsistencies between national legislation and requirements under the Convention, such as an obligation to notify of planned measures or to conduct an EIA. This would not only be useful for supporting the efforts of the parties to systematically identify difficulties, but if coupled with technical and financial assistance, would help address implementation gaps and build trust amongst the parties. Similarly, where a party is struggling to exchange data due to technical capacity issues, a transparent and regular means of reporting such difficulties would help build trust between the parties and assist in finding a solution. Additionally, reporting could help to engage non-state actors in the efforts to review progress in implementing a state's commitments under a transboundary water agreement and identify solutions to individual or collective challenges in meeting the commitments under the agreement.

Then, there is a question of whether there is any merit in providing an expert body with the mandate to review compliance and implementation of a transboundary water agreement. Again, much will depend on the context. Within the context of bilateral arrangements, it might be that the pre-established institutional arrangements, such as a river basin organisation, can play such a function. To a greater or lesser extent, states perform such a role through their regular meetings, such as their annual conference of the parties, or through regular working group meetings. However, unlike a compliance or implementation committee, such a review would not be independent. An additional option might therefore be for countries to have the option to refer a compliance or implementation issue to an independent expert body. In some of the treaties examined in Chapter 4, the option to involve a third party already forms part of a more general provision to settle disputes in a peaceful manner. States could rely on such provisions to establish a body made up of legal and technical experts, such as envisaged in the implementation committee of the Water Convention.

This approach has similarities with the fact-finding commission envisaged within the Watercourses Convention.[74] Pursuant to the Watercourses Convention, a fact-finding commission must be established where states are unable to resolve a dispute through other diplomatic means. In justifying its inclusion, ILC Special Rapporteur Stephen McCaffrey observed that such a commission would be sensitive to the nature of water disputes, which 'rely heavily on technical expertise'.[75] McCaffrey went on to comment that, 'a non-binding expert report possibly accompanied with a recommended course of action, will frequently result in resolution of an actual or potential dispute without the need to have recourse to a procedure that results in a binding settlement'.[76] Along similar lines, Tanzi and Farnelli comment that, 'an expert's neutral input into an emerging, or ongoing, dispute may enable the disputing parties to best define such a dispute, which can often deflate, and, hence facilitate its resolution'.[77]

However, a further observation that can be taken from the Watercourses Convention is the reluctance that some states expressed over the involvement of third parties. In a vote taken on Article 33 of the Watercourses Convention, five countries voted against, 25 abstained, and 33 voted in favour.[78] The compulsory nature of third-party intervention in any dispute was the main reason for countries voting against the provision.[79] It may therefore be unlikely that certain countries would incorporate any third-party role into their treaty arrangements – although such an option may find favour in other agreements.

---

[74] Article 33, Watercourses Convention. See also Attila Tanzi and Gian Maria Farnelli, 'The Settlement of Disputes through Non-judicial Means (Article 33(1)-33(9))' in Laurence Boisson de Chazournes and others (eds), *The UN Convention on the Law of the Non-navigational Uses of International Watercourses – A Commentary* (OUP 2018), 353–355.

[75] ILC, 'Sixth report on the law of the non-navigational uses of international watercourses, by Mr Stephen C. McCaffrey, Special Rapporteur' (1990) II.1 Yearbook of the International Law Commission 41, 66.

[76] Ibid.

[77] Tanzi and Fernelli (n 74), 354.

[78] UNGA 'Report of the Sixth Committee convening as the Working Group of the whole (A/51/869)' UN Doc A/51/PV.99 (21 May 1997).

[79] Stephen McCaffrey, 'The UN Convention on the Law of the Non-navigational Uses of International Watercourses: prospects and pitfalls' in Salman M.A. Salman and Laurence Boisson de Chazournes (eds), *International Watercourses: Enhancing Cooperation and Managing Conflict* (World Bank 1998), 26.

Where those agreements are adopted by parties to the Water Convention, it may be that the implementation committee under the Convention could perform such a 'fact-finding' task.

Also, a distinction can be made between a committee set up or invoked with the aim of resolving a dispute between two parties and a committee that could support a party having difficulties in implementing or complying with its obligations under an agreement. In the latter instance, a party that is reticent to involve a third party in a dispute may be willing to utilise a compliance or implementation committee if it believes that the committee can provide a supportive environment by which to address the technical and/or financial issues it is facing.

Finally, there is a question of whether transboundary water agreements might benefit from the availability of direct assistance to support incidences of weak implementation or non-compliance. In a scenario where countries might be regularly reporting on their progress in implementing a transboundary water agreement, the value of that reporting would certainly be enhanced if there were a facility that the parties could draw upon to help address any difficulties they face. Such a fund might be supported by both by the parties and external donors that have an interest in the successful implementation of the agreement. An example of something similar is the efforts of the Mekong River Commission to develop the Mekong Fund, which is designed to provide both direct and indirect aid to communities impacted by climate change and the negative consequences of water infrastructure development.[80] Such a fund might be expanded to support countries that are having difficulties in implementing the requirements of an agreement, such as developing a joint monitoring and assessment system, conducting a joint EIA, or engaging stakeholders in basin management plans.

9.5 CAN A FOCUS ON IMPLEMENTATION AND COMPLIANCE MECHANISMS ENCOURAGE MORE STATES TO ADOPT TRANSBOUNDARY WATER AGREEMENTS?

The SDG indicator 6.5.2 report notes that only 43 out of the 154 countries that share transboundary waters have 90% or more of their territory covered by an operational arrangement, with major gaps present in Asia and Latin America.[81]

[80] Anoulak Kittikoun, 'A Conversation with Dr Kittikoun, CEO of the Mekong River Commission Secretariat' (*CWR*, 22 March 2024) <https://chinawaterrisk.org/interviews/a-conversation-with-dr-kittikoun-ceo-of-the-mekong-river-commission-secretariat/> accessed 22 January 2025.

[81] UNECE and UNESCO (n 6).

This can be contrasted by strong global calls to adopt transboundary water agreements, which are considered an important means to progress sustainable development at the transboundary level.[82] As noted in Chapter 2, a range of factors are likely to influence whether or not countries enter into transboundary water agreements. In the case of upstream hegemons, such as China and Turkey, the likelihood of the countries agreeing to detailed basin-wide agreements for their major transboundary rivers would appear to be low. However, Chapter 2 also demonstrated how a multiplicity of benefits can be derived from transboundary cooperation and can therefore act as an incentive for states to enter into transboundary water agreements. Some scholars therefore observe that, 'in order to reach agreements, states must … feel that they will gain more from cooperating than from maintaining the status quo, and trust that their counterparts will not renege once the agreement is signed'.[83]

Where states therefore see a benefit in cooperation, a discussion of CIMs during the negotiation of a transboundary water agreement could assist in reaching an agreement. Such a discussion has the potential to allay any concerns that the other country or countries may have that their counterpart may renege on their treaty commitments. As Brochmann and Hensel put it, 'unless each party believes that the other party intends to comply with an agreement, an agreement is unlikely to be reached in the first place'.[84]

A discussion of the three key components of CIMs during the negotiation of a transboundary water agreement could therefore help countries address any concerns and barriers they may have in progressing their cooperation. A commitment to regular reporting on the implementation of and compliance with an agreement might help countries address any trust issues that they may have with the other party or parties. Regular reporting would provide a transparent means by which each party would be able to assess the progress of the other party or parties. Reporting could potentially build confidence amongst the parties, as they could see the reciprocal benefits that derive from each party meeting its commitments under an agreement.[85] Initially, reporting might focus on commitments that deepen knowledge and understanding of the basin, such as data and information exchange, notification and consultation, and joint monitoring and assessment. By regularly reporting on the progress in implementing

[82] UN (n 6), 17.

[83] Marit Brochmann and Paul R. Hensel, 'The Effectiveness of Negotiations over International River Claims' (2011) 55(3) International Studies Quarterly 859, 862.

[84] Ibid.

[85] Francesco Parisi and Nita Ghei, 'The Role of Reciprocity in International Law' (2003) 36 Cornell International Law Journal 93.

provisions related to these aspects, countries will not only be able to build trust amongst themselves but will also build up a shared understanding of the basin and how it might be managed in an equitable and sustainable way. As cooperation evolves between the parties, the reporting might focus more on provisions related to basin planning, such as the development of joint management plans, their implementation and continuous review. Regular reporting of such plans and their implementation also offers an opportunity to build trust and progress cooperation.

While regular reporting in such a manner helps build trust and deepens shared knowledge and understanding of the basin and its collective management, reporting may also act as an important deterrent for breaching treaty commitments. A party may be more reluctant to renege on its treaty commitments if it knows that its actions or inactions would be clearly called out through the regular reporting mechanism. Upholding its reputation as a state committed to complying with its transboundary water agreements might, therefore, act in itself as a powerful means to promote compliance and implementation.[86] In turn, the prospect of including a reporting mechanism within a transboundary water agreement during neogotiations might allay fears that a state may have over whether or not its neighbour may commit to the implementation of the agreement.

Further assurances might be given to negotiators of an agreement through the prospect of having a mechanism in place whereby periodic reports are analysed, either by the secretariat or a third party. Analysing periodic reports would help develop a better collective understanding of the transboundary river, lake or aquifer in question, and the challenges and opportunities that are present. In identifying gaps and weaknesses in the implementation of commitments, such a review could also support more general efforts to implement the agreement, such as through a basin management plan. Another opportunity that regular reporting and the analysis of such reports might offer is to reward 'good' practice and exchange experiences and lessons learned.[87] Highlighting where the parties have made good progress in implementing their agreements could in itself encourage parties to implement their commitments in an effective way. Again, these types of advantages to reporting could help address certain concerns that a country may have in adopting a transboundary water agreement with its neighbour.

Having a mechanism in place whereby parties can seek technical and financial assistance in cases where they are having difficulties in implementing or

[86] George W. Downs and Michael A. Jones, 'Reputation, compliance, and International law' (2002) 31 Journal of Legal Studies 95.

[87] Anne van Aaken and Betul Simsek, 'Rewarding in International Law' (2021) 115(1) American Journal of International Law 198.

complying with an agreement might also provide an incentive for countries to enter into an agreement. For countries that have concerns about their domestic capacity to implement commitments within an agreement, the prospect of such a mechanism, which may have to be provided by a third party, may allay concerns. Such incentives and rewards are increasingly recognised as an important driver of treaty compliance.[88] The international community could play an important role in supporting such mechanisms through innovative finance. This is something that was highlighted by the High-level Panel on Water and Peace, which recommended that the international community create 'financial and other incentives to promote transboundary water cooperation'.[89]

9.6 CONCLUSION

The analysis in this chapter has demonstrated how there is potential for transboundary water agreements to take on board some of the lessons learned from both theory and practice related to CIMs, particularly within the context of MEAs. The philosophy of 'managing compliance', which is embedded in many MEAs, resonates well with the types of challenges faced by countries sharing transboundary waters. Moreover, experiences from the Espoo Convention and the Water Convention already provide early examples of how CIMs might support transboundary issues of both a bilateral and multilateral nature, and can do so in a way that might rival the traditional dispute settlement mechanisms that have been utilised by countries in attempts to resolve their transboundary water disputes. In this regard, the CIM of the Water Convention holds much promise given that it is already up and running at the global level. However, it also has its limitations. As only around a third of countries sharing transboundary waters are party to the Water Convention, enhancing the role of the Water Convention's CIM must go hand in hand with increased accession to the Water Convention. While the uptick in accession to the Water Convention in recent years, and the growing interest among other states, is encouraging, it is unlikely to reach universal coverage among all countries sharing transboundary waters in the foreseeable future. However, there remain other ways in which CIMs can assist in the implementation of transboundary water agreements. Systematic reporting on the implementation of a transboundary water agreement offers opportunities to build trust and deepen shared knowledge

---

[88] Ibid.

[89] Global High-Level Panel on Water and Peace, 'A Matter of Survival' (December 2017) <https://www.genevawaterhub.org/sites/default/files/atoms/files/a_matter_of_survival_www.pdf> accessed 20 August 2024, 67. See also UNECE, 'Funding and Financing Transboundary Water Cooperation' UN Doc ECE/MP.Wat61 (2021).

and understanding between the parties to an agreement, and to enhance transparency among parties and non-state actors. Parties to transboundary water agreements might also benefit from the type of compliance or implementation committees found in CIMs to assist them with the challenges they might face in implementing their agreements. If such assistance is coupled with the provision of financial and technical assistance, this may provide additional support to implement transboundary watercourses agreements. Moreover, the chapter has demonstrated that these benefits may incentivise countries to enter into transboundary water agreements, or may help to address bottlenecks in negotiations, particularly where the parties lack trust in each other to fulfil their treaty commitments. Ultimately, the chapter therefore shows that there is great value in parties to existing and future agreements considering how they might incorporate mechanisms that report, review and address compliance and implementation; and many lessons can be learned from the use of CIMs within MEAs.

10. Conclusion to *Implementing Transboundary Water Agreements*

This book set out to analyse the extent to which transboundary water agreements might benefit from the incorporation of compliance and implementation mechanisms (CIMs). A key driver of such an analysis was the current state of transboundary water agreements and the importance of advancing transboundary water cooperation. Whilst transboundary water cooperation is indispensable in progressing sustainable development and addressing climate change, transboundary water agreements are lacking in many transboundary rivers, lakes and aquifers. Moreover, where agreements do exist, they may not be fully implemented. Conversely, CIMs are a common feature within the context of multilateral environmental agreements (MEAs), which in turn begs the question of whether transboundary water agreements might profit from this MEA experience.

In consideration of this question, the book identified multiple disciplinary perspectives on why states cooperate over their transboundary waters. The analysis showed that there are no clear answers on what influences cooperation. Different accounts suggest that power has some influence on cooperation, whereby the most powerful states within a basin, i.e., the hydro-hegemon, can influence transboundary relations. Where the hydro-hegemon is upstream, such as in the case of China and Turkey, there is less likelihood that detailed basin-wide arrangements will be entered into, compared to where the hydro-hegemon is downstream, such as in the case of India. The research also showed how the benefits of cooperation can be an important driver of cooperation. Examples such as Canada and the United States, as well as relations between India and its upstream neighbours, show how cooperation among states sharing transboundary waters has led to benefits for all the countries concerned. The analysis also demonstrated how norms and ideas can influence cooperation, and international law provides an important basis upon which states structure their negotiation and implementation of transboundary water agreements. Ultimately, the multiple perspectives on transboundary water cooperation suggest that, whilst dependent on context, there is an important role that transboundary water agreements can play in fostering cooperation between countries sharing transboundary waters.

A review of the types of CIMs found in MEAs was also key to addressing the research question. This analysis highlighted both an extensive practice of adopting CIMs within MEAs, largely dating back to the introduction of a CIM within the 1987 Montreal Protocol and its subsequent success. The analysis revealed three elements that most CIMs hold in common, namely reporting, review, and the availability of measures to address incidences of weak implementation or non-compliance. While these elements were held in common, the analysis also showed variation in how reporting was carried out, how compliance and implementation were reviewed, and how issues of weak implementation or non-compliance were addressed within MEAs.

The three CIM core elements found within MEAs provided an important basis upon which to analyse the extent to which similar arrangements might be found within transboundary water agreements. Through an analysis of transboundary water agreements, it was clear that few contain explicit provisions concerning compliance and implementation. The Sava Agreement, with its requirement to develop a methodology for reviewing the agreement's implementation, and the Zambezi Agreement, with its requirement for parties to self-report non-compliance issues, stand out as amongst the few agreements that explicitly make reference to core CIM features. Most agreements include more general provisions related to the exchange of data and information, or joint monitoring. A common trend is for river basin organisations to be afforded a general role in supporting the implementation of an agreement, although no agreement included a systematic process by which compliance and implementation with the agreement were periodically reported on by the parties and reviewed by the joint institution.

The analysis of global and regional approaches did however reveal a different perspective. The relatively recent adoption of SDG indicator 6.5.2 showed that a system was in place whereby countries periodically reported on progress in the adoption of operational arrangements for transboundary water cooperation. In parallel, developments under the Water Convention align well with the type of CIMs found within MEAs, especially in relation to the reporting mechanism under the Convention and its implementation committee. Given the linkage between reporting under the Water Convention and reporting under SDG indicator 6.5.2, it appears that the basis upon which a CIM related to transboundary water agreements might grow can already be found. Moreover, the experience of the Revised SADC Protocol on Shared Watercourses and the EU Water Framework Directive highlights that, particularly in relation to reporting, parties are already incorporating CIM elements into their activities related to transboundary water cooperation – albeit with a particular emphasis on technical aspects rather than the systematic review of their legal obligations.

The analysis of the Danube, Mekong and Orange-Senqu River Basins offered critical insights into how states tackle compliance and implementation in practice. None of the three case studies squarely address compliance and implementation in the way that the CIMs found in MEAs do. In terms of reporting, the case study analysis revealed that countries were more willing to report on the scientific and technical aspects of water management rather than their legal requirements. The analysis of each case also revealed the sensitivities involved in reviewing and addressing issues of weak implementation and non-compliance. By and large, countries shied away from addressing such issues within their basin commissions, which are constrained by the expectation that countries will make decisions by consensus. Compliance and implementation issues are rather tackled indirectly through the adoption of strategies, policies and programmes, and their subsequent revision. Third-party intervention is rare, although in the case of the Danube, the benefits of involving the Espoo Convention implementation committee were clear. This might offer an important lesson for other countries who might be struggling to resolve their compliance and implementation issues bilaterally and/or within the confines of their river basin organisation.

Ultimately, the analysis in this book has revealed that important lessons can be learned from the types of CIMs found in MEAs. While it is unlikely that CIMs will become a common feature within existing transboundary water agreements, there is scope to include elements of CIMs within those agreements both to enhance the way in which they are implemented and to help engage non-state actors in their implementation. For states negotiating new agreements, a discussion on incorporating CIMs into an agreement has the potential to overcome potential bottlenecks in the negotiations, particularly in relation to the uncertainty that might be present within the basin and the lack of trust amongst the parties. Given the huge challenges faced by countries sharing transboundary waters, and the central role that transboundary water agreements can play in progressing cooperation, any opportunity to enhance their contribution must be seized upon.

Index